# LEARNING TO LEAVE

## THE IRONY OF SCHOOLING IN A COASTAL COMMUNITY

**Michael Corbett**

WITH A NEW PREFACE

WEST VIRGINIA UNIVERSITY PRESS
MORGANTOWN

First edition published 2007 in Canada by Fernwood Publishing
West Virginia University Press edition published 2020

ISBN 978-1-949199-53-6 (paperback)

Library of Congress Cataloging-in-Publication Data
Names: Corbett, Michael John, 1958– author. | West Virginia University Press.
Title: Learning to leave : the irony of schooling in a coastal community / Michael Corbett.
Other titles: Irony of schooling in a coastal community | Rural studies.
Description: Second Edition. | Morgantown : West Virginia University Press, 2020. | Series: Rural Studies | "With a new preface." | Includes bibliographical references and index.
Identifiers: LCCN 2019053602 | ISBN 9781949199536 (Paperback)
Subjects: LCSH: Dropouts—Nova Scotia—Case studies. | Dropouts—Canada—Case studies. | Education, Rural—Nova Scotia—Case studies. | Education, Rural—Canada—Case studies. | Rural youth—Education—Nova Scotia—Case studies. | Rural youth—Education—Canada—Case studies. | Rural-urban migration—Canada—Case studies.
Classification: LCC LC146.5 .C67 2020 | DDC 371.2/91309716–dc23
LC record available at https://lccn.loc.gov/2019053602

Cover design by Than Saffel / WVU Press
Cover image: Michel Gerard Doucet, Trout Cove Wharf, Centreville Digby Neck, 2018. Oil on canvas.

# Contents

# Preface to the 2020 Edition

*Learning to Leave* attempted to address the historical, sociological and economic transformation that occurred in a particular rural coastal community in the North Atlantic from the 1960s through to the end of the twentieth century. It was developed in its original form while I was at the University of British Columbia under my mentor Don Fisher and completed the day after the George W. Bush–Al Gore presidential election of November 2000. At the time there was little contemporary Canadian scholarship dealing with rural education other than the work of a small contingent of historians. Some sociological work did consider rurality as a variable in quantitative analysis, but there was nothing contemporary that focused exclusively on rural schooling experience although approximately one in five Canadians lived (and continue to live) in what is defined by Statistics Canada as a rural area.

When I was asked about my research interests by a senior colleague, his response was, "Oh, you're interested in international education." This comment illustrates how rurality is understood and misunderstood as a space elsewhere, either in the past of "modern" societies or in the Third World. As the G.W. Bush administration was followed by the Obama administration and on into the current political climate, much is made of how rural angst, perhaps a crucial part of a generalized white working-class ressentiment, has come to matter electorally and ideologically not just in America, but around the world. Indeed, explaining rural angst has become something of a cottage industry for scholars, memoirists, essayists, journalists and others. I think this book can contribute to an understanding of the complex social forces and landscapes of reflexive decision-making that provide a backstory to contemporary rural phenomena. Educational issues are not peripheral to rural development cultural and socioeconomic problems; it is my argument that they are foundational, but not in the simple, linear sense in which deficits in education are used as a catch-all explanation for rural angst and voting patterns (Biddle and Hall, 2017).

*Learning to Leave* explores a deep, yet ambivalent skepticism in a single-industry peninsular coastal community about the power of education to transform lives in a positive way. This was illustrated by research participants who experienced the industrialization of the fishery through the 1970s and '80s and who hung on through the 1990s to fashion lives and livelihoods through hard work and without much formal education. Many of my research participants spoke of how their community and their industry was exploited by urban corporate interests and abandoned by government. But deeper than this was the unexpected idea that formal education was seen by many as a kind of conspiracy of urban liberal elites who used their money, institutional positions, bureaucratic influence and linguistic sophistication to control, undermine and cheat the hard-working producers who serve as the backbone of the economy. This sentiment is not significantly different from phenomena, such as the "empathy wall" (Hochschild, 2016) or a feeling of being "left behind" (Wuthnow, 2018), articulated by contemporary scholars and journalists who endeavour to explain rural angst to apparently uncomprehending metropolitan audiences. *Learning to Leave* is about the human geography of education in a community undergoing structural change, and while it is located in time and space, many of the tensions in this study continue to resonate today.

*Learning to Leave* takes its place as part of a history of early warnings about the political and ecological consequences of ignoring and demeaning the 20–25 percent of North Americans who do not live in urban and suburban environments. I learned how the political and the ecological are fundamentally entangled, and how the protracted dismissal of rural issues and the corollary complacency of political and economic leaders around the marginalization and selective depopulation of rural North America are key problems that have been largely ignored. *Learning to Leave* is about a pragmatic, down-to-earth people of the land who have figured out how to piece together a life largely without the support of government or the help of well-resourced professional services. This includes formal education, which was, as often as not, experienced as irrelevant and even a waste of time, contrasting the "real work" that was immediate, necessary and comprehensible. At the same time though, the book also illustrates the transformative power of education as a mobilizing force that opens up horizons of choice and possibility for those offered success in its selective institutional processes.

Fundamentally, *Learning to Leave* is an oral history that asked research participants to think back to their schooling in an Atlantic Canadian coastal village and retrospectively make sense of their experience. I was particularly interested in how formal education influenced life trajectories and mobilities, and not surprisingly, I found that people generally understood education to be an important but ambivalent force both in their own lives and in the development of the community. These accounts are situated within the transition from the small boat

*Grundrisse*, Marx saw the origins of capital in the mobilization of people and things. This process effectively required an ongoing severing of any deep connection between people and place, abstracting the modern self into a flow of exchange represented by money, but also by commodified indicators like school grades, test scores and credentials. Yet, a persistent tension remains in a corollary longing for a place to belong, a place that is ours. The mobile imaginaries that dominate formal education generate tensions and opportunities that create emergent and rhizomatic networks and connections that spawn new ways of seeing and being.

*Learning to Leave* explores the contours of choice and compulsion. Is leaving a rural community a choice, and if so, what kind of choice is it? Is this choice equally distributed? The tension in aspirations discourse between choosing what is right for the individual, as the individual sees their interests and capabilities, and what might be considered "realistic" by powerful actors like parents, teachers and others remains a central problematic. How choices are structured, presented and understood as more or less coherent in the lives of different individuals living in particular intersections of time, social position and geography is key in this study drawing on and critiquing the seminal analysis of Pierre Bourdieu. *Learning to Leave* is about how decisions were made and how individuals retrospectively understood what they thought they were doing when they left or continued on in formal education.

I generally agree with Margaret Archer (2012) that Bourdieu, his intellectual descendants and much of mainstream sociology mischaracterize contemporary socialization processes that have been radically reshaped by what she calls the "reflexive imperative" in the last couple of decades. Yet, there remains, for most rural youth, what I have termed a "mobility imperative," or the idea that a successful life requires a move out of the community, probably into some form of urban space either for education, employment or both. The rural Nova Scotia learning-leaving dynamic has been complicated in recent years by work in the oil patch of Alberta. Atlantic Canadians make the "long commute" shuttling four-thousand-plus kilometres for fly-in–fly-out deployment. Ironically, in rural Atlantic Canada, temporary migrant labour has been brought in for primary industry labour and the development of niche agriculture and ecotourism. Still, people have different capacities to move (motility); different relations to place; different economic, social, educational and cultural resources; and different dreams. Choices are made, with imperfect information in ever-shifting environments of uncertainty and ubiquitous change. *Learning to Leave* analyzes the intersection of history and biography, as C. Wright Mills put it, and offers an account of schooling and fishery of the 1950s and '60s, through the period of industrializati and capitalization of the 1970s and '80s, and on through to the peri of restructuring and downsizing of the industry that began in the l: 1980s, carrying on to the present day.

In this book I attempted to bring an analysis of schooling i conversation with sociological, anthropological, historical and so change literatures to illustrate how institutional processes are in enced by economic and state transitions and how schooling itself come to be understood independently as a motor of developm and social change under the rubric of human capital and neolib theories. Such an approach problematized the idea of choice, no dismissing it, but rather by situating educational decision-makin the context of economic and technological change, institutional velopment, social class, culture and gender. Complementary line research and theorization are now emerging in the field of rural cation as a new generation of scholars begins to move away from American rural education tradition, which tended to focus on intir and often congratulatory studies of good, community-focused ed tional practice and resistance struggles confronting the centrali juggernaut of amalgamation and consolidation of rural services.

In the wake of the most recent U.S. presidential election growing right-wing political movements/drift in much of Eur there is interest in understanding rurality as a mythic construct i ferent national contexts. I largely agree with Daniel Gamson (2 who wrote recently in the *Oxford Handbook of the History of Edu* that "there is surprisingly little work that focuses directly on th ture and dynamics of the transition from rural to urban school occurred in virtually every industrialized and industrializing n during the nineteenth and twentieth centuries and that has co ued into the early twenty-first." This very transition is the subjec ter of *Learning to Leave*, which focuses on the modernizing s tivization processes and resistances that contemporary social c involves. While Gamson has a point, his disciplinary specializati the history of education may well cause him to miss relevant disciplinary and transdisciplinary work emerging in the field of education (i.e., Corbett, 2018).

Today, a considerable amount of contemporary work in rura cation takes up the mobile, mutable imagery I attempted to deve *Learning to Leave*, providing new ways of conceptualizing rural sp dynamic and connected rather than static and isolated. What I tempting to show in *Learning to Leave* is how the development of co porary capitalism requires multiple levels of mobility. Particularly modernization in a community riding the waves of three and a half decades of social and industrial change, waves that continue to break on uncertain shores far from the city lights.

Finally, I would like to thank my rural education colleagues who have provided me with critical commentary and friendship over the last two decades. These include (and I apologize to those I've forgotten) Karen Eppley, Craig and Aimee Howley, Dennis Mulcahy, Ursula Kelly, Kim Donehower, Paul Theobald, Amy Azano, Mara Tieken, Jayne Downey, Michael Barbour, John Madden, Bill Green, Jo Reid, Phil Roberts, Pam Bartholomaeus, John Halsey, Simone White, Sharon Fraser, John Williamson, Christine Gardner, Elaine Sharplin, Unn-Doris Baeck, Andrew Kristiansen, Gry Paulgaard, Linda Hargreaves, Rune Kvalsund, Cath Gristy, Dawn Wallin, Dianne Gereluk, Aniko Varpolotai, Dianne Looker, David MacKinnon, Ann Vibert and Jennifer Tinkham.

Kai Schafft suggested this reissue of *Learning to Leave*, and I am grateful for his ongoing support. Spencer Woods brought this project together and has supported this second edition. Michel Gerard Doucet has graciously allowed me to use the image from one of his wonderful paintings for the cover, and I am very grateful. Michel's work documents the rare beauty of the landscape that every single research participant involved in this work referred to as a beloved geography.

Michael Corbett
23 July 2019
Lower Rose Bay, NS

## References

Archer, M.S. (2012). *The reflexive imperative in late modernity*. Cambridge, UK: Cambridge University Press.

Biddle, C., and Hall, D. (2017). How education is failing rural America. *Education Week*, January 17. http://www.edweek.org/ew/articles/2017/01/18/how-education-is-failing-rural-america.html.

Corbett, M. (2018). Review of Forgotten Places: Critical Studies in Rural Education. William M. Reynolds (Ed). *Journal of Research in Rural Education* 33, 5: 1–4. http://jrre.psu.edu/wp-content/uploads/2018/09/33-5.pdf.

Gamson, D. (2019). Transitions from rural to urban schooling. In J.L. Rury and E.H. Tamura (eds.), *The Oxford handbook of the history of education*. London: Oxford University Press.

Hochschild, A.R. (2016). *Strangers in their own land: Anger and mourning on the American Right*. New York: The New Press.

Wuthnow, R. (2018). *The left behind: Decline and rage in rural America*. Princeton: Princeton University Press.

# Foreword

I began my teaching career in a First Nations community in northern Manitoba in the early 1980s. For several years I worked as a high school social studies teacher in a small K–12 school in a Cree and Métis community. Very early into this teaching assignment, I realized that the high school did not work very well, at least in terms of the expectations I had at the time. Literacy and numeracy standards were low. There were major drug and alcohol issues in the community, and young people were introduced into the culture of substance abuse at a very early age. Teenage pregnancy was common. Attendance was sporadic, and, with the exception of a few individuals, general academic achievement was very weak. Many students dropped out of school. Those few who managed graduate mostly remained in the village living lives that were not significantly different from those who dropped out of school. A tiny fraction of my students tried their luck in post-secondary education, but they typically ended up back in the community, again living in much the same way as everyone else.

I began to see that the whole project of secondary schooling was set up to usher young people out of the community and into opportunities in the south, despite the fact that the overwhelming majority remained close to home. There were powerful precedents for this orientation. In the Platonic vision, the word education means "to lead out." Young people are stuck in ignorance in a shadowy cave and the teacher's job is to lead them out to apprehend reality. In the Christian tradition, the educator worked hand in hand with the cleric to steer the "savage" away from primitive and pagan ways toward civilization and true religion. In northern Manitoba, we were in the missionary business trying to save a few souls and transport them safely to a middle-class life in the south, or minimally an honest trade or working-class job.

The whole process was a moral exercise but one with crucial geographical content. The location of success was clearly not in the community itself; the space of the local was explicitly defined by teachers and school administrators as dysfunctional. The local was the cave, it was the darkness from which our students needed to be delivered. As I began to spend time outside the small circle of the teacher accommodations and started to meet people living in the community, it slowly dawned on me that while the community was significantly troubled, it was a safe, familiar home to the people who lived there. On the invitation of Ron Cook of Grand Rapids, Manitoba,

I fished on Lake Winnipeg from small boats and in the winter from Bombardiers, the ladybug-shaped snow tractors that traversed the five-foot thick frozen lake ice. I came to understand that my students and their families had deep knowledge of this place and that this knowledge was threatened by the kinds of abstract knowledge and cultural assumptions we applied quite unwittingly in the everyday practices of our professional work as teachers. My pedagogy was, as one student put it, "White-man's stories."

I came to know a hard-working group of people and began to take part in some of the early phases of a revival of traditional First Nations spirituality. I also began to understand that the intimate connection between Cree and Métis people and the land from which they made a living was a great deal more than a set of words mumbled in ritual fashion; it was a living relationship that had been twisted and changed irreparably by industrialization and the needs and practices of my tribe living in the south. I heard stories told by men and women my own age about the day they were playing in the woods and the bulldozers came through the trees at the head of a parade leading a road building crew followed by construction crews that built a bridge over the great South Saskatchewan river that flows through the community. The river was subsequently diverted and dammed, and some of the community's traditional lands were flooded because of the growing need for power in the south. With the link to the south and the boomtown atmosphere during the years of construction, the community was changed forever in ways I can only begin to understand or even imagine.

I learned that despite all of these problems, most of these friends had no intention of leaving and that they were quite troubled by the idea that they ought to leave. Their ancestors had walked this land for countless generations before European contact, the advent of the fur trade, the incursions of religious and education missionaries, and later the hydro project that arrived in the mid-1960s to change people and the places they lived. As one elder told me, "Eventually you will all be gone from here, but not us." The community was home to these people and it would continue to be home.

From the point of view of education, which was what I was supposed to be doing, I became increasingly concerned about the way the curriculum, prescribed materials, our preferred transmission pedagogies, our ways of individualizing instruction and testing, our standards, disciplinary and behavioural expectations, our cultural assumptions and generally the whole matrix of institutional practices and practitioners (most of whom were "White" southerners) seemed out of place and misguided. I started to believe that by educating, or attempting to educate, these youth for a life outside the community, we were missing the opportunity to really connect with and teach them. I remembered vague notions from my teacher training about how learning must begin from the experience of the child.

I have written some of the story of the way this experience changed me as a teacher elsewhere (Corbett, 1999), but the point is that I became less interested in the generic "what" (content) and "how" (methods) of education and more interested in the "why" and particularly the "where" of the process.

After four years in northern Manitoba, I began what was to be a fifteen-year public school teaching career in coastal communities in the Digby area of southwestern Nova Scotia. There I encountered something similar to what I experienced in Manitoba. Many of these students also seemed to stay close to home after graduation, fitting into the local economy and the family-based network that had an intergenerational history of work in resource industries, particularly the fishery. Many of these students graduated from high school, but the majority of the boys, it seemed to me, did not. My students in this new situation were somewhat more successful academically, and there was a fairly sizeable cadre that did "go on" and pursue post-secondary education, never to return to the community. These youth were considered by the teachers to have been the success stories of the school system. It seemed as though the further away a student went, the more pride teachers took in the part they played in the process. The larger group who remained was lumped into a category with the demeaning prefix "just." The just had just stuck around here, or just gone fishing, or became just a housewife, or just took a job in town.

In the coastal community formal education was viewed by some people as an unqualified good. However, many considered it to be an expensive and time-consuming means to an end that was not achievable locally or by "people like us," as Pierre Bourdieu (1984b, 1990) put it so cryptically in an exposition of his core concept of cultural capital. Like in northern Manitoba, there was a significant disconnect between what was going on in school and the real and imagined lives of that large group of students who had no intention of leaving the local area.

I had no real way of knowing for certain if my sense of the failure of schooling for these young people was really as profound as it seemed to be. I really did not know who left, who stayed and what role education played in these mobility trajectories. I also had, and continue to have, a limited understanding of the informal education practices and processes through which a person learns to fish or the multiple skills necessary to manage a household in a fishing family. Finally, I wanted to find out more about how people in a coastal community actually experienced schooling and the choices and life paths involved in deciding to stay or leave school and to stay or leave the community. I expected that these two latter decisions were intimately connected.

This book documents a research project that began formally in 1997 and carried on through 2001. The general research question driving the project was simple: "In this coastal community who stays, who goes and why?" The methods I used to answer my question included two surveys of individuals who attended the local elementary school from the time it was consolidated in 1957 until 1992 (the potential high school graduating classes of 1963–1998). This survey work was accomplished with the generous help of a number of Digby Neck women and men who "tracked" virtually everyone who attended the elementary school through these years to where they currently reside. From this survey work I interviewed a sample of eighteen individuals who stayed on Digby Neck after their schooling. I then interviewed a sample of eighteen individuals who were living further than 250 km from Digby Neck. Finally, I interviewed a sample of twelve educators and former educators who taught children from Digby Neck from the early 1940s through to the late 1990s. Through 1998–2000 I conducted field work on Digby Neck that included several fishing trips.

Chapters 1 and 2 lay out some of the theoretical and conceptual issues that I think connect to the problem of learning and leaving in rural communities, and perhaps of learning and leaving more generally.[1] In essence these chapters document my own transition from attempting to explain poor school performance and low achievement in terms of the concept of resistance developed by Paul Willis and Marxist curriculum and education theorists from the late 1970s, toward an engagement with a broader range of sources in cultural studies and in sociology. While I still find the idea of resistance useful and appropriate, I argue, especially in Chapter 2 for a reformulation of the concept that incorporates a more complex and nuanced idea of power. The title of this book is a rather obvious genuflection to what I consider to be the importance of Willis's classic study *Learning to Labour* (1977). Chapter 3 is an analysis of documentary sources that provide a demographic background for Digby Neck in historical and contemporary terms. In this chapter I also discuss the results of my own survey work that looks specifically at the contours and magnitude of the relationship between learning and leaving.

The plan of the rest of the book was developed out of the categories and concepts I developed with key informants in the field work part of the research. These informants identified three key historical periods through the thirty-six years covered by this study. The first period begins in 1963, the year in which the eldest group would have reached the age of potential high school graduation, six years after leaving the elementary school in grade 6 (1957). This first historical period ends in 1974, the beginning of limited entry licensing in the lobster fishery and the widespread regulation of the coastal fishery. I call the people who "came of age" between 1963 and 1974, Cohort 1. Chapter 4 relies heavily on their accounts of their experience of schooling and life in a community still very much dependent on the small-boat inshore fishery and a developing offshore industry.

Chapter 5 is based on the accounts of the group I call Cohort 2, who came of age between 1975 and 1986. This period was defined locally as the "boom" time that followed the widespread industrialization of the fishery. It is remembered as a period of relative and in some cases great local prosperity, large catches, modernization, abundant work and the expansion of consumer opportunities for well placed families. Chapter 6 develops the accounts of the third cohort, who came of age between 1987 and 1998, a period that began with relative prosperity that quickly transformed into what can only be described as something of a panic about the state of fish stocks after years of industrial harvesting. This time in generally understood as one of "downsizing" in many areas of the fishery.

In the final chapter I return to some of the core concepts and problems identified in the opening chapters and some of the pragmatics that follow from my analysis. This study concludes, as it begins, with a deep ambivalence. I have no direct answers to the problem of mobility as a central feature in contemporary education.[2] I am deeply ambivalent about the way that young people in isolated and rural communities are put in a situation where a serious engagement with formal education pretty much always leads away from home. Education failure and immobility is often tragic at the individual level in contemporary Canada, but so too is education success and the depopulation of rural places. Recently, the novel problem of labour shortages in Atlantic Canada has revealed an unexpected challenge in the region. There are no easy answers at the level of curriculum and instruction, education policy or economic development strategy. Keeping young people in rural communities is not necessarily the answer. In fact, I tend to believe that educators need to be more explicit about their typically implied notion that rural youth must learn to leave. While I do believe that children in rural and coastal communities need to be taught in ways that strengthen their roots and understanding of place, I also believe that both physical travel and imaginative literate travel are particularly important in isolated schools. To promote this end, and to recognize the inspiration of the children of Digby Neck (my former students), royalties from the sale of this book will be donated to Digby Neck Consolidated School for books and for educational travel.

## Notes

1. It has been suggested to me that learning to leave and learning to be mobile are essential features of contemporary schooling. I draw heavily on the work of Anthony Giddens and particularly Zygmunt Bauman who have been making this kind of argument for some years now. To be modern/postmodern is to be

incessantly and irreversibly in motion.

2. It is also the case that as the present decade has unfolded, young people in coastal and rural communities face new challenges and opportunities as Ontario, Alberta and British Columbia have experienced economic boom periods not entirely dissimilar from those of the 1950s, 60s and 70s. These boom conditions have created new opportunities -or perhaps more importantly, the perception of opportunity, the for migrants who lack formal education.

# Acknowledgement

This work would not have been possible without the help of many people from Digby Neck who opened something of their world to me over the years both as a teacher and in this research project. I know that I have not gotten everything right but I hope that my ignorance causes a minimum of offence. I learned on one of my first fishing trips that a novice can cause a lot of trouble mucking about in a highly coordinated, high stakes enterprise like a working fishing boat. I hope I have not done that here. I would like first of all to thank Fred Horner and Donna and Roger Tidd for their ongoing support of this work through many informal conversations. The survey part of this book would have been impossible without the assistance of a number of people, including Deanna Frost, Pam Frost, Susan O'Neil, Karen Mosher, Junior Theriault, Dianne Theriault, Margaret Titus, the late Elizabeth McCullough, Cindy Graham, Anna Marie MacKenzie-Kelly and Dorothy Tidd. Tony Kelly and Arthur and Ruth Bull provided me with feedback and critical commentary throughout the research process. In the academy, I have benefited from critical feedback from several anonymous reviewers as well as from readings of earlier drafts of the book by Don Fisher, Kjell Rubenson, Ralph Matthews, Brian Elliot, Dianne Looker and Don Wilson (in whose seminar on the history of Canadian education the idea for this study was originally conceived). My colleagues and students in the School of Education at Acadia University have also supported my work in numerous ways over the past several years. I would also like to thank the anonymous reviewers. The cover photo, from Eastern Head looking out over the mouth of Little River harbour, was taken by Audrey Oldershaw and her ongoing support has been incalculably important through the years.

This research was funded by the Social Sciences and Humanities Research Council, the Nova Scotia Teachers Union and a University of British Columbia graduate fellowship. The fieldwork and other parts of this research were also made possible by a sabbatical leave granted by the Tri-county District School Board. The publication of this study as a book has been funded by the Aid to Scholarly Publication Program of the Federation for the Humanities and Social Sciences. Finally, thanks to Errol Sharpe of Fernwood Publishing and the others who assisted with the publication of this book: Beverley Rach, Brenda Conroy and Debbie Mathers.

Chapter 1

# Introduction

> On the first day of May the boats raced out as they had always done, laden down almost to the gunwales with their heavy cargoes of traps. They were almost like living things as they plunged through the waters of the spring and maneuvered between the still floating icebergs of crystal white and emerald green on their way to the traditional grounds that they sought out every May. And those of us who sat that day in the high school on the hill, discussing the water imagery in Tennyson, watched them as they passed back and forth beneath us until by afternoon the piles of traps which had been stacked on the wharf were no longer visible but were spread about the bottom of the sea.... And the spring wore on and the summer came and school ended in the third week of June and the lobster season on July first and I wished that the two things I loved so dearly did not exclude each other in a manner that was so blunt and too clear. (MacLeod, 1976: 143–45)

Paul Willis's (1977) ethnographic study of working-class life and schooling in an English industrial city is introduced with the direct and poignant subtitle: "How working-class kids get working-class jobs." Indeed, one of the central questions for the sociology of education continues to be the role that schools play in reproducing class structure. Willis's question is central to understanding the relationship between schooling and class in urban communities.[1] A similar yet seldom analyzed problem confronts rural education researchers. Alistair McLeod's fiction (cited above) works with similar kinds of questions. If Willis's "lads" learned to enact a working-class identity that rubs hard against the urban, middle-class norms of school, Alistair McLeod's fictional characters wrestle with both how and where to construct their identities. In rural communities, school plays a number of roles, including the reproduction of labour in traditional local industries and migration to urban centres.

In fact, the history of rural education can be read as one part of a larger history of urbanization, the movement of populations from the country to the city. This is a history that charts national development out of colonization and the struggle for land, through the establishment of "founding" cultural enclaves in eastern Canada and a general oppression of First Nations peoples, through the development of an increasingly multicultural society from the early part of the twentieth century. This book is an account of education in one of those rural communities that persist in a reliance on a single resource industry in a social and cultural space that remains largely Anglo-European. A multitude of social, economic and cultural forces are bearing down on such communities, and keeping things as they are is a struggle that the inhabitants of isolated communities are bound to lose in part because education offers up opportunities for youth in a different kind of social space beyond the village. This study attempts to understand how it is that certain people remain in Atlantic Canadian coastal communities while others leave. In other words, how do some rural youth "learn to leave," while others "learn to stay?"

A central theme in Atlantic Canadian sociology is geographic mobility. This theme articulates with larger problems of the development of the Canadian state and the underdevelopment of Atlantic Canada (Brym and Sacouman, 1979). Mobility is very often presented as the solution to the region's problems (George, 1970; Courchene, 1974; Florida, 2002). But coastal communities in Nova Scotia not only have a history of more or less sustainable resource extraction, they are understood as a partially secure home-place by many youth who are not successful in school. These young people are discursively cast as the losers in the education drama; they are the "dropouts," the ones who cannot read the "writing on the wall" and make the "obvious" choice, which is to acquire an education as means to buy passage elsewhere. Contemporary work in the sociology of education has begun to raise questions about how these discursive constructions of the "good student" actually frame and position groups of youth as "successful" and other groups as "failures" (Walkerdine, 1990; Lesko, 2001; Hicks, 2002; Kenway and Kraak, 2004). Post-secondary education presents most rural youth with a problematic juxtaposition of their home communities and elsewhere, usually an urban environment or a small town in a more prosperous region of the country.[2]

Like Willis's "lads," many rural youth resist formal education and make what are considered to be the "wrong choices." Whether the "resistance" of these students to the project of education represents what Willis called a "penetration" of the false promise of the education system is an interesting question. The fact that resistance exists is well established, but what it means to those rural youth who enact it has not been well explored. Indeed, the idea of resistance assumes the hegemony of a particular set of values and structural arrangements. Rural life itself may simply be resistant to the juggernaut of industrialization and urbanization, an experiential base for resistance to modernity and to a set of "rational" values (Bonner, 1997; Ching and Creed, 1997; Theobald, 1997). In other words, rural places may represent competing discursive frameworks that offer different definitions of who is and who is not able and successful (Brandau and Collins, 1994; Porter, 1996; Wotherspoon, 1998).

In order to exploit marine resources "efficiently," capital has required a flexible and relatively immobile work force in coastal communities, a work force sufficiently adaptable and responsive to survive boom and bust in the industry and respond to the ebb and flow of fish stocks in particular areas. Education decisions are always made in a context. The industrialization of the fishery after World War Two provided young men in coastal communities with certain community-based opportunities, which stood beside opportunities offered by formal education. In fact, many frustrated teachers and guidance counsellors in rural places are community "outsiders, "cultural bridge" workers and "gatekeepers," who have adopted placeless urban values (DeYoung, 1995; Haas and Nachtigal, 1998) and have little understanding of the economics, social networks or indigenous local knowledge that has sustained coastal communities for generations (Bowers, 2003).

Rather than support place-based ways of knowing and established social, economic and cultural networks in rural and coastal communities, the school has typically stood in opposition to local lifeworlds. The nature of professionalism among teachers has tended to privilege placeless, generic and technocratic ideas about what counts as education. If education is to be democratic and serve the purpose of social and cultural elevation, then it must be generic and transcend the specificity of the locale. It must transcend the bounded realms of place and move its object (the student) into the unbounded universe of space (Lefebvre, 1991; Casey, 1998). Place attachment and local knowledge are precisely what many rural educators struggle to subvert in the interests of democracy and what is often called "broadening the horizons" of rural children and youth. Continuing high rates of high school non-completion among youth in coastal communities and particularly among young men illustrate the failure of this project.

In the case of Digby Neck, Nova Scotia, which is the location of this study, place attachment has related to a labour-intensive fishery and the services often provided by family members (notably women and children) that supported it. Ironically, many Nova Scotians forged their identities and honed multiple skills and strength working in the industrialization and capitalist development of a fishing industry that has slowly but surely undermined the viability of coastal communities. The modern fishery is not a nostalgic pastiche; it is a business, and a business with a history. Most modern fishers resemble small business owners and factory workers in their daily activity rather than the "fisherfolk" Ian McKay (1994) describes in his historical work. As McKay argues, contrary to the "folk" stereotypes of the slow moving, primitive rustic, Nova Scotians survived through "(G)eographic mobility (moving from place to place in search of waged work or better access to fish stocks), occupational pluralism, and from the mid-nineteenth century on, widespread out-migration to cope with diminishing opportunities in the region" (1994: 28). The connection between formal education and this migration is by now iconic and enshrined in twentieth-century Atlantic Canadian literature (Kristiensen, 1994).[3] Atlantic Canadian coastal communities are places that people learned to leave.

Historians have documented the rise of the state and its growth out of urban centres and into the rural periphery. The process of state normalization has been much more troublesome in rural areas, as institutional practices like schooling fit more readily into the productive industrial spaces of the city or large town (Curtis, 1988). In remote areas like the northern parts of most Canadian provinces or in coastal fishing communities, economies were based upon resource extraction, and communities were, for many years, relatively insulated from both mechanized industrial production and the institutional "tutelary complex" of modern society (Donzelot, 1979). On the rural margins, the evidence is that the routines of secondary schooling were not effectively established until at least the post-World War Two period, despite the establishment of free schools in Nova Scotia in 1865 and mandatory schooling in 1882 (Wilson et al., 1970; Axelrod, 1997: 35–36). In rural Canada, a complex structure of opportunity existed, and patterns of informal education and direct socialization to adult roles stood in opposition to the school and the training it offered (Davey, 1978; Gaffield, 1987; McCann, 1982; Wilson and Stortz, 1993). Additionally, rural communities offered active, systematic and sustained resistance to early efforts to impose the normalizing regime of schooling upon their children (Curtis, 1988).

Very often the practical contingencies of relentless physical work in rural communities and apprenticeship-style socialization of youth made the establishment of formal schooling problematic, and resistance to schooling remained prominent. The institutional discourse of formal education continually met the practical discourse of life in the community, and the world it enjoins them to imagine is typically a shadow of the local places in which these rural children live out their lives.

Lucas's (1971) work contains the most detailed ethnographic and quantitative analysis of the connection between education and migration I have found in the literature. Lucas's general conclusion is that education is one of the principal and "easiest" exit routes from single-industry communities. He writes: "one of the easiest ways to emigration is to continue along the education lines that link the community to the outside world" (1971: 366). "Furthermore, the educational system represents an established bridge into other places and other lives, a series of "well marked route… for the fortunate who persist in school" (1971: 368). In his review of several quantitative studies of migration from Canadian single-industry communities, he found that around 60 percent of youth migrate and that a high percentage of those who do have the highest levels of education. In his own survey of 817 students over a twenty-three-year period in a single-industry community, Lucas found what he termed a "remarkable connection between grade completed and location of occupation" (1971: 382). For instance, 100 out of 126 people who attained less than grade ten remained in the community, while only 18 percent of high school graduates stayed. Lucas asserted that "all respondents in all communities agreed that youth very quickly educated themselves out of the jobs offered in the community and out of the community itself" (1971: 363).

> By supplying symbols of qualification, the educational institution has great power over the pupil and his occupational orientation. In a community of single industry it provides the youth not only with upward mobility, but also with one of the most useful emigration routes from the community. (Lucas, 1971: 302)

Lucas also showed how work opportunities in single-industry communities were not universally available but were distributed on the basis of social class and gender.[4] Implicitly, we can also discern a tension between life in the community and an education enterprise that operates principally as a "link" to elsewhere, particularly when that link seems to function as a one-way street.

How the strain between informal work socialization and formal schooling has played out in coastal communities is unknown. No one has yet studied ordinary people's experience of schooling in fishing villages, or how the lure of work, ready money, established patterns of family formation and gender roles, and a deep knowledge of the land and the ocean were counterpoised by the uncertain promise of school. The tension between school and community in Atlantic Canada is also nested within a larger tension between rural and urban places on a global scale (Berry, 1977; Theobald, 1997; Roy, 2001). In the uneven development of the Canadian economy, Atlantic Canada remains a "hinterland" region. Although complicated by globalization, the theme of marginality remains the same. In coastal places, this has led to the historical development of ambiguous social-class formations and what Marxist analysts call semi-proletarian household-focused forms of production (MacDonald and Connelly, 1989; Kearney, 1993; Brym and Sacouman, 1979). The persistence of these economic forms through the evolution and industrialization of rural resource communities has consequences for education (Ricker, 1978b) as well as for economic, institutional and social development in the region.

At the level of local lives, these tensions can mean that dropping out of school is constructed as the positive decision to drop in to community life and to reject the denigration of that community life implicit in the education message (Kenway and Kraak, 2002; Smyth and Hattam, 2004; Kirby, 2005). This is effectively what many ethnographies of working-class resistance have shown (Hall and Jefferson, 1976, Corrigan, 1979; McLaren, 1980; Willis, 1979; McRobbie, 1991; Wexler, 1992; Gaskell, 1992; LeBlanc, 1999). In Willis's study, the "lads" resisted school only to end up in an alienating factory routine, but they seem to have found integration into a customary way of life. Similarly, in Nova Scotian coastal communities, "the boys" find integration into a culture that, although it contains significant elements of hardship, exploitation, alienation, sexism and racism, is not experienced as oppression, but rather is accepted as a familiar way of living grounded in community and regional culture (Kelly, 1993). The fishery also provided at least some young men *petit bourgeois* opportunities in the loosely regulated fishery that remained alive until the 1970s. What women may have found is less clear.

## Migration and Regional Dependency: The Brain Drain

> A suggestion to provide "generous assistance" to those people who might wish to move to other parts of Canada where, "'there may be better opportunity'" was met with derision. Obviously decades of out-migration had not served the region very well as a development strategy. (Conrad, 1997: 410)

Atlantic Canadian folklore routinely associates migration and education. Both academic and non-academic commentators use the notion of "brain drain" when discussing education. This familiar Atlantic Canadian tale is often told in the context of regional inequality. Education institutions in the region tend to educate young people for employment opportunities elsewhere. But is this an accurate picture? Do residents of coastal communities facing declining fisheries migrate en masse? How do they decide whether to stay or leave? Where do they go? And what role, if any, does formal education play in this drama?

The quantitative literature that explores the connection between migration and education generally supports the brain-drain hypothesis.[5] Large-scale Canadian and international quantitative analyses show that highly educated individuals are more mobile than other less educated segments of a given population (Afsar, 1996; Amit-Talai, 1993; Banerjee, 1996; Braio-Ureta et al., 1996; Dasgupta, 1988; Dublin, 1998; Frey, 1995; Gibbs, 1994; Liaw, 1990; Michalos, 1997; Moomis, 1990; Newbold and Liaw, 1994; Newbold, 1996; Tolnay, 1998; Goldscheider et al., 1999). The positive correlation between education levels and migration rates has been so well established and so often repeated that it is simply assumed that more educated people are more mobile. Dasgupta writes:

> A positive association between education and propensity to migration is often assumed by sociologists. Mobility is increased as members of the labor force acquire superior skills, professional training and education of all kinds. (1988: 37)

Yet, Dasgupta argues that lack of formal education can also be seen as a "push" factor stimulating migration. Two studies of internal migration in Canada conducted in the 1960s found higher rates of out-migration among those people who had lower than average levels of education attainment (Leavitt, 1960; Stone, 1969). In his classic analysis of historical census data, Stone commented that:

> The general expectation would probably have been that a purely economic model of migration would give better results for a more highly educated group than for persons with only elementary schooling. The results of this case study indicate that the reverse may be the case. (1969: 196)

Stone went on to raise questions about the "economic model of migration" that underpinned his research because he found that less educated people in fact tended to be more mobile than more educated individuals. While farming areas were indeed losing population, Stone found a rural non-farm population that was very stable, actually gaining population in Canada and in Nova Scotia from 1956 to 1961 (1969: 56).[6] Leavitt was also unable to find the clear link she expected to find between education and migration in Atlantic Canada (1960). These studies both deal with data from pre-1961, but their findings raise questions about the link between migration and education and also foreshadow the movement of population back to rural areas that are in close proximity to urban places.

The connection between education and migration in Atlantic Canada is both an emotional and a political issue. From the point of view of conservative economic theory, migration is an "adjustment mechanism" through which the market moves (pushes and pulls) labour into places where it is needed (George, 1970; Courchene, 1974). Pierre Trudeau retorted in the late 1970s, when confronted by Maritimers who complained about unemployment in the region, "why don't you just get off your asses [and move to a place where there is employment]." From a Marxist perspective, the migration problem is a manifestation of the needs of capital to maintain a "reserve army" of labour waiting on the periphery to be deployed in the metropolis in times of capital expansion or "boom" (Veltmeyer, 1979;

Sacouman, 1980). There has been significant debate about both the Marxist and conservative economic visions of the state of social and economic life in Atlantic Canada. For instance, Ralph Matthews has consistently argued that the neo-conservative economic analysis of migration and regional dependency is demeaning and dismissive of Atlantic Canadians and largely ignorant of the history of economic development in the region (1983, 1993). Southcott argues that the structural Marxist analysis of regional dependency in Atlantic Canada in the 1970s and 1980s effectively sapped energy for research in this area because it presented such a hopeless, dismal picture of the role of human agency and community (1999).[7] Both of these critiques call for a focused research program that investigates the cultural experience of underdevelopment with the objective of mobilizing local understandings toward generating positive policy decisions and social change.

With respect to migration, both neo-conservative and political economic analyses agree that individuals respond to structural forces over which they have little control. Both also seem to agree that educated individuals are drawn in and out of "peripheral" regions to serve the needs of the market. Neither theory offers much immediate hope for the region. Papastergiadis argues that both of these perspectives rely on what he calls the "water pump model" of migration theorizing, where people are seen as being driven to and fro by the needs of capital (2000). He states that neither conservative nor radical structural models of development, or the migration analysis contained within them, actually stand up in the face of less predictable human agency and culture.

> Marxist theories of dependency and Weberian theories of modernization both tended to relegate cultural differences to a sign of underdevelopment that would be overtaken by a progressive movement of modernity. Cultural differences have proved to be both more resilient and contradictory. (Papastergiadis, 2000: 94)

In sociological studies of migration and of education, the conundrum is to find a way between analyses that track the broad structural contours of a problem and studies that are so focused and particular they are not generalizable. Political economy studies of migration lack cultural sensitivity and explain population movement entirely in terms of the ebb and flow of the "needs" of capital (if the account is Marxist) or of society (if the account is functionalist). One is positive, the other is negative, but they amount to the same thing. How the pursuit of higher education impacts on the lives of individuals and how it contributes to the stress and ambivalence found in rural schools is not well understood. There is, it seems, something deeply problematic about both the cultural and physical spaces and places that formal education can open up for rural youth.

It is equally clear that structural analysis needs to be combined with methodologies that focus on culture, local understandings and the lived experience of knowledgeable human agents (Giddens, 1976). Looker and her colleagues' work on rural youth's aspirations do recognize the problematic nature of leaving home (Looker, 1993; Looker and Dwyer, 1998; Looker and Andres, 1998).

> The rural youth were more tied to their communities, were more concerned about family relationships, but they were also more likely to leave. They perceived few, if any, options if they remained. The respondents planning to stay were those for whom family and community ties were more important than occupational advancement. (Looker, 1993: 59)

Combining quantitative and qualitative methods, Looker found that this leaving problematic has a significant impact on rural youth participation and outcomes in higher education and far fewer rural youth either start or finish post-secondary programs (Looker, 1993; Looker and Andres, 1998; Looker and Dwyer, 1998). How rural living and education and migration decision-making interact is beyond the scope of these studies. Looker and Andres suggest Bourdieu's theory of practice as a way of framing the problem (1998), but most work of this sort contains little theoretical direction.

Gill Jones' (1995, 1999a, 1999b) qualitative work in Scotland investigates the migration decisions of rural youth. Jones studied how young people develop what she calls "socio-spatial identities" — how they come to forge identity with respect to place. Jones' work responds to migration studies that ignore the role of agency and operate at the level of gauging the relative "rationality" of the migration decision-making process in large populations. Most migration studies investigate the extent to which people leave areas of relatively low wages and low levels of employment and move to places where wages are higher and jobs are more plentiful. Jones is interested in how individuals living in rural communities interpret the field of options before them and how they go about making migration decisions in the context of their lives.

Jones (1999a) found that intracommunity dynamics played a powerful role in the migration decisions of the individuals she studied. Using the theoretical work of Giddens and Bauman, Jones draws a continuum of community attachment from traditional, place-bound identity, through Giddens' (1990) modernist notion of the self as a "project," to Bauman's (1995) transient postmodern idea of a kind of floating identity that avoids all ties to place. Jones finds elements of all three kinds of socio-spatial identity at play in the responses of her sample population. Her central finding is that those individuals whose identity is rooted in place and situated at the "traditional" end of her socio-spatial identity continuum are least likely to migrate. Those most likely to migrate from rural communities are children of in-migrant parents, who because of their family mobility experience have developed more modern or postmodern identity structures, which have fewer and weaker linkages to the rural communities in which they were raised.

Jones' work investigates migration as a decision-making process in which agency is the central feature. She does not, however, analyze the role of schooling and formal education trajectories in the migration decision. In a Nova Scotian study, Jane Jensen (2002) analyzed adult education in a deindustrializing community, finding that most adult level training has limited practical value in the context of the local economy.[8] Jensen too focused on agency in her anthropological analysis but did not explore the implicit connection between formal education and out-migration. So while the education-migration connection is well supported in the quantitative literature on migration, and implied in the sociological literature on education decision-making, it is not well understood at the level of particular communities. An additional problem is that most sociological studies of education decision-making are not longitudinal, and so the dimension of the historical transformation of rural economies is not connected to the decision-making of individuals through time.[9]

## The Migration Imperative in Rural Education

> It is a great error to assume that people are rendered stupid by remaining always in the same place. —William Cobbett, 1830

> Such winds as scatters young men through the world to seek their fortunes further than at home where small experience grows. —Shakespeare (*The Taming of the Shrew*, Act 1 Scene 2)

Neoclassical economics views migration as driven by rational economic calculation on the part of individuals and groups and by the "natural" evolution of markets at the macro level. People move from areas where there is little economic opportunity to areas where there is abundance.[10] In addition to the scholarly literature on the problem of schooling and migration in rural areas of Nova Scotia (Looker, 1993; Looker and Dwyer, 1998; Looker and Andres, 1998), there is a wealth of fictional material that explores migration, and some of it deals with the role that education plays in re-placing individuals in a social and psychic landscape larger than that of the rural Nova Scotian community and local attachments. This re-placing is often infused with a fundamental rejection of home (the rural community).

In the Atlantic rural fiction of Alistair MacLeod, Earnest Buckler,

Charles Bruce, Lynn Coady and Connie Barnes, to stay in school, beyond secondary education particularly, typically amounts to a decision to leave or dropout of the community. Schooling in suburban and urban environments carries no such implication. Thus, continued schooling in rural communities is a different order of decision for the young people who live there, and it represents taking the first steps toward severing important ties to place, community and family. These days, leaving home may be a much more problematic enterprise than ever before (Jones, 1995), because the post-modern world is understood to be an exciting and choice-filled, yet chaotic and dangerous, space. The central sociological macro-imagery of the last decade illustrates this tumult in the form of Anthony Giddens' "runaway world" (1999), in which the central social image is a juggernaut; Ulrich Beck's liability-fixated "risk society" (1992); Manuel Castells' equally uncertain and tumultuous "network society" (2004), replete with unseen knowledge conduits; Richard Sennett's floating, relocating knowledge workers (1999); and I think most powerfully the uncertain, mobile, wasteful "liquid modernity" described by Zygmunt Bauman (2000, 2004b). In late modernity, everything seems to be in flux and everyone who counts as successful seems to be in motion. We learn to leave places for spaces.

A large number of studies in the sociology of rural education have also identified the strong connection between learning and leaving — and the ambivalence about schooling this equation generates — in rural communities. The decision to stay or leave the home community is a significant and often traumatic milestone for rural youth (Donaldson, 1986; Gibbs, 1995; Theobald, 1997; Beggs et al., 1996; Ley et al., 1996; Pollard et al., 1990; Hektner, 1995; Ovando, 1984; Hawley, Harmon and Leopold, 1996; DeYoung, 1995; Elder, King and Conger, 1996; Seyfrit and Danner, 1999; Jones, 1995, 1999a, 1999b; Looker, 1993; Looker and Dwyer, 1998; Looker and Theissen, 1999; Looker and Andres, 1998). Each of these decisions (staying or leaving) has significant implications, both for the individual and for small communities (Theobald, 1997). This difficulty contributes to lower participation rates for rural students in post-secondary education and elevated high school dropout rates. These lower rates of participation and high school completion are not new. The "rural school problem" has been discussed for at least the past hundred years in both Canada and the United States. At least part of this problem is that education may be presented to and perceived by rural students as preparation for elsewhere. For some students this perception is liberating, for others unthinkable, and for most it is problematic and conflicted (Hektner, 1995; Elder, King and Conger, 1996).

Several U.S. studies investigate place attachment and the weighty decision to leave rural communities associated with school completion. Elder, King and Conger (1996) found in their large-scale quantitative study (part of the Iowa Youth and Family Project) of rural adolescents' psychological well-being, that the period at the end of a rural student's high school career is typically fraught with intrapersonal conflict, feelings of depression and unhappiness. Those youth who had made the firm decision to leave their home communities to further their education or to work experienced higher levels of personal distress and less of a sense of control over their lives. To quote the study: "Leave-oriented adolescents are most apt to believe that life is not going well… stayers… the boys in particular, have a relatively positive view of self and life, whatever the future may hold" (Elder, King and Conger, 1996: 416). Elder, King and Conger also discovered that once adolescents committed to staying in the community, their perceptions of employment prospects in the community became more positive (1996). By committing themselves to remain, rural students actually came to see their prospects, and those of their community, in a more positive light.

Hektner found that rural children expressed greater conflict between the importance of staying close to their parents and home and moving away from the local area (1995). In this study rural youth expressed higher levels of desire both to "get away" and to "live close to parents and relatives" than did urban youth (Hektner, 1995: 8). These strong contradictory desires led to higher levels of personal distress, particularly for rural males. Hektner also found high levels of conflict between leaving and staying to be positively associated with lower education aspirations. Those students who experience the most ambivalence about moving away from home tended to want less post-secondary education. As Hektner puts it: "Given two mutually incompatible wishes, whatever decision a conflicted adolescent makes may not be without emotional costs" (1995: 12). Unlike their rural counterparts the decision to pursue post-secondary education for most urban and suburban youth will not necessarily involve separation from home.

Drawing on the High School and Beyond study, Ley, Nelson and Beltyukova (1996) investigated education aspirations of rural youth, specifically the interaction of youth, parental and teacher aspirations. This study attempted to understand how migration was offered to rural students as a means of personal advancement and how the pursuit of opportunities "elsewhere" fit with concerns for the long term sustainability of declining rural communities. The hypothesis was that rural community members would see youth as the future of their communities and would understand education as a key strategic point for inculcating values of stewardship, community leadership and activism. On the contrary, the study found that parents, youth themselves and particularly teachers placed "traditional community values" of mutual aid, caring and sharing at the bottom of their list of factors they considered important for successful adulthood. While they may have been committed to building sustainable communities, no one saw the school as significant in the process. Instead, these rural residents held highly individualistic visions of school as a personal opportunity for rural youth. In a study of an Alaskan high school, Ovando also found that teachers are the principal promoters of school as a mechanism for personal as opposed to social advancement in rural communities (1984).[11]

Theobald (1997) argues that contemporary schools are fundamentally liberal institutions, concerned primarily with the promotion of individualism at all costs. For Theobald, the dissolution of community and massive rural out-migration are unintended consequences of this orientation. Rural teachers and school administrators are often highly committed to the ideals of providing what they consider to be a "modern education," which has involved promoting school closures, consolidation and out-migration (Cuban and Tyack, 1995; DeYoung, 1995; Theobald, 1997; Wotherspoon, 1998). Ley, Nelson and Beltyukova comment that "those who hold those positions often fail to see the bleak future it offers for rural communities. When rural youth migrate from their home towns their communities are deprived of talent and vitality that contributes to the development of a desirable future for these communities" (1996: 133).

Ironically, there is evidence that as more money is funnelled into rural schools, communities do not necessarily prosper. Again using the High School and Beyond database, Pollard, Oltare and Berg (1990) found that as a community's per pupil high school expenditure increased, so too did the probability of out-migration among rural youth. This research suggests that rather than contributing to community stability, well funded rural schools have resulted in rural decline. Rural schools tend to float above the communities in which they operate, apparently ushering certain "successful" individuals out of increasingly destitute rural areas and launching them into space.

## Challenges to the Migration Imperative in Rural Schooling

> The only escape from victimization has been to "succeed" — that is to "make it" into the class of exploiters, and then to remain so specialized and so "mobile" as to be unconscious of one's life or one's livelihood. (Berry, 1977: 4–5)

The formally educated young person who is retained in a rural community strengthens the way of life there, while the one who is lost contributes to its demise. Paul Theobald (1997) sees this paradox of liberal education as a dual-edged sword that presents individual rural youth with access to "opportunity" but which simultaneously erodes community. Theobald critiques this problem by claiming that contemporary American education is predicated upon a vision of the autonomous "self." Theobald situates the preoccupation with the individual in the classical liberal tradition, and particularly in the work of Locke, whose thought provided the framework for the character of American individualism and its particular incarnation of democracy. Theobald writes: "A self has come to be defined as someone who acts upon the world to achieve individual ends and desires.... Constructing life as an individual enterprise, as modern liberal thinking does, necessitates a government based on rights, an economy based on accumulation, and an education system that reifies the notion that life is an individual enterprise" (1997: 31).[12] The consequences for particular places, particularly rural places, are irrelevant because schools serve individuals. In fact, Theobald goes on to make the claim that this conception of education contributes inevitably to the crippling of rural communities. Following Wendell Berry, he writes: "When a society openly embraces political, economic, and education theory that hinges on an individualistic and anthropocentric conception of human nature, community disintegration is logical and predictable" (Theobald, 1997: 66).

Drawing on an alternative philosophical tradition that he associates with Montesquieu, Theobald opposes this autonomous individualism with a communitarian vision of individuals with interdependent and what he calls "intradependent" connections to people and places. Theobald's pedagogical vision is a model of place-based education predicated upon service and responsibility to others.

Canadian education sociologist Terry Wotherspoon argues that assumptions and priorities that are established, normal and even effective in urban schools need to be examined critically in the context of the rural school (1998). Ultimately Wotherspoon concludes that education agendas, which are becoming more "global" in scope, ought to be formulated in connection with "strategies that promote the sustainability of local places in rural areas" (1998: 140). Wotherspoon sees at the heart of contemporary education the inherent mobility imperative that effectively shunts rural youth to urban centres.

> Ironically, escalating demands for educational credentials and the integration of formal education into global realignment have created conditions in which educational success means that youth must leave their communities in order to pursue opportunities for higher education and meaningful employment. Consequently, the institution that communities look to as a guarantor of their future is, in fact, the gateway that channels valuable human resources out of these communities and into urban centres. (1998: 138)

Wotherspoon calls for education research that tries to sort out what kinds of education outcomes rural people want when they lend what he calls "strong support" to their schools. Rural parents are notoriously supportive of their community schools, but are they supporting the currently ascendant notion of schooling as preparation for global "market driven vocational and education plans," or conversely, "local concerns that focus upon the rebuilding and sustainability of communities" (Wotherspoon, 1998: 140). A good example of this kind of concern is contained in the comments made by rural residents across Canada in a series of workshops conducted in 1998 by the then newly constituted Canadian Rural Secretariat (Canada, 1999). Participants in these workshops consistently resisted the idea that children in rural communities must and should use higher education to move to urban areas.

> many young people in rural areas are leaving in order to find jobs or to go to school. The shrinking population of young people in many rural communities was identified as a key challenge.... Many rural youth must leave their communities or travel for long periods of time in order to access post-secondary and sometimes even high school... young people do not feel they had [sic] a future within their rural communities. (Canada, 1999: 9)

Not all rural youth want to "escape," nor do their families and communities unambiguously support their exodus. Notwithstanding the work of Ley, Nelson and Beltyukova, a common theme in studies of rural schooling is that rural students, and very often their parents too, may continue to resist the individualizing imperative of the contemporary school. As Porter discovered in her ethnography of a rural Appalachian high school, parents support and desire schools that, from a bureaucratic perspective, are dismal failures. A 50 percent dropout rate, as Porter discovered, means that at least half of the students stay in the rural mountain communities she studied. This fact, in the context of a deep sense of loss, is not particularly problematic.

> In Hickory County there is a poignant sense of accelerating loss of both land and close family ties. At the same time residents expressed the desire to reassert their distinctiveness and to preserve their mountain spaces, especially their schools as belonging to them, as vehicles for them to transmit valued cultural ways of being and relating to one another. In this process, they are actively engaged in constructing definable and bounded "imagined communities," deeply rooted communities that offer alternatives to the (mainstream) values of transience, consumption, individualism and material measures of success. (Porter, 1996: 109)

Which schools "work" or are "effective" is a matter of perspective. Those schools that "work" from the point of view of bureaucratic efficiency, change-fixated liberal individualism (Bowers, 2003) and mobile norms are those that effectively ease the rural student's transition out of the community. From the point of view of at least some rural communities, however, schools that work are those that provide opportunity but do not exacerbate de-population and out-migration.

In a study of what they called "bright rednecks," students attending a specially developed school for gifted rural Appalachian students in West Virginia, Hawley, Harmon and Leopold found that many of the most able students chose to use their abilities to establish a rural lifestyle, foregoing better occupational and economic possibilities available to them in cities (1996). These students articulated a definition of the "good life" that rested on rural values of community, family, close contact with nature and personal autonomy, values these students thought they would be unable to realize in urban environments. Gibbs also suggests that "educated" rural students who stay in their communities may be making a conscious decision to forego income in order to be closer to their families. Gibbs concludes that family ties and employment opportunities are the principal influences constraining post-secondary participation among rural youth (1995). He also discovered that approximately 65 percent of rural youth who leave for post-secondary training return to their communities of origin. Dropouts and those high school graduates who pursued no post-secondary training "comprise a much larger share of young people who stayed in rural areas than those lost to urban areas" (Gibbs, 1995: 40).

Rural areas do remain attractive for some students because of the lifestyle offered there. Brandau and Collins (1994) found that many Appalachian rural working-class youth choose community life and integration into "unskilled" or "semiskilled" marginal employment and social assistance over migration to more stable and lucrative urban opportunities. They investigated the tenuous relationship between work in the adult world and the socialization available to rural children in school. This study was motivated by a concern that national and state level education initiatives failed to consider the complexity of the relationship between school and work in rural communities. The interplay of what school offers and what working life demands is more problematic than the simplistic "stay-in-school" and "school effectiveness" rhetoric imagine.

Brandau and Collins reject theories commonly used to explain the alienation of many rural students. They claim that reproduction, resistance and mismatch theories are inadequate and argue that teachers and students often understand one another's position; they simply reject one another's agenda. Brandau and Collins surmise that rural students often consciously exchange the promise of prosperity and alleged comfort offered to those who conform in school for the relative autonomy that comes with irregular employment and the outdoor life of the rural community. These students understand they are sacrificing stable employment and career possibilities. Brandau and Collins write: "Rather than being prepared by school for routine jobs with little autonomy, many male Appalachian youth sidestep school and enter into menial work that allows considerable autonomy in the broad margins of the so-called informal economy" (1994: 120). They go on to claim that resistance is an inappropriate concept for understanding the kind of withdrawal from academic participation this entails: "We do not analyze this as resistance aimed at transforming school (or society). Rather, we analyze it as *skepticism*, rooted in a particular class culture and a choosing of local life over education based social mobility" (1994: 120, emphasis in original).

In one of the few such studies of rural schools in the literature,[13] an ethnographic approach allowed Collins and Brandau to gain a clearer understanding of the dynamics of the choice of coherent life paths in particular communities.[14] The decision to stay in rural places is not irrational but represents what is seen as a normal socialization pattern — integration into community habitus and following in one's parent's footsteps. Parents who spend much of their time hunting and fishing and riding in the back country on "four-wheelers" and who love camping-out and living a physical life serve as primary role models to their children, offering a vision of an interesting and autonomous future. The urban industrial work routine demanded in school grates against the structure of work in the rural community, which is predicated on complex social contacts, flexibility of skills and control over work time (Lofty, 1992; Cochrane, 1987). These studies illustrate the case made by Bourdieu (1984b) that social class is embodied and embedded in habitual practices and ways of thinking and acting.

The rural working-class habitus represents a coherent and functional lifeworld for those whose identities are situated within it, and it is a space in which the structures and processes of formal education often play a minimal role. This habitus is also a set of cultural lifeways in what Wenger (1998) calls "communities of practice," and these competencies can be very difficult to transform into education credentials (Jensen, 2002; Rose, 2004; Livingstone and Sawchuk, 2004; Bailey, Hughes and Moore, 2004; Kenway and Kraak, 2004).

These contemporary studies of rural education are not unlike historical studies of nineteenth- and twentieth-century rural resistance to schooling (Davey, 1978; Gaffield, 1987; Curtis, 1988), or those in contemporary anthropological and sociological literature (Blythe, 1969; Weber, 1976; Wylie, 1977; Reed-Danahay, 1987; Demerath, 1999; Deyhle and Margonis, 1995;

Lawrence, 1998; Jensen, 2002). For example, Reed-Danahay describes how children in rural France quietly balance the demands of teachers and curriculum, which focus on the child as "an individual learner and encourages middle-class/urban values and modes of conduct," and the community values of "the perpetuation of the family farm as both a kinship and an economic unit" (1987: 85). Robert Critchfield, echoing anthropologist Robert Redfield, argues that there is something common in the rural experience that cuts across culture and historical time — a view of the "good life," which is intimately connected to place (1994: 19). In the same vein, Deyhle and Margonis (1995) describe how young Navajo women find their way into the cultural space of their communities, assuming adult roles that preclude and/or render formal education useless.[15]

All of these studies of rural schooling demonstrate how the call of authentic adult experience is a strong and powerful form of cultural capital that is acquired and traded in local markets. In rural communities, that experience often included periodic and/or part-time employment in primary resource extraction industries and also in secondary or tertiary sectors, multiple work and social skills, friendship networks, outdoor living, traditional gendered subjectivities and deep kinship roots. The studies also demonstrate the limited penetration of the institution of schooling into the social fabric of many rural communities. One hundred and fifty years of state normalization (including the project of public schooling) and industrialization have not yet entirely infiltrated the rural community. It is therefore crucial to understand the history of a community as well as its culture when we attempt to make sense of common rural school crises like education "failure" and "underperformance." It is also important to understand the ways in which contemporary social forces such as economic globalization, risk society, migration, cultural hybridity, network society and the media explosion have transformed the kinds of experiences described in these studies.

These large scale social transformations have changed rural places at a number of levels. The notion of the rural community as a space outside modernity has been critiqued for at least a generation (Pahl, 1966; Williams, 1973; McKay, 1994). While many Canadian coastal and rural communities remain relatively homogenous in racial and even ethnic terms, they are situated within an increasingly diverse national and international context. Modernity has also challenged traditional gender roles. So, while rural residents fight to protect their home places and traditional spaces, broader social developments offer significant challenges to the maintenance of traditional lifeways, values and sets of inclusions and exclusions. As Gwynn Dyre put it, one of the critical political fault lines in Canada seems to be the gulf between monocultural, poor rural places and rich, multicultural urban ones (2001). School is one of the key flashpoints where modernity, cultural hybridity/multiculturalism, globalization/international capitalism and other change forces meet a certain resistance.

## Why Would Young People Stay?

> Once upon a time, before progress robbed us of our innocence, life was full of content. People were truly individuals. They were happy then. They lived in balance with nature on an island outside history. Everyone was, as Livesay says, of an equality, they lived beautiful and simple lives, as their ancestors had done before them, never questioning their place in the world, never troubled by the politics of an uncertain age. They still live this way, pure and unspotted in a troubled and difficult world. (McKay, 1988: 41)

According to Ian McKay, tourists consume what they think is Atlantic Canadian resistance to modernity and find in it a manufactured reassurance that community exists and time stands still (1988, 1993, 1994).[16] Part of this resistance is a connection to a "simple life," in which economic relations are egalitarian and people are friendly. Another part of it is a deep connection with cultural traditions and heritage that link directly with Anglo-European traditions and peoples. Tourism advertising continues to focus on traditional fiddle music and dance, rural vistas, down-home hospitality, traditional gender relations and a virtual ethnic monoculture. While this vision of resistance is a cultural construction to be sold to tourists, Atlantic Canadian coastal communities and the people in them do resist becoming just like any other place. In other words, in rural areas of Nova Scotia, there is a certain amount of truth to the picture despite the absent presence of gays, lesbians, bisexuals, ethnic and racial minorities and the steady incursion of "newcomers," particularly to increasingly scarce and expensive waterfront property.

The resilience of coastal communities in Atlantic Canada has been something of a puzzle for state normalizers and academic theorists alike. Against the consolidating logic of corporate capitalism, petty capitalism and "peripheral" places have survived and evolving out of the colonial dependency relationships that established many Atlantic Canadian coastal communities. The steady march of capital concentration ought to have by now "rationalized" the Atlantic fishery, and as yet it has not (Brym and Sacouman, 1979; Clement, 1986). Explicit state policy designed to "modernize" the Atlantic fishery and create a small cadre of "professional fishers" has been in place since the late 1940s (Matthews, 1993; Davis, 1991; Blades, 1995; Apostle and Barrett, 1992; Kearney, 1993; Rogers, 1995).

This policy has supported such initiatives as controlled and limited licensing systems restricting the number of people fishing; transferable licences, which have concentrated the allowable catch in the hands of increasingly fewer fishers; low-interest and no-interest loans for capital expansion in the industrial fishery that allow some fishers to invest in intensive and increasingly high-tech harvesting technologies; and, most recently, massive "adjustment" packages and educational programs (Jensen, 2002) designed to ease people living in coastal communities out of the fishery.

By contrast, in Atlantic coastal villages and small towns, life is made up of a network of long-term, largely face-to-face commitments. The small-boat fishery persists, and people continue to inhabit the villages that have virtually no economic reason for existing other than the fishery. Despite several generations of "development" efforts, many rural and coastal towns remain classic Canadian one-industry towns as described by Lucas (1971). To be sure, there is concern, even a kind of panic, about the future, but there is also resistance to what is presented as the inevitable demise of the Atlantic coastal community. Indeed this alleged demise is hotly contested by ongoing struggles between local and state forces, characterized best by small nascent fishers' organization and community defence groups against the Department of Fisheries and Oceans and corporate fish companies (Clement, 1986; Kearney, 1993). The case of Newfoundland outports is instructive because they were the first Atlantic communities to have been explicitly declared redundant. Matthews studied the resettlement initiative and the resistance to resettlement carried out by communities whose residents decided forcefully to defend their homes, declaring, "There's no better place than here" (Matthews, 1976). Matthews comments on the definition of success and failure in the communities he studied, definitions of the situation that appear strangely quaint to a mobile middle-class ear.

> Failure for them would mean moving their families to live permanently in Toronto, St. John's or Corner Brook. Success on the other hand, has come to be associated with the ability to supplement traditional sources of income with outside seasonal employment, so that one's family can live in the rural community throughout the year. (Matthews, 1976: 24)

If the logic of capital demands a transcendence of what Marx called the feudalistic bondage and "idiocy" of rural life, remaining rural people were passed by in the evolutionary march of the history of capitalism, like Foucault's "determined inhabitants of space," standing their ground in resistance to the "pious descendants of time" (1986: 20).

Matthews has followed up his early work with a series of community studies that found similar levels of attachment to place and a traditional life supplemented by periodic migration and government assistance (1993). Rural economies are also hybrid constructions linked intimately to production and consumption, to the state and to global capitalism (Winson and Leach, 2002; Hodge, Dunn, Monk and Fitzgerald, 2002; Vias, 2005). As a Digby Neck dragger fisherman told me in conversation, "Make no mistake, fishing isn't a guy in a little boat, fishing is big business." Although it employs only a small proportion of the labour force, fishing remains the single most important resource industry in Nova Scotia in terms of export dollars (Davis and Kearney, 1999: 2). Fishing is indeed big business, but it is also small business, wage labour and a way of life (Newell and Omer, 1999; Binkley, 2002). The independent small-boat fisher in his own boat, the deck hand who works as wage labour or "on a share" on an offshore dragger, the dragger captain, the person who owns the company, the shareholder, the woman who does the books for her husband, the fish plant worker, and the First Nations fisher who may not require a licence are all players in the contemporary Atlantic fishery. Contemporary fishing is a complex web of state, corporate, class, family, ethnic and gender relationships (see Clement, 1986; Durrenberger, 1997; Grzetic 2004; Kearney, 1993; MacDonald and Connelly, 1990a, 1990b; Sinclair, 1992; Palsson, 1994, 1999).

But why would youth remain in "dying" coastal communities dominated by an industry as troubled and conflicted as the Atlantic fishery? Part of the answer lies in what Zygmunt Bauman (1998) calls "glocalization" — the phenomenon of highly mobile privileged individuals on the one hand (Sennett, 1999; Urry, 2000) and on the other, marginalized players doomed to stay in one place because of scarce resources. Bauman refers to this as "globalization for some, localization for others." Formal education, particularly higher education, confers mobile credentials, or what might be called generic and mobile cultural capital, which can be exchanged in a variety of labour markets. O'Grady (1995) and Felt and Sinclair (1992, 1995) found that for young Newfoundlanders in regions that offered few employment prospects, migration was still not a particularly desirable option. While O'Grady found considerable personal distress among unemployed youth in the northern peninsula of Newfoundland, he also found a strong sense of place attachment. This attachment was not rooted in an ignorance of other places in which work and education opportunity are better, nor even in a strong desire to stay, but rather in knowledge of the high cost of living and social isolation in urban areas. To quote one of O'Grady's informants:

> I was living in a one-bedroom apartment in Scarborough over a store in an old strip mall for $600 a month. Even though I had a full time job as a fork lift operator in a chewing gum factory, I was no better off than I am here. Although work is hard to find, at least

> I don't have to pay rent living with my parents. And all me buddies are here. (1996: 41)

This young man offers what seems to be a rational assessment of his life situation. Like him, O'Grady's other informants were interested in becoming independent and self-reliant; they simply did not see out-migration and marginal urban employment as a sensible way to achieve these goals. Felt and Sinclair also found that for many Newfoundland youth, migration was not an attractive proposition because of the investment it involved, one that typically brought poor returns. Migrants expected to find a lifestyle that was more difficult and generally inferior to the one they were used to at home (1995). The economic returns which served as a "pull" factor in times past now appear to be considerably less attractive. Additionally, these young people had low levels of formal education and understood that in order to access reasonable wages in the 1990s, they needed "an education." Formal education is a type of mobile capital ready for exchange in distant markets, and without it many youth find themselves unable to survive outside a place where they are known and where they possess networks and kin. Urban areas have also been producing an indigenous "reserve army" of labour (Weis, 1990, 2004), an underclass of unemployed youth who are available to fill marginal service positions and move into the full-time labour force in times of capital expansion, thus usurping the traditional role of flexible, multi-skilled Atlantic Canadian migrant labour.[17]

The Newfoundland studies cited above seem to suggest that the "lure" of education and migration is far less seductive in modern rural and coastal communities than theories of modernization, brain-drain speculation and a generation of "going' down the road" fictional literature might have predicted. Indeed, as Press, Galway and Collins (2003) have pointed out, the Newfoundland education system is itself challenged by a range of demographic factors that include out-migration and teacher shortages. Since education has traditionally been seen as a ticket out of rural places, it is not surprising that O'Grady found a preponderance of youth with low levels of formal education in the communities he studied (1995: 41). Could it be that rural resistance to formal education can be understood as recognition that one's social capital is localized and of little value in the face of the placeless and individualistic mobility ideology of liberal schooling? Kincheloe and Pinar suggest that the placeless liberal ideology of schooling is at the heart of Southern (U.S.) resistance to formal education because this form of learning is not sensitive to any particular place or the particular complex of practical skills needed to thrive there (1991: 152).

It may also be that acceptance of education challenges and opportunities offered through formal schooling amounts to rejecting a powerful and well known community-based habitus (Bourdieu, 1990), with its own hegemonic and economic power to define reality. In the 1970s, 1980s and 1990s, it might have been an act of resistance, for instance, for a young man to walk away from a fishing boat and the strong expectation that he will follow his father in the family fishing tradition. He would be resisting economic enticement as well as community ideological pressure. For young women, the choice may be less problematic. While she too might have to resist certain pressure to follow her mother's example, the community habitus may appear more as a default option or the result of early sexual experience drawing her into community life in lieu of other visible options.[18]

But few people are simply "reproduced" in terms of a family/class tradition. As Bauman points out, choice is the inevitable chronic feature of modernity, and, "whether we like it or not we are doomed to choose, to go on choosing and to justify our choices and to be painfully aware that choosing and being pressed to prove ourselves right is our fate" (1999: 134). And it is in school that choice is presented and managed, fretted over and contemplated. In single industry and rural communities, choice assumes mobility. For urban youth, it is a normal condition to have to choose from an unpredictable array of options. In many coastal communities, the family "norm" is to stay, and leaving means moving into a foreign space, where outcomes are unknown, a space where the known habitus cannot map the future. In less economically privileged sectors of rural and coastal communities, the idea of choice is a cruel fiction, a form of symbolic violence perpetrated by educators and bureaucrats looking for a victim to blame.

A range of social forces, including globalization, the traditional interface between the town and the country, the deindustrialization of the urban landscape and massive youth unemployment, all converge on youth in both urban and rural communities. Are rural schools any longer perceived as a cultural bridge out of those resistant places that cling to the map for no apparent reason, as DeYoung (1995) and Theobald (1997) suggest? Do rural schools in coastal communities of Nova Scotia continue to play their traditional role of moving educated individuals out to greener urban pastures (Lotz and Welton, 1997: 6–12)? Could it be that the current certain economy and persistently high levels of youth unemployment in urban areas have created the conditions in which marginal, sporadic employment in coastal communities and family networks actually provide many youth with their best chance for a decent life (O'Grady, 1995)?

A sociological focus on place as a location for identity has challenged visions of both working-class revolution and functional notions of social mobility in an ossified industrial heartland (Papastergiadis, 2000; Florida, 2002). As Orun writes (echoing a host of others): "Many people have shifted their efforts to reconstruct the world of their neighborhoods, their communities, their places" (1998: 8). At the same time the modern state is reaching into the "community" as a new and more efficient site of governance (Rose, 1997; Valverde, 1997) with a variety of grassroots development initiatives and adjustment and training schemes aimed at constructing and governing rural subjectivities. Two strong disciplinary forces in the modernization of rural people and places have been education and migration. Education institutions have shown rural people their alterity and the importance of places other than their own (Popkewitz, 1998; Theobald, 1997; Haas and Nachtigal, 1998; Vanderbeck and Dunkley, 2003). A part of rural governance strategies aimed at developing communities is the notion that globalization and the "information economy" present new high-tech options for rural communities. Rural youth view the "community development" rhetoric of the "high tech" future in their remote fishing villages as dubious. If they want to become computer programmers, they know that they will have to leave. If they want to fish or work in most close-to-home jobs, higher education will be of little obvious value to them. The discourse of rural education now contains a significant level of ambivalence around the complex problems of the troubled relationship between community sustainability and youth out-migration.

## Schooling and Migration in Atlantic Canada

> If rural development is to flourish, for example, the education system must be changed so as to train people for rural living. Unwittingly, schooling in Newfoundland since Confederation has been essentially training to get people out of the outports. The brightest and most highly motivated have been trained to leave, while those who aspire to a rural lifestyle have found little meaning in what school has to offer. (House, 1988: 114)

I have suggested that definitions of "success" current among contemporary school promoters may be at odds with those found in traditional coastal communities. In rural and coastal places, community success stories are often simultaneously stories of school failure; dropouts typically stay and contribute to the community. The way these categories (success and failure) are constructed in terms of allegiance to place is seldom considered. This 1992 exchange between veteran Digby Neck teacher Laura Tidd and lobsterman Fred Horner at a planning session for a community-based curriculum project at Digby Neck Consolidated School illustrates the ambiguous position of schooling and the gulf between community and school, between life's curriculum and formal pedagogy (Portelli and Vibert, 2001).[19]

Laura: These kids have got to have a good education so that they have some choices when they get out of here.

Fred: I agree, they need a good education, but they need to learn some responsibility and respect for work. You know they got to get out of bed in the morning and go and get after something like I done. The problem is there ain't nothing to do any more for a lot of em'.

Laura: And that's because you're stuck. Maybe you wouldn't be if you had kept on. My son wanted to quit school when he was in grade 10 and I told him OK, but pack your things while you're at it. Well, of course, he stayed and that's why he's got his engineer's papers and landed that job in Yarmouth.

Fred: Well, you know I quit school in grade 9 to go fishing. I haven't had any use for anything but math, that's the only thing I wish I had'a learned because it stopped me from getting my navigation papers. That's all. The rest of it I never would have used; I never even used what I had much.

Laura: And your choices are limited by that. If you wanted to change jobs right now or if you had to, you wouldn't be able to do it very easily.

Fred: What me and Conrad (another fisherman sitting beside Fred) got is an education from life. We learned how to work and how to fish. We're educated people, it's just that we're not educated according to [pause] in the eyes of school. In fact, I can turn my hand to a lot of things. Look, ask him [pointing to male teacher Tony Kelly], ask him if he could find a job easy if something happened to this one.

Tony: No I don't think I could easily.

Fred: And he's got his education and I've got mine.

For young men, resistance to school is simultaneously resistance to migration and to a construction of manhood that stands in opposition to one that is valued in the community (Kenway and Kraak, 2004; Rose, 2004; Palsson, 1994, 1999). In a study of male labourers in the inter-war years in England, Hussey (1997) discovered that manliness and the self-worth of a rural working man was in the ability to turn his hand to many things. In coastal communities, multiple skills are learned through extensive socialization and informal apprenticeship in the company of established and respected experts and teachers in the fishery (Gatewood, 1984, Palsson, 1994, 1999). Ferland and Wright (1996) also comment on the tendency in historical studies of the working class to ignore the uniqueness of labour patterns in rural communities. They use the examples of "remote" resource extraction areas as prototypical examples of situations in which workers have tended to be multi-skilled and highly flexible. A similar pattern is evident in Atlantic coastal communities, both historically and in the modern context (Matthews, 1976, 1993; McCann, 1994; Burrill, 1992).

As Matthews' work shows, useful everyday skills, supplemented by social benefits, community barter, reciprocity and family interdependence allow people to survive in rural coastal communities, often far better than they might in urban environments (1976, 1993). Such a life represents a set of procedures for coping with and surviving the Catch 22 of the migration imperative and resisting the apparent need to venture into the uncertain waters of cities and higher education. As Hektner (1995), Porter, (1996), Lofty (1992), Ching and Creed (1997), Smyth and Hattam (2004), Kenway and Kraak (2002), and Brandau and Collins (1994) have shown, leaving school is not necessarily opting for an impoverished or a less complex life experience. As one of my informants claimed in *Dropping Out in Digby* (Corbett, 1991), working-class young people do not stay in school because they are "smart," they do so because they are not considered particularly gifted by community standards, not able to handle a complex and difficult life of entrepreneurial risk-taking, raising a family on limited resources, physical toil and manual skills in the "real world" of the community and on the water. In other words, they may be unable to function within one or more localized communities of practice (Bourdieu, 1984b; Wenger, 1998). Those "forced" to rely on school may also lack connections to employment networks and other forms of social capital necessary for finding work in rural areas. Formally educated individuals may, in many respects, appear stupid and isolated in rural community terms because they typically lack the variety of skills, connections and experience that are seen as constituting a proper practical education for competent living (Gatewood, 1984; Cottom, 2003).[20] This irony is powerfully illustrated by Gisli Palsson's ethnographic studies of learning to fish (1994) and to become a successful fishing boat captain (1999).

When the rural community is considered in education discourse it is typically presented as a problem, the "rural problem,"[21] a vaguely defined sense of retrogressive life associated with the countryside. Canada's "rural problem" has been featured in education discourse for at least a century, and it is slowly being "solved" by urbanization, out-migration and the consolidation of schools. The link between the implicit migration/escape message embedded in schooling routines and curriculum and the decline of rural communities is sometimes even made explicit. In a classic ethnography of coastal communities in Digby County, Hughes et al. (1960) identified the idea that "people must migrate if they are to make anything of themselves" as a key community sentiment. They elaborated:

> The main purpose of education as now conceived is to prepare the student for the possibility of a successful position somewhere away from the island. The minimal meaning of a successful career is a white collar job and the fullest hopes are for a professional position. For years Fairhaveners have been proud of their record of supplying a large number of teachers, clergymen and other professionals to the outside.... Fishing is seen as a satisfying occupation for those who are already in it but the evaluation is quite different for young men. For them there is only one course: leave the island.... Nevertheless, migration from Fairhaven is attended by strong feelings. Parents hate to see their children go away, and the young people themselves find the prospect of moving to a strange city disturbing whether to finish their education or to seek employment. (Hughes et al., 1960: 222)

The "rural problem" in contemporary education theorizing effectively constructs the rural community itself as a problem. So rather than the "rural problem" we now see emerging the rural *as* problem. Individuals living in "backward" places are potentially functional, so long as they can be turned into modern tourist promoters or small-scale entrepreneurs or moved to "places that work." I suggest that a central part of the specialized governance in rural areas is an implicit migration curriculum for the young, ensuring that backward spaces are not reproduced but transformed, reduced and significantly depopulated. The simplest and most "efficient" means of transformation in Atlantic Canada has always been out-migration.

Yet, notwithstanding modernity, community allegiances and place attachment remain. For this reason, Ralph Matthews' informants in rural Newfoundland (1976, 1993) and the respondents in the Stirling County Study interviewed in Digby County in the 1950s (Hughes et al., 1960) could hold the seemingly contradictory view that the community was a wonderful place in which to live but that it held nothing for their children. In each of these cases, education was seen to be the passport out of the trouble facing the community. As Matthews quips, "the road to school leads out of town" (1993). In neither of these cases was education seen as having anything to do with confronting the problems faced by the community, but rather as a rocket in which the "motivated" individual might escape the gravitational pull of local ties.

In addition to the power of place and questions of identity, there is also an odd anomaly at the heart of the migration dilemma in Atlantic Canadian coastal communities. On one hand, mass media trumpet the demise of rural Canada, and Atlantic coastal communities are often used as prototypical examples of depopulated and impoverished backwaters (Catto, 2003; McMahon, 2003). In this swan-song for rural places and coastal communities, formal education is typically presented as a kind of necessary evil. High-school and post-secondary graduating classes are said to leave their home communities *en masse*, using their credentials to buy employment and better lives in sustainable places, typically in central and Western Canada, or in the United States.[22] On the other hand the value of fish landings in Nova Scotia has been steadily, notwithstanding inevitable fluctuations, increasing since the early 1990s (see Table 1.1), when much of the rhetoric around the collapse of the Atlantic fishery was in the news and the federal state developed a series of programs to ease "redundant" people out of the fishery.

The rather obvious anomaly illustrated in Table 1.1 is that while catch values were rising steadily, people in coastal communities were being encouraged to leave the fishery and pursue formal education as an alternative life trajectory leading ultimately to out-migration. There are a number of questions that need to be asked at this juncture. If the economic worth of the Nova Scotian and Atlantic fishery is on the increase, why is the state actively involved in ushering people out of the fishery? And finally, should we be surprised that many fishing people in Atlantic Canada see themselves as victims of a state/corporate alliance conspiring to uproot and dislocate them?

Fishers have long argued that the answer to these questions can be found in the very forces that have "modernized" the Atlantic fishery, i.e., corporate concentration and state policy that has consistently supported the privatization/commodification of the resource. Essentially, I have found a four-part answer to this question: 1) corporate concentration of fish quotas and licences have forced small-boat and inshore fishers out of the business; 2) the use of more expensive and more invasive technologies and gear (often supported by state guaranteed loans at low interest) have allowed the "big players" to expand their industrial fishing operations and harvest more fish using fewer employees; 3) the federal state has created an open market in fish quotas and fishing licences commodifying fishing privileges and inflating the value of quotas and licences to the point where it is very seductive for established fishermen to sell out and far too expensive for young fishermen to buy in; and 4) as the big players concentrate capital and maximize "efficiency," they make it increasingly difficult for small-boat fishers to find fish to catch, given that they are competing with high technology and big money.

**Table 1.1**
**Commercial Catch Value 1977-2002 (in thousands of dollars)**

| | Atlantic Canada | Nova Scotia |
|---|---|---|
| 1977 | 288,252 | 133,145 |
| 1982 | 589,174 | 259,592 |
| 1987 | 1,129,962 | 524,135 |
| 1992 | 984,195 | 511,572 |
| 1993 | 959,260 | 478,254 |
| 1994 | 1,127,813 | 504,552 |
| 1995 | 1,359,239 | 512,158 |
| 1996 | 1,148,885 | 466,225 |
| 1997 | 1,211,390 | 511,817 |
| 1998 | 1,287,206 | 542,508 |
| 1999 | 1,589,596 | 629,429 |
| 2000 | 1,789,531 | 704,551 |
| 2001 | 1,791,981 | 784,619 |
| 2002 | 1,859,945 | 808,778 |
| 2003 | 1,906,395 | 847,152 |
| 2004 | 1.902,451 | 742,752 |

Source: Nova Scotia Department of Fisheries and Agriculture (2006).

The result of this array of forces is an ongoing struggle for small-boat inshore fishing operations to survive even though the value of caught fish is actually rising. Young people are not forced to move, fishers say, because of a lack of fish; they are forced to move because the available harvest is being steadily and relentlessly concentrated into fewer and fewer hands. The great myth is that coastal communities are being depopulated by the forces of nature and declining stocks and a coming together of a series of "natural disasters," including the so-called "tragedy of the commons," which essentially blames individual fisher's greed for the decline of stocks. People living in coastal communities in southwest Nova Scotia understand all too well that they are being driven out of their communities by the forces of corporate concentration and hostile state policy. The education and mobility dilemmas and opportunities available to differently placed actors in coastal communities are nested within the context of these structural forces, and it is within this context that youth decide whether to stay or to go.

## Notes

1. Questions of schooling and class have a long history in the sociology of education in Britain. Stuart Hall and his colleagues (Hall and Jefferson, 1976) also used ethnographic methods to investigate the lived experience of class and schooling in urban Britain, inspiring many similar studies throughout Europe and North America. The work of Pierre Bourdieu (1974, 1984b, 1990) in France and a generation of critical ethnographers of schooling in the United States have extended this analysis, virtually all of which is urban in its focus.
2. Referring to the work of Father Jimmy Tompkins, one of the founders of the Antigonish Movement, Lotz and Welton write:

   > His own university Saint FX, took the brightest of the local youth, educated them in traditional academic ways, and gave them credentials, then saw many of them leave the region. This out-migration increased as times became tougher in eastern Nova Scotia after the first world war. Father Jimmie believed that educated ordinary people who stay were the key to revitalizing the region and creating prosperity for all. (1997: 6)

3. For a survey of Atlantic Canadian fiction see Kristiensen, 1993 and Kulyk-Keefer, 1987. In both of these accounts the idea of leaving plays a significant role. Specific sources include: Bruce, 1954, 1959; Day, 1928/1989; Raddall, 1957; Coady, 1998; Barnes, 1997; Buckler, 1952; MacLennan, 1951; MacLeod, 1976, 1999; deFreitas, 1997. Virtually the entire corpus of Nova Scotian folk music of the last two generations has had as a central theme the decision to stay in the province or leave for uncertain and typically alienating prospects in other parts of the country. Nostalgic nonfiction accounts of staying and leaving are also common (cf., Bruce, 1988; Burrill, 1992).
4. With respect to class, Lucas writes:

   > The world opened for a young man depends on whether his father has knowledge of a few or many occupations... it is mainly in connection with the occupations of his father and his father's friends that the child is likely to receive occupational models. (1971: 287)

   This is also a piece of gendered discourse given the way girls are left out of the picture. With respect to gender and education, Lucas cites a teacher who sees schooling as a feminine pursuit, which explains the much better academic performance (and subsequent higher rates of out-migration) of young women in single-industry communities.

   > School is a feminine world in the vocational sense. It prepares the girls academically for their careers in the work world... for the boys it's otherwise... there seem to be few places where skills learned by boys in school, even in vocational school, can be applied to a specific job. (1971: 299)

5. The relationship between out-migration and economic development has been the subject of considerable controversy for years. Analyzing historical migration patterns from Atlantic Canada between 1871 and 1921, Thornton argued

that large scale out-migration can be seen as a cause of underdevelopment rather than an effect.

> It may be suggested that massive and sustained net losses of about fifteen percent of the region's population per decade must have seriously jeopardized the potential of the region to complete its industrial transformation. (1985: 8)

6. Stone's work identified what would become something of a demographic surprise beginning in the 1970s as rural areas and small towns actually experienced population growth. Most of this growth was however in small communities within commuting distance of urban centres.
7. DeVries and McNab-DeVries make a similar argument when they document their methodological migration from an approach to the problems of rural Cape Breton informed by political economy to a more culturally sensitive postmodern ethnographic approach (1991). These researchers became interested in ethnography as a way of avoiding the problem of reducing people's lives to the effects of structural (capitalist) forces.
8. If formal education has appeared in rural areas as an irrelevance for those who stay, it is quite probable that recent state-sponsored training for jobs that do not exist simply extends the generalized sense that education is a kind of ethereal pursuit. People in coastal and rural communities are faced with the contradiction generated by state admonitions to "stay in school," or the notion that education is "essential," and the practical experience of formal education and mandated training as a total irrelevance to their lives.
9. Exceptions to this problem are some of Looker's studies that are is longitudinal and the work of Shanahan, Meick and Elder (1998), who use longitudinal analysis of census and OCS survey data to track historic education attainment levels in the United States. McCann (1994) has also done historical work charting the funding of the education system in Newfoundland against the backdrop of the fluctuating economics of the fishery. There are no Canadian longitudinal studies of migration and education. Dublin has recently combined an analysis of historical census data with ethnographic analysis of the migration experiences of rural residents of Pennsylvania (1998). Using high school enrolment data as the basis for his sampling, he found that only 30 percent of graduates of the classes of 1946–1960 currently reside in the communities of origin. Those who completed high school were much more likely to migrate and post-secondary education was positively correlated with out-migration. Dublin asserts that higher education has become a prerequisite for out-migration from rural communities.
10. From the point of view of human capital theory the mistaken assumption is that a social investment in education will result in a work force better able to produce, as well as attract and generate investment. Eric Ricker points out, though, that human capital theory is not particularly sensitive to geography and where educated individuals will end up living and working (1978b: 8). For many individuals, the departure is permanent, and in human capital terms there is simply an enormous loss to the "donor" region. On the other hand,

Mountford argues that a "brain drain" can be positive for the "source" economy because the exodus and relative good economic fortune of highly educated out-migrants raises the status and perceived utility of formal education raising human capital value in the source as well as in the receptor region. Mountford writes that: "brain drain can change the dynamics of the 'class' formation so that an undereducated class fails to develop" (1997: 288). Others argue that migration is the principal source of cultural diffusion and is effectively the well spring of all human capital and intellectual vitality which creates truly vibrant contemporary cultures (Bhabha, 1994; Said, 1993; Kasabarian, 1996; Sowell, 1996).

11. Commenting on the role of teachers or "guru" in rural Malaysia, Ong writes:

    > In almost daily contact with students, teachers (guru) are highly regarded for their learning, their kerajaan (shorthand for government employment) stamp, and orientation to Malay society. They set local standards for aspiring kampung boys and girls, the majority of whom seek career paths out of agricultural work. Gurus not only display the accoutrements of urban lifestyle such as cars, plastic sheathed furniture, electronic gadgets, and expensive clothes, but they also speak in authoritative tones about Malay problems, sprinkling their speeches with technical terms and English phrases. As the varied representatives of a rural intelligentsia, teachers, policemen, office clerks and party functionaries furnish rural folk with workaday knowledge of the wider society, a bureaucratic elaboration of the increasing diet of Televeshen Malaysia and popular magazines eagerly consumed by village families. Situated in government offices and public institutions, guru and officials are strategic nodes in the bureaucratic system linking rural Malays to the national society. (1987: 79)

    In this study Ong explains the periodic resistance of normally docile female workers in Malay electronics plants. She argues that institutions like the school are designed to promote conformity and capitalist work discipline, but that this project has never been entirely successful, as the resistance she documents demonstrates.
12. Chet Bowers (2003) makes essentially the same point criticizing the liberal individualism he see sitting at the heart of contemporary pedagogical theory, not only in its conservative forms, but also in the allegedly less socially conservative and more innovative constructivist, progressivist and Frierian conceptions of schooling. For somewhat different reasons and from considerably different perspectives, Kieran Egan (2002) and Tom Popkewitz (1998) have also levelled criticism against the biases and limitations of currents of ascendant pedagogical thought that flow from the Deweyan tradition.
13. See Porter, 1996; Reed-Danahay, 1987; Lofty, 1992; and Ovando, 1984 for other examples.
14. Looker and Andres (1998) also use Bourdieu's conceptual apparatus to understand aspirations of rural students. They argue that community level "habitus" must be considered in order to understand the education and occupational decision-making of rural youth. Jentsch and Dey (2000) critique the Scottish

rural youth policy agenda for providing "good jobs" to rural youth in their home communities, arguing that the policy, however well intentioned, misses the complex nature of kinship and community structure, which offer differently placed rural youth different levels of access to community work. The key argument Jentsch and Day make is that the interests of communities and individual rural youth are often conflated, resulting in insensitive and ineffective policy.

15. McRobbie (1991) also found that many young women dismiss school in favour of traditional women's roles in the home and in the community. She writes: "They found little in school with which to identify actively. The ideas and values they preferred to identify with were those of their mothers and other female members of the family" (1991: 58). Gaskell (1992) found similar patterns with young urban women. Trying to understand how young working-class women who were educated "alongside men" came to have different education outcomes, Gaskell concluded that: "most of the young women believed their choices arose not out of unequal giftedness, but out of a quite sensible inability to tolerate the pointlessness and childishness of school… they did not think that what they could learn there was useful" (1992: 43). School appeared to these women as a waste of time in meaningless pursuit of "irrelevant academic information" (Gaskell, 1992: 44). Even watching other people's children and doing menial domestic labour proved more "real" and engaging for these young women than school.
16. See Blakie for an analysis of how coastal communities are constructed in British tourism and retirement literature as nostalgic vestiges of an older communitarian and harmonious moral order (1997). Of course, Williams' *The Country and the City* (1973) contains the quintessential treatment of the rural idyll in British culture. For an analysis of the commodification of culture on a global scale in the context of international tourism see Tilley (1997).
17. It can be argued that the traditional Atlantic Canadian migrant is precisely the kind of worker being demanded by neoliberal, post-Fordist employers. Atlantic Canadians have been providing just-in-time, multi-skilled, flexible service to Canadian and international capital for at least a century and a half. This history is documented in a variety of places. Brookes' pioneering study of migration from the Maritimes is a basic source (1976, 1981), as are Thornton (1985) and the Forbes and Muise survey of Atlantic Canadian history (1997). Burrill uses oral history to document the working lives of more recent Maritime out-migrants.
18. In his anthropological analysis of space and place in a Newfoundland village, Pocius discusses the different kinds of gendered space that men and women learn to negotiate (1991). The male space is outside the house and its immediate environs, the bush, the shed and on the water. Pocius shows how men and women both learn how to negotiate these different geographies. This gendered concept of space is linked to kinship and the economy of the fishing village because fishing operations and licences are handed on to males in the family. Thus, men tend to remain working in the same places as their fathers. Women on the other hand will have to move to different communities upon marriage because in small coastal communities the restrictions of consanguinity restrict

the availability of "marriageable" men. Pocius argues that because of this temporary attachment to particular landscapes and local geography, women are socialized to learn how to construct the interior geography of the house, a geography which can be found in any community (1991: 99). Similarly, gendered structures of opportunity in the Atlantic fishery have been analyzed by other sociologists (MacDonald and Connelly, 1990a, 1990b; Connelly and MacDonald, 1983; Porter, 1985).

19. I am using the names of these individuals with permission. The context of the discussion was an ongoing series of school-community planning meetings at Digby Neck Consolidated School. This excerpt was transcribed from videotape. Thanks to Laura and Fred for allowing me to use this excerpt.
20. This is precisely the problem that motivated a series of curriculum reform projects in North American schools in the early decades of the twentieth century. Influenced by Dewey's pragmatism and responding to rapid urbanization and industrialization of Canadian and American society variants of "progressive" education sought to introduce into the school curriculum less academic practical subjects, including agricultural education (Jones, 1978, 1979; Norman, 1989), domestic science (Riley, 1992), commercial and vocational education (Anstead and Goodson, 1993) and physical education (Mott, 1986). These movements represented early attempts to integrate the formal curriculum of school with the pragmatic socialization of life.
21. Marx contributed perhaps the classic formulation of the "rural problem," writing in *The Communist Manifesto* about the demise of rural regions. "The bourgeoisie has subjected the country to the rule of the towns. It has created enormous cities, has greatly increased the urban population as compared with the rural, and has thus rescued a considerable part of the population from the idiocy of rural life" (cited in Berger and Mohr, 1976: 36).
22. Or increasingly in Asia working in the burgeoning English as a Second Language (ESL) teaching industry.

Chapter 2

# Reconceptualizing Resistance

## Habitus, Discourse and Place

### Resistance Theory in the Sociology of Education

> The existence of distinguishable and irreconcilable social groups upon which the mode of production depends also means that each group can and will create cultural forms and life-worlds which are based upon different definitions of reality and relationships with the material world.... We need to be able to decide, for example, whether those pupils who passively accept the label "educational failure" and their placement low down in the education and occupational hierarchy do so as a response to the message of schooling, or alternatively, as a response to communication which has little to do with education and its directives and signals, and may well contradict them. (Meighan, 1981: 251)

The opening chapter began with a brief look at the seminal work of British education sociologist Paul Willis. Willis's *Learning to Labour* was the key work that linked close-up qualitative analysis in the phenomenological and interpretive traditions with broad structural analysis in the critical tradition (Dolby and Dimitriadis, 2004). Willis's book led to a still evolving series of critical ethnographies and works in education resistance theory most notably and voluminously represented in the oeuvre of Henry Giroux (1981, 1983, 1988, 1992, 1994; Aronowitz and Giroux, 1985) and the work of Peter McLaren (1980, 1985, 1989).[1] This body of work was designed to critique the "correspondence" theory of social class reproduction, developed by American Marxist sociologists of education in the 1970s (cf. Bowles and Gintis, 1976; Apple, 1979). The general thrust of Willis's work is that some students, at some level, come to understand their class exploitation and the way that institutions of formal education function to serve interests contrary to their own. Out of this realization come forms of consciousness and behaviour that not only push against hegemony but that contain the seeds for creating a more just social order. Resistance theorists were interested in mapping the inventive nature of defiance, and through the use of ethnographic methods, they were often able to present intimate accounts of the logic of working-class youth resistance.

*Learning to Labour* remains the exemplary study in the resistance theory tradition. Over a period of more than two years, Willis conducted an ethnography that probed the intricacies of the school and out-of-school lives of a group of working-class boys on the cusp of leaving school for work. Willis then followed them into their employment placements for six months, developing a very comprehensive picture of the school-to-work transition of these youth. *Learning to Labour* is an account of misbehaviour, defiance, sexism and academic self-sabotage, and yet, Willis finds among his informants an odd sort of insight into class oppression, which he takes to contain emancipatory potential. Willis's working-class "lads" resist the limited opportunities available to them in a class segregated society, the logic of which they see through, or, to use a term that proved to be particularly provocative to his feminist critics, "penetrate." Despite its theoretical and empirical contributions to the sociology of education, resistance theory has been subject to significant critique in the 1980s and 1990s.

Critics question the extent to which working-class youth "penetrate" class exploitation; they argue that, in fact, youth seem to be strikingly ignorant of how their own agency positions them. Additionally refuted is the suggestion that adolescent play, trendy folly, simple rudeness, violence and destructiveness represent valid resistance.[2] For Rikowski, a "dangerous romanticism" and a vagueness of definition lurks beneath the surface of resistance theory and research, in which "actions ranging from students day dreaming, picking their noses in class, through to fighting and staging a strike fail to mark 'resistance' out as a specific phenomenon" (1997: 561). Rikowski goes on to wonder how illiterate, violent, sexist, racist figures like Willis's lads (and the host of other miscreants other ethnographers have discovered) can be seen as a vanguard leading the charge against social injustice. This critique is neither new nor unique. Feminist scholars such as Roman and Christian-Smith (1988) and Kelly (1997) have had similar misgivings, as have curriculum theorists William Pinar and his associates in a survey of a century of curriculum theorizing (Pinar et al., 1995). Dale (1989) has also argued that resistance is a poor concept, incorporating an often unrelated variety of behaviours into a general "rag-bag."

In a more sympathetic critique, Gibson adds that the anti-intellectualism inherent in the resistance Willis found effectively erases the possibility of emancipation, which is supposed to be the key motivation of his Marxist ethnography. Gibson writes: "Resistance without knowledge merely strengthens the status quo" (1986: 60). Ethnographies that attempt a less ideological analysis of the complex, nuanced relationships between school knowledge and what Roman and Christian-Smith call the "knowledge and meanings acquired outside school in other institutional and informal contexts" (1988: 21), find richer and more ambiguous and meaningful accounts than those found in resistance theory. Resistance theory as it is presented by Willis, McLaren and Giroux presumes to interpret meaning in advance, to know better than the informants what they are saying and doing, and to have the benefit of a deeper level of consciousness, as opposed to a different theoretical framework for interpretation. As Ellsworth (1989) showed convincingly, the results can be oppressive and alienating.

Willis's study (along with many that have followed) does deliver unfortunate testimony to the way marginal youth actively reproduce their own subordination. The "lads" are not being shifted into a disadvantaged place in the class structure; they rebelliously and joyously seize it, apparently of their own volition. They enthusiastically support and actively facilitate their own subordination and realize too late that they have been seduced into engineering their own passage into exploitative work relations. While his analysis is rich in ethnographic detail, Willis's *Learning to Labour* is a qualitative analysis of class with a predictable theoretically driven conclusion. Willis's lads are trapped by a social class system that operated behind their backs. By shifting emphasis from the theoretical abstractions of Marxist and quantitative functionalist analyses of working-class "oppression," Willis, and others who used the techniques of ethnography to explore schooling in Western societies, shifted the political emphasis away from accounts of domination to accounts of resistance to that domination (Game, 1990: 29–30).[3] However, the results remained the same, and these ethnographic accounts of schooling were faced, in the end, with explaining how oppression is grounded in resistance to oppression, an apparent contradiction. Game and others have argued that resistance theory is insufficiently attuned to the way that resistant identities are discursively produced.

Despite these problems, I believe the concept of resistance has value. A wide variety of students resist formal education in a lot of ways for many reasons. Resistance needs to be understood in the context of particular locations. As an attempt to consider location, McLaren and Giroux have each argued in different ways that popular culture is a "site of resistance" in the face of the hegemonic power of schooling. It seems rather obvious that both schooling and popular culture are different and often complementary hegemonic sites, the latter being probably the most powerful and entrenched set of ideological levers currently available to contemporary capitalists and normalizers alike. As critics suggest, Giroux and McLaren seem caught in their own ideological meta-narrative of class reproduction.

## Bourdieu's Logic of Practice

> I came to understand that school leaving was a fundamental part of schooling in low income communities, not an aberration. (Fine, 1996: xii)

Bourdieu's idea of the logic of practice and what he calls "habitus" can be used to explain the way individuals are reproduced in particular social class positions through the practices they encounter in the course of their schooling. Bourdieu's concept of the habitus is dynamic and agency-focused, investing creative interaction of ordinary, "objectively" positioned social actors within the context of a field of limited possibilities. Bourdieu writes:

> Through the *habitus*, the structure of which it is the product, governs practice, not along paths of a mechanical determinism, but rather within the constraints and limits set on its invention. This infinite yet strictly limited generative capacity is difficult to understand only so long as one remains locked in the usual antimonies... of determinism and freedom, conditioning and creativity, conscious and unconscious, or the individual and society. (1990: 55, italics in original)

What Bourdieu calls the "logic of practice" is the situated decision-making that operates in particular circumstances. Rather than being forced by structural constraint, as was the case with resistance theory, individuals make the decisions they do on the basis of a practical assessment of their life chances and "reasonable" options. As such, individuals see an array of choices before them, but tend to gravitate toward those choices that are most coherent, given their own assessment of their chances. Bourdieu takes care to distinguish practical logic from formal logic, just as he draws the line between practical and scientific reasoning. Scientific reasoning arrives on the scene after the fact, once the action is over, and it attempts to categorize and theorize around what has happened much in the way that Willis did in *Learning to Labour*.

The logic of practice, the reasoning that social actors use when they make ordinary life decisions, affords no such luxury. Practical logic operates in the middle of the action and represents an active engagement with the context of real social affordances and constraints, not theoretical possibilities. People choose on the basis of what they understand to be their array of reasonable options. They tend to choose "sensibly" by selecting for themselves what Bourdieu calls "coherent" and "convenient" options (1990: 86). The structures and history that render certain kinds of options coherent and convenient are understood by agents only at the level of practice. The logic of practice is no abstraction; it "understands only in order to act" (Bourdieu, 1990: 91) and "can only be grasped in action" (92). Therefore, in order to understand how Bourdieu's practical logic works, social researchers are required to understand the context in which action happens as well as the creative way that agents "play their cards," given the affordances of that context.

Decisions, in the end, are made on the basis of an assessment of an individual's resources or access to various kinds of what Bourdieu calls capital. For Bourdieu there are many forms of capital; some are tangible and materially based, but others are symbolic and, generally speaking, linguistically based. Symbolic cultural capital appears in the form of taste and manners, the ability and inclination to make certain kinds of judgments and distinctions and privileged experiences and dispositions (Bourdieu, 1984b). In terms of formal education, Bourdieu describes the way that symbolic capital is constructed as a method of inclusion and exclusion; since educational and educated discourse is the language and subject matter of the privileged classes for the most part, symbolic capital operates in tandem with economic capital. Those excluded from privileged circles by a lack of symbolic capital are subtly constructed as losers in education institutions. However, individuals may also have symbolic capital that connects them to particular locales, where their place-specific symbolic capital is useful for profit and identity construction "around here." This local, non-academically certified symbolic capital has its own value in its own spaces, or what Bourdieu calls fields. An example of a particular field might be the small-boat fishery in a coastal community. In this field, players learn to develop and utilize forms of symbolic capital, including an embodied ease around fishing boats, a discourse that is used in the work of fishing and a way of speaking, eating, dressing and presenting and using the male body that can only be achieved through a deep immersion in the culture of fishing families and communities (Gatewood, 1984; Palsson, 1994, 1999; Durrenberger, 1997).

Bourdieu's notion of the logic of practice and the habitus are essentially structuralist, despite their dynamic aspects. The general scheme within which the action happens is a structural frame of constraint and enablement. Agents make "logical" choices within the ambit of the reasonable — set out by entrenched structural and embedded habits. But where in the system of oppositions are there alternatives?[4] Bourdieu's logical social action frame posits that sensible choices are dictated by the logic of a particular social position and a particular set of what he calls "objective" social conditions. Social actors however draw their action orientations from a number of places simultaneously, an array of "objective conditions." In Bourdieu's scheme, both choice and resistance seem difficult to conceive because the habitus is so tight and powerful. If people resist the habitus, where are the "alternative," "opposing" or even "oppositional" modes of discourse that allow them to do so?

This, I think, is where the Foucauldian notion of multiple discourse spaces and the play of resistances in power relations can add to Bourdieu's conceptual scheme. The school, which is one of Bourdieu's chief research locations, is a clear example of this kind of contested terrain (at least in

North America), where competing forms of the habitus come together and where competing logics of practice mesh, negotiate and clash, as Giroux and others have often pointed out (e.g., Aronowitz and Giroux, 1985). These multiple logics present themselves in the form of more or less resistant identity formations carried into school by children from different "backgrounds." But even this is problematic, because it imagines children growing up in a particular neighbourhood or a particular community as unified subjects. From the moment of birth, children are immersed in a variety of spaces composed of multiple crosscurrents.[5] For example, some youth from fishing backgrounds "resist" their interpellation into a way of life and a social-class position that provides them with "coherent and convenient" roads into manual work, often because they are actively recruited to do so within an academic habitus. In this case, school may offer an alternative sort of coherence and convenience framed in a discourse that presents coastal communities and life in the fishery as a pre-modern vestige. The scope of choice is not as tightly bound to social class and familial habitus as Bourdieu suggests; rather this habitus is one among many competing and overlapping discourses. In fact, the particular habitus of any given family may contain significant elements of academically valuable symbolic capital as well as locally valuable symbolic capital. More recently, the spatial turn in social theory has introduced what is now understood as multiple geographies of youth, each containing differential developmental trajactories and patterns of habitus (Atiken, 2001; Holloway and Valentine, 2000).

Bourdieu shows, in a vivid and powerful way, how structural imperatives are made all the more powerful because they are not mechanistic abstractions, but rather the result of individual social actors having a personalized sense of social structure that is incorporated into their bodies and their practical reasoning. Social behaviour becomes habitual and appears as a contingent "series of irreversible choices, made under pressure and often involving heavy stakes... in response to other choices obeying the same logic" (1990: 101). Still, social actors have certain degrees of freedom and the ability to engage in agency that is not predictable in terms of the logic of the habitus, a field within which boundaries are permeable. These acts are resistant precisely because they cannot be predicted and because they confound the strategic logic of theory (deCerteau, 1984). Bourdieu uses chess or ballet as examples of formal systems within which creativity is not only possible, it is celebrated, however rare it may be. So there is a range of performance, a set of limits and standards which are embodied in "ways of using the body or the gaze... in the automatisms of language and thought through which a man asserts himself as a real, manly man" (1990: 103). These understandings Bourdieu describes are buried in consciousness and may not be discursively available, as Giddens points out (1979). They represent embodied practical knowledge, the ability to "go on" as Wittgenstein suggested, the commonsense "know-how" out of which a life is fashioned. The habitat is the field of practice and the habitus is its enactment, playing the game, constructing and reconstructing it in time and through time, changing everything subtly and incrementally. However, Wittgenstein spoke not of a single language game, but of multiple language games or discourses. Any given habitus is pervaded by "outside" or alternative cultural influences; in the context of economic globalization and international mass media, the "traditional" habitus is challenged but more importantly, it is transformed and exploded by the changes introduced into it. In these days particularly, no unified habitus operates unchallenged or unaltered by its encounters with others.

Indeed, it appears that many of the informants in this study learned to play social life games that are rooted in habit and tradition and that are supported and buttressed by the way space is produced and geography is transformed (Lefebvre, 1991; Soja, 1989). Many informants wrote themselves off as suitable subjects for extended formal education and fit into a habitus which tends to "generate all the 'reasonable,' 'common sense' behaviours," which "without violence, art or argument tend to exclude all 'extravagances' ('not for the likes of us')" (Bourdieu, 1990: 55–56). Bourdieu's work shows how the education system works as a regulatory agency in the reproduction of the habitus, effectively supporting standardized routines and norms, the objectification and quantification of knowledge as though it were neutral, and "teaching" variously positioned individuals what they can expect to achieve for themselves in a subtle physically non-violent (yet symbolically violent) and ostensibly "objective" manner.

On the one hand, we see the community habitus drawing youth into the orbit of the kinds of practice that are routine and considered natural, or "in the blood" for "people like us." The habitus of the school, with its own set of routines and expectations, is simultaneously constructed as being for "people like them." These two competing spaces stand in resistance to one another; each creates its own criteria of intelligence and legitimate ("real") work and each sets up its "own" as the people who have the "natural gifts" to do the work that is done by "people like us," because each is considered to be "naturally" suited to a particular habitat. Just as it is said that only those "born into" fishing can become truly successful at it, it is also understood that the children of teachers and doctors have other "natural" gifts that allow them to succeed in school. Bourdieu's great contribution has been to help us understand how these alleged "gifts" are not at all natural, but derived form the social position of individuals who possess them by virtue of the luck of their birth.

> the educational system helps to provide the dominant class with a "theodicy of its own privilege"... by making — under the overt connection that it guarantees, between qualifications and jobs — the relationship which it surreptitiously records under cover of formal equality, between qualifications obtained and inherited cultural capital. (1991: 133)

In another place Bourdieu calls this "le racism de l'intelligence" (1984a). By this he means that schools create an allegedly generic (but actually class-based) notion of intellectual merit out of the cultural practices of the dominant class and then encode it "objectively" in formal curriculum and testing regimes. This knowledge — which is differentially available on the basis of social-class position — is presented as the essence of intelligence or "natural gifts" of the girl who always felt at home in school and who "took to" the work given her there. The same process is carried out in the male dominated community habitus by my informants when they speak of fishing being "in a boy's [never a girl's] blood." The extension of this discourse is the notion that the only people who can fish effectively, authentically or well are those men who have been born in coastal communities and who have spent a lifetime acquiring the complex and subtle skills and intuition necessary. This intuition is sometimes thought to be an inherited characteristic, as the notion of "blood" implies, but it can also be conceived as a social gift acquired through years of immersion and observation.

Both the habitus of school and the habitus of the community fishery had very specific mobility implications for young men on Digby Neck. If one is to be a fisherman, one must resist the temptation to stay in school, accepting its discourse and "rational" admonition that the fishery is in irreversible decline, or to secure a "steady" job (typically outside the coastal community) that requires little physical exertion and no local knowledge. On the other hand, if one is to enter into the habitus of the school, and particularly higher education, then the embodiment of masculinity and local knowledge that is crucial to becoming "gifted" in the context of the fishery becomes irrelevant. It may even be that the school and its personnel sympathize with the plight of fishing families and fishing communities, but, as one educator in this study asserted, the "hard truth is these people need to face the fact that things have changed, sad as it is for some of them; they need their education."

These two differing contexts stand in opposition to one another, particularly in the context of the older cohorts in this study. Yet, the narratives of decline and survival still sit opposite one another, often in a state of dynamic tension if not in open contradiction. Nevertheless, this conflict seldom surfaces because Digby Neckers are both committed to their communities and families and "realistic" at the same time.

This study is an account of the slow, uncertain rise of a school-based middle-class habitus and the transformation of the community-based habitus of work in the fishery. As the fishery industrialized in the decades between the early 1960s and the late 1990s, there have been significant changes in the structure of opportunity in the fishery, the class relations that distribute the resource and harvesting capacity, the technology used to do the work, the state regulatory function, the commodification of fishing licences and the imposition of quotas, all of which have an impact on the way life is lived by men in the community.

Women have always been much more likely to leave; fishing is usually not their business in the same sense that it is for men and fishing privileges are passed on from father to son. The nonacademic education or socialization system that formed the heart of the small-boat, community-based fishery saw its importance diminish relative to the importance of the academic education system. Now everyone seems to want schooling, and even if they "hate it." Prolonged schooling is seen as a practical necessity and a moral imperative. Young people are drawn into formal education for longer periods, and the results have been particularly problematic for young men caught in the transition between constructions of masculinity requiring little formal education and the emerging narratives that include the acquisition of formal education credentials (Weis, 2004; Kenway and Kraak, 2004; McGrath, 2001).

The tension between fishing and schooling creates a play of resistances that set up specialized mythic metaphors in coastal community schools. The school is the "ladder," the "bridge," the "gate" and the "stepping stone," while the community is "static" and "dying." The discourse about rural education contains strong elements of despair, decline and even death" (McMahon, 2003; Catto, 2003; Press, Galway and Collins, 2003). This discourse of decline is mediated by a questionable "community development" discourse about entrepreneurial high-tech information industries, or tourism. Youth are not convinced, and in the absence of better alternatives, many remain "around here," not because they see exciting new opportunities, but because it is a known space and one in which they can negotiate a livelihood and survive. As people are quick to point out, there are no homeless people on Digby Neck. There is family, there is shared work, there is access to known resources, and there is caring and tradition. This contrasts with the competitive structures and routines of schooling, where, as one informant put it, "it's every man for himself, clawing and scratching for every mark he can get to try and crawl over the next person for a spot in a community college." Many Digby Neckers understood higher education to be the road out of the community into a world that appears more unstable and uncertain every day.

## Poststructural Resistance Theory

> Moreover, the final word on power is that *resistance comes first*, to the extent that power relations operate completely within the diagram, while resistances necessarily operate in a direct relation with the outside from which the diagrams emerge. This means that the social field offers more resistance than strategies, and the thought of the outside is a thought of resistance. (Deleuze, 1988: 89–90, emphasis in the original)

Bourdieu's ideas of the habitus and the logic of practice turn the attention of education ethnographers away from trying to understand how agency resists structural domination toward looking at how agency is enacted "logically" in the context of particular social spaces. While the logic of practice is a powerful tool for understanding social actors' life choices, Bourdieu's general conceptual apparatus seems too monolithic. As Foucault's work shows, agents are not positioned in a coherent and unified habitus but rather in multiple positions responding to multiple discourses, which act as frames within which language games are played. Bourdieu's habitus is a metanarrative that, like Giroux' Marxist metanarrative, ending up envisioning and reproducing a dominated subject (Ranciere, 1995: 52–55). Subjects can always resist and the motivation for resistance as well as its short- and long-term consequences are highly complex.

Poststructural, postmodern and feminist sociologies present a vision of a more or less organized or conflicted interface of smaller narratives, voices, micropowers, response and counter-response. Sociologists struggle to make sense of societies in which power is bound up tightly with desire and consumption, and where formerly powerful core ideas "basic" to the discipline of "society" seem to have been passed by in the mobile, shifting space of contemporary globalism (Urry, 2000). Foucault's work demonstrated how power is produced and reproduced not from the centre in large sovereign institutional or legal gestures, but rather in everyday events by ordinary social actors within multiple spaces, e.g., families, schools and hospitals. Various social and identity politics movements have been quick to seize the opportunity opened up by anti-essentialism, challenging the hegemony of grand theory. As Soja (1989) maintains, Foucault's work turns scholarly attention away from time as a unified epochal force that transforms all places in the same way, to space and place and the particular locations in which time passes in a multitude of ways.

This poststructural idea of power (and perhaps any notion of power) has been difficult for educators and even education theorists to embrace, partly because it seems to offer a rather dismal vision and one which appears to fly in the face of the emancipatory values at the core of public education in liberal democracies. The grand modernist dream of institutional education has been one of homogenization, progress, mass transformation and secular elevation of populations. Criticism of this dream is often considered to be a fundamental challenge to what education is all about (Corbett, 2004). This is unfortunate. Poststructural theory demands an analysis of both multi-layered power and its other (i.e., resistances), as well as an analysis of how the two articulate in practice. Poststructural theory can provide a basis for a positive view of teaching. Why indeed does an understanding that power is produced discursively lead to the dismal conclusion that there is "no way out"? Why not just the opposite? Foucault once commented: "I am sometimes asked: 'But if power is everywhere, there is no freedom.' I answer that if there are relations of power in every social field, this is because there is freedom everywhere" (quoted in Rabinow, 1997: 292). In fact, Foucault's interest in what he came to term governmentality and biopower was precisely a concern with how freedom was enacted, countered and enacted again in a continual relationship of the constitution of power and resistance.[6]

What remains problematic for critical theorists interested in the emancipatory possibilities contained in poststructuralism is the vague and problematic nature of resistance this theory suggests. While Foucault constructed an intriguing and formidable picture of the workings of power in contemporary societies, he did not significantly elaborate what to do about it in terms of emancipatory strategy. For Foucault, power is always contested in discourse rather than out of the machination of structures of domination. Because power is discursive, it can, therefore, be resisted discursively, which indeed it is and must be. This resistance, of course, sets off a counter response, and power relations are produced and reproduced anew. Foucault saw resistance as central to the operation of power. Resistance is simply one face of a multifaceted and constantly shifting power struggle; indeed, there is little else but opposing resistances, or as Foucault wrote, "where there is power, there is resistance" (1990: 95). Thus, power and resistance are everywhere. In fact, resistance is crucial to the very constitution of the power relations Foucault found at the heart of social life.

> You see, if there was no resistance, there would be no power relations. Because it would simply be a matter of obedience.... So resistance comes first, and resistance remains superior to the forces of the process; power relations are obliged to change with resistance. So I think *resistance* is the main word, the *key word* in this dynamic. (quoted in Rabinow, 1997: 167, emphasis in original)

Resistance drives power relations and gives them their form. Conversely,

Giroux, McLaren, Willis and other 1980s resistance theorists see resistance as a by-product of dominance, as something driven and given shape by domination. Foucault's conception of resistance is that it is the play of difference that shapes institutional power. Difference is controlled principally through the generation of knowledge about its character and through charting a strategic response to alterity. Since difference can never be mapped in its entirety and because its character is constantly shifting, power is a dance between strategic knowledge and the ever resistant tactics of the intractably unpredictable object of study (deCerteau, 1984).

Resistance has continued to engage poststructurally oriented theorists and researchers. DeCerteau developed an analysis of resistance out of Foucault's work, arguing that everyday life is a skilled accomplishment in which ordinary social actors accommodate and resist the kind of disciplinary regime Foucault described in his earlier books (1984). While Foucault was most interested in mapping the contours of the regime of truth, deCerteau was interested in the small-scale tactical resistances that grow up in response to what he called the "cancerous growth" of strategic vision. His central idea was that the "victims" or "targets" of disciplinary strategy make use of the ideas that are presented to them as moral guideposts by powerful agents, but what follows from this is an unpredictable creative act of what deCerteau calls "poesis." DeCerteau writes:

> The presence and circulation of a representation (taught by preachers, educators and popularizers as the key to socioeconomic advancement) tells us nothing of what it is to its users. We must first analyze its manipulation by users who are not its makers. (1984: xiii)

DeCerteau argues that this pragmatic usage of disciplinary ideas by the very people at whom they are aimed (i.e., Foucault's "docile bodies") often runs counter to the strategic intent of cultural transmission, resulting in tactics,[7] resistances, compensations and deflections that result in what he calls "antidisciplines." DeCerteau uses the image of the social actor as "reader," claiming that the meaning of power strategies is never fixed and that each social agent reinvents disciplinary strategy in the constructive act of reading normative directives. Given a careful analysis of the practice of everyday life, social analysis which is grounded in a particular context can unravel the interplay of structure and agency, of disciplinary practice and the response of its object.[8] Resistance, in deCerteau's sense, is the symphony of all those disparate acts that are unpredictable from the point of view of discipline and that confound theory in their everyday complexity. Resistance is the tactical response to discipline by individuals who have no space of their own and so are forced to respond in the terms of power itself in a hybrid thirdspace (Bhabha, 1994; Soja, 1989). Resistance is then:

> [The] innumerable ways of playing and foiling other games, that is, the space instituted by others, [which] characterize the subtle stubborn, resistant activity of groups which since they lack their own space, have to get along in a network of already established forces and representations. (deCerteau, 1984: 18)

An example of this sort of resistance is found in bell hooks' account of her childhood resistance to her father's violence, her mother's capitulation and to the reproductive work done to institutionalize the patriarchal family (1994). Through experiences of powerlessness and oppression in her educational biography, hooks came to theory, as she puts it, out of a kind of desperate necessity. Theory allowed hooks to see the play of oppositions and locate her own pain within larger struggles.[9] Without the discursive tools of theory, her resistance and challenges would remain personal problems experienced by a person who does not understand the context in which she lives, much like Willis's lads.

Unlike the pantheon of spectacularly anti-school (typically male) "heroes" found in most critical ethnographies of schooling, hooks found intellectual work to be liberating. By learning to think differently, hooks could confront the assimilationist thrust of her education and learn to work in instead of against schools, universities and other institutional sites that make rural, working-class, Black students feel uncomfortable and pressured to assimilate into the mainstream by learning to "change speech patterns, points of reference, and drop any habit that might reveal them to be from a non-materially privileged background" (hooks, 1994: 181). In other words, hooks was able to use the disciplinary apparatus of the academy to cut out a space for herself that did not have the predicted assimilatory consequences. An understanding that the whole academic enterprise rests on discursive pillars allowed hooks to use theory itself to affirm her roots and ties to home and resist the pressure on working-class students to reject the place from which they come by incorporating a hybrid discourse. Theory and an understanding of power allowed her to see through class-biased territoriality in the academy.

> It was assumed that any student coming from a poor or working-class background would willingly surrender all values and habits being associated with this background.... During my student years, and now as a professor, I see many students from "undesirable" class backgrounds become unable to complete their studies because the contradictions between the behavior necessary to "make it" in the academy and those that allowed them to be comfortable at home, with their families are just too great. (hooks, 1994: 182)

Hooks' survival strategy, both for herself and for her working-class students, is discursive. She urges them to become comfortable in both circumstances, to "cross borders" and to not renounce one for the other categorically, but rather, to seek a space in between and revel in the tension. Just as importantly, hooks' biography serves as one narrative example of resistance, the story of a subject who was not predictably socialized into "her place." Unlike Marxist resistance theory, which comes with an *a priori* oppositional matrix, hooks' resistance operates at the multiple levels of biography and social structure, race, class and gender, and thus, it is more nuanced than most education resistance writing. Hooks' resistance operated on a number of levels and it continues to provide grounding in her present teaching practice, which continues on as a resistant struggle.

Foucault used the plural to speak of resistance (i.e., resistances). A single grand meta-resistance imagines that a wide variety of disparate activity will be folded into a single categorical resistance to the logic of dominance. Resistance here means standing up against the determining monolithic thrust of social reproduction. The conception of multiple resistances brings into view a different panorama of active contestation operative on a number of fronts, each of them specific locales. This place then becomes a locus of resistance. Schooling is clearly an important part of this governance.

## Resistance and Community

> The boat is a floating piece of space, a place without place, that is closed in on itself and at the same time is given over to the infinity of the sea.... In civilizations without boats, dreams dry up, espionage takes the place of adventure, and the police take the place of pirates. (Foucault, 1986: 27)

Bell hooks uses the idea of place to inform her resistance theory. Hooks resists being placed, preferring to cut out her own hybrid location "in between" home place and the academy. In doing so she resisted the seductive invitation to leave home while at the same time refusing to remain locked in place. In his classic treatment of resistance to schooling, Stuart Hall also understood the importance of place in relation to oppositional behaviour in British working-class neighbourhoods (1976). The post-World War Two capitalist development Hall and his colleagues saw emerging in urban Britain in the 1970s was also a systematic destruction of working-class neighbourhoods and communal spaces (Hall and Jefferson, 1976). Hall writes that, "what was destroyed was a concrete set of relations, a network of knowledge, things, experiences — the supports of a class culture" (1976: 37). The decline of the working-class cultural space in urban Britain was facilitated by consumerism and by the expansion of public institutions of normalization like the school. These "developments" substituted what Hall calls a "mobility matrix," which came to characterize working-class culture and working-class space as places from which youth ought to escape. Hall writes that post-war development depopulated working-class neighbourhood and broke up old family and neighbourhood patterns, narrowing family and friendly attachments. Families cut adrift in this way were drawn into the mobility matrix, either "upward into the ranks of the new suburban working-class elite or downward into the lumpen" (1976: 31).

The hegemonic power of "development" can be seen in the commonsense acceptance of a "better life" in suburban growth areas. Urban working-class residents in decaying industrial cities understandably fled their declining neighbourhoods, encouraged formal education for their children and effectively facilitated the dissolution of their solidarity and communities in favour of a mobile ethic. Likewise, the rural community-based, kinship/friendship network had to be smashed by its own hand. Part of this destruction is the way the dissolution of community is presented as evolution and as the only option in the face of modernizing structural forces. The school figures in this coaxing, slow process of ideological formation. The hegemonic message to the old working-class has been: "You had better prepare your children for a life that was different from your own, a life that will be lived in other places." This insistence on flexibility and mobility calls into play a multi-faceted and often unconscious resistance as urban and rural people resist the incursion of capital into those spaces they consider their own. As they defend their spaces, rural dwellers, like those displaced from urban settings, defend their "right" to remain who and where they are (Ching and Creed, 1997; Kincheloe and Pinar, 1991; Smyth and Hattam, 2004). Hall writes: "(T)hese are 'rights' not of ownership or force, but of territorial and cultural possession, the customary occupation of the sitting tenant" (1976: 43).

Hall described the school as an institution that used "double binding," both "horizontal binding" of people to localities in community, but also "vertical binding" of people to "those structures which tie them to dominant institutions and cultures" (1976: 43). This makes the local school a key point of intersection between two disconnected cultures, that of the dominant society and that of the street and the working-class neighbourhood and family. In this intersection, school becomes a "theatre of struggle" into which working-class youth bring "a repertoire of strategies and responses — ways of coping as well as resisting" (Hall, 1976: 44). This resistance is situated within a community context of inter-generational conflict infused with a vision of the appropriateness of staying or leaving and of work and schooling. Hall claims that generational consciousness

> is likely to be strong among those sections of youth which are upwardly and outwardly mobile from the working class… the upward path, through education, leads to a special focusing on the school and the education system as the main mechanism of advancement: it is this which "makes the difference" between parents who stay where they are and children who move on and up. It involves the young person valuing the dominant culture positively, and sacrificing the "parent" culture even when this is accompanied by a distinct sense of cultural disorientation. His experience and self identity will be based around mobility. (Hall, 1976: 51)

To resist schooling is therefore to resist mobility, or at least to grasp the multiple problems mobility entails for working-class youth. In isolated rural places, to resist schooling is to commit at some level to membership in a community of others who stay put. As Bourdieu's empirical work and a great deal of evidence in the sociology of education have shown (Riordan, 2003; Berliner, 2006), education offers "escape" to relatively few. Bourdieu (1984b) also shows how even working-class youth who are educationally successful find themselves always on the margins, never quite "getting it" because their cultural capital is "schooled" rather than transmitted "naturally" and deeply in a middle-class home (Lareau, 1989, 2003).

The powerful logic of capitalism, state control and rational managerial/bureaucratic discourse, along with the highly competitive nature of the global economic order, should by now have smashed local resistance; instead we find the hybridity Bhabha describes (1994), "modular" spaces and selves (Bauman, 1999), migrant multi-spatial identities (Said, 1993; Papastergiadis, 2000), robust local/global identity politics (Luke, 1997, 2002) and produced spaces (Lefebvre, 1991). What has emerged is a struggle between local discourse and structural discourse raising persistent questions about: "a) the relationship between the power relations evident in the local 'micropolitics' of everyday statements and 'macro' systemic social formations, and b) the relationship between change in discourse statements and practices and material, social and economic change" (Luke, 1997: 345).

Manuel Castells has taken up this theme in Volume 2 in his series of books investigating the rise of the "network society" (2004). Castells points to the unexpected emergence of powerful social movements, vibrant identity politics and community-based resistance to the forces of globalization, massification and, indeed, to the whole project of institutionally based civil society. Just when many social theorists were beginning to speculate about the triumph of state and capitalist normalization, and even the "end of history" (Fukuyama, 1992), the 1990s saw the rise of a wide range of resistance movements that relied on some features of the network capabilities introduced into advanced capitalism through technologies like the fax machine, the cell phone and the Internet. As Castells puts it, "When the world becomes too large to be controlled, social actors aim to shrink it back to their size and reach" (2004: 69). Castells argues that these resistance movements have become a more powerful location for the organization of identity in contemporary societies, in some ways more powerful than the institutional mechanisms employed by the key institutions of the state and corporate capital.

In other words, state institutions like schools have become far less important to the construction of individual identity than networked resistance movements that actually represent a fundamental critique of both state institutions and the forces of global capitalism that Benjamin Barber (1995) characterizes as McWorld. What is more, Castells' "resistance identities" (2004: 8–9) result in the formation of communities of resistance that stand in opposition to the meta-community of civil society, the democratic ideal citizen, which is the object of most visions of key state apparatuses (Gramsci, 1971; Althusser, 1971) like public schooling. Place once again matters, and identity is increasingly likely to be located in opposition to large social forces, institutions and totalizing visions (Bauman, 2004b). As Castells puts it:

> Thus, so emerged the paradox of increasingly local politics in a world structured by increasingly global processes. There was production of meaning and identity: My neighborhood, my community, my city, my school, my tree, my river, my beach, my chapel, my peace, my environment. But it was a defensive identity, an identity of retrenchment of the known against the unpredictability of the unknown and uncontrollable. Suddenly defenseless against a global whirlwind, people stuck to themselves: whatever they had, and whatever they were became their identity. (2004: 64–65)

The network society that was built to eradicate the importance of established institutional relationship and to draw everyone, particularly privileged consumers, into the ambit of post-industrial consumer spaces in which society no longer mattered, has, Castells argues, failed. In fact, the very network mechanisms employed to do the job have become the field in which this exclusionary project has been subverted by the creation of resistant micro-communities and social movements that are themselves more or less networked (Castells, 2004: 166–67). It seems to me in some ways that rural people and rural spaces have become unlikely heroes in this new configuration of resistance because they have always been an irritant to the grand project of normalization or the establishment of civil society (Corbett, 2001b).

## Rural Identity Politics

While there has been a great deal of attention paid in recent years to the explosion of identity politics, as Ching and Creed point out, remarkably little of this attention has addressed what they call the "rural urban axis" (1997: 3). They argue that "rusticity," which is a rooted rural identity and connected to particular geographic locations, operates as a form of resistance to the placeless, urban values that characterize contemporary cultural and social theory.[10] They also point out that education plays a crucial role in creating character structure that articulates with urbanism.

> In the West, few intellectuals have deep rural roots, and for those who do, education often severs those connections. The traditional pedagogical agenda, with its emphasis on enlightenment through the liberal arts, has long been opposed to the supposed essence of rusticity — lack of cultural sophistication and a preference for practical know-how over erudition... education [is described] as tantamount to an urbanization of the mind. (Ching and Creed, 1997: 10)

"Rustics" are deviant precisely because of their attachment to particular places and their apparent unwillingness to engage the contemporary, the urbane and the global, the urban and the sophisticated. Rustics resist modernity and confound educationalists in no small part because they refuse to leave the country.

Kieran Bonner has found an ironic tension between the radical mobility of late modernity and the desire for connection to place represented by rural living (1997). Developing a contemporary analysis of the rural-urban debate that animated the development of North American sociology in the early twentieth century, Bonner examined the mundane notion that rural communities are seen by their residents as "a great place to raise kids." His analysis of what this commonsense rural notion actually means leads to the conclusion that rural living is resistant to "the pluralization of life worlds that makes the practice of consumerism seem reasonable" (1997: 178). Bonner argues that attachment to any particular place is, in the face of post-modernity, a form of resistance. Drawing on Bauman and Giddens, Bonner identifies radical mobility or the form of phenomenological homelessness (Berger, Berger and Kellner, 1973) as a central feature of contemporary life.

The development of modernity was marked by a displacement and mass migration of rural people to urban environments. People who had formerly been tied by tradition to the land were forced into the new industrial urban landscape as industrial labourers. Bonner argues that postmodernity is now marked by its preoccupation with consumption rather than production. A key part of this shift is the idea that place has, along with everything else, become commodified. In other words, the place one lives becomes yet another consumer choice along with everything else rather than a fundamental expression of identity or belonging. In the bargain, the roving consumer of place must be mobile in order to be open to a variety of consumption and place choices constructed in contemporary society. Bonner argues that place attachment in his community of "Prairie Edge," Alberta, represents a form of resistance to the mobility imperative implied by postmodernity. But the kind of resistance he finds is hybrid, not a simple throwback to a relatively "immobile" traditional society. This resistance itself is also postmodern and rooted in the enhanced ability of rural individuals to visualize and move through space to carry out surveillance both of their own families (especially, but not exclusively their own dependent children) and the community at large. The key part of Bonner's account is the idea of place-based resistance, or more precisely, an attachment to place that forms the basis of a resistance against the insecurity and chronic fear in the drive to total mobility and consumerism.[11]

The analysis of mobility as a chronic feature and a central problematic in the development of contemporary capitalism is also prominent in Richard Sennett's (1999) return to the core ideas in *The Hidden Injuries of Class* (Sennett and Cobb, 1973). Sennett describes the differences between the working-class men he interviewed in Boston in the early 1970s and the lives led by their children in the late 1990s (1999). Sennett finds a highly mobile, unsatisfied restlessness in the latter generation. While education for their children was the dream of Sennett and Cobb's 1970s informants, the irony is that this very education has created a new kind of alienation in the present generation. Education plays a key role in the character formation of the mobile, flexible individual. Describing the career trajectory of his key informant, Sennett claims, "school prepared the young couple to move and change jobs frequently, and they've done so" (1999: 18). More particularly he argues that the right-wing, conservative values expressed by this informant are a reaction to their immersion in the flexible, mobile, short-term, instrumental ethical environment of the modern "efficient" corporation.

Much of Zygmunt Bauman's recent work has also focused on the relentless mobilization of people on a global scale (1998, 2000, 2004a). The winners in contemporary modernity are those attached to no particular place and whose lives represent an endless flight from one site of consumption to another, leaving behind a trail of equally endless waste. Relentless mobilization, which flows from the globalization of capitalism, has impeded the ability of more and more locales and the people committed to them, to support population, leading to what Bauman eerily describes as surplus humanity and "human waste" (2004a).

> Where family and communal businesses were once able and willing to absorb, employ and support all newly born humans. And at most times secure their survival, the surrender to global pressure and the laying of their own territory open to the unfettered circulation of capital and commodities made them unviable. Only now do the newcomers to the company of moderns experience that separation of business from households which the pioneers of modernity went through hundreds of years ago, with all its attendant social upheavals and human misery but also with the luxury of global solutions to locally produced problems — an abundance of 'empty' and 'no man's lands' that could easily be used to deposit the surplus population no longer absorbed by the economy emancipated from familial and communal constraints: a luxury not available to latecomers. (Bauman, 2004a: 72)

This new form of alienation is rooted in the sense that nothing is permanent, neither values, nor kinship networks, nor attachment to any particular place. Sennett's young informant and his family have moved a total of four times in fourteen years since university graduation. Bauman writes that late modernity is characterized by what he calls "modular" forms of identity. Identity, work, personal relations and indeed the total environment are fragmented to the point where "instead of alienation we should better speak these days of 'unsettlement' or 'unhomliness'" (1999: 160). This is precisely the kind of consciousness Sennett describes. Sennett's informants find ways to resist this unsettlement by supporting simplistic values and political agendas that appear to them to resist the erosion of long-term commitments and enduring values. In the process, they become static and petty because they cannot come to grips with a world in which everything is in motion.

## The Organized Rural Community as a Resistant Site

> She knew what they wanted most was for her to stay. None of their ideas about what she should do with her life involved her leaving. (Coady, 1998: 149)

> Recognizing the vulnerability of the commitment, and confronting the emptiness of materialism and the consequences of rootlessness in a world made increasingly homogeneous by mass production and modern communication, we must stress the many good humanitarian and social reasons for maintaining communities in which people can reap the emotional benefits of belonging and know the satisfaction of meaningful employment. (Wynn, 1988: 51)

Raymond Williams was interested in the conditions under which people become "massified," and central to this is the transformation of communication in modern societies. Mass communications construct a plane of understanding that transcends the face-to-face, experiential world of locale. Williams wrote: "The old rural culture, which is so widely and sometimes sentimentally admired, rested on generations of experience within a general continuity of common condition" (1958: 311). The importance of the local community is subverted by the mass media and in the communication practices embodied in the public school and mass education. Mass communication then is a prototypical domination technique, a subtle one, a manipulation of ideas. But transmission must be connected with reception at the concrete points to which it descends in order to be effective (Williams, 1958: 314). At multiple local points of reception, mass communication must connect, and this is why it never really dominates. Again in Williams words: "mass communication… has failed and will continue to fail when its transmissions encounter not a confused uncertainty, but a considered and formulated experience" (1958: 313).

Williams imagined organized communities as sites of resistance to the mass normalization project of popular media and perhaps the tutelary complex as well. He was politically committed to articulating a vision of society in which communal values confronted those of atomistic individualism. Williams understood that communities represent an obstacle to normalization because, particularly when they are organized, they represent experiential grounding in a functioning habitus against which mass communication chafes, but never entirely conquers. In this sense, communities are resistance to what Williams calls "massification" and what Foucault calls normalization (1979).

Anticipating Foucault's idea of power/knowledge, Williams saw the conception of mass society as useful to elites, which can now (through mechanisms like opinion polls and market research) use distancing and objectification to understand the tastes and preferences of large numbers of consumers. "The 'masses' exert their influence on the direction of society, not by participation, but by expressing a pattern of demands and preferences… and this for the elites is a starting point: to be carefully studied and then worked on" (Williams, 1961: 110). Education works in a similar way, serving to impart a curriculum of "fixed knowledge," which includes "social character training" (Williams, 1961: 126), but also to provide a social laboratory in which children might be studied, understood and improved. But against this project, specific places and resistant spaces illustrate by practical example the range of alternate social characters and unique knowledges from which the child might choose. For Williams: "children while at school, learn from their whole social environment as well as from the particular curriculum, to say nothing of the fact that when they leave school they have to compare what they learned with the actual practices of their society" (1961: 120).

Community itself is a discourse space into which competing and supplementary institutional discourses have been be introduced. Contemporary education historians have helped us understand how the normalization process, which inserts protracted schooling into particular spatial and temporal locations, is predicated on a long-term negotiation between educators and those to be educated (Prentice, 1977; Curtis, 1988; Gaffield, 1987; Corbett 2001b). This is to say that the institutions, habits, discourses and norms that surround contemporary schooling had to be actively built and legitimized amongst populations and even governmental bodies (Bouchard, 1997). Schools are part of a state-sponsored attempt to mobilize a normalizing discourse and thus become one of the central locations of modern governance. They were developed initially to inculcate norms of time consciousness, industrial routine and hygiene and to further religious and patriotic ideologies. Today they continue to be mobilized to normalize populations around contemporary discourses such as literacy, numeracy, health (e.g., drug, alcohol and obesity campaigns), information technologies and numerous individual and social pathologies. Each of these discourses now contain both specific pedagogies, curricula and an entourage of research experts and curative agents. Contemporary schooling is a massive, coordinated, bureaucratic social project that up until recently has appeared so firmly entrenched that schooling has become almost synonymous with modernity, civilization and progress.

However, as Castells (2004) shows, social movements and communities, either imagined or enacted, emerge from resistance to organized large-scale attempts by both bureaucracies (civil society) and organized capitalism (neoliberal globalization) to form identities and control life. This way of looking at rural schools should help to explain why they are very often such contested and ambiguous spaces. At one level, the institutional discourse of formal education continually meets the practical discourse of place, and the world it enjoins children to imagine operates as a shadow of the local spaces in which these children live out their real lives. At another level, it is eminently clear in coastal communities that both state-level planning (as represented quintessentially by the way the federal Department of Fisheries and Oceans has mismanaged the many fisheries to the point of collapse) and the trajectory of corporate concentration in the open markets of the contemporary fishery have combined to create a disaster that has fundamentally compromised community sustainability. In rural communities, locale is important, often generating resistance to the massification, globalization and mobilization project represented in part by contemporary schooling. In other words, in communities like Digby Neck, many people retreat into an often nostalgic community survival mode when the pressure is on.

In fact, community is now a discursive governance tool. Deploying Foucault's concept of governmentality, Rose (1997) suggests that the metaphor of locality and community has emerged out of the ashes of the state. Rose maintains that the "social" is no longer the principal zone of governance, having been replaced by the "community." Rose calls the community, "a new spatialization of governance: heterogeneous, plural, linking individuals, families and others in contesting cultural assemblies of identities and allegiances" (1997: 327). In the modern "advanced liberal" state, community is invoked as a friendly site for the generation of activity and the mobilization of publics. Decentralization is the order of the day as neoliberal states devolve functions once centralized in bureaucracy to local initiatives controlled by the "grass roots." Rose writes:

> The social and the economic are now seen as antagonistic, and the former is to be fragmented in order to transform the moral and psychological obligations of economic citizenship in the direction of active self-advancement. Simultaneously, government of a whole range of previously social apparatuses is to be restructured according to a particular image of the economic — the market. Economic government is to be de-socialized in the name of maximizing the entrepreneurial comportment of the individual. (1997: 340)

In the interests of creating self-governing agents imbued with the appropriate consumer/market values, the "community" is mobilized to provide the cultural context for an interconnected yet unique economic network of self-regulating consumption and production. Anti-communities, which lack the social cohesion to be trusted to steer their own affairs, come to be colonized by what Rose calls "a plethora of quasi autonomous agencies working within the 'savage spaces,' in the 'anti-communities' on the margins." Rose goes on to argue that this regulative work reproblematizes these savage spaces as a matter of the lack of individual and marketable skills among the un-employed themselves to be countered by a multitude of training organizations that are private and compete in the market for public contracts" (1997: 347).

Rural communities (and I think Atlantic coastal communities stand as good examples) are often cast as dysfunctional or backward spaces that exist on the fringes of civil society and its institutions. Their schools, operating as they do within "savage spaces," as Rose calls them, are typically perceived as dysfunctional education sites. Popkewitz's *Struggle for the Soul* (1998) focuses on the discursive production of educationally problematic spaces in the Teach for America (TFA) alternative teacher training program. Specifically Popkewitz is interested in how "urban and rural" is constructed as a unified category of children placed in a position of educational alterity as "historical discourses about the capabilities of children are mobilized… [and] function to place the urban and rural child outside reason" (1998: 48). Urban, in this context, is code for "inner city" or suburban poor, while rural is code for country backwater. In this construction the urban and rural child is conjured as a deficient stereotype against the absent presence of the "normal" middle-class child living in an advantaged affluent environment. This absent presence is the "successful" child juxtaposed against the deficient, incompetent and unsuccessful urban/rural child. Success, in this cosmology, is having one's life set in a middle-class home.

> The successful child is one who can sleep at proper hours, study, and who is allowed to develop self-motivation and responsibility…. The lack of English language skills stand within the grid of ideas whose normalization testified to the child's lack of competence and achievement. The students are positioned as anthropological "others" who stand against reason — they "can't study," are "just so disruptive" and are "pressured not to learn." The children occupy an oppositional space to what is "normal." The nonsuccess of the child is embodied in the normalized capacities of "being" which the child in school lacks. (Popkewitz, 1998: 37)

In this matrix, schooling becomes a focus for governing spaces and "rescuing" or "saving" rural and urban children from the social decay in which they are ensnared by virtue of an accident of birth. Urban and rural become code words for marginal spaces populated by non-middle-class, non-white, non-affluent children in need of specialized forms of governance in order to, "discriminate, distinguish and normalize what the child is and is to become" (Popkewitz, 1998: 22).

The idea of the backward community is heard increasingly in the discourse about education and development in Atlantic Canada. And it is in the resistant and backward space that specialized normalization work needs to be done. Social rehabilitation programs abound, and "life skills" (a ubiquitous education concept striking if only because of its arrogance) and various types of "retraining" for the "information economy" are being "delivered" to adult learners on every street corner. Backward rural spaces are defined as doomed places to be left behind as soon as one is able to move on to their antithesis: progressive spaces, urban spaces where a person can be useful, productive and a burden to no one.[12] Their brains, it seems, must be made fit for the drain. Such prospects are largely a joke for a large proportion of the current generation of fisheries workers deprived of their livelihood. But it does seem as though the children of these people staying in school longer, acquiring portable credentials. Are rural schools doing their part and facilitating the migration that will ultimately spell the end for many coastal communities as working settlements?

## Conclusion: To Choose and to Move

> It is the power which the children have to resist everybody and everything outside the village.... I've come to the conclusion that this strangeness I am trying to describe has nothing to do with this (insularity). The village children aren't jealous — on the contrary, they are convinced that they have something which none of the newcomers can ever have, some kind of mysterious life which is so perfect that it is a waste of time to search for anything else. I used to wonder at their slowness at absorbing things but now I am beginning to realize that they know from an early age that they don't need to take in what I am teaching them.... They will do anything you tell them but never that little extra original thing. (village teacher quoted in Blythe, 1969: 177)

Resistance theory as it was presented in the 1970s and 1980s is inadequate for explaining the complexity of response of working-class youth to the experience of schooling. Giroux commented in a seminal work from this tradition (1983) that in order to separate real acts of resistance from false ones, resistance theory needs to isolate those acts that are useful to what he (or some enlightened/privileged observer) considers to be legitimate political struggle.

> Thus, central to analyzing any act of resistance would be a concern with uncovering the degree to which it speaks to a form of refusal that highlights, either implicitly or explicitly, the need to struggle against the social nexus of domination and submission. In other words, resistance must have a revealing function, one that contains a critique of domination and provides theoretical opportunities for self-reflection and for struggle in the interest of self-emancipation and social emancipation. (1983: 108–109)

This, I think, is precisely what is wrong with this version of resistance theory. When the idea of resistance is removed from the context in which it occurs and when its motivation is written into a political/theoretical account that assesses its meaning and its worth, then resistance is relegated to an ideological division between legitimate resistance and false consciousness. Giroux uses the term "function" to describe what he sees as the role of resistance because in this formulation it is a tool in a larger political struggle. This emphasis on evaluating and sorting different forms of opposition also removes them from their context, from the place where they happen because location is irrelevant in the larger play of political emancipation.[13] Rather than subsuming all sorts of resistance under the theoretical umbrella of structural theory, it seems to me more productive to attempt to understand varieties of resistance in their own terms as much as possible. To do this requires research, preferably a protracted engagement in a social location, in this case, a coastal community in Atlantic Canada.

More recent studies of both resistance and the importance of place have shown that resistance needs to be understood first of all in the context in which it occurs and against the backdrop of its other, the set of disciplinary procedures that attempt to shape behaviour in particular directions in particular locations. Foucault discussed power in terms of "structures of domination" and micro power relations (in Rabinow, 1997: 291–93). The question often arose in his interviews as to why he seemed to have so little to say about these larger structures of domination in his own epoch (i.e., class, gender and race), structures that most theories of power take to be of primary importance. His response was that in societies like those in which he lived his life (including Nazi-occupied rural France, where he spent part of his early youth), there was a great ambit of possibility for action despite the obvious weight of structures of domination. For Foucault, it was precisely the possibility of resistances that creates the space for power relations. To really understand how structures of domination get and keep power relations moving in a particular direction, one needs to understand both what "they" encourage us to do and how we interpret this encouragement and respond to it. This is the intricate dance of micro-politics in what Dorothy Smith calls the "everyday world as problematic" (1987).

For instance, Pocius's (1991) study of place attachment in rural Newfoundland, Berger and Mohr's photo essay of migrant workers in the 1970s (1977), Sennett's mobile contemporary corporate employees (1999) and Burrill's oral history of a generation of Maritime migrants in New England, Ontario and Alberta (1992), each represents different kinds of exchange *vis-à-vis* the disembedded, placeless, homeless, mobile urban world of modernity described theoretically by Berger et al. (1973); Giddens (1990, 1991); Bauman (1995, 1999); Urry (2000); and Papastergiadis (2000). Resistance to the invocation to move takes many forms, some of which may be "emancipatory" in the face of particular kinds of dominance. Only a detailed and nuanced analysis of particular forms of resistance in particular places at particular times can explain this order of problem. In the particular case of this study, I am interested not so much in the way that resistant behavior supports or disables emancipation, but rather, what indeed is being resisted, how, where and, particularly, with what results.

Commenting on his rural boyhood, Wallace Stegner wrote, "I was educated for the wrong place" (quoted in Ching and Creed, 1997). What he meant was that his education did not prepare him for staying in the place where he was educated and migration was an implicit and hidden but well understood curriculum. The story is a common rural variant of Pygmalion and it has been a staple of Western fiction, as Raymond Williams has shown in his scholarly work (1958, 1961, 1973) and in his novels.

> It was really as if, oppressed by an enemy, a people had conceived of its own liberation as training its sons for enemy service. And they would even boast how well they were doing and how much the enemy thought of them. (Williams, 1964: 137–38)

Foucault's vision of power locates resistance in all social relations. Bhabha's idea of intransitive resistance helps us understand how opposition can be immanent and not necessarily intended within unequal power relations (1994). Bell hooks (1994) teaches us that home is a location for education resistance and a point from which agents can form a hybrid, migrant, border-crossing identity. Rural sociologists Matthews (1976, 1993), Bonner (1997) and Ching and Creed (1997), as well as rural education theorists Theobald (1992, 1997), Haas and Nachtigal (1998) and DeYoung (1995), all demonstrate how rurality itself can be a site of resistance. Contemporary social theory recognizes the central place of migration and mobility in late modernity (Bauman, 1991, 1999; Urry, 2000; Papastergiadis, 2000). Some people in coastal communities become mobile while others resist and remain rooted. By analyzing the stories of both stayers and out-migrants from a single Atlantic Canadian coastal community, we can begin to understand the nature of this contemporary call to move and keep on moving and the ambivalent struggles individuals encounter to stay and to leave. Why indeed have some people remained in a place that is discursively constructed as crumbling. If choice is the predominant metaphor of a consumer society, then mobility is the key metaphor of the rural school. To have education choices, young people are almost always required to move.

In Castells' (2004) formulation, social movements and communities have been forming since the 1970s in creative reaction to the placeless forces of globalization and consumerism. The technologies of the network society produce information, and it seems to be Castells' argument that information is more democratic than neoliberal power brokers ever imagined. It is becoming increasingly clear that not everyone wants into McWorld. Many people are looking for a position from which we might resist the neoliberal forces that were thought for awhile to mark the end of history. It is my sense that they find it largely outside Castells' "space of flows," in what he terms the "space of places" (2000: 453–59), the face-to-face locales where the most people fashion identity and hunker down to meet and often resist the challenges of the networked capitalism controlled by a mobile, wired elite who live nowhere. The search for community is a creative process of constructing what Castells calls "resistance identities," which oppose the "legitimized identities" constructed for us in the context of civil society and its state apparatuses. By looking hard at the stories that constitute this community and how those stories articulate with the institutional vision of public schooling and the identities this vision contained, I want to explain the persistence of people living in places that have been declared dead of natural causes. Apparently they are not quite dead yet.

## Notes

1. In addition to Willis's study, which is the most thoroughly researched and theoretically sophisticated of its genre, there is a similar body of British ethnographically informed resistance analysis and theory dating from the late 1970s (Hall and Jefferson, 1976; Corrigan, 1979; McRobbie, 1991).
2. Giroux does take some pains to distinguish between legitimate resistance and irrelevant and conservative forms of oppositional behaviour (1983: 107–11). However, the distinctions he argues for simply seem to intensify problems of essentialism and presumptuousness. What indeed are the criteria for making the distinction between what Giroux sees as resistance and what defiant students themselves define as resistance?
3. Game argues that the growing use of ethnographic methods by urban sociologists in Western societies has created what she terms a slide from studies of cultural "production" to political resistance (1990: 29). What she seems to mean by this is that studies of schooling influenced by the work of Willis and Hall have focused on agents' accounts, which understandably present not a picture of domination but one of resistance to it. Game suggests that this slide is a discursive one and the shift from studies of dominance to studies of resistance are generated primarily by the techniques and concepts used by the sociologists who employ them.

   > The inversion from oppression to resistance is effected through a particular approach to research: lived experience has become the object, with the assumption that experience is more authentic than either the abstractions of Marxist theorizing or the numbers of quantitative sociology. (Game, 1990: 29)

4. Bourdieu himself is clearly committed to supporting various kinds of "resistant" social causes. A recent collection of his conference interventions, addresses and political writings demonstrate a strong activist stance that supports strong questioning of the political orthodoxy of neoliberalism (1998). Bourdieu has always maintained that his studies of reproduction have political implications in that they show a kind of benign institutional social control that needs to be recognized and identified in order to be countered. Perhaps Bourdieu is

responding to the critique that his work, in the end, presents a depressing, over-determined view of human agency that is so tightly controlled by the articulation of institutional and cognitive repression that it ends up stifling the democratic oppositional potential (Ranciere, 1991, 1995). This critique is powerful, because it argues that it is the very agency of subordinate classes that closes off their ability to resist. Without the ability to resist we are left with a hollow and politically impoverished account of the world.

5. In fact, some sociologists are now arguing that core sociological concepts like society (Urry, 2000) and community (Bauman, 2000) may be irrelevant in the highly fluid and mobile space of globalization and hybridity.
6. In fact, as Deleuze has asserted, it is essentialist discourses of knowledge (i.e., freedom, man, and life) that are static and repressive but that are continuously and necessarily resisted by what he calls life. When the human sciences, for instance, sought to categorize and administer life itself, it is the very substance of life that resists. Deleuze writes:

   > Life becomes resistance to power when power takes life as its object.... Is not the force that comes from outside a certain idea of Life, a certain vitalism, in which Foucault's thought culminated? Is not life this capacity to resist force? (1988: 92–93)

7. DeCerteau used the concept of tactics in opposition to the idea of strategy (1984). For deCerteau, strategy is the operative planning of those who hold social power. Tactics, on the other hand, are the less coordinated responses of less organized agents who are the objects of strategy.
8. In *Portraits of "the Whiteman*, Keith Basso (1979) has shown carefully how the discourses and practices of a socially dominant group can be read creatively and in a resistant fashion by subordinated people.
9. As Eagleton (2003) argues, theory is an ethical tool that allows its users to make judgments outside a framework of absolute truths and fundamentalist logic.
10. Soja (1989), Harvey (1990), Day and Murdoch (1993) and the contributors to Benko and Strohmayer's *Space and Social Theory* (1997) argue that social theory developed from the essential idea that place does not make much difference. These scholars argue that social theory has aimed at generality and the production of knowledge that holds true across places and across time. Giddens' work has been an attempt to address this, among other problems in social theory, which he found to be developed on a nineteenth-century philosophical base that is inadequate for dealing with both the complexity and dynamism of social life (1971, 1976, 1979, 1981) and the specific problems of modernity (1990, 1991, 1995, 1996). Referring to his own work with sociologists on Digby Neck, one of my informants calls this placelessness in sociological thinking, the view from nowhere. In education studies, space and place are just beginning to come into view on the theoretical landscape (Reay and Lucey, 2000; Comber and Thompson, 2001; Gruenewald, 2003; Hutchinson, 2004).
11. In his analysis of the development of the classical sociological tradition, Bonner hypothesizes that the analysis of modernity found in Weber, Marx and Tonnies particularly and later developed by Wirth and the Chicago School can be

read as a protracted argument in support of the notion that rural communities were doomed, if not to die, to become urbanized and indistinguishable from their hegemonic urban counterparts. As this theme is developed into contemporary and postmodern social theory the relevance of rurality becomes even less significant, a point made equally forcefully by Ching and Creed (1997), Berry (1977) and Theobald (1997). Bonner cites the work of contemporary Marxist Frederic Jamieson and critical geographer Edward Soja to make this point. This disappearance of the rural thus represents the disappearance of resistance to the dominance of capital (1997: 32). His point seems to be that rurality may well be the last bastion of potential resistance to this dominance. Ching and Creed also make a similar point that what they call rusticity is a fundamentally resistant identity choice in the face of urban-centric capitalist development (1997).

12. Marxist theorists have used the language of the needs of capital and the idea of the reserve army of labour to describe this phenomenon (Veltmeyer, 1979, 1990). The difference here is that the reserve army now requires specialized training for mobility just as immobile stayers now need to be educated to both leave and stay.
13. A recent study of resistance in an elementary classroom demonstrates that the idea that resistance can be utilized for behavioural control of children (Spaulding, 2000). Drawing on the work of Ball (1987), which uses the notion of micropolitics, Spaulding uses the idea of resistance theory to analyze the oppositional behaviour of young children. Her intent is to provide teachers, and teachers in training particularly, with the social control skills necessary to counter student resistance. Another more critical study of student resistance using poststructural theory is briefly described in a research note in the *Canadian Journal of Education* (Field and Olafson, 1999).

Chapter 3

# Who Stays, Who Goes and Where

## Education and Migration on Digby Neck, 1963–1998

Digby Neck is a 30-km long, narrow peninsula jutting into the Bay of Fundy in southwestern Nova Scotia. Never exceeding five kilometres in width, it is bounded on the north by the Bay of Fundy and on the south by St. Mary's Bay. To the west are a narrow passage and two small islands and to the east are several small villages and the town of Digby. "The Neck" is comprised of nine villages, which extend from the head of St. Mary's Bay in the east to East Ferry (so named from the point of view of the island joined from the east to the mainland by this ferry) at the western extremity. I refer to this collection of villages as a community because the discrete settlements that comprise the Neck are generally seen as belonging to the larger collective. Older residents remember the time, dating back to the mid-1950s, before school consolidation and the paving of the highway, when each village on Digby Neck had more of its own identity, but today the "community" is generally meant to refer to the nine villages. These villages are similar in that they were all settled in the early to mid-nineteenth century to access the rich fishery on both St. Mary's and the Bay of Fundy.

The houses along the Neck are predominantly wood frame, painted white and set close the main road (Highway 217) or one of the community access roads that branch off to either the Fundy or St. Mary's shore. The properties are generally well kept and neat in appearance. Some have the look of prosperity about them while others do not, but the norm is a modest respectability. Beside most houses are workshops and wood sheds. Many families in the community heat their homes with the abundant softwood that grows on family wood lots. A typical male Digby Necker is described by most informants as a man who likes to work hard, do things with his hands (such as cut wood), hunt, fish and spend his time on the water or in the woods. Most properties have signs of this kind of lifestyle. Four-wheel-drive vehicles and half-ton pickups are the conveyance of choice, and motorized "four wheeler" cycles are seen around most houses. The interior spaces of the house and the landscaping that surrounds them tend to be managed by women. The typical Digby Neck woman is also seen as "a worker," someone who is always "busy" keeping the house in order, doing the cooking, decorating, "running around" for groceries and ferrying children to "town" (Digby) for activities not available on the Neck. Many women also participate in outdoor labour and recreation with their partners around the property and in the woods but typically not on the water. While they worry about the future and what their children will do to make a living, most people take pride in their ability to make do and to survive in a place they call home. Many homes show signs of a connection to the fishery. Lobster traps and assorted kinds of fishing gear are often stored near houses in the off-season.

Most of the villages continue to have more or less active wharves, which continue to the focal point of the economic life. During any given part of the year, there is some fishery in operation, and the wharf is the landing and departure point for all fishing operations. Some wharves, like those in East Ferry, Little River and Sandy Cove, are equipped to handle small-boat draggers, which typically measure 45–65 feet in length. Centreville was a dragger port until the 1980s, but the wharf has fallen into disrepair and washouts have filled the harbour with sediment, making it impossible for larger boats to berth there. Other communities have smaller wharves in various states of repair. Fishers in Whale Cove on the Bay of Fundy side of Digby Neck still winch their boats fully out of the water and up onto a slipway at the end of most working days because of the volatile weather and limited shelter offered by their small wharf. The wharves at the eastern end of Digby Neck, in Waterford and Gulliver's Cove, are in disrepair and are virtually unusable.

The Neck is an extension of Nova Scotia's North Mountain, which itself is a part of the Appalachian system. The North Mountain runs from Brier Island, just west of Digby Neck, to the Minas Basin, near the far end of the Annapolis Valley.[1] In fact, "the Valley" is formed in the space between the North and South mountains. The land on Digby Neck is rugged and hilly, with acidic, rocky soil and is wooded primarily with spruce and fir. Prominent and accessible basalt deposits on the Fundy shore of Digby Neck have recently become the source of new debates around a controversial proposed megaquarry project. Highway 217, which begins in Digby, connects the sporadic communities, most of which were established around sheltered coves and harbours along the two bays. The Neck is strategically located for fishing because of its proximity to both the Bay of Fundy to the north and St Mary's Bay to the south.

Despite fears that the population and economic vitality of Digby Neck are in decline, historical village level population figures show that the population remained relatively stable from the nineteenth century into the 1980s, when significant population decline began (See Tables 3.1 and 3.2).

**Table 3.1 Pre 1951 Census Counts for Digby Neck Communities, 1871–1941**

| | 1871 | 1881 | 1891 | 1901 | 1911 | 1921 | 1931 | 1941 |
|---|---|---|---|---|---|---|---|---|
| Rossway | 385 | 514 | 431 | 391 | 343 | 376 | 318 | 355 |
| Sandy Cove and Centreville | 738 | 708 | 687 | 754 | 711 | 683 | 668 | 687 |
| Little River | 397 | 382 | 373 | 448 | 407 | 448 | 464 | 460 |
| Digby Neck | 1520 | 1504 | 1491 | 1593 | 1461 | 1507 | 1450 | 1502 |

While the enumeration areas used by Census Canada and the Dominion Bureau of Statistics changed over the years, the overall population of the communities of Digby Neck fluctuated about 20 percent between 1871 and 1981, peaking at 1593 in 1901 (see Table 3.1) and falling as low as 1234 in 1961 (see Table 3.2). By 1991 the population had risen to 1366, its highest point since 1941, but fell dramatically to 1055 just five years later, in the 1996 census. Generally the population has shifted "down the Neck," with numbers remaining far more stable in the western as opposed to the eastern part of Digby Neck. This is probably due to the decline of the small-boat hook-and-line fishery and the rise of the small-boat dragger fleet, which has been documented by other studies of the area (Hughes et al., 1960; Davis, 1991; Kearney, 1993). This population movement is also reflected in the state of wharves in the communities along the Neck, with wharves in better condition at the western end.

The fishery has been, and continues to be, the economic lifeblood of Digby Neck. Digby Neckers remain close to land and sea, particularly the latter with the intensification of fishing in the last thirty years. This is obvious to travellers and residents alike. Communities are organized around fish plants and wharves, and both land and sea show signs of fishing gear. Older residents of the Neck can still remember when agriculture was more important, and the fishing/farming family was common.[2] Many residents of the Neck have always kept household gardens and cut small amounts of firewood, pulp or saw logs. In recent years though, pulp and paper companies and the provincial Department of Natural Resources have begun to petition local residents to sell off their wood lots for saw logs and pulp in the face of an infestation of the spruce bark beetle. Some residents have decided to accept this analysis, and it is not unusual to see clear-cuts while driving along Highway 217.

Fish and lobsters are landed at seven different wharves in six different communities. With the decline in ground fishing, lobstering has become the principal remaining viable fishery on the Neck. This is almost exclusively a small-boat, family-based fishery. Both traditional and modern methods of fishing for groundfish have been in decline on Digby Neck for at least

**Table 3.2 Population of Digby Neck Communities, 1951–1991**

| | 1951 | 1956 | 1961 | 1966 | 1971 | 1981 | 1991 |
|---|---|---|---|---|---|---|---|
| Roxville | na | na | na | 23 | 52 | 64 | 29 |
| Rossway | 237 | 214 | 127 | 137 | 117 | 142 | 137 |
| Gulliver's Cove | na | na | 65 | 89 | 93 | 94 | 91 |
| Waterford | 94 | 87 | 87 | 74 | 62 | 68 | 72 |
| Centreville | 293 | 297 | 304 | 278 | 266 | 257 | 206 |
| Lake Midway | na | na | na | na | 35 | 33 | na |
| Sandy Cove | 210 | 178 | 169 | 176 | 170 | 173 | 129 |
| Mink Cove | 63 | 66 | 82 | 82 | 86 | 84 | 56 |
| Little River | 213 | 197 | 182 | 202 | 210 | 210 | 190 |
| Whale Cove | na | na | na | na | na | 33 | 29 |
| Tiddville | 121 | 75 | 87 | 95 | 106 | 105 | 83 |
| East Ferry | 129 | 117 | 131 | 131 | 123 | 111 | 129 |
| Digby Neck | 1360 | 1318 | 1234 | 1287 | 1285 | 1366 | 1055 |

Sources: Population figures for unincorporated places: Census Canada Catalogue # 92-535, Bulletin 1.1-6, 19/10/1962; Catalogue 92-771, SP-1, March 1973; Catalogue 93-306, 1993. This table contains no data for 2001 because this catalogue item appears to have been discontinued.

the past decade and both remain a shadow of their former economic and social importance. Some lobster operators fish with handline and/or gill net ("fixed gear")[3] for ground fish from the end of the lobster season at the end of May until the late fall when lobstering opens again. Recently these fisheries have been so poor that many multiple licence holders and small boat inshore fishers "don't even bother" hand-lining and gill netting. Small-boat fishers have been declining in number as a combination of regulation, licence buy-back programs and a scarcity of fish all combine to induce operators to "sell out." The large government wharves in Sandy Cove and Little River also serve as home for a mostly offshore dragger fleet ("mobile gear"), which continues to operate on a limited basis despite restrictive government quotas and dwindling stocks. Several fisheries have emerged periodically in formerly ignored species such as herring roe or sea urchins, sold mainly on the Japanese market.

Each community on Digby Neck has at least one church. The population is predominantly Baptist, with a significant minority of evangelical Protestants. Many churches continue to be active on Digby Neck although it is clear that in most cases their membership is aging.[4] Ethnically, people on the Neck are almost exclusively of English extraction (via New England) and long ago assimilated Acadians (Bull, 1978). The English descendants emigrated to Digby Neck as part of the Planter migration following the deportation of the Acadians in 1760. These settlers established fishing settlements around family land grants in sheltered coves and these settlements grew slowly into villages. By the middle of the nineteenth century the current villages of Digby Neck were established, and the bulk of the population was engaged in subsistence farming, ship-building, fishing and the carrier trade. Bull comments in her history of Sandy Cove that this cosmopolitan community was the place of origin of many successful international sea captains (1978). A few Acadian families migrated across St. Mary's Bay in the nineteenth and early twentieth centuries, especially to the communities of East Ferry and Waterford. These families are now assimilated linguistically and culturally with the anglophone population of the Neck although they retain Acadian surnames like Theriault, Thibodeau and Thibault.

The population of this area remains remarkably homogeneous. The limited amount of immigration of full-time residents to Digby Neck that does occur comes in the form of women relocating to the area from surrounding villages in the Digby area to marry or co-habit with a Digby Neck fisherman. Few Digby Neck women bring husbands or lovers to live on Digby Neck. To my knowledge no openly gay, lesbian or bisexual people live in the community. Recently, a small number of African Nova Scotian and Asian residents have come to Digby Neck either as partners or as adopted children. There is a well established and growing immigrant population of mostly retired and part-time, mainly Anglo-Canadian and Anglo American, summer residents, particularly in the village of Sandy Cove. This group is said to be slowly but surely changing the way of life and the Digby Neck real estate market. Despite the future potential of immigration to alter the face of the community, in most respects Digby Neck remains a "White" community.

A handful of small convenience stores and one small general store currently operate on Digby Neck, replacing the village general stores, which supplied virtually all community needs until the paving of the Highway 217 in the mid-1950s. Recently a gasoline outlet has been opened midway between East Ferry and the "head of the bay," which marks the eastern end of geographic Digby Neck. Several fish plants can still be found on the Neck, but most of these are either out of business or operate for only limited periods. Most of the local fish processing is now done on Long and Brier Islands, to the west, or in the Acadian District of Clare, across St. Mary's Bay.[5] These plants are owned by local families that have expanded their operations, buying gear and licences, and controlling an increasing share of fish production in the area, particularly since the establishment of quotas and regulatory regimes in the mid-1970s. By the mid-1990s several aquaculture ventures were in operation on Digby Neck.

Digby Neck has been a tourist destination for more than a century, and older residents remember several hotels and summer camps catering to tourists in the early and middle decades of the twentieth century. Tourism is now often promoted by community activists, local development authorities and state bureaucrats as an industry with unexplored and unexploited potential. An expanding modern tourist trade is developing, particularly during the warm months of May to October. Obvious examples of modern ecotourism development are whale watching and bird cruise operations that have opened up since the early 1990s. The Neck also has a provincially operated tourist park.

In many ways, the local elementary school, Digby Neck Consolidated, is the focal point of the Digby Neck community. The school is the single institutional forum where all of the children of Digby Neck meet for at least a brief period of their lives, and residents of Digby Neck and staff of Digby Neck Consolidated unanimously oppose closing the school. School closure is a persistent threat because the student population has declined rapidly from peak enrolments of more than 200 students in the mid-1960s to the current student population of less than 60. This decline reflects lower birth rates and out-migration of young people of child bearing age, particularly since the 1980s. The school serves students from grades primary to six. For secondary schooling, the students are bussed to Digby or to Freeport on nearby Long Island. A number of community projects have operated out of the school, including an association of small-boat, fixed-gear fishers, a local development agency, a learning co-op, which promoted education activity in the community, a community access computer centre, a daycare program for working parents, short-term state supported community development projects, a hot lunch program and periodic community suppers, socials, adult education, conferences and workshops. The school's regular "events," such as the talent shows, benefits, Thanksgiving Dinner, Christmas Concert or Leaving Ceremony in June are, along with weddings and funerals, the premier regular social events in the community. Digby Neck Consolidated School is a community-integrated rural school, and the current principal has worked to expand the role of the school as a multi-service community site.

The community has been, up until very recently, the source of significant employment for certain youth. It follows that Digby Neck has not been constructed historically by inhabitants as a place to leave behind, but rather as a place in which one might make a living, albeit a difficult one that requires a variety of skills and capacities. Significantly, this complex of abilities is rooted in the traditional community, and despite challenges it offers both rewards and the comfort of the familiar (Brandau and Collins, 1994; Porter, 1996). As Ursula Kelly comments, "without a vision of the future, the past beckons with its familiarity. However terrible the terrain was, one has already coped" (1993: 80). Indeed, traditional notions of masculinity and femininity are built around the toughness, native intelligence (work and survival skills known as "common sense") and the resourcefulness needed to cope and prosper in the local environment.

## The Economy

It is difficult to understand clearly the "rationality" of migration decision-making without understanding some characteristics of the economy migrants leave behind. While Digby Neck is a traditional one-industry community, the nature of the economy on Digby Neck is somewhat distinct. Table 3.3 demonstrates the heavy concentration of the Digby Neck labour force in fishing and trapping related industries. In addition, the majority of other occupational categories found on Digby Neck are in industries that support the fishery or distribute its products. For example, Digby Neck people listed in census data as working in processing and manufacturing for the most part work in fish plants; those listed in transportation mostly haul fish. My earlier analysis showed that the majority (71.3 percent) of male "stayers" work directly in the fishing industry (Corbett 2001a: 122). This percentage includes the 58.1 percent of males who fish, the 7.8 percent who work in fish plants and the 5.8 percent who work in other fishing related occupations like trucking fish or aquaculture (see Table 3.4). Female "stayers" work almost exclusively as homemakers and in service industries. A considerable number of respondents worked at several different occupations and

**Table 3.3 Percentage of Labor Force Working in Fishing and Trapping (1996) and in Primary Industries (2001)**

| | Percentage in fishing and trapping 1996 | Occupations unique to primary industries 2001 |
|---|---|---|
| Canada | 0.3 | 4.3 |
| Nova Scotia | 2.2 | 6.1 |
| Digby Municipality | 10.1 | 11.7 |
| East Digby Neck | 20.8 | 25.8 |
| Central Digby Neck | 36.7 | 30.0 |
| West Digby Neck* | 33.3 | 41.4 |

Source: 1996, 2001 Canadian Census Micro data.
*This census enumeration area includes the communities on Digby Neck west of Little River and Tiverton and Central Grove on Long Island.

**Table 3.4 Principal Occupations of Digby Neck "Stayers" by Gender, (70% sample, percentages in parentheses)**

| | Male | | Female | |
|---|---|---|---|---|
| Fishing | 75 | (58.1) | 0 | |
| Fish Plant | 10 | (07.8) | 3 | (05.6) |
| Other Fishing Related | 7 | (05.4) | 1 | (01.9) |
| Home maker | 0 | | 24 | (44.4) |
| Private sector service | 15 | (11.6) | 14 | (25.9) |
| Public sector service | 7 | (05.4) | 7 | (13.0) |
| Other | 15 | (11.6) | 5 | (09.2) |
| Total | 129 | (99.9) | 54 | (100.1) |

had some difficulty declaring a "principal" occupation. In a 1965 study of the economic base of Digby County, Harvey noted difficulties involved in investigating an economy dominated by a few resource industries (which makes things simpler), but where many residents engage in more than one occupation in the course of the year (which makes things more difficult). Available statistics continue to operate on the assumption that individuals have a particular unified "occupation." More research is needed into the way residents of coastal communities combine a variety of occupations to make a living. Nevertheless, most of the work men do on Digby Neck is still rooted in the fishery. This is obvious to anyone living in the area. Referring to Digby Neck in the mid-1960s, Harvey commented that:

> fishing is of considerably greater importance to Digby Neck than to the rest of the county. In fact, fishing is practically the only source of income for Digby Neck if fish processing is also included. (1965: 10)

As Davis found in his 1991 study, this concentration on the fishery remains consistent on Digby Neck. Tables 3.3 and 3.4 provide updated statistical support for the centrality of the fishery in the area. Table 3.3 also shows that a large segment of Digby Neck women defined themselves as "housewives." Approximately one in four of these women worked outside the home and outside family fishing operations in the private sector service industry, mostly commuting to Digby to do so.

While the economy of Digby Neck is still dominated by the fishery, Table 3.5 shows an increasing reliance on government transfer payments as well as how Digby area incomes compare to those of other Canadians. There are two sorts of polarized myth[6] surrounding this question. One myth

**Table 3.5 Income Levels (in Dollars) for Canada, Nova Scotia and the Municipality of Digby, 1971–2001**

| | 1971 | 1981 | 1986 | 1991 | 1996 | 2001 |
|---|---|---|---|---|---|---|
| Canada | | | | | | |
| Family | 9,600 | 27,328 | 37,877 | 51,342 | 54,583 | 66,160 |
| Male | 6,538 | 16,918 | 23,265 | 30,205 | 31,117 | 38,347 |
| Female | 2,883 | 8,414 | 12,615 | 17,577 | 19,208 | 24,390 |
| % low income | na | na | 14.3 | 13.2 | 19.7 | 16.2 |
| % of income from transfers | na | na | 11.1 | 11.4 | 14.0 | 11.6 |
| Nova Scotia | | | | | | |
| Family | 7,858 | 21,872 | 32,938 | 44,001 | 46,110 | 54,786 |
| Male | 5,388 | 13,918 | 20,492 | 26,406 | 27,009 | 32,328 |
| Female | 2,430 | 6,998 | 11,017 | 15,005 | 16,100 | 20.338 |
| % low income | na | 14.2 | 14.3 | 12.9 | 18.8 | 16.6 |
| % of income from transfers | na | na | 15.3 | 15.7 | 19.1 | 16.1 |
| Municipality of Digby | | | | | | |
| Family | 6,360 | 17,823 | 26,551 | 35,466 | 35,311 | 40,123 |
| Male | 5,720 | 11,279 | 16,383 | 21,326 | 21,642 | 31,608 |
| Female | 1,160 | 5,438 | 9,100 | 11,676 | 12,038 | 19,318 |
| % low income | na | 17.9 | 17.6 | 14.1 | 19.5 | 12.0 |
| % of income from transfers | na | na | 24.7 | 24.3 | 29.3 | 25.9 |

Sources: Census Canada: Income, Nova Scotia, Catalogue #93-951, Vol. 2, Provincial Series 1981; Profiles: Nova Scotia, Part 2, Cat #94-106, 1986; Profile of Census Subdivisions, Part A, Nova Scotia, Cat# 95-312, 1991; Profile of Census Divisions and Subdivisions in Nova Scotia, Cat. # 95-184-XPE, 1996; Census 2001 Internet Data, <http://www12.statcan.ca/english/profil01/CP01/Details/Page.cfm?Lang=E&Geo1=CSD&Code1=1203004&Geo2=PR&Code2=01&Data=Count&SearchText=digby&SearchType=Begins&SearchPR=01&B1=All> (accessed Oct. 31, 2006); Nova Scotia Government Community Counts Data, <http://www.gov.ns.ca/finance/community-counts/subject.asp?ptype=sub&gtype=Province&gname=Nova%20Scotia&gview=1&gnum=pro9012&s=income> (accessed Oct. 28, 2006).

is that fishers earn a great deal of money although the income is sporadic and uncertain. The other is that fishing is a poorly paid occupation and most of the people working in the fishery are economically marginal. The reality is that the fishery contains its own class structure that has extremes,

**Table 3.6 Population, Digby Neck and Digby Community Health Board Region**

| | 1991 Census | | 1996 Census | | 2001 Census | | Change |
|---|---|---|---|---|---|---|---|
| | # | % | # | % | # | % | 1991–2001 (%) |
| Nova Scotia | 899,945 | 100 | 909,280 | 100 | 908,005 | 100 | 0.9 |
| Digby Community Health Board Region | 11,365 | 100 | 10,953 | 100 | 10,273 | 100 | -9.6 |
| Digby Neck | 2,240 | 100 | 2,075 | 100 | 1,890 | 100 | -15.6 |

Source: Nova Scotia Community Counts. <http://www.gov.ns.ca/finance/communitycounts/default.asp> (accessed Oct. 27, 2006).

such as a few wealthy "fishtocrats" (who manage fleets of boats, large fish quotas, bait and processing facilities and trucking operations) and fish plant workers, who struggle to find enough work to "get their stamps" (qualify for Employment Insurance). Historical census data allows comparison of the Municipality of Digby (the municipal district in which Digby Neck lies), Nova Scotia and Canada. Table 3.5 shows that average incomes, both individual and family for the Municipality of Digby, have been approximately one-third less than the national average and approximately 20 percent less than the provincial average since the early 1970s. In 1970, men in the Municipality of Digby reported incomes above the provincial average and 87 percent of the national average. Women in the municipality earned less than half the provincial average and only about 40 percent of the national average income for women in 1970. By 1980, Digby area women saw their wages rise relative to provincial and national averages, while men's earnings decreased in relative terms. For instance, in 1971 women in the Municipality of Digby earned one-fifth of their male counterpart's income. By 2001 women's average income rose to 61 percent of the male average. Between 1970 to 1996, Digby area men's wages remained fairly stable at around 70 percent of the national average and 80 percent of the provincial average for men, probably reflecting the strength of the lobster fisher and the rebound of the scallop fishery. In the municipality, women's wages rose between 1981 and 1986 and have hovered at around 75 percent of the provincial average and 65 percent of the national average. However, by 2001, women's incomes in the Municipality of Digby rose to 95 percent of the provincial average and 80 percent of the federal average income for women.

Table 3.5 also shows that while in recent years the percentage of low-income earners in the municipality has fluctuated, the percentage of income

**Table 3.7 Average 1995/2000 Family Income as a Percentage of the Canadian Average**

| | 1995 | | 2000 | |
|---|---|---|---|---|
| | Average family income | Std Error (in dollars) | Average family income | Std Error (in dollars) |
| Canada | $54,583 | 36 | $66,160 | 51 |
| Nova Scotia | $46,110 | 138 | $54,786 | 221 |
| Digby Municipality | $35,311 | 1003 | $40,123 | |
| East Digby Neck | $28,805 | 3704 | $48,860 | 13716 |
| Central Digby Neck | $30,735 | 2814 | $39,583 | 6437 |
| West Digby Neck* | $40,118 | 2203 | $41,865 | 5762 |

Sources: 1996 Canadian Census Micro data and 2001 Canadian Census Micro data. 1996 data reflects census enumeration areas. 2001 data reflect census dissemination areas. These differently labeled regions encompass exactly the same geography.
*This census enumeration area includes the communities on Digby Neck west of Little River and Tiverton and Central Grove on Long Island.

derived from government transfer payments was more than double the national average between 1986 and 1996. Many residents of the municipality are heavily dependent on government transfers. On the other hand the landed value of fish in the Scotia Fundy region continues to show consistent strength from the late 1990s (Nova Scotia government, 2006). As Davis (1991) points out, while the value of landed fish has been increasing fairly steadily since the mid-1970s, the development of a social class structure on Digby Neck and nearby Long and Brier islands has led to income disparity. This class structure has been created by the growth of the small-boat dragger fleet, situated mainly in the western end of Digby Neck. Average family income figures from the 1996 census micro data confirm this hypothesis. Furthermore, as population on Digby Neck has declined (see Table 3.6), income levels have risen both in absolute terms and relative to provincial and national averages. In other words, outmigration and better economic conditions seem to be occurring simultaneously on Digby Neck. As Table 3.7 shows, average family income increased from east to west along Digby Neck in 1995. Still, even in the wealthiest area of the Neck, 1995 average incomes are significantly below the Nova Scotian and Canadian averages, but slightly above Digby Municipality averages. By 2001 all regions of Digby Neck appear to be at least equivalent to income averages in the Municipality, but due to high standard error in the data it is impossible to know conclusively.

The picture is similar regarding individual income for residents of

**Table 3.8 Average 1995/2000 Individual Income by Gender, Canada Census Micro Data**

| | 1995 | | | 2000 | | |
|---|---|---|---|---|---|---|
| | Total | Male | Female | Total | Male | Female |
| Canada | 26,474 | 31,917 | 20,162 | 31,757 | 38,347 | 24,390 |
| Nova Scotia | 21,940 | 26,701 | 16,322 | 26,632 | 32,328 | 20,338 |
| Southwest Nova | 20,662 | 26,007 | 13,507 | 22,437 | 27,716 | 16,058 |
| Digby Town | 16,418 | 20,833 | 12,809 | 20,231 | 25,496 | 15,747 |
| East Digby Neck | 15,345 | 13,732 | 17,779 | 26,564 | 25,496 | 18,608 |
| Central Digby Neck | 14,013 | 16,187 | 10,780 | 23,873 | 27,567 | 17,463 |
| West Digby Neck* | 18,648 | 24,098 | 11,391 | 23,163 | 30,713 | 13,821 |

*West Digby Neck includes the villages of Tiverton and Central Grove on Long Island.

Digby Neck. Table 3.8 shows personal income data by gender. For men in 1995, total income increased moving east to west along Digby Neck. For women, the pattern is different, with women living in the eastern part of the Neck earning significantly more than other Digby Neck women, and indeed, more than men in all but the western region. This phenomenon is probably explained by the proximity of this area to the town of Digby and to feminized service work and in professional jobs, many of which are also in female dominated fields such as teaching and nursing. Personal income levels are also well below provincial and national levels with the exception of men in western Digby Neck and women in Eastern Digby Neck. In eastern Digby Neck in 1995, women appear to have reported personal income levels above the provincial average. Similarly, men in western Digby Neck reported incomes slightly below the 1995 provincial average. 2001 data show however that Digby Neck men's wages appear to have increased markedly relative to provincial and regional averages, whereas women's wages have actually decreased relative to these averages (with the exception of central Digby Neck).

Given 1996 income figures for women on Digby Neck, one would expect their out-migration rates to be high. For men the picture is less clear. Men living on Digby Neck may actually have little to gain economically through migration, particularly short-range migration. Digby Neck is a case of a one-industry community where most available employment opportunities have been tied directly to the fishery. Therefore, it seems reasonable to suggest that for men whose lives were most integrated into the fishery, formal education had (and may continue to have) limited relevance and economic value. By 2001 however, it is much less clear that either men or women would had as much to gain economically by moving out of their villages into the surrounding region.

**Table 3.9a Highest Degree Achieved Expressed as a Percentage of the Population 15+ for Canada, Nova Scotia, and Digby Neck Census Enumeration Areas, 1996**

| | Canada | Nova Scotia | East Digby Neck | Central Digby Neck | West Digby Neck |
|---|---|---|---|---|---|
| No degree/diploma | 36.8 | 41.0 | 58.7 | 50.8 | 70.4 |
| Grade 12 diploma | 23.1 | 17.2 | 10.9 | 18.6 | 14.8 |
| Some post-secondary | 28.9 | 29.5 | 32.6 | 26.2 | 30.7 |
| University | 12.0 | 11.4 | * | * | * |

*Fewer than 10 persons. Data massaged to protect identities of individuals.

**Table 3.9b Highest Degree Achieved Expressed as a Percentage of the Population 20+ for Canada, Nova Scotia, and Digby Neck Census Disssemination Areas, 2001**

| | Canada | Nova Scotia | East Digby Neck | Central Digby Neck | West Digby Neck |
|---|---|---|---|---|---|
| No degree/diploma | 22.7 | 26.4 | 42.9 | 50 | 61 |
| Grade 12 diploma | 23.9 | 18.2 | 19.0 | 13.5 | 9.1 |
| Some post-secondary | 31.8 | 35.2 | 38.0 | 28.9 | 23.1 |
| University | 22.6 | 20.2 | * | 7.7 | 6.1 |

*Fewer than 10 persons. Data massaged to protect identities of individuals.

Sources: Census Canada data table <http://www12.statcan.ca/english/census01/products/highlight/Education/Page.cfm?Lang=E&Geo=PR&View=1b&Code=0&Table=2a&StartRec=1&Sort=11&B1=Distribution&B2=Both>; Nova Scotia Community Counts Educational Attainment data table <http://www.gov.ns.ca/finance/communitycounts/table_e1.asp?gnum=pro9012&gname=Nova%20Scotia&gview=1&gtype=Province&ptype=geo&acctype=education>; Census microdata.

## Education Levels

Local lore suggests that education is not necessary for income security if one is going to stay on Digby Neck. Census Canada micro data also showing education levels for the Digby Neck enumeration areas seem to confirm this notion (see Table 3.9a and 3.9b). Over 70 percent of the total population fifteen years of age and over living in the western section of Digby Neck reported no degree or diploma as of 1996.[7] This is nearly twice the national average of 36.8 percent. If anything, the pattern is strengthened by the 2001 data. These data show that the percentage of people on Digby Neck possessing no degree or diploma fell in absolute terms. However, relative to the provincial and national populations the preponderance of non-formally educated people has actually increased.

Yet western Digby Neck reported the highest average male income and the highest average family incomes in 1995, out-pacing other areas of Digby Neck by 30 to 40 percent. In other words, in the part of Digby Neck that has the lowest rate of high-school completion, men and families appear to have the highest incomes by a considerable margin. Despite high standard errors in the data, 2001 census material reported in 3.7 and 3.8 seem to indicate that income levels on Digby Neck are actually rising to at least regional levels and even close to provincial levels for men and women, with the exception of women in the western section of Digby Neck.

These data raise some questions about the link between formal education and earnings in rural areas. This equivocal relationship between "earning and learning" in rural communities has been noted previously. For instance, Bollman (1999) found a negative relationship between education and income, supporting the idea that there is a lower "payoff" for formal education in rural communities. Bollman also found that the more "rural" the community, the lower the average education levels. For those who wish to remain in their rural communities, the decision to forego higher education actually appears to be economically "rational." Pittman et al. (1999) found something similar in their analysis of the relationship between education and income in rural areas using 1940–1990 United States census data. They found a positive correlation between education and 1998 income, it was much weaker in rural than urban areas. Pittman et al. conclude that, "rural educators and citizens should treat as doubtful, claims that education improvement will lead to improvement in rural economies" (1999: 29).[8] Other international studies confirm the tenuous link between education and income in rural areas (Jolliffe, 1998; Demerath, 1999; Banerjee, 1996; Rothstein, 1996).

While education and income may be related in larger populations (for instance, at the level of province or nation), the relationship may be one that "works" considerably better in urban areas. For individuals who remain in rural regions, the link between learning and earning may not be as simple as stay-in-school propaganda suggests. Men in coastal communities seem to have been correct when they claimed that those who wished to stay "didn't need education" for economic success. When this sentiment and the economic reality it reflects is understood by young men in coastal communities, it undoubtedly has clear consequences for school performance. When these factors are compounded by the retreat of the state from funding education and a general decline in public sector employment and the opportunity to access "government jobs," it follows that higher education has not been seen as a high priority. In rural communities, particularly those with relatively limited occupational diversity, the strength of public sector employment is very often the basis of rationalizing higher education. The question perhaps is not so much whether education is beneficial to people in coastal communities, but rather, what are its benefits for differently placed individuals?

Finally, outmigration is typically assumed to be an indicator of economic decline, and few studies investigate the economic and life fortunes of those who stay behind and who do not leave. Low levels of education and high levels of outmigration are simply assumed to indicate general economic decline in divergent rural micro-contexts. The data reported above suggest that outmigration may ironically result in improved economic conditions for those who stay on and ride out the inevitable fluctuations of life and work in a resource industry. As I have learned through my years in the community, this discourse of struggle and survival in certainly a core feature of what it means to be a Digby Necker. For those who have survived the boom and bust cycle of the lobster fishery and held on to licenses and gear through hard times, this logic has actually paid off quite handsomely. It may be true that education is very important for those who wish to migrate and for women but not necessarily for those men who remain.

## Mobility

Given relatively low incomes, high unemployment rates and a heavy dependence on a single "declining" industry, Digby Neck ought to be a prime example of a community that is losing population to out-migration. Yet, in his analysis of national level 1996 Canadian census data, Finnie found that the smaller the community and the more rural it is, the less mobile are its residents (1998). But this data measures mobility in five year segments: it does not help understand the long-term migration behaviour of people who may have left coastal communities, never having lived as adults on Digby Neck. My survey of migration from Digby Neck explores a somewhat different form of mobility data. The Community, Schooling and Migration Survey (511 respondents) and Basic Data Bank (714 respondents) tracked the long-term migration behaviour of all individuals aged from approximately twenty to fifty-six who originated on Digby Neck. Thus, we see a snapshot of the migration results for thirty-six years of students who reached grade six in the local elementary school (Digby Neck Consolidated, DNCS), that is, virtually everyone who grew up on Digby Neck from the mid 1950s through to the late 1990s (see Tables 3.10 and 3.11).[9] The population appears to be becoming slightly less mobile through the thirty-six-year period

**Table 3.10 Potential Grade Six Graduates Remaining on Digby Neck by Percentage**

| | N | Deceased or unknown | N Revised 1999 | Digby Neck | Percent-age |
|---|---|---|---|---|---|
| Cohort 1 (1963–74) | 306 | 25 | 281 | 73 | 26% |
| Cohort 2 (1975–86) | 236 | 12 | 224 | 66 | 29.6% |
| Cohort 3 (1987–98) | 214 | 5 | 209 | 69 | 33.0% |
| Total (1963–98) | 756 | 42 | 714 | 208 | 29.1% |

Source: Basic Data Bank (99 % data)

**Table 3.11 Out-migration from Digby Neck by Cohort and Destination, Potential Graduating Classes of 1963–1998**

| | Cohorts N | N Revised | Stayers & Around here | Not far | Away |
|---|---|---|---|---|---|
| Cohort 1 | 306 | 281 | 155 (55.2%) | 62 (22.1%) | 64 (22.8%) |
| Cohort 2 | 236 | 224 | 144 (64.3%) | 53 (23.7%) | 27 (12.0%) |
| Cohort 3 | 214 | 209 | 137 (65.6%) | 39 (18.7%) | 33 (15.8%) |
| Total | 756 | 714 | 436 (61.1%) | 154 (21.6%) | 124 (17.4%) |

Source: Basic Data Bank (99 % data)

this survey covers; an average of less than 30 percent of people who grew up on Digby Neck from the mid-1950s to the late 1990s still remain there in 1999. Rather than becoming more likely to emigrate from Digby Neck in times of economic downturn, these data shows the opposite effect. Both the "boom" of the 1980s and the "bust" of the 1990s are accompanied by lower rates of out-migration. This would seem to support Finnie's analysis of the Canadian Census data (1998). However, with a more than 70 percent out-migration rate, this is certainly a highly mobile population.

The Canadian Census mobility data and the data presented here are not directly comparable as my data show a longer term of mobility. In terms of Census Canada classifications, people who leave Digby Neck become residents of their destinations if they remain five years. The brain drain hypothesis and both Marxist and conservative economic analyses would contend that if they were "rational" economic migrants, the majority of these individuals would have migrated to central or western Canada, where greater economic opportunities exist. Table 3.10 shows the present location of out-migrants from Digby Neck. Destinations are organized by four categories: "stayers," which includes those still living on geographic Digby Neck; "around here," which includes those who have stayed on Digby Neck or within 50 kilometres of Digby Neck; "not far," those who have moved farther away than 50 kilometres but not more than 250 kilometres; and "away," those who have moved farther than 250 kilometres from Digby Neck. Because key informants made little distinction between "stayers" and those who remained "around here," and because (as later tables will show) the education profiles of these two groups are similar, I have combined these two categories. These data show that over the thirty-six years of the study reported here, Digby Neckers are indeed becoming less mobile. The largest proportion of the population, more than 60 percent through the study period, remained in the local area (i.e., within 50 kilometres). More than 80 percent (82.7 percent)[10] remained inside the "not far" region or closer, i.e., within 250 kilometres of the Neck. So while the population is "mobile," the range of mobility is limited in the majority of cases.

Some communities on Digby Neck appear to have been more mobile than others. The most mobile community, Sandy Cove, is a part-time home

**Table 3.12 Out-migration from Digby Neck by Community of Origin and Present Location, Potential Graduating Classes of 1963–1998 (percentages in parentheses)**

| | Stayers & Around here | Not far | Away | Total |
|---|---|---|---|---|
| Waterford | 25 (53.2) | 10 (21.3) | 12 (25.5) | 47 (100) |
| Centreville | 133 (69.3) | 38 (19.8) | 21 (10.9) | 192 (100) |
| Lake Midway | 19 (61.2) | 6 (20.0) | 6 (16.7) | 31 (99.9) |
| Sandy Cove | 32 (41.0) | 21 (28.2) | 25 (30.8) | 78 (100) |
| Mink Cove | 41 (69.5) | 6 (10.2) | 12 (20.3) | 59 (100) |
| Little River | 71 (54.2) | 35 (26.7) | 25 (19.1) | 131 (100) |
| Whale Cove | 11 (73.3) | 1 (06.7) | 3 (20.0) | 15 (100) |
| Tiddville | 50 (58.1) | 21 (24.4) | 10 (10.5) | 81 (100) |
| East Ferry | 54 (68.4) | 16 (20.2) | 9 (11.4) | 79 (100) |
| Total Digby Neck | 436 (61.1) | 154 (21.5) | 124 (17.4) | 714 (100) |

Source: Basic Data Bank (99 % data)

to a transient summer population and their presence may have influenced the children of that community (see Table 3.12). Waterford is situated at the eastern extreme of the DNCS elementary school catchment area, closest to the regional service centre of Digby. The other community with a relatively high "not far" and "away" migration rate is Little River, which is one of the principal homes of the small-boat dragger fleet and relatively higher incomes. Contrary to economic rationality arguments about out-migration from Atlantic Canadian coastal communities, the wealthier communities tend to produce the most mobile populations.

Given that the fishery presents a gendered structure of opportunity, it might be expected that women would have higher rates of migration. On the other hand, this gendered structure of labour and social relations may also result in women being less mobile and less able to break out of gendered role expectations. In her focus-group discussions with young rural Nova Scotian women, Day (1990) found these women aspire less than young men to leave despite the dismal prospects they saw in their communities. Table 3.13 shows that men were more than twice as likely as women to stay on Digby Neck, but that women showed a much greater propensity to migrate short distances in the "around here" and "not far regions." As one school administrator put it: "The girls around here see that the pool of local guys is pretty small, but when they go to Digby or Weymouth there are guys there that look and act like their guys." The decision to move into the "away" region was taken by roughly similar proportions of each gender (18.4 percent of men and 16.2 percent of women).

**Table 3.13 Out-migration Rates from Digby Neck by Gender and Present Location, Potential Graduating Classes of 1963–1998 (percentages in parentheses)**

| | Male | Female |
|---|---|---|
| Stayers | 145 (40.5) | 60 (16.9) |
| Around here | 101 (28.2) | 130 (36.5) |
| Not far | 46 (12.8) | 108 (30.3) |
| Away | 66 (18.4) | 58 (16.2) |
| Total | 358 (99.9) | 356 (99.9) |

Source: Basic Data Bank (99 % data)

## The Education/Mobility Connection

> As work like *The Master's Wife* reveals, "escape" has been for ambitious young Maritimers what "success" was for Richler's Duddy Kravitz — escape not merely from the drudgery of the family farm or fishing boat, but also from the inevitable constrictions of Maritime society. Three avenues of escape have traditionally been open: running away to sea; finding work in New England factories or western cities; or getting an education and going not on, but out to university. (Kulyk-Keefer, 1987: 211)

The results I report above are very similar to those found by Dublin in mining communities in the Pennsylvania anthracite region in the United States, where he found that only 15 percent of the high school classes of 1946–1960 "migrated beyond this narrow band reaching roughly 100–150 miles from Panther Valley" (1998: 45). He also found that since the 1960s out-migration has stabilized and the bulk of the population has chosen to remain in the region despite declining economic fortunes. Residents of Panther Valley chose to reject opportunities available through out-migration in order to stay close to family and community networks. Even though they "persisted" in the region, Dublin reports that his study group, now presumably in their late fifties and sixties, encouraged their own children to migrate and pursue formal education.

> Choosing to accept the limited economic opportunity available in the anthracite region, persisters indicated the value they placed on family and community networks as opposed to more strictly economic considerations. Still, even as they made these particular choices for themselves, persisters typically encouraged their children to gain an education and leave the area. (Dublin, 1998: 52–53)

But Dublin also found that education was proving to be a dubious strategy for the children of his study group. While the relatively strong social safety net protected persisters through the 1980s, it became more "porous and unreliable" in the 1990s. The irony is that migration was also becoming a "less promising strategy" as recession constricted the economy and job opportunities in urban areas as well. As overheated rental and real estate markets boomed in urban areas of North America through the 1990s and beyond, it became increasingly difficult if not impossible to leave a rural home without skills and formal education.

A similar pattern can be seen in Digby Neck. Relatively more Digby Neckers migrated in the 1960s and early 1970s compared to the 1980s and 1990s. The 1960s and early 1970s was a period of transition in the fishery, but not necessarily one in which employment opportunities were significantly less than in previous decades. The population of the Neck was relatively stable and fish landings were on the rise (Davis, 1991). The introduction of the small-boat dragger fishery and its consolidation in the 1960s led to increased opportunities in fish plants, fishing support work and crewing on boats. Through the 1970s and 1980s the dragger fishery expanded, as did fish landings and processing activity, and the population remained stable, with out-migration rates declining. However, when the fishery began its downturn in the early 1990s, the population of young adults does not appear to have become significantly more mobile than were previous cohorts, especially when mobility is defined as moving out beyond the "around here" area. It is quite probable that declining opportunities elsewhere for unskilled labour created this situation and that it was exacerbated by cuts to social programs, which made it more difficult for marginal young workers to sustain themselves independently away from their families and communities.

Education is becoming a prerequisite for migration to urban jobs, and without it, one is destined to remain in place in the coastal community. Without a family habitus that included prolonged secondary and post-secondary experience, young Digby Neckers (especially young men) from non-elite fishing families developed locally focused socio-spatial identities (Jones, 1999a) in which formal education played little part (Kenway and Kraak, 2002; Kenway and Kraak, 2004). At the same time, many young people, especially young men, on Digby Neck see the weak or even negative relationship between earnings and education. Added to this experiential knowledge was widespread exposure via cable television to popular media of the 1980s and 1990s, which was highly critical of the formal education system in terms of its ability to give students "marketable skills," even to highly educated youth.[11]

Tables 3.14–3.16 document the relationship between education attainment and the propensity to migrate. The data for these tables was compiled from the Community, Migration and Schooling Survey. While the foregoing analysis shows some of the contours of the economic, education and mobility profile of Digby Neck in comparison to trends regionally, provincially and nationally, the central problem for this work is the link between education and migration. Less than one-fifth of the population of Digby Neck has gone "away." The rest remain within an afternoon's drive of the Neck. The majority, both male and female, are within a half hour drive from the Neck. Is it true that these people who have stayed closer to home have obtained less formal education than their counterparts who migrated "away?"

**Table 3.14 Highest Level of Education Attainment and Out-migration from Digby Neck, "Stayers" and "Away"**

| | Stayers | Away |
|---|---|---|
| Less than grade 10 | 40 (23.8%) | 5 (05.7%) |
| Some high school | 59 (35.1%) | 20 (23.0%) |
| High school graduation | 62 (36.9%) | 33 (37.9%) |
| Post-secondary | 7 (04.1%) | 29 (33.3%) |
| Total | 168 (99.9%) | 87 (99.9%) |

Source: Community, Migration and Education Survey (70% data)

Comparing the two populations most easily defined as "stayers" and "leavers," i.e., those still living on Digby Neck and those who have migrated to the "away" region, Table 3.14 confirms this basic hypothesis. On average, stayers have significantly lower levels of education attainment than leavers. As anticipated, education is strongly linked with out-migration, particularly at the post-secondary level. Out-migrants who moved to the "away" region were more than eight times as likely to have attended post-secondary education and 30 percent more likely to have graduated high school.[12]

"Away" migrants were also four to five times less likely than "stayers" to

**Table 3.15 Highest Level of Education Achieved by Migration Status and Gender (70% data)**

| | Stayers | | Around here | |
|---|---|---|---|---|
| | Male | Female | Male | Female |
| Less than grade 10 | 36 (30.2) | 4 (08.2) | 22 (32.3) | 10 (10.3) |
| Some high school | 44 (37.0) | 15 (30.6) | 23 (33.8) | 17 (17.5) |
| High school grad. | 34 (28.6) | 28 (57.1) | 19 (27.9) | 62 (63.9) |
| Post-secondary | 5 (04.2) | 2 (04.2) | 4 (05.9) | 8 (08.2) |
| Total | 119 (99.9) | 49 (100.1) | 68 (99.9) | 97 (99.9) |
| | Not far | | Away | |
| | Male | Female | Male | Female |
| Less than grade 10 | 1 (04.3) | 4 (05.9) | 5 (12.2) | 0 |
| Some high school | 5 (21.7) | 10 (14.7) | 13 (31.7) | 7 (15.2) |
| High school grad. | 9 (39.1) | 33 (48.5) | 9 (22.0) | 24 (52.2) |
| Post-secondary | 8 (34.8) | 21 (30.9) | 14 (34.1) | 15 (32.6) |
| Total | 23 (99.9) | 68 (100.1) | 41 (100) | 46 (100) |

Source: Community, Migration and Education Survey

be in the lowest education group, never having entered high school. When the same data are analyzed by gender, the differences between male stayers and leavers becomes even more stark (see Table 3.15). Male stayers are represented far more pervasively in the lowest education category (less than grade ten).[13] Both male and female migrants have acquired considerably more high school and higher education credentials than their stayer counterparts. The differences are particularly acute among males, where high-school completion rates for the "stayer" and "around here" populations were 32.8 percent and 33.8 percent respectively.[14] By contrast, more than 60 percent of women in all migration groups have completed at least high school. Also striking is the similarity of education profiles between stayers and those remaining in the "around here" region.

Males who migrate into the proximal "around here" area tended to have very low levels of formal education compared to men who stayed on Digby Neck. Women who moved into this proximal area had acquired marginally more education credentials than their stayer counterparts. In other words, these data show the limited utility of formal education for both stayers and for those who migrate but remain "around here." Those who migrated further into the "not far" and "away" regions were much more likely to have acquired higher-level credentials.

Table 3.16 shows a consistent rise in levels of formal education for women across the three age cohorts. High-school graduation rates for wom-

**Table 3.16 Highest Level of Education Achievement by Age Cohort and Gender (70% data)**

| | Cohort 1 (1963–74) | | Cohort 2 (1975–86) | | Cohort 3 (1987–98) | |
|---|---|---|---|---|---|---|
| | Male | Female | Male | Female | Male | Female |
| Less than grade 10 | 31 (33.3) | 5 (05.1) | 15 (19.5) | 7 (08.0) | 12 (16.7) | 3 (03.6) |
| Some high school | 29 (31.2) | 25 (25.5) | 35 (45.5) | 19 (21.8) | 25 (34.7) | 7 (08.3) |
| High school grad | 21 (22.6) | 54 (55.1) | 17 (22.1) | 40 (46.0) | 27 (37.5) | 56 (66.7) |
| Post-secondary | 12 (12.9) | 14 (14.3) | 10 (13.0) | 21 (24.1) | 8 (11.1) | 18 (21.4) |
| Total | 93 (100) | 98 (100) | 77 (100.1) | 87 (99.9) | 72 (100) | 84 (100) |

Source: Community, Migration and Education Survey

en have increased from just under 70 percent in Cohort 1 to slightly over 90 percent in Cohort 3. The only anomaly in generally increasingly levels of education attainment is the unexpectedly high percentage of women in Cohort 2 with less than grade 10. This is perhaps explained by the ready availability of fish plant work for young working-class women through the boom period. By the mid-1970s women were "getting into the fish" (i.e., fish plant work) more than in previous or subsequent generations. With increased demand for this work, which required few formal education credentials, a greater number of women dropped out before entering high school.

The general trend, which has remained consistent through thirty-six years, is that women are about twice as likely as men to complete high school. High school has become the basic prerequisite for most forms of post-school education, and thus for mobility beyond the local area, so it is logical that women are more mobile than men. Men as a group remain well behind women in terms of all education credentials except in the Cohort 1 post-secondary group, where they nearly matched women's participation rates. While Digby Neck men too have been acquiring more formal education credentials, fewer than half of all males in any cohort have graduated high school. For males, generally increasing levels of formal education are broken by an anomaly. Males in Cohort 2 are significantly less well represented in the post-secondary group, reflecting lucrative fisheries opportunities for young men from elite fishing families who might otherwise have accessed higher education.

Previous analysis has shown that those individuals in the "around here" area have education profiles similar to those who stayed on Digby Neck. Those who moved into the "not far" region were also found to have education profiles similar to those who migrated to the "away" region. When the three age cohorts are broken down by migration group the picture is more complex (see Tables 3.17 and 3.18). Table 3.17 shows that education levels for women "stayers" and "around here" have generally risen. The striking anomaly in data for women in this migration group is the high percentage of women in the post-secondary group for Cohort 2. This seems to show that through this period, young women in elite fishing families were able to use family resources to access higher education and that a considerable number of them were able to return to the area to find employment in the expanding public service sector in nearby Digby. An alternate explanation is that these women acquired education credentials and returned to the local area to traditional gendered occupations and family roles. The data in Tables 3.17 and 3.18 also further explain the anomaly for Cohort 2 noted in Table 3.16, with men continuing to be under-represented in the post-secondary level group. Table 3.17 also shows a relatively high percentage

**Table 3.17 Highest Level of Education Achievement by Age Cohort and Gender for Stayers and "Around Here" (percentages in parentheses, 70% data)**

| | Cohort 1 (1963–74) | | Cohort 2 (1975–86) | | Cohort 3 (1987–98) | |
|---|---|---|---|---|---|---|
| | Male | Female | Male | Female | Male | Female |
| Less than grade ten | 26 (41.9) | 3 (06.0) | 15 (27.8) | 7 (13.0) | 11 (18.3) | 3 (06.3) |
| Some high school | 18 (29.0) | 18 (36.0) | 29 (50.0) | 12 (22.2) | 24 (40.0) | 5 (10.4) |
| High school grad | 15 (24.2) | 27 (54.0) | 11 (19.0) | 27 (50.0) | 22 (36.7) | 37 (77.1) |
| Post-secondary | 3 (04.8) | 2 (04.0) | 3 (05.2) | 8 (14.8) | 3 (05.0) | 3 (06.2) |
| Total | 62 (99.9) | 50 (100) | 58 (100) | 54 (100) | 60 (100) | 48 (100) |

Source: Community, Migration and Education Survey

**Table 3.18 Highest Level of Education Achievement by Age Cohort and Gender for "Not Far" and "Away" Migrants (percentages in parentheses, 70% data)**

| | Cohort 1 (1963-74) | | Cohort 2 (1975-86) | | Cohort 3 (1987-98) | |
|---|---|---|---|---|---|---|
| | Male | Female | Male | Female | Male | Female |
| Less than grade ten | 5 (16.1) | 2 (04.2) | 0 | 0 | 1 (08.3) | 0 |
| Some high school | 11 (35.5) | 7 (14.6) | 6 (31.6) | 7 (21.2) | 1 (08.3) | 2 (05.6) |
| High school grad | 6 (19.4) | 27 (56.3) | 6 (31.6) | 13 (39.4) | 5 (41.7) | 19 (52.8) |
| Post-secondary | 9 (29.0) | 12 (25.0) | 7 (36.8) | 13 (39.4) | 5 (41.7) | 15 (41.7) |
| Total | 31 (100) | 48 (100.1) | 19 (100) | 33 (100) | 12 (100) | 36 (100.1) |

Source: Community, Migration and Education Survey

of women in Cohort 2 who completed less than grade ten who live in the "around here" region. In fact, this entire population is still within 50 kilometres of Digby Neck.

Men in the "around here" group demonstrate consistently increasing levels of formal education. The principal anomaly in this data is the very low male graduation rate for Cohort 2. Apparently the boom period in the fishery was accompanied by a bust in education credentials for young men of that cohort, and graduation rates actually fell below those for men in Cohort 1.

Table 3.19 shows consistently increasing rates of education for migrants who have left the "around here" region. Those who migrated to the "not far" and "away" regions have acquired more education credentials at all levels than their stayer counterparts. In Cohorts 2 and 3 virtually all members of this groups graduated high school and approximately four in ten attended post-secondary institutions. It appears as though the basic hypothesis is confirmed: secondary and post-secondary education goes hand in hand with out-migration from Digby Neck. This also demonstrates a strong segment of the population accessing post-secondary education and settling outside the area. The "gender effect" noted in the "stayer" and "around here" populations is attenuated considerably in the "not far" and "away" population. With the exception of Cohort 1 (which faced very different employment and migration prospects than either Cohorts 2 or 3), male graduation rates fell only approximately 10 percent below female rates. In other words, mobile males seem to require and acquire nearly

**Table 3.19 Migration by Gender, Age Cohort and Present Location (99 % data)**

| Male | Here & Around here | Not far & Away | Total Male |
|---|---|---|---|
| Cohort 1 | 87 (59.2) | 60 (40.8) | 147 (100) |
| Cohort 2 | 83 (74.1) | 29 (25.9) | 112 (100) |
| Cohort 3 | 76 (76.8) | 23 (23.2) | 99 (100) |
| Female | Here & Around here | Not far & Away | Total Female |
| Cohort 1 | 68 (50.7) | 66 (49.3) | 134 (100) |
| Cohort 2 | 61 (54.5) | 51 (45.5) | 112 (100) |
| Cohort 3 | 61 (55.5) | 49 (44.5) | 110 (100) |

Source: Basic Data Bank

as much higher education as their female peers. If one goes, education is important regardless of one's gender; but if one stays, then it is a different story, and masculinity has its privileges in terms of the amount of schooling one requires.

## Summary

Perhaps the most striking finding from this survey is that out-migration flows from Digby Neck have remained stable through the thirty-six years of this investigation. Out-migration rates have actually decreased slightly from the early 1960s to the 1990s on Digby Neck. This seems to support Dublin's finding that rural communities can act as havens during economic hard times, as well as the Marxist "reserve army" hypothesis. But since the out-migration rate remains remarkably stable throughout fluctuations in the economy of the fishery, I would agree with McCann (1994) that even in a highly culturally homogenous single industry "fishing society," economic explanations alone are not adequate and that we must take into account social and cultural factors. Both "good" and "bad" times seem to generate conditions conducive to staying for significant numbers of youth "born and bred" on Digby Neck. The Basic Data Bank data show that most who "migrate" move only short distances to areas that are culturally and economically similar to Digby Neck. Women are also more mobile than men in terms of settling off Digby Neck. So while the large numbers of women who migrate to the "around here" region do not marry and settle on Digby Neck, they do tend to marry and settle in nearby communities much like those of Digby Neck.

Given that the area "around here" is in many respects a macrocosm of Digby Neck, these data suggest that short-range migrations do not really represent movement into a significantly different cultural space. While the "village" no longer exists as an economic and social entity that holds many individuals, the area "around here" does. Short-range migrations are not considered by most Digby Neckers to be migrations at all, and indeed, the education profiles of short-range migrants are similar to those who stay on Digby Neck. Nearly two-thirds of the population studied here remained within the "around here" area, within 50 kilometres of Digby Neck. This shows that a majority of Digby Neckers remain within easy reach of their communities of origin, suggesting that this coastal community remains somewhat resilient, albeit in a slightly larger geographic space. Digby Neckers are mobile, but at the same time they manage to retain communal bonds from a short distance. As several informants put it: "I didn't want to go too far." This phenomenon may itself be a product of an increasingly mobile society. Improved highway travel and communication technology in the past several decades allows individuals to remain connected to their "home" communities while living closer to services, employment and recreation opportunities for their children. It may also represent what Zygmunt Bauman (1998) calls "glocalization," the mobilization of educated elites and the simultaneous localization and even entrapment of others whose knowledge and economic resources limit them to a restricted geography.

What I describe above may be part of the fundamental changes in coastal communities that are now organized around small, remote "service centres," a phenomenon perhaps best illustrated by the expansion of the Wal-Mart chain (Vias, 2005). Wal-Mart establishes the bulk of its locations in rural and low-income areas. Ghemawat and Mark (2005) have discovered for instance that 80 percent of Wal-Mart's square footage is located in the 25 percent of zip codes with the greatest percentage of poor households. The small town of Digby is a case in point. This community of slightly more than 2000 residents offers a wide and expanding array of services and large retail outlets that service surrounding villages, which themselves are simultaneously losing infrastructure, but not necessarily "dying."[15] Fast food franchises and major grocery chains have noticed the potential for consumer business in Digby and through the decade of the 1990s have set up in the community forcing smaller and independent retail operations out of business. If postmodern social theorists are correct and contemporary culture is organized around consumption rather than production, then what I am describing here may be the incursion of consumerism into the rural margins. Digby Neckers are quick to point out that they can now "get anything" one could find in a city in the town of Digby. Indeed, not all urban consumers can access a full range of shopping services within a half hour of their homes. By the late 1990s, it had become as easy to be a consumer on Digby Neck as in many parts of suburbia. Further expansion of the service sector in the Digby area created new (albeit marginal) working-class opportunities.

While women in the sample are better educated as a group, they are not in a better economic position if they stayed on Digby Neck. With the exception of women living in the eastern part of the Neck, all women earn significantly less than their male counterparts despite having much higher levels of formal education. This fact serves to illustrate the tenuous connection between formal education and income in this coastal community. Women "do well" in school and acquire many more of virtually every kind of education credential, and yet their incomes remain significantly below those of their male counterparts, who have comparatively little formal education. From a "practical" point of view, this negative relationship between education and income demonstrates support for the local (male) knowledge, which argues that, "You didn't need a good education to be successful if you stay on Digby Neck." Women's success in school and relative economic and social disadvantage in life may have actually reinforced the idea that formal education is useless and even counterproductive in terms of making a living on Digby Neck. Additionally, a man who takes school too seriously might lose out on the critical informal education required to become a successful fisherman, an education that begins in early adolescence for most young men, if not before.

Conversely, those bound for places beyond the "around here" area have a very clear need for education. The commonsense perception that education is necessary for life and work in other places is confirmed, particularly in the two most recent cohorts. While education levels actually dipped for the segments of the "boom" (Cohort 2) group of "stayers" and "around here" migrants, they rose sharply for "not far" and "away" migrants of this same cohort. It certainly appears that in this coastal community outward bound young people did learn to leave through the course of their formal education. Corollary evidence confirms that men who stayed "learned" in the pragmatic spaces of the fishery that formal schooling was of limited value, and they resisted the idea that they ought to acquire significant formal education credentials. As one fisherman put it cryptically, echoing a local aphorism, "When education came in, common sense went out." His comment was directed toward the "educated" but ignorant scientists and bureaucrats who, he argued, ruined the small-boat fishery. Formal education was also understood by many men as passive and even unproductive. Many young men were drawn out of school and into, if not lucrative at least "active" and appropriately masculine work in the fishery. The intensification of this "pull" is mirrored by high male dropout rates among stayers.

What is perhaps surprising in this data is the high rate of high-school completion levels among women who remained. It is clear that those who pursue their lives outside the "around here" circle require higher levels of formal education. The only demographic that is "insulated" from the need for a protracted education are men considered to be "born and bred" in fishing families. They can survive because they have largely exclusive access to a skill set and "connections" to communities of practice that, while they are diminishing and under threat, continue to harvest fish. In fact, dedication to the preservation of this community of practice has been one key measure of masculinity. Digby Neck is also a place with strong traditions of education achievement. Digby Neck women's education achievement, whether they remained within the "around here" circle or not is relatively strong. Comparative high-school graduation rates actually appear to be well above national and provincial averages historically. Whether they stayed or went, Digby Neck women have acquired education credentials at a much greater rate than have men. This finding supports Lois Weis's (2004) analysis of the deindustrialization and subsequent social transformation of a white working-class community in the United States. Weis found that women made the transition to life after the collapse of traditional industrial work and family life by engaging with institutions of formal education more than did their male peers. What Weis fails to note is that they probably had no other choice.

Why are younger Digby Neckers less mobile than their predecessors? This contradicts the notion that coastal communities that were once relatively "stable" in terms of population and out-migration are now characterized by a mass exodus. The population of Digby Neck for both genders has become consistently less mobile across the three age cohorts studied here. Table 3.19 shows that greater numbers of both men and women are remaining within the "around here" region and that this trend is particularly strong for men. By the time members of Cohort 3 were coming of age (i.e., the 1990s), more than three out of four Digby Neck men were remaining within the fifty kilometre "around here" circle.

While Digby Neck is a classic example of a community that can provide only limited opportunities for its youth, out-migration appears to have become consistently more challenging from the early 1960s to the late 1990s. How can we explain this phenomenon? First of all, the erosion of work in industrial centres for "unskilled" youth with low levels of formal education creates a climate of diminished opportunity for Digby Neck youth who might otherwise migrate. While plentiful service sector work may be available in urban centres, the work is very often part-time, and wage levels are insufficient to support a young person from a rural community, who will probably need to "set up housekeeping" independently. In order to survive in a marginal part-time job, a young person generally needs to live at home. The option of working at an urban "McJob" and living at home does not exist for Digby Neck youth, unless they have strong family connections in urban areas.

Second, the community contains its own expanding roster of McJobs. Some of these are in the fishery, but increasingly they are found in the local service sector. These jobs typically do not require significant levels of formal education, although more and more of service sector employers demand secondary school completion from their workers. These jobs are "marginal" and often part-time, but they are seen as a kind of "opportunity" for rural youth to remain in their communities, whether to "buy time" for future mobility and/or education, or to "settle down" more permanently. Through the 1990s, expansion of the local service industry was also buttressed by a parallel expansion of something similar to what Winson and Leach (2002) called the ruralization of industrial labour in Ontario. By the beginning of the 2000s, a decommissioned military base has now become a small industrial park providing employment in manufacturing and in the burgeoning call-centre industries. A New Jersey-based basalt mining operation has its sights on the western part of Digby Neck and has a proposed quarry operation under federal environmental review (see http://www.ceaa-acee.gc.ca/010/0001/0001/0023/registry_e.htm [accessed Oct. 2006]). It seems as though national and international capitalists are beginning to understand what Atlantic Canadian developers have known for generations: Nova Scotians are a compliant, cheap and increasingly well-educated labour force. In addition, the province's resources are up for grabs, often royalty-free, as is the case with North Mountain basalt.

Third, the ability to be mobile is increasingly connected to the possession of higher education credentials. In Cohorts 1 and 2, Digby Neckers who had relatively little formal education had the opportunity to move their work-related skills to Ontario or Alberta in industrial, clerical or secretarial applications. These jobs were often stable and well paid, and out-migrants could not only establish roots and a home, they could also look forward to a future that contained "steady" work. If they exist at all, these kinds of opportunities outside the "around here" area now exist primarily for individuals with post-secondary credentials. In other words, one needs an education to move more than ever before.[16] Even though they have higher education levels than their predecessors, more than 50 percent of men and 10 percent of women in Cohort 3 have not completed secondary education. Without higher education, Digby Neckers have been virtually unable to migrate, whether or not they want to. Fourth, the high percentage of youth currently living in the area creates a community of stayers. This may create a youth "subculture" on the Neck or in nearby communities that has the support of immediate and extended family and locally oriented peers.

As a result, the community remains remarkably stable despite transformations in its economic base. Slightly less than two in three Digby Neckers through the thirty-six years that this study covers remained within fifty kilometres of "home." The "community" has expanded out of the frame of individual villages with relatively complete infrastructures to the "around here" area. Short-range mobility allows Digby Neckers to access work and services relatively close to home in an environment that remains similar to Digby Neck in cultural terms. These data also show that higher education continues to be economically unnecessary to "survive around here," for men, many of whom seem able to make a living with very little in the way of formal education credentials. Contrary to expectations and rhetoric about the importance of "getting your grade twelve" and higher education, this trend continued into the late 1990s. Indeed, it could be argued that as the service sector in Digby expands, greater numbers of immobile individuals will be required by capital in the emerging economy of the "around here" service sector (Winson and Leach, 2002, Hodge et al., 2002; Vias, 2005). This trend has been consistent, and it appears to intensify as the traditional resource-based economy continues to mechanize and constrict, and as mobility becomes the prerogative of the privileged few who are able to access higher education. Could this be a kind of postmodern transformation of coastal communities, fuelled by a strange mix of globalization, resource exploitation, consumerism, tradition and social networks, and marginal employment? And what will be the impact of more recent trends like the current Alberta oil boom, which is understood by a segment of local youth to generate considerable high wage, low skill resource industry employment? As time passes, the "around here" area seems increasingly to represent community for Digby Neckers, the place where life is lived, jobs are found and identity is forged. As Bauman writes, the contemporary world represents "globalization for some and localization for others" (quoted in Beilharz, 2001: 298).

## Notes

1. See Cruise and Griffiths (1997) for a poetic description of the natural history of the Annapolis Valley. Bull (1978) and Davis (1991) offer descriptions of the natural history of Digby Neck.
2. *Life Magazine* published a photo essay in 1946 that focused on one farming and fishing family living on Digby Neck. For another idyllic description of the way of life on Digby Neck prior to the paved roads and modern communication and trading links, see Bird, 1956: 123–58.
3. Fixed gear is the type of fishing gear normally associated with the small-boat fishery. In fixed gear fisheries, nets, hooks and lines do not move through the water pulled by the power of a motorized boat. Fish, therefore, come to the bait in a fixed-gear fishery. Mobile gear, on the other hand, is pulled through the water, trapping fish in catchment nets or bottom raking apparatus. The distinction is somewhat arbitrary and does not always serve to distinguish between small and large boats or between more or less "technological" fisheries. For instance, longliners fishing offshore for swordfish are as large and powerful and have as much catching potential as large offshore fish draggers.
4. Although it should be noted that Hughes et al. (1960), commenting on data from 1952, made the same observation.
5. There is now general concern about both the state of the fish stocks and the way that more and more fish are being shipped offshore for processing.
6. I am using myth in the sense of the generative meta-narrative around which identities are formed, stories are told, assumptions are made and practices are enacted. I do not mean to suggest that myths are entirely fictional; they have powerful pragmatic consequences.
7. This designation includes a high school leaving certificate as a "diploma." Those in this category have not completed high school or any other form of certified post-secondary education.
8. Another face of this problem, and one that is probably more commonly articulated, is the mismatch between the needs of local labour markets in rural communities and credentials and qualifications provided in higher education

(Jensen, 2002; McGrath, 2001).

9. For the methodological details of these surveys, see Corbett (2001a: Chapter 5, Appendix A, Appendix B and Appendix C).
10. This figure was calculated by subtracting the "away" percentage (17.4 percent, i.e., those living farther than 250 km from Digby Neck) from the total percentage.
11. Many informants commented on how one was "always hearing" how even educated youth struggled to make a living in urban places. These stories came to Digby Neck largely through mass media, but also through the first-hand accounts of out-migrants who return to visit or to stay.
12. This claim is supported using Table 19 by combining the post-secondary group (which necessarily graduated high school) with the group whose highest education attainment is high school graduation. Forty-one percent of "stayers" and 71.1 percent of "away" migrants fall into this category.
13. This cutoff point was chosen rather than the grade nine division used by Census Canada because in Nova Scotia high school begins with grade ten.
14. High-school completion rates are calculated by combining post-secondary and high-school graduate groups.
15. For an analysis of the transformation of a rural village in Digby County in the face of industrialization, resource depletion and technological change, see Hornsby, 1996.
16. Given the growth in local McJobs, Digby Neck youth may still not perceive education as necessary in order to stay.

Chapter 4

# Parallel Education Systems

## The Classes of 1963–1974

This place here is one of the most beautiful places in the world. You can go out here anywhere and cut a truckload of wood. We can go down to the beach and pick penny winkles[1] and mussels, we can go down to the wharf and catch a few fish for supper and run in the woods and shoot rabbits. We've got lots of land there to put a little garden in for a few vegetables.... What more would you want? And all these beautiful people. I've never locked a door in my home. I've never took a key out of a vehicle in my life around here. You know they come from the city and tell about how they got to chain everything up to bolts in the ground. (KS-MS-71)[2]

By the early 1960s the dragger fishery was established and the traditional fixed-gear small-boat fishery was stable and expanding in two of the three Digby Neck communities analyzed by Davis (1991: 55). Davis shows a marked rise in the value of the fishery on Digby Neck beginning in the mid-1970s (1991: 53). Despite yearly fluctuations, catches remained relatively stable overall, average price per pound (unadjusted for inflation) increased more than five-fold between 1963 and 1983. More than three-quarters of this increase occurred after 1974 (Davis, 1991: 53). In the 1960s, policy thinking around the Atlantic fishery was dominated by the view that the fishery needed to be modernized by transforming the seasonally employed multi-occupational fishermen into full-time "professionals." Davis also shows that the small-boat fishery continued to dominate through this period with the number of this kind of vessel actually increasing through the period.

In education, elementary school consolidation was complete in 1957 with the opening of Digby Neck Consolidated School (DNCS) in Sandy Cove. The eldest members of the 1963–1974 cohort took their early schooling in one- or two-room village schoolhouses, finishing their elementary school careers at DNCS. By 1963, the usual school trajectory was the completion of at least a few years of secondary schooling in the rural high school that was opened in the town of Digby in the early 1950s. In 1968, a regional vocational school opened in Middleton (approximately 100 kilometres from Digby Neck in Nova Scotia's Annapolis Valley) offering trades training. Well-established paths of work in the fishery and in the home were now juxtaposed against life strategies that involved formal education and mobility, at least in theory. In the 1960s and early 1970s, there was also ample "reserve army" (Veltmeyer, 1979) work opportunity for "unskilled" labour in central and western Canada. Many young women also took secretarial training at the regional high school in Digby.

The paved Highway 217 was completed in 1956, allowing for improved transportation, communication and the ready availability of mass produced goods and services, including fresh "store bought" foods. The eldest informants in the sample (born in the mid to late 1940s) can remember the farmer-fisherman and remnants of the kind of multi-occupational co-integrated economy described by Bouchard (1997) and Johnson (1999).

> They had a few dairy cows and they would sell milk and cream. And they all had a few vegetables to sell in the fall. I used to help Joe hay in the summer. And then I used to help Dad set lobster traps at the first of the season, and then bring 'em in at the end of the season. Most of the kids there did it. (IS-ML-63)

Informants born in the mid to late 1950s remember a working community nearly exclusively focused on the fishery. The value of landed fish rose steadily, with average prices for cod and lobster nearly tripling, between 1963 and 1974 (Davis, 1991: 53). In addition, government remittances played an important role in the broad social change that swept coastal communities beginning in the 1950s. All of these developments supported a transition to an increasingly specialized and concentrated fishing economy (Davis, 1991; Kearney, 1993; Johnson, 1999: 69–71; Schrank, 1997: 69). As unemployment insurance and other forms of social assistance became widespread, the persistence of small farming and logging as well as trading in traditional crafts became both less necessary for household income and too poorly rewarded relative to better returns in the fishery or in wage work now within commuting distance.

## Family and Work: An Education for Staying

> It wasn't hard to find work around here in them days. There were six, seven, eight fish plants going, boats going everywhere. When I got out of school they was fish draggin' and they was just starting to get into it good in the early sixties. (FN)

Through the 1960s and into the early 1970s there was abundant paid work for young men and to a lesser extent for young women in the villages along Digby Neck. Young men were expected to engage in fisheries work as a matter of course. In a labour intensive fishery, the work of young people was essential, unlike education, which was often perceived as something that had dubious value to the community.

> It was a natural thing. If you weren't working, you were lazy or you had to go somewhere to hide because there was work to do. Christ, if you wanted the day off you had to go hide 'cause somebody would see you and say to you: "You doin' nothing? Come here, I've got something for you to do." (GG-MS-71)

Through this period most fishing operations were family-based. Young women were expected to do fisheries support work as well as domestic work. This work was done with and for family in support of the work of male relatives employed in the fishery. Women were also largely responsible for maintaining the domestic and social relationships that make small communities viable. This finding is consistent with Porter's findings in Newfoundland regarding the gendered structure of labour in coastal communities (1993). Young men were expected to watch their fathers and learn from them. These men describe having been drawn to life in the family-based fishery and into the larger circle of life in the fishery. While most young men worked toward more permanent positions in the fishery, usually on the deck of a boat in some capacity, many young women were working in fisheries support work on land doing particular gender- and age-segregated jobs.

> You know the whole family knit (lobster trap) heads, all the kids helped knit heads. By the time you were six years old you could knit a head. TV wasn't big back then. So you went in the kitchen and you had an eye hook under the counter and you sat there in the chair and you knit heads. (IS-ML-63)

The discourse is distinctly different around what male and female children were doing when they worked baiting trawl[3] for longliners or baiting bags and knitting heads for lobstermen. The boys were "learning to fish," while the girls and women were "helping."

> Oh, we helped out from time to time. Nothing too serious, just when they needed some help because they were behind. (EF-FS-74)

Young men wishing to stay in the fishery had to establish a reputation as a capable and knowledgeable person around fisheries-related skills. Young men said to be "born and bred" were given access to the cultural capital of the craft of fishing. The quote below comes from a man who eventually went on to co-own a fish and scallop dragger. He began his career by demonstrating his ability to work at shore-based tasks in the fishery.

> My first job was for my father pitching fish at night. I done that probably from when I was fifteen to when I was eighteen. And that's how my name kind of got around down the shore that I would do that. And that's what I done. I just went every night and pitched my father's fish out. You had to get your name around. That was very important. (FN)

From an early immersion in shore-based fisheries work and fishing trips aboard fathers' and grandfathers' boats, young men became immersed in the working culture of the coastal community. They learned to deal with seasickness, long hours and weather. Some educators recognized this "alternative" education system that trained boys for the fishery.

> You're not going to learn it in school, not what you want to know. You've got to drop out to get it. To go to this college [informal apprenticeship in the fishery] you've got to drop out of this one [school]. And why not, there's a good livelihood there, you're doing what you want to do. (ES-FE)

As adolescents, Digby Neck boys had varying degrees of "connection" to the fishery and varying degrees of commitment to working in the fishery. Some young men "just didn't have the interest" or "didn't want to go fishing for the rest of their lives." Others could not imagine doing anything else. These different identity constructions had considerable impact on whether or not a boy continued through secondary school and whether or not he remained "around here."

On Digby Neck very few women went to sea. Women worked on gear and supported the fishermen in a number of ways, and their work was seen as essential, but the central activity in the fishery was the "men's work" of getting aboard the boat and going out to catch fish. Young women were more typically seen as "earning some spending money" by working in the fishery. For a young woman who needed to work, it was equally important to establish a good reputation as a reliable, hard worker in the gendered spaces of the coastal community of the 1960s and 1970s.

> I did house work for a disabled lady and I had babysitting places that I would go and they would sometimes want ironing done or just light housekeeping. I carried the mail for some senior people who couldn't get to the post office. If you were a dependable reliable person and they could entrust their children with you then babysitting jobs were no problem at all. (DL-FS-69)

Education was not seen as important for success and prosperity in the fishery of the 1960s and 1970s for young men. For women though, formal education was considered important and girls seemed to "fit in" to school better than boys.

> Girls seem to have fit in to school better than boys. And it just goes to the next level for kids [boys] who come with the kind of background and attitude and say that this is sissy stuff and I hate it. And I've got some really good alternatives. (SF-ME)

Informants look back on the situation differently today and encourage their children to stay in school more forcefully than their parents had with them. Yet, male informants in this cohort were typically content with their career and education choices. Fisheries work is seen as interesting, engaging and lucrative for those who own their own boats and licences. Many Digby Neck families have this level of "direct" entrepreneurial connection to the fishery. A "direct" connection to the fishery meant having a father and/or extended family who were established, licence-holding fishermen.

In licence-holding families with few boys, male children could inherit *petit bourgeois* resource production capacity in the form of boats and gear. They could also acquire the readily available local cultural capital necessary to be successful fishermen through a long-term immersion in daily life in a fishing village. The young men of this cohort acquired the cultural capital necessary for fisheries work by assuming incremental responsibility and through a slow but steady advancement in responsibility and rewards. The community offered these male informants an apprenticeship into a highly visible industry, with the feeling of adult responsibility and of being a part of a working enterprise with a volatile but established structure of rewards. On the other hand, school was seen by male stayers as an infantilizing, disconnected, disempowering experience.

> You just felt like a little kid in school. I just sat there and stared out the window a lot of the time. I was working around the shore and making pretty good money for the time. That schoolhouse[4] [pause] well the work wasn't like [pause] it just seemed like elementary school all over again, sitting in desks and a lot of talk.... You set and listened most of the time, just like a little kid. I couldn't see myself standing that. I wasn't going to college. (FN)

The love of the water and a love for the area combine with an excitement for fishing and the result is a person who understands himself to be rooted in a place and in a way of life. This position is known as being "brought up" in the fishery, or being "born and bred" a fisherman.

> Just born and bred. I'm a thirteenth generation fishermen from my forefathers who came here in 1637. And it's been in my family ever

> since. When I was twelve or thirteen, I wanted to get on the water, and when I was fourteen my father took me aboard the boat. He never wanted me to do it, he always wanted me to go to school. Go to school, do something else. When I was fourteen, I owned my own boat and fished it a little after school, just a rowboat. When I was fifteen I quit school. Even in school, I just wanted to be on the water. It was a good living, everybody was making a good living. I mean I owned my first boat, a 30-foot powered boat when I was sixteen years old. And I was into the ground fishery and lobstering and I never looked back. You know, just straight ahead. (KS-MS-71)

These men describe fishing as being in their "blood." This means that they were exposed to the fishery as children and came to understand it as a lucrative set of opportunities that could be had by any man who had "direct" or "blood" connections to Digby Neck, without "paper," or the qualifications conferred by formal education. Up until the imposition of limited entry licensing in the mid-1970s, the simple possession of the cultural capital available to most boys in the community was enough to "make a start" in the fishery, even if one's family had few tangible resources like boats and gear.

Today though, fishing is too rich for the blood of most young men, as the price for a licence can now cost up to a million dollars. Up to the mid-1970s, fishermen remember paying twenty-five cents for their lobster licences at a local store. "I can remember going in and flipping that quarter on the counter," one informant from this cohort commented, remembering the days of open access to the common property ocean resource. The apprenticeship for this career involved living and working around men and older boys in the community and waiting for an opportunity to be helpful in practical tasks and economically productive at an early age. Significantly, cultural capital was acquired through the tacit and powerful deep socialization experience of watching life unfold.

> When I got old enough to be allowed to play with my friends we would go down to the "pond," which was a tidal pool that flooded every day when the tide was up but when the tide was down a pool of water was left. Here we would take our model boats and pretend to be fishermen, sailing our boats to one end of the pond to fish and then sail our boats back to the other end of the pond to come home with our load of fish. It was fun, but also educational in that it introduced us to the tools and language of the fishermen and taught us to think in terms of fishing. This is how we were introduced to the technology of fishing at an early age. (FN)

For women, a community-based skills complex involved shore-based fisheries support work like knitting lobster trap heads, baiting lobster bags, baiting trawl, working in fish plants (in peak periods particularly), preparing food for family, workers and community functions, maintaining households, doing a variety of community organizational work, acting as bookkeeper for fishing and other businesses and organizations, supporting children's education and purchasing supplies for the family fishing operation, among other tasks (Neis, 1999; Binkley, 2002).

> It's work, work, work all the time around here, especially in lobster season. You know, he's out there in the Bay freezing his ass off, so I feel I have to contribute too. Why shouldn't I? So when he's fishing he don't cook and I take care of the house, the shopping and everything else. He comes home and he's got to get some sleep. They work hard old days, so he can be pretty cranky with the kids. So I try to keep them out of his way. I'm always running around for something. And there's the books. He don't have nothing to do with that. He don't go down to the school house neither. He says he feels just like a scared little kid again when he goes in there. (EF-FS-74)

Women are proud to claim quietly that they "run the community," and nobody disputes that women "run" families. Women were more successful than men in formal education on Digby Neck and see a more direct connection between school learning and the kind of work they do in the community in gendered roles (e.g., periodic or permanent wage work in the "around here" area as well as unwaged bookkeeping, family and community organizational work, and dealing with the school). Additionally, women tended to be less resistant in school and more likely to do what they were "supposed to do," probably because of their inability to establish "direct" connections in the patriarchal structure of the fishery. For women stayers of this cohort the typical path was from school to a marriage.

> If I had stayed to grade twelve there wouldn't be any difference because I'd be here and married and I'd have had my family. That was it because that was all I knew growing up. You see it growing up and you say, this is what I'm supposed to do. And to me being a wife and a mother was a very important job. It was not even like a job, it was something that I just thought I could do. (DS-FS-69)

Educators comment that through the 1960s and 1970s a typical career trajectory for many young people involved early marriage and establishment of well worn patterns of domestic life.

> When I first started teaching it was nothing to see kids just graduated from school getting married. And the guy was on the boat and the girl was home keeping house and that was it. (CD-ME)

Popular high school secretarial programs also offered women of this cohort immediate work opportunities, which could be easily combined with other traditional women's family responsibilities. Most women who took this route ended up leaving Digby Neck or moving into the "not far" and "around here" areas to be closer to employment opportunities, but some managed to remain on Digby Neck, commuting to Digby or taking advantage of local opportunities available for secretarial or service industry work. As Table 3.5 shows though, through this period, women's wages were depressed both in relation to men's wages and in comparison with provincial and national averages. If anyone had economic motivation to leave the "around here" region it was young women of this generation. It should come as no surprise that the women of Digby Neck would be more successful in the education system and more committed to attaining the kind of mobile cultural capital it offered.

An example of the gender divisions found in shore-based support work is the division of labour in the fish plants. While almost no women "go fishing," they do "work in the fish." "Working in the fish" means working in plants processing fish the men catch. Both men and women work in the fish, but the wage structure continues to favour men, who are thought best able to do better-paid "heavy" work. No one questioned the division of labour or the differential pay scale; both seemed to be understood as "natural" and justified by both the nature of the tasks and "primary breadwinner" position of men.

> Women and men both, ya there would be. And in the fish plants you had both men and women. They might have a little different job. The men would do some of the heavier work. This is when you did a lot of it by hand. (SS-MS-71)

Women were typically employed as fish "cutters" and "trimmers" and generally did the more precise knife work of skinning and filleting the raw fish. Men tended to work at the tasks involving heavy lifting like fish packing, icing the fish and loading it onto trucks for shipping. Fish plant work requires endurance and the ability to withstand difficult working conditions, much like fishing. The work is considered to be skilled. The informant quoted below spoke with pride about being considered a "clean cutter" although she was not one of the fastest on the floor. The skill required to save as much of the valuable flesh as possible was a source of considerable pride. Fish plant work often carries a stigma outside the community, but on Digby

Neck most people understand and even admire fish plant workers most of whom are now women.

> I worked hard. You know how to work hard if you've worked in the fish plant. I admire anyone who works in the fish. Anyone that can stay and work in the fish plant all day and not get home until 5:30 at night, and stand in the same spot for nine hours. (DL-FS-69)

## The Hand on the Shoulder: Socialization for Leaving

> Your family was a really big influence on what kind of job you went into later in life once school was over. They were a big influence on even who you married at that time. And I think that gave you a sense — right or wrongly — it gave you a sense of belonging. People were looking out for you. (IS-ML-63)

In the 1960s and 1970s, the community provided a known work and social matrix. But at the same time other alternatives were becoming accessible as well. Men who stayed tended to be positioned in families that had "direct" connections to the inshore and the developing dragger fishery on Digby Neck. The most financially successful of these men were those whose families owned independent processing facilities, fishing rigs and licences, and these individuals felt the strongest pull to remain in the community and the fishery. Women in this cohort who stayed reported financial compulsion and the weight of family expectations as influencing them to make the decision to stay on Digby Neck. This "career" trajectory was opposed by educators, who report trying to encourage young women to "broaden their options."

> With the grade twelve girls I used to say, I've interviewed all the boys and there's not one of them told me they were getting married. So I said to them, who are you going to marry? And in the second place, that's going to take you ten minutes; then what are you going to do? (OI-FE)

Gendered careers in the service industry or in the "helping professions" as well as the traditional housewife role were available for women who wanted and were able to leave. Most women who stayed gravitated toward local "options" of marriage and part-time work for the social benefits and family support it gave them, or because they could see no other choice. Given the size and "close-knit" nature of the community it is no surprise that family connections were important for leavers as well. But leavers in the sample tended to be individuals whose family connections were less local in nature. Leavers had family members who were connected to communities beyond the Neck, either through previous emigration or because they had at least one parent who came from another community. This finding is consistent with the ethnographic work done by Gill Jones in northern England, where she found that the most mobile rural young people tended to be those whose own parents are in-migrants from other places (1999a).

> You know, a lot of the ones that left over the years, they had some family up in the [Annapolis] Valley or in the city [Halifax] or in Yarmouth. And they'd go stay there until they got, you know, on their feet. (NS-FE)

In the 1960s and 1970s, the Canadian post-secondary education system was expanding offering the promise of new forms of training that could be used outside the community. The leavers of the 1963–1974 cohort were post-secondary pioneers. Some reported having significant family or family friendship connections outside the community, but most frame their decision as a pioneer experience or a journey into the unknown. In order to facilitate out-migration, significant family-based encouragement was seen as crucial. This support ranged from subtle encouragement to leave fishing and homemaking for opportunities elsewhere, to conversations with summer residents about life in other places, to the realization that the gendered structure of opportunity on Digby Neck offered few opportunities for women outside marriage or for men whose connection to the fishery was marginal. There are then several kinds of connection that come to light in an analysis of leavers' interviews. In these cases, families very often made it clear to young people that they ought to explore a wider range of options than those available locally. For young men, this was generally framed in terms of a rejection of fishing as a way of life. It was all right for the previous generation but not for this one.

> There was never any pressure on you to go fishing. There was more pressure on you to stay in school and get an education and get away from fishing. You know [pause] my mother and father wanted me to be better than just a fisherman. (IS-ML-63)

Some families saw the industrialization of the fishery as an opportunity, while others saw it as the end of a way of life. Opportunities existed for most young men locally, and one needed a kind of family support to leave the opportunities available in the familiar world of the fishery. Parents of leavers tended to promote the idea that fishing was a way of life that did not offer sufficient stability, income and comfort. There were, they argued, "better" options.

> Oh, he [father] liked fishing. It was in his blood to fish. He started out with his father in a dory. You know, it was his life. He always said there was something better for us to do than fishing. You know, he didn't say we couldn't but he always wanted us to be better. (FN)

In this cohort, gender roles appeared to be fairly static, regardless of whether men and women stayed or left the community. Mobility trajectories led to gender specific roles in other places (e.g., secretarial or clerical work for women and labour or professional work for men). Locally though, prospects were seen by mobile families as particularly dim for women, and one informant had an overt gender analysis.

> They never really said, like they never discouraged, nothing like that. I hate to keep bringing up gender all the time, but really like if the roles were reversed and I was the mother, I would want my daughter to move on, just because there's nothing there for her. You know there's no jobs. (FE-FL-73)

In the 1960s, a variety of options were available for those who were willing to emigrate to urban areas, including secretarial and clerical work for women and trades, the armed forces and abundant labour opportunities for men. Leavers also report being "unusual" because they chose to go when it seemed as though most of their peers were staying close to home. This perception is borne out by my analysis in the previous chapter. Fewer than one in six people in the full sample of 714 individuals migrated further than 250 kilometres from Digby Neck, and this percentage remained stable from the 1960s through the 1990s.[5] What all of these mobile individuals have in common is encouragement and a "hand on the shoulder" facilitating the migration process. Typically, staying, like leaving, was intimately connected to family ties.

> Well my mother, I told her that these guys were going out, and she said, well you should go and see if you can find something. See what it's like. I had uncles… well one's in BC. I think I had another uncle who lived in Montreal. And there was a few other ones around so I knew that I wouldn't be stuck. I could travel around a bit. (HL-ML-69)

For male leavers who were not "streamed" by the secondary school for university, vocational training and the work skills learned fishing with family on Digby Neck were easily transferable to construction sites or to trades in western and central Canada in the 1960s and 1970s. These leavers report a migration involving work similar to that found aboard fishing boats. "Work is work, it took you a few days at the most to catch on and then you're away," commented one leaver (FN). In the 1960s and 1970s, it was common for groups of young men (both stayers and leavers) to set out for Ontario or "out West" in search of work. The masculine labouring sensibilities learned in the coastal community were easily transferable to abundant jobs in other places.

> We just got together and said let's go out and see what she's [Northern British Columbia] like. So all of us who come out all worked in the woods all together all on one crew. They've all gone back now. (HL-ML-69)

The women's version of this migration tended to be of shorter distance. Women report looking to the middle range "not far" area identified in Chapter 3 (within 250 km of Digby Neck), and particularly Halifax, as a place where one could find "good work." With opportunities in the "helping professions" and in clerical and secretarial work, female leavers set out to make their connections with other women who had blazed the trail before them. In the 1960s and 1970s, groups of women working in Halifax formed support networks for one another, helping to keep each other apprized of work, supporting the initial migration transition and providing a friendship circle in the city.

> You never even thought about going up the Valley or Yarmouth. It was always Halifax. There were lots of jobs, mostly finance and insurance companies and in banks.... And we all got apartments together and went out to shows. That was really good. (TL-FL-65)

Once they found work in Halifax, these women acquired the experience they needed to find jobs in a variety of urban settings and in larger rural centres in southwestern Nova Scotia or in the Annapolis Valley. These "not far" migrants typically retained ties with their families and close friends on Digby Neck, but they mostly married men from and settled outside the "around here" region.

In other cases, the hand on the shoulder came from summer visitors from Ontario or from the United States. The highest rate of out-migration is from Sandy Cove, the community on Digby Neck with the largest population of summer residents and the traditional centre of the tourist trade. This community boasted not only a number of permanent/transient summer residents from Ontario and the United States, it also had two youth summer camps through the 1960s and 1970s, one of which operated up until the early 1980s.

> I guess I used to have these friends that used to visit from Oakville.

> And they were very, like, different. They were more sophisticated. They went to school and one was going to be a teacher. So I guess I just knew that they were doing this so I had to do this too. (TL-FL-65)

> When I was growing up there were two large camps in the village. That's where I made some friends. And those two people I told you about, friends I'd made. There were those supports for going on beyond high school and going on to university and doing something else other than living on Digby Neck. (SF-ML-67)

## Formal Education: Streaming for Leaving in the 1960s and early 1970s

> The Captain's voice stopped and changed and lowered. There was a note of irritable apology in it. John could catch only a word or two. "Don't… talk about it… him leaving… more than I have to.… In a couple of years away to school." He tried to study his history after supper in the kitchen lamplight, but he couldn't get the facts to stay. He went to bed in a kind of sober exaltation, and the future lay with him in his dreams. (Bruce, 1959: 206)

> I knew I wanted to leave and the way of doing that was to become educated. (SF-ML-67)

Leavers in this cohort made a clear connection between formal education and leaving the community. Education took a variety of forms, ranging from university, to vocational school, to secretarial, nursing and clerical training. Additionally, opportunities in the military requiring minimal secondary education and on-the-job learning in labour jobs in central and western Canada in the 1960s and 1970s provided opportunities outside the formal education system. Children of elite fishing families could choose from privileged options outside the local area just as they could access similarly privileged options on the Neck.

School streaming supplemented and supported the differential menu of "options." Those streamed into an academic college preparatory program starting in junior high school ended up leaving, first for university and then for elsewhere. This segregation of students created an effective barrier of social exclusion and differentiation between the two groups. The streaming system created a two-track academic and social world and there was only minimal contact between the two categories after the beginning of the seventh grade. University-bound informants have difficulty even remembering their elementary school classmates from Digby Neck, most of whom were streamed into non-academic programs.

> Um [pause] the ones that just stayed behind. I'm having a hard time remembering some of those people. Usually the ones that just stayed behind didn't just finish school. We [academic stream students] didn't associate with them much in high school. (FE-FL-73)

The junior high school presented children at the age of twelve or thirteen with a set of experiences that differed on the basis of presumed academic ability. Stayers typically report confusion and disjunction between their interests and school activity. Leavers report satisfying social and recreational involvements through sports, clubs, outings and school organizations throughout their high-school careers. This complex of activity represents the cultivation of a form of cultural capital that enabled academic success. As one teacher put it, "You could just tell who was going to make it [graduate]; they were the ones in the clubs and the sports" (OI-FE). The students in the academic stream were assumed to be "going on" to university, while the others were assumed to be staying "around" or to be moving into vocational training, and the result of these assumptions was a tightly controlled regime of academic and mobility offerings.

> I know we're not supposed to say this today, but we knew who was going on and who wasn't. You knew when they were just small children. I think we were just more honest about it in those days (FL-FE)

The entire business of "placing kids" is a more or less conscious forecasting of the education and mobility future of young people. Some educators saw the social class dimensions of this migration message. The children who are given the view that their chances lie elsewhere tend to be the children of professionals, small business owners and wealthy fishing families.

> I think the message that our kids, or professionals' kids or teachers' kids, get is that, yeah, you don't belong here. If you then decide that this is where you want to come back, that's good. But I know that somewhere in there there's a pressure to achieve, and achievement means to go off to university and off to the big city and get a responsible job. (CD-ME)

These streaming decisions resulted in the formation of friendships and associations that would influence education and mobility decisions. The "hierarchy" that streaming created sent messages to students about who was and who was not worthy of teachers' attention and capable of getting beyond high school. In the 1960s and 1970s, the secondary school system was overtly elitist and designed to usher the academic cadre out of the community and into higher education. Students came from the feeder schools around Digby and were "placed" according to "academic ability," ranging from the middle-class, mobile, academic class, to the rooted "dumb class," as one stayer called his placement.[6] Educators understood that the placements made in the streamed system of the 1960s and 70s were based upon their own projections.

> You first had the separation of kids into A, B and C classes, and were sorting them out according to ability. A lot of times it was not actual ability, or it didn't seem to be as much as it was perceived where they seem to be going.... They're only going to go to grade eight or they're only going to be fishermen. They'd just be staying around here so what was the point. (HL-FE)

Many young Digby Neck boys were placed in the non-academic stream because they were considered to be "destined" to make what was for them the "natural" choice to work on father's boat as soon as he was old enough. As educators point out, there was no "shame" or "prejudice" associated with this assessment; it was simply seen as a common-sense assessment of differently placed student's education "potential." Fishing was seen by some educators as a "good" occupational choice for a boy slotted into a non-academic stream in the 1960s–late 80s. The work, though very hard, was generally lucrative by community standards.[7] This was the known path, the way that "most of them" went. One educator tells a story of a young man who graduated high school in the early 1970s.

> When Hector was in high school and choosing his courses he was encouraged to take the general route and not the academic because he was the son of a fisherman and he lived on the Neck and that's where he'd end up. And he would in no way shape or form be going to college [even though he said he was going to Acadia]. So what was the point of taking the academic? (HL-FE)

Non-academic and academic students alike saw the school as being responsive only to the top echelon. Leavers were particularly aware of the social class dimensions of streaming for the distribution of education resources in high school.

> That seemed to those who got poked away into what I think they called general education, uh, those kids didn't... a lot of them were poor and they came from bad homes, I shouldn't say bad homes, difficult homes. Those kids didn't have a chance. They were poorer kids. (SF-ML-67)

Family background lurked behind educators' assessments of who would and who would not "go on." These assessments also worked to shape students' understanding of themselves and their abilities. Those in the general stream were defined as being "incapable" of acquiring more than a basic education and, at best, trade training in vocational or business programs. Streaming also created "cliques" of Digby Neck children who did not "mix" with children from other communities. Educators claim that these "non-mixers" (as one informant called them) tended to have significantly lower education aspirations than children who integrated into the larger secondary-school community.

Being part of the elite stream gave select Digby Neck students access to the encouragement and support necessary to assist some of them to become pioneers, among the first members of their families to go to university. The general character of the discourse around education and the future was higher-education and mobility oriented. These students also understood the nature of the streaming system and how it worked to create exclusive categories of individuals in school, but also different structures of opportunity and expectation. Elite students learned to define their mobility options in terms of "smart" identity constructions.

> I was the first person in my family ever to get a high-school diploma. I have to say that teachers did always encourage me. You were in the academic class and you were going to be the ones to break out and do something different. The rest of them were put in classes that weren't going anywhere. We were put in different worlds when we went to Digby [secondary school]. (RR-FL-70)

Stayers needed to resist school-generated definitions of their academic intelligence. This mirrors Stern's ethnographic finding that in Inuit communities intelligence is constructed in terms of an individual's ability to learn "through observation and experimentation [from which] individuals are expected to draw their own conclusions" (1999: 505). He goes on to comment how, "I have never heard adults equate being smart with success in school" (1999: 510). The community and the fishing industry provided a different forum for intellectual work and self esteem, one which seemed to be more relevant, even superior to, the way learning was presented and assessed in school.

> You know learning and education is a funny thing. I can remember being called up to the board in grade six to do some simple multiplication problem or some math that wasn't too hard and my mind going right blank, I was that scared. But I'm not stupid. I've been on jobs where I figured out things that licenced carpenters and college trained engineers couldn't. I've learned more out workin'

> than I ever did in school. I learned there because it was all part of doing something and I always had the confidence to look over a job and figure out how to get it done. I never had that in school because I couldn't see the job that had to be done there. Fishing is my roots; that's what I grew up around so it's work that's natural to me. (FN)

Educators saw this stigmatization of youth from rural communities and they understand how the inferiority complex that this process generated truncated the school careers of many people.

> It's not so much with this generation, the ones that are in school now, as with previous generations. They may have been in school and very capable, but had this feeling that they weren't going to be accepted because they speak this way and they come from this kind of background. (SF-ME)

The education track was constructed, both in and out of school, as a kind of moral imperative. In order to be "good" or "successful" people, they had to remain focused on the structured environment of school. Leavers used mobile analogies like "track" or "stepping stones" to describe their education trajectories. On the other hand, the establishment of a working-class masculinity typically involved developing an anti-school persona. Stayers used static imagery like "wall," "tunnel" and even "jailhouse" to describe their schooling. For many male stayers especially, education was a sentence to be endured. For leavers, each stage in an education career was a step into something different, and this new place then revealed a different set of possibilities.

> It was like a chain reaction, or a snowball effect or even an addiction. It was you've gotta' finish each step: now you've gotta' get your grade eight and now your grade nine, because quitting and being somewhere isn't going to get you anything. It was no good, and if you dropped out what would you do? (FE-FL-73)

These choices may have been difficult and fraught with unknown elements, but these students were able to place trust in the formal education system because the system placed trust in them. Because they lacked a "direct" connection with the fishery, the steps or trajectory of a coherent life path involved formal education. The streaming system reassured elite students that they were "chosen" and certified as capable of making the leaps of faith necessary to abandon the familiar world of the community.

> It was like we were chosen to leave and the others weren't [pause].

> But it's not that simple. Nobody stood in anybody's way. I don't know how to put this. In the fish plant they could work hard and they did work hard, but in school it was totally different. They just didn't see anything else, they wanted to stay I guess. (RR-FL-70)

In this period, a minimal amount of formal education was still sufficient to provide a reasonable standard of living. And this is perhaps the single most important difference between this cohort and those that follow in later decades; having an "education" did not necessarily mean university graduation or even vocational or high school completion. The view was that you got as much education as you "needed" to do what you wanted to do.

From the point of view of differently placed individuals making strategic decisions about their lives or their children's lives, education was an investment and a resource like any other. It made no sense to purchase an education credential that one was not going to be able to "use." Perceptions of "rationality" were structured by unequally distributed "necessities" opportunities available to men in the fishery. Anything more than "the basics" or "what you're going to use" was frivolous and wasteful and represented foregone income to many stayers, who, as Bourdieu put it, "made a virtue of necessity," celebrating their practicality and lack of affectation. Given the volatile nature of the fishery, procrastination meant lost opportunity. Only those with no direct connection could afford to fool around with education.

Ironically then, education was taken very seriously, so seriously in fact that it was seen as wasteful to acquire formal education and not use it. Education was an instrumental investment, an expenditure of valuable time and money with an eye to future returns. In the context of a stable and expanding industrial fishery, men's education investment decisions were high stakes in terms of potential material losses for the person who "set in school" or in post-secondary study. Minimal secondary credentials were enough to give an aspiring worker a foothold and an entry point into the world of work. More than that was only necessary for people who wanted to leave and work "outside" the area. Education was a mobility ticket purchased with precious earned money and time, and neither of these commodities could be squandered.

> If you wanted to get out of there and go to Halifax or Toronto or somewhere, you needed an education, or job skills of some kind other than fishing. Education was your key to get away from there I suppose. A lot of them looked at it like that, and that's maybe why they dropped out of school, so they wouldn't have to leave, I don't know. In my generation grade ten got you a job anywhere. (IS-ML-63)

## Learning to Do: The Construction of Intelligence and Identity in a Coastal Community

> I've got a different kind of education, and it's an education that allows me to actually get my hands on tools and work on something. If you ask any fisherman he'll tell you the same thing. When we were growing up there was lots of work for anyone that wanted it. School didn't let you do that. You didn't feel you were good at the things they were teaching in school, and you didn't feel the things they were teaching in school were really good for much anyway. They saw us as a bunch of dummies and so we went where we could feel like what we did mattered. (FN)

Practical skills are highly valued by the stayers in this generation of Digby Neckers. Most are proud to describe themselves as hands-on people who are able to "figure things out" and who can work with a wide variety of tools. Women on Digby Neck also spoke of the multiple skills that they use to negotiate everyday life. Family and friendly connections are economically important on Digby Neck, and these allegiances provide a context for barter and sharing of goods, services, skills, knowledge, advice and talent. Many informants spoke of the way families work together to "live on love," as one informant put it, during slack times in the fishery.

> I can fix most things really, or there's somebody around here who can and I can trade with them. That YK2 that they're all worried about, that don't bother me no more than nothing. (KS-MS-71)

One of the distinctions between stayers and leavers is that those who leave are seen as "specialized" people, some of whom were unable to master the multifaceted and arduous work necessary to make it in the "tough" world of the small-boat inshore fishery. In terms of locally negotiable cultural capital, it is the formally educated person who is disadvantaged. In a certain sense education was seen as the only option for men who lack the resourcefulness, mechanical ability, stamina and ability to withstand seasickness and cold. In other words, this was a man who could not cut it in the man's world of the fishery. Such a man was not "fit to do anything else," and in certain respects he was "doomed" to "settin in school" (and later in an office) because he lacked the physical and intellectual abilities necessary to make it as a fisherman.

> They've gone to school and they've took a trade or a specialty and they're probably very good at it. But I got my degree at the University of the Bay of Fundy. You take, if I'm out there in the bay

> and a goddamn engine stops, I've got to try to get it going. I'm a mechanic. You know, you figure it out most of the time. I consider myself to be as educated as that guy out there living somewhere else, only it's in something different. (GG-MS-71)

In the fishery, practical skills are only acquired by active engagement in physical tasks (Palsson, 1994, 1999). For men in this cohort school experience was anything but active and involved a great deal of rote learning, physical inactivity and concentration on questionable, abstract tasks. When asked what kinds of people seemed to do well in school, informants described a person able to follow orders and think mechanically rather than analytically. This reverses popular perceptions of the academically successful individual as an intelligent person capable of abstract thought. In the context of the working life of the community, the ability to conceptualize work situations and act counts as learning.

> Who did good in school? I'd say somebody that could sit and listen for one thing. Some people are more hands-on. Rather than be content to listen and think about things that way, some people are more active, some people have more social interests. (SS-MS-71)

To be a "good worker" is to have a particular orientation to the job, to be able to analyze a situation and take appropriate, decisive and rapid physical action. To be a man in this space is to be capable of coordinating your physical movement with that of others in very tight quarters (without getting sick), in the intricate dance that is work on the deck of a fishing boat. This is a sort of practical, common-sense, working intelligence developed over many years of experience in the fishery, typically from childhood. The following quote from my field diary illustrates this kind of knowledge.

> Some guys, they just never get it. Workin' takes more than a strong back and a weak mind like they say. You've got to have some common sense is what I call it. Some "fullers" can't do that, you got to push them out of the way and do it for 'em. All the schoolin' in the world, but they can't figure things out. (FN)

This cohort have all had to adapt to modernization, changes in the fish stocks and government regulation by refitting their fishing rigs or working boats for other fishermen in other fisheries. All male informants have worked in a number of fisheries and a number of different fishing support activities through their careers. A normal fishing career involves work in at least a half dozen different fisheries.

> I've been at lobstering for thirty-two years. But I done long lining

> for quite a few years. And I seen as the draggers got building and coming to this area, we seen that they was kind of taking the fish before we could get 'em hooked on, so it came to the point where I said if you can't beat 'em join 'em. Then we decided to go scallop fishing because the ground fishery was getting bad. And then I went from the scalloping to the whale watching. Every year I've done the lobstering. I've done some drift net herring fishing and set net herring fishing. I had different licences so there was always one we could go to. (KS-MS-71)

Versatility and flexibility have meant that fishermen have had to read the environmental and political waters and make appropriate adjustments in their operations. Each change of fishing gear requires the application of a different skill set, and each fishery is a risky entrepreneurial activity requiring management and administrative skills. Adaptations must be made very quickly in order to exploit the stock "before it's gone." Some informants spoke of the tenuous nature of community and traditional fishing practices in the face of the industrialization of the fishery. They now recognize that fishing has become more of a business than a community and family-based enterprise. Recent conflict in the fishery over poaching and First Nations fisheries have intensified the competition for what is seen as dwindling stock.

> Basically, for the most part I would say that traditional rules and boundaries have been [pause] well, they're gone. They don't have that respect for traditional territory or things like that because government rules have come in and that is the legal standard. I'll exploit this and then I'll find something else to move on to. A lot of the mentality in the fishery is "get it before it's gone." (SS-MS-71)

The process of industrialization and regulation combined with declining stocks and competition from mobile gear has forced a lot of the smaller operators out of the fishery, with boat and licence ownership becoming concentrated in the hands of fewer and fewer big owners. Uncaught fish are now owned by "men in offices who never put on a set of oil-clothes," as one fisherman put it (FN). Many small-boat fishers blame state policy for this situation, claiming that it represents a deliberate attempt to downsize the Atlantic fishery and destroy the viability, economy and culture of coastal communities. The Individual Transferable Quota (ITQ) system, for instance, as well as government licence buy-out programs and adult education initiatives are all seen as part of a general conspiracy aimed at depopulation of communities, concentration of control of fisheries resources in the hands of a small cadre of what are being called "core," or "professional," fishers. The ultimate end of this program, many Digby Neckers claim, is the engineered destruction of both the small-boat inshore fishery and their way of life.

## They Wanted Me to Go to School: Schooling, Identity and Family

> It might be that you were kept in school when the winter woods work was on, and steered away from other responsibilities you would like to take a crack at, but working with the pulpwood in hot weather was nasty work.... But it was sharing a man's work... a known enterprise on the Channel Shore. (Bruce, 1954: 184)

The stories of stayers contain an apparent contradiction. None of the men report being actively encouraged to go into fishing, and none of the women report being actively encouraged to marry fishermen. Young people watched their parents and responded eagerly when adult opportunity presented itself. Fishing and support work offered a class and family structured menu of opportunities, income and the invaluable reputation of a "practical" and resourceful housekeeper, a man who could "stand it" on a boat and generally someone "willing to work." While not everyone could "get rich," as some young men from elite fishing families were able to do, everybody had "something to do." By comparison, school was viewed as infantilization, irrelevance and drudgery by most male stayers, who wanted to get on their feet and do "something constructive." They resisted school despite parental pressure to keep them there.

> I had to get in fishing by myself. But he [father] did show me a little that first couple of years, enough to get me started, you know. But I always went out with him as a young person, you know, five, six, seven years old. I'd go in the summertime with him and just watch him, watch how he done things. I was educating myself there. I didn't care about school. I mean, to set in them school houses all day to learn things that I knew wasn't much use [pause]. I was fifteen years old. I just knew that I had to get on the water. I didn't care if I could speak, I didn't care if I could write, I didn't care if I could read, I didn't care if I could add, I just needed to catch fish. It was just such a pull. I'd sneak away from the school and come down here and get in a rowboat, you know ten, twelve years old, get in a rowboat and go out fishin'. (KS-MS-71)

For women the situation was more complex. Getting a "good" education (defined as completing grade twelve) was desirable.

> The females are more mature about looking at education as having some value as compared to men. Well, certain guys will play hockey. But as far as student government types of things, yearbook, debates, liberal arts kinds of activities.... If it's not a physical kind of thing, males shy away. It doesn't fit their persona or something. (CQ-FE)

However, it was understood that obstacles were quite likely to intervene to cut short a school career. For men it was a question of how long a person could "stand" school and put off earning a full-time wage. Women in this cohort claim to have enjoyed school, but encountered obstacles, including lack of financial resources to continue education further than high school, confusion concerning education and career options, self-esteem issues, pregnancy and relationships with men, and the corollary pressure to slide into the well-worn groove of traditional women's roles.

> Back in 1970 now, it's like most of my friends and I, we all got married young. And that was sort of more what you thought was expected of you. You know, get married by twenty, and have your children by twenty-one, and then raise your family. It was different with my daughter. I can see that now. (DL-FS-69)

Most women who stayed became housewives, just as most of the men who stayed became fishermen. None of the women I interviewed in this cohort were in full-time employment, but all of them had worked outside the home, full- and part-time, at some point in their adult lives. None of the men ever worked at anything other than fishing or in a fish plant or fishing support work. Gender lines are clear and powerful for this generation.

Young men watched their friends going into the fishery, and they watched their father's generation of fishermen modernizing and investing in technological innovation and larger boats, often with government financial support. Just at the time that education opportunities were becoming more accessible, money in the modernizing fishery steadily improved. While most families supported the idea that young people ought to stay in school, the reasons for this view are unclear. The stronger the fishery, the less relevant school seemed for young men. For young women, a strong fishery meant more money in the family and better access to higher education.

As one man commented, "You kept the wolf from the door by workin', not by piling up a bunch of degrees" (FN). While the work retained much of its physical rigour, advances in fishing technology also took some of the physical misery out of the job, both creating a better level of comfort for fishers and the sense that the industry was entering a more sophisticated and lucrative phase. In what was perceived to be a low-risk climate, few men who were positioned to take advantage of the fishery saw much need for education "insurance." Taking time and money out for education, especially beyond high school, would take a man away from some potentially productive years, years when he might otherwise be establishing a position in the community and in the fishery.

> You know, we thought, what did he have to do all that for, he's just back here fishing. Here I am a few years ahead of you, I've got my own car and my own boat: what have you got? (GG-MS-71)

Schooling was also marginal to the experience of many stayers because of the relative or perceived poverty of families in the communities. Post-secondary and even secondary education were generally seen as an investment in impractical cultural capital that only the rich could afford. In the early 1970s the modernization of the fishery was beginning to create class divisions on Digby Neck. With social class formation came the accoutrements of privilege. Included in the array of middle-class advantages is access to higher education and the safe sort of social mobility that money facilitates.

> Well [pause] who's paying the tuition? Somebody's got to pay the tuition. The ones who went to college didn't have to worry too much about work because their families had money. (GG-MS-71)

Post-secondary education, even vocational education, was still seen by some respondents from non-elite fishing families as a burden families could ill afford.

> Well, I would have liked to have even gone to that business course at St. Pat's [high school in Digby]. Like I couldn't even afford that because it would have cost more money. My father and mother worked in the fish and there was just not even a thought of it because there was just no money. (TL-FL-65)

People had to act "responsibly" when they were old enough to work and help the family by becoming productive and independent. To be responsible was to opt for practical known ways to "help out" the family and, as Bourdieu put it, "make a virtue of necessity" (1984). This is prominent in the discourse of women in the sample, all of whom were "successful" in their high-school careers. These women were in a position where they felt they had to get into the work force as quickly as possible because there was insufficient family income to support a protracted post-secondary education experience.

> There wasn't any money. University was for people who had the

> ability to financially put themselves through. So my easiest way out was to switch into the secretarial program. I could come out of school with work. I could help out at home. Then I won't to be a financial burden. (DL-FS-69)

These accounts are consistent with the literature on working-class obstacles to learning and the kinds of "hidden injuries of class" described by Sennett and Cobb (1973) and Bourdieu (1984b). Male stayers felt these injuries in school, and they often constructed their identities as intelligent, hard-working, practical people against the way they were defined in school. One educator articulated how the "hidden injuries" are subtly inculcated in children from coastal communities.

> In our subtle way… we stigmatize it [rural identity], we make it agony. We go one step further than saying this is where you'll end up for your life. And because we're part of that institution where we think what we offer is mobility, we don't recognize that perhaps what is out there available to these people [in their communities] is equally important and equally as valuable. (CD-ME)

Given the nature of the community and the importance of multiple practical, hands-on skills, it should come as no surprise that so many young men left school before graduation. Beyond a basic level, male stayers did not see schooling as real learning at all. Rather they remember a process of confusion, character destruction and identity stripping. Most male stayers offered some variation on this general theme: that school was a place that bore little relationship to the identities they were building in their communities in the context of work in the fishery, in the home and in the community.

> It's your identity. I'm a fisherman. And like I say, in my day there was a lot of fishermen out there that's educated, they just, they kept their roots rather than using their wings. That's all they done. They're just as educated as that guy out there that's flying around in Toronto, but they stayed here. (GG-MS-71).

One informant articulated this analysis of what he calls the "missionary" work of the schools.[8] He saw in teachers' attitudes an implicit denunciation of the way of life in the community and the way people made their living.

> You weren't made to feel great about yourself and where you were from. You were conditioned that way in school. You know, a lot of teachers felt like they was almost like a missionary coming to liber-

ate you from this type of life. Those who don't make it, well maybe you can go fishing. (SS-MS-71)

The respondent above claimed that the education system has not served people in coastal communities well because it set its own vague agenda above work and life in the community and effectively provided a vision of a better life elsewhere. The difficulty is that this vision was virtually unattainable for a large part of the population, whose families lacked the resources as well as the sense of self necessary to attain it.

> That was always [pause] it seemed like that was the attitude when I was in school and stuff. You know, fishin', that's almost the same as working [pause]. Well, there was something wrong with that kind of job. (KS-MS-71)

Leaving school to do fisheries support work in peak times or otherwise continues to be a common practice in a limited way for young men, and to a lesser extent for young women, in the remaining fisheries, notably lobstering. There is an abundance of work at peak fishing times, and young people are trained to do it from a very early age. This informal training partly created a stigma around Digby Neck as a community. Teachers remember that from the 1960s through to the late 1980s, it was common for boys in fishing families to "disappear" for lengths of time and eventually permanently. For the young men of this cohort particularly, fishing clothes, lobster sandwiches in the lunch pail and coming from outside "town" were all marks of a lack of sophistication.

> Generally they ["town" people] looked down on it [fishing] and it was [pause] you were just an ignorant fisherman from Digby Neck or from wherever. And they used to kind of look down their nose at you. That was just part of your identity being off the Neck. (IS-ML-63)

While in later years these differences became positive badges of identity, this 1963–74 age cohort reported feeling very much outside the mainstream social world of the regional high school. Women tended to be less resistant to the implicit stigmatizing messages they too encountered in their schooling. Criticism of Digby Neck as a "primitive" place full of "ignorant" fishermen was generally understood to be levelled against men. But women also express similar perceptions and how only recently people in the community have begun to think differently about their own experiences and abilities.

> Today a lot more people believe that life experience can make you an educated person. I consider myself to be an educated person because of the things I've done. I've had an administrative job for

> seven years. Ten years ago I would never have thought that I'd be able to do that. It's experience that makes you educated. (FN)

The reflective perspective of these middle-aged informants reveal a clear understanding that they have been educated in the course of their lives, but it is an education that would not have been possible in school. Community experience and family life for instance have provided women with a practical education much as working in the fishery has provided men with their particular skill sets.

> As far as being educated... we're educated. Education is not just education from grade primary up to grade twelve in a classroom. You're educated in everyday life going from one thing to another. There's lessons that we have learned all through our lives that you could never get behind a classroom door. (DS-FS-69)

Men never spoke of their education careers in terms of an exploration of their interests or talents. Women did and felt disadvantaged in comparison with their own children, who had the benefit of counselling and what they saw as a more humanistic form of schooling. These women claim they were not given an opportunity to "look inside themselves" and evaluate their own potential. In the absence of this opportunity or training to analyze the self, these women found themselves drawn into the well-trodden life paths on display in the community.

In the emerging therapeutic culture of the contemporary mass media many women now see in their life histories a failure to gain a clear sense of modern reflexivity, to imagine their lives as what Giddens (1990, 1991) calls a "project," where one has significant choices to make and where the self is something one "constructs" rather than inherits. They simply "fit in" to what they considered at the time to be the expected woman's role. Connected to this weak sense of reflexivity, the women in the sample also report a strong strain of uncertainty about the purpose and the ends of the whole enterprise of formal education, particularly beyond high school. Comparing her own experience to that of her adult children this informant spoke quite clearly of this ambiguity about the ends of education or the possibilities to which schooling might be connected.

> There was nobody telling you to look within yourself and think about what you're gonna' do or what you're interested in. When I thought about high school I thought, what was I going to do, and I couldn't see anything. You were told to go to school, but the "why" wasn't very clear. (DS-FS-69)

This respondent now understands her life in retrospect as a reflexive "project," but her community contained limited role models, and subsequently, a limited vision of what education was indeed for. In order to construct a self reflexively, one needs to have a sense of alternative possibilities or to see the self as an open set of options rather than a set of fixed roles. Giddens argues that this is a key feature of life in a post-traditional society. To see options one needs both a choice oriented or individuated perspective as well as access to resources and the absence of material and ideological constraints. Some informants saw school as a place where things just didn't fit with the world as they knew it. Nebulous, frightening or unattractive "opportunities" were offered in school, and school learning tasks were often constructed as "invisible" and related to skills and materials which had no tangible place in the community. For instance, informants routinely commented that they could see no purpose in what they were learning or where the trajectory of formal education was leading. As they continued in school, the work expected of students became more and more disconnected from the habitus of life in the community.

> There was no boredom that I can remember, it was work, work, work and everyone did it. But school, well that was work, work, work too, and I liked it, but [pause] I don't know, it just seemed like a crossword puzzle or a trivia contest. It didn't have anything to do with anything people did around here. (FN)

## Leaving Home: Education and Occupational Pioneering

> When I left Nova Scotia to go to university in Ontario, I wasn't prepared for what confronted me. Other students were light years ahead of me, in some areas. And I'd never lived in a city before and I was terribly homesick. (SF-ML-67)

> Well, I think a lot that came out here [Western Canada] got homesick and wanted to go back. But I got out here and there was hunting and fishing and all that I liked to do, and so I stayed. We have fog here and seagulls here and they come up here and holler and scream, just like home. (HL-ML-69)

All informants (including educators) report that in this period, Digby Neck remained relatively isolated and insular in social terms. While family vehicles had become common by the 1960s, they were not used in many families for journeys beyond the "around here" region.

> When I was young, well if we went to town (Digby), that was a big event. You might go once a month. (DS-FS-69)

Those who left Digby Neck in the 1960s and early 1970s faced a variety of significant challenges and an uncertain future that could not be mapped by local knowledge. Educators who began their teaching careers in the 1960s and 1970s were amazed at how many of their high-school students had never travelled outside the local area. This lack of exposure of other places contributed to a particular kind of resistance to mobility and education-related life options.

> I remember when I came to this area being blown away by the number of kids who had never been as far as Halifax. There was just no desire, no inclination, no effort to know anything beyond immediate confines. (GG-FE)

Living in other places has presented and continues to present significant emotional, social and financial challenges for youth from coastal communities regardless of their social position.

> I was eighteen or nineteen when I got out of school and never been out of Centreville before in my life so I was so homesick. [But] I didn't want to stay around the Neck. (RR-FL-70)

The visceral experience of living in a city alone was sufficiently traumatic to influence a great many prospective migrants to turn around and return to Nova Scotia. Most leavers reported missing the physical setting of the coastal community and the comfort of the ocean, even if they saw the place as unsustainable or unsatisfying in many respects. Digby Neck is home for leavers as much as it is for stayers.

> I mean you love it. You love it there, I think we have the best house, right next to the ocean. When I moved, I was like a fish out of water. (FE-FL-73)

> I miss the people. They're friendly and that. I got a lot of relations back there. It's a nice place to go, quiet and peaceful. (HL-ML-69)

For people raised there in the 1950s and 1960s, the coastal community is a known universe, a place where most people felt comfortable not only at a social level and in terms of their families, but also at the level of the physical environment. Yet, the vast majority of this cohort who went on to post-secondary education left the community. Despite unsupported local folklore about a number of fishermen with university degrees, very few people in this cohort with any post-secondary education remain on Digby Neck. Most of the stayers in this cohort understood education as a "toolkit" for those who wished to make their lives elsewhere. "Most of the ones who stayed in school are somewhere else," is a more accurate common perception. When the education enterprise was "successful," the person would leave the community for the array of "opportunities" in other places. When the individual "failed" or defaulted on the mobility offered by schooling, the community provided a life.

> You know the whole thing through school was get your education and move on to something different. If you were successful, then you'd be able to move on. If you weren't, well, you'd probably have to stay here and find something to do. And I don't really think [pause] I think it's a thing people have had to learn to live with.... You're told to look at this group of people away over here and that these people are doing great. Well, how come this other one stayed here all his life? Well, he's not noteworthy. (SS-MS-71)

For those who left Digby Neck, post-secondary education was a social as well as a geographic migration. University-bound leavers tended to feel unsophisticated and out of place in university. While they found the experience fulfilling in the end, they report significant transition difficulties, ranging from feeling unprepared academically to feeling "at sea" socially. Urban students already had significant support networks in place, and university was, for them, an extension of high school.

> I went to university and I then left and came back home after about six weeks. And I remember the trip back, and I knew that I had made a terrible mistake about leaving university and I knew that I had to do it. But I was very lonely because I didn't know anybody. I was confronted with high-school students who went to university with all their buddies. They had sort of moved one community into another. Well, I didn't have that luxury. (SF-ML-67)

The university-educated leavers in this cohort really saw no options for themselves other than pursuing higher education and moving to another place no matter how difficult this transition might be. In contrast to the "rooted' stayers of their generation (who were generally unable to imagine a life outside the community at the decisive point in their adolescence), university-bound migrants were unable to imagine life in the coastal community. The privilege of seeing options outside the community made leaving a foregone conclusion for university- and professionally-bound women.

> I couldn't see myself staying there although some of my friends did and all of my mother's generation. I guess you sort of felt like it was nice and comfortable for them anyway. It's a nice place to visit kind

> of thing, you know? I went into nursing and I knew I wouldn't be coming back except to visit. (RR-FL-70)

A combination of the strong desire to do other things and see other places, access to financial resources, as well as a strong repulsion to traditional work in the fishery or in traditional women's roles made the difficult move to other places palatable for migrants. While they continue to have strong attachments to family and to place, leavers could not have imagined themselves staying and doing work they "couldn't do." So while other places were intimidating in a number of ways for leavers in this cohort, the alternative to leaving was even less attractive.

> My friends back then wanted to keep everything the same. I guess they found that comfortable. It's funny, it's changed and it hasn't. I see a lot fewer boats, but I see a lot of familiar people doing the same things they were back then. I don't know how they can put up with that. But then they probably don't know how I could just up and leave like I did. (RR-FL-70)

Both the urban environment and the university setting provided a significant social challenges to leavers of this cohort, who were accustomed to a familiar social environment in the coastal community. The "luxury" of an urban upbringing includes the visibility of universities, other cultures, people of different social classes working in a variety of occupations and the general mix of difference that is absent in many rural communities and coastal villages. Part of this urban privilege is daily immersion in a diverse social space and economic geography. This is a story of a doubly challenged individual, challenged not only by the social-class habitus of higher education, but also by the isolation of urban living, an isolation made particularly acute because this man left a tightly structured, family-based, predictable life in a coastal community. The familiarity with difference, combined with the presence of school friends, made university a more comfortable and predictable place for this leaver's urban classmates.

> I knew when I was fairly young that I was going to leave but I wasn't prepared for the shock of leaving the village and everything familiar. I was afraid, kind of lonely. I think I was more sort of bewildered than anything else. It was a totally different culture, a culture that I wasn't familiar with at all. (SF-ML-67)

## I Didn't Want to End Up…

> And it's a shame they just stay there because the world is so beautiful. I'm just not one to be stagnant, there's just too much out there and life is too short. I'd hate to just sit here and think, gee, I didn't really accomplish anything with my life. I want to be able to look back and say I had a great life. I don't want to say, well yeah, I had fifteen kids and now I got ninety-nine grandchildren or something. That's just not enough. That's a wonderful thing and I'm not knocking it, but that's just not enough. (FE-FL-73)

> But the people around here [a western Canadian city] talk about the Maritimes in a funny way. I guess it's a place you love to visit but you still can't figure out why people stay there all the time. Maybe it's like visiting Disney World. I mean you don't want to stay in Disney World all the time. And that seems to be it, the Maritimes is a place where not much happens and that's why it's a good place for a vacation. Nova Scotia is like a summer cottage, a place you go to relax, but it isn't a real place. (FN)

Leavers tend to see Digby Neck as an almost mythical place, a childhood home that is remembered with fondness, but with a sense of unreality. They think of it as a romantic, pastoral vacation place. What emerges is a picture of a place that has been both tainted by modernity and capitalist relations of production but which at the same time retains elements of the rustic, quaint, folkloric fishing village (McKay, 1994).

> We just couldn't understand why all the other boats were taking everything that was there, the U.S. boats and I can't remember who all was there. But they were taking anything and everything. It was harder and harder all the time for the little guy to make it. The bigger companies were buying up the small companies and most of the work was on a company boat. (FN)

Given the changes in the fishery, staying was seen by leavers as a kind of stagnation. This perception is typical of both men and women, who did not want to "end up" spending their whole lives in what was seen as the very limited environment of Digby Neck. Male leavers particularly saw staying as not only stagnation but struggle. All leavers reported that those who remained in the Neck faced a struggle, implying that those who did stay were both willing to suffer hardship and to be adaptable and resilient. Not only have stayers faced the hard work that is traditional in the Atlantic fishery, they are also now faced with having to learn how to survive in the context of globalization, capitalist development and industrialization of fisheries work, and the concomitant demise of fish stocks.

> If I didn't have that [education] I imagine I'd be fishing or trying to anyway. It's not so easy right now. Hard to figure out how to make money down there 'cause all they knew is fishing. Right now my brothers are kind of stuck. They're kind of old now to try to do anything else. (HL-ML-69)

While work in the Digby Neck fishery was a struggle and something all of the leavers in the sample were subtly encouraged to escape, the struggle and its familiar setting on Digby Neck and on the Bay of Fundy made it attractive to many male stayers. One stayer described this environment aptly as "comfortable tough," echoing Ursula Kelly's comment about life in rural Newfoundland being rough, yet familiar territory, or Paul Willis's evocation of the way the "lads" came to accept the brutal work they saw as their lot (1977). Stayers struggle on against the odds. Leavers in this cohort find this to be a particularly insecure way to live.

> I think a lot of 'em [leavers] thought of it as a struggle. I mean it wasn't that horrible. And there are some who like a familiar struggle, the same life your parents had. Even if it's tough you still want it because it's a comfortable tough. (FN)

The industrialization of the fishery changed the nature of the familiar struggle, introducing new elements of risk and uncertainty that developed more fully in the next decades (the late 1970s–1990s). By the mid-1960s, family strategies and assessments of prospects in the fishery varied, with some elite families making major investments to modernize their fishing operations with the support of low-interest loans and grants. Leavers point out that it was mainly established fish-dragging families that were able to take advantage of this kind of opportunity. The irony is that it is also this kind of family that was best positioned to take advantage of post-secondary education as well. Male children of elite fishing families were "lured" out of school and into the fishery. Without reasonable prospects that education and other places could provide viable alternatives, young people from less advantaged families were willingly forced into the fishery.

Women leavers describe leaving behind a place in which their options were restricted to the point of stagnation. They were typically careful not to criticize their parents and brothers who inherited fishing privileges, as well as members of their own peer groups who remained on Digby Neck

> I love where I come from but it just didn't have anything to offer for women. We didn't buy boats, we didn't go fishing. So if you didn't

> do that [pause] and if you didn't just marry someone, heaven forbid, and that to me was just like ending your life, you had to move on. There, it's like [pause] well, you don't have a choice. You either have to go on or you're stuck behind. (FE-FL-73)

Approximately 40 percent of men stayed on Digby Neck while only 15 percent of women remained there through the thirty-six years that the survey covered. Women leavers and stayers both understood school to be the principal means of social mobility. School was seen as something that a woman could do in the 1960s and 1970s if she wanted to forge a different kind of life. If a woman did not want to remain in the community, and could afford it, then education was seen as the way to avoid "getting stuck." Like their stayer counterparts, women in this sample of leavers describe generally positive, if bland, secondary-school experiences. By contrast, male leavers claim that they were able to migrate and build successful lives outside their home communities in spite of their high-school experience rather than because of it.

Women leavers report never having "gotten serious" with a local man. For leavers, a romantic involvements with a local man leading to pregnancy was a significant threat to mobility aspirations, because having a child meant the termination of a young woman's school career in virtually all cases.

> I think a lot of them [stayers] had boyfriends really, really young and they were [pause] they got more involved with them. So they were married earlier. I never really got serious about anyone. But I find when they did get serious over someone they married and then they don't get any further. (TL-FL-65)

Female leavers in this cohort assumed that they had to both acquire education beyond the high school level and leave the community. There were, as they put it, "no opportunities" available for women of their generation. Young men were given the opportunity to go fishing even if it was not always the path encouraged by parents. For young men, fishing was the locally based default option.

> Well my father was very generous with him [brother]. You know he took him in. He wanted to fish and they didn't stop him. They let him do it. (RR-FL-70)

> I think, like before, when I was in school, the men, they almost always stayed there. But I think, for girls, that is how they saw it definitely, you had to leave. (TL-FL-65)

Regardless of their family's position in the fishery, women did not inherit fishing privileges and licences; in fact, women leavers in this sample report being actively discouraged from doing fisheries related work. While they were not actively encouraged to leave, they were actively discouraged from engaging in the only kinds of activity that would have allowed them to stay.

> I don't think my mom really wanted me to [work in the fish plant]. She'd say that's no place for a girl, your hands are in cold water all day. It wasn't a glamorous job. (FE-FL-73)

Since fisheries related work was virtually the only work available on Digby Neck, the logical conclusion to be drawn by young women is that their opportunities lay outside the community and that these opportunities were accessible only through education. Women of this cohort were effectively forced to continue with education at least to the high-school level unless they "chose" to marry a fisherman. This compulsion is reflected in the consistently higher levels of both education credentials and out-migration for women reported in Chapter 5.

Marriage was seen as a legitimate "career choice" and served as the default option for women in this sample. As one educator commented, "There was certainly no stigma attached to marrying a fisherman in those days." Still, default options are denoted by the prefix, "just a." If one chose the default path, one became "just a fisherman" or "just a housewife." All women in the sample of stayers in this cohort were married before the age of twenty. None of the women leavers I interviewed in this cohort were married until the completion of some post-secondary training or education. Women could achieve community-defined success by marrying a successful fisherman and being in a position where she did not have to work and could afford a well appointed house, very often built on family land.

> Anybody that… I don't know why people decided to stay, unless that was their goal, to grow up and get married. Um, certainly it wasn't mine. I mean I guess, go to school and if you got your grade twelve and lucky enough to get a boyfriend and marry him and if he had a good job like fishing and he was doing well, I guess you were looked at as doing pretty good. (FE-FL-73)

Educators expressed frustration at what they perceived to be the majority of young women of this cohort moving directly from school into domestic situations. Female leavers saw no options other than to move, and stayers saw no options other than to stay. Educators could see habitual patterns being recapitulated.

> And it was off to get married, right out of school. They thought it was wonderful, their mothers thought it was wonderful. It's supposed to be bliss, but you could see those old patterns being repeated. (OI-FE)

While many women did move into domestic situations, the large majority of them did so off Digby Neck. The further they moved from Digby Neck, the less likely it is that they report "housewife" as their principal occupation. The traditional image of domestic femininity and reliance on the earning power of men was rejected by female leavers. Village life held few attractions for them other than the physical beauty of the place and family ties. Leavers saw little comfort in well known daily routines. Where stayers spoke of family based enterprises, comfort and familiarity, leavers tended to see oppression and a lack of challenge.

> At that time in my life I really wanted badly to get out of there. I saw people doing the same things that their own mothers had done. That wasn't for me. I didn't want to marry a fisherman, I wanted to do something for myself. Maybe I just never fell in love in high school [laughs]. (RR-FL-70)

The older members of the cohort can remember sexist and anti-education attitudes in the community. Women had to resist the idea that formal education was a dead-end that represented a prolonged childhood. Without the economic opportunity the fishery provided young men of this cohort, young women were faced with few options should they choose to stay. Women's activity was stratified into the very narrow band of domestic labour and on-shore fisheries support work. Describing the climate of gendered opportunities in the mid-1960s in the community, this male leaver commented:

> Once they [women] got married, say seventeen or eighteen, well that was it, they just dropped out of school, they weren't interested at all. And nobody pushed them in those times either because education, especially for women, wasn't a big thing unless she was an exceptional student. (IS-ML-63)

These accounts explain the gap between male and female migration rates from Digby Neck reported in Chapter 5. Gender quite clearly structured local opportunity available to stayers and provided a strong influence on migration and education decision-making in the 1960s and early 1970s.[9] The power of gender segregation in traditional resource-based labour markets is remarkably entrenched.

## Resisting Displacement

> I think again of a family in the community. This is my boat, this is my wife, these are my eight sons and my six daughters or whatever and we know who we are and this is our place. In all the layers that this applies to is a real sense of who I am and pride in that. There's that clear sense of who I am and what I believe in, there's no wishy-washiness about it. They know who they are. (SR-FE)

The 1963–1974 cohort are now parents of young adults in and out of the community. They are also community leaders attempting to understand and respond to what appear to be massive changes in the structure of life on Digby Neck. While they see formal education as an important strategic resource for young people in the emerging community, credentialism is also thought to be the principal justification for ignoring "uneducated" voices from coastal communities. The paradox of education is that it is constructed as a functional necessity, but one that holds questionable and largely unexplored utility "around here." Many Digby Neckers support their own children's education but are often nervous about the estrangement and mobility implications it contains. Some felt that education would probably take their children away. Others argued that education is now necessary to develop Digby Neck in the emerging tourist industry and the regulation and political/legal struggles ahead in the fishery.

> I don't know what you'd do [without formal education]. Live on welfare around these areas. We, as an area around here, need so much and we've got so many resources. I mean our lobster fishery is still good, and there's other fisheries out there. We need managers, we need scientists, we need it all. The area's got potential for tourism and we haven't tapped it; we need to be smart. (KS-MS-71)

All of these informants are more or less aware of the forces at play, at the level of the state and at the level of the corporate fishery, working to undermine the economic basis of the small-boat fishery and by extension of the community itself. Fisheries problems are often set in terms of tradition and family inheritance. Fishing licences and boats are traditionally passed along from father to son. While only one of the women in this cohort mentioned the sexism inherent in this practice, most of the men bemoaned the lack of opportunities faced by their own male children in the fishery, even if they themselves are licence holders and boat owners. The twin forces of state policy and the corporate offshore fisheries sector have, in community discourse, steadily and relentlessly conspired to usurp the small-boat family-based inshore fishery. The idea that this process of state-supported, corporate resource concentration will triumph is the single most important source of Digby Neckers' resistance. They realize that the central struggle is one of basic community survival against a hostile corporate fishery and a "government" that has consistently "sold us out" to "big players." Lobster licences are now worth as much as a million dollars on the open market. As one resident put it, if stayers are "rooted" in the community, there are a lot of "shovels" digging away at that root.

> I will survive and I will be happy. Take away my [fishing] licence and my children can't stay here. They are forced, they have to leave. They have to eat, and they have to have shelter to live. And if you take that root away, that's what I am, and here are them old shovels digging around it and it may get loose. It was just like I told you about one fishermen who has had a few bad years, and his ass is up against the wall. If you offer him enough money, he'll sell.... He's forty or more years old and his wings have never been tried. You take his roots and he's adrift I guess. (GG-MS-71)

Digby Neckers understand that every time a fisherman sells out and his "rights" are cashed in, there are young men who will not be able to make a living in the community. Education plays an ambivalent role in this whole drama. Many people in coastal communities see themselves as an endangered species, or as this informant put it, as rooted plants threatened by a multitude of "shovels." Education is not seen as another shovel *per se*, but educated people are thought to use their credentials as "shovels" against people in coastal communities. The informant quoted above went on to speak of the way that bureaucrats are complicit in community destruction and forcing young people to move by offering their parents lucrative buy-out packages.

> It says in this letter that he'll [the federal minister of Fisheries and Oceans] give me this much money to buy all my licences and all my privileges. That's just bait in front of me. Right now I'm not hungry, but some day I might have to bite, whether I want to or not. And it'll hurt me. I could get a half million dollars. Geez, that's a lot of money, isn't it? I oughta' go for that. I could take that right to the bank and probably, if I did it right, I could live on that. You hear me saying, "I could live off her." Well what about two boys that I got, and two girls, what are they going to live off of? If I sell out, they're gone. (GG-MS-71)

All of the stayers interviewed in this cohort have both male and female children living and working in the community, many in family fishing operations. The men have been integrated into the fishery, and the women living on Digby Neck are either homemakers or between jobs. Those who stay tend to conform to traditional gender patterns. And those who go, women particularly, tend not to go very far away. The analysis of data in Chapter 5 showed that while women were more prone to out-migration they mostly moved into the near regions "around here" and "not far." One fisherman offered this comment about his daughter's prospects:

> She felt at the time that she'd have to leave the area, and I felt it too. I says, "Mary, probably the only way you're gonna' be able to use that course is you're gonna' have to leave." There's not much work for her in her field around here, not yet anyway. She knows that to use that education [pause] hopefully she can use it around here. (KS-MS-71)

Because of their relative success in secondary education, women were able to glimpse something of the vista of education opportunities that might have been available to them. But the lure or the necessity of making ready money was paramount. Many of the women who took secretarial training or hairdressing (which were the options of choice for young women who needed to get out to work quickly) migrated to the middle-distant "not far" region. These career choices allowed them to remain in southwestern Nova Scotia but to still have some occupational mobility in traditional gendered trades. Only a select few in this cohort had the resources to access significant post-secondary education. Few families had yet established the resources necessary to offer elite post-secondary education to their children.

For men, the lure of the ready money in fishing and the sense that higher education is designed for those who want to be somewhere else (a perception that was well supported in the community and in the school) ended the school careers of many aspiring fishermen. From there they attended what some fishermen in this cohort call the "University of the Bay of Fundy."

> It always seemed to me like school was for those ones that wanted to go on to university. I knew I was going to stay around here and I was going to go fishing. It was just a matter of when. And I stayed in school there until my old man told me [pause] well, until I figured it was time I got to work full time. School was starting to get in the way of making real money. So in grade eleven, I quit. (FN)

## Conclusion

Class, race and gender are generally considered to be differences that matter in terms of education outcomes. Teacher training programs and academic publications include critical, interpretive, postcolonial, poststructural, phenomenological and feminist discourse, all of which serve to help teachers understand how education is a fundamentally political enterprise and one which requires investigation of the relationship between the teacher and the taught, and between the society and the school. Yet, the bulk of this discourse seems to ignore the fact that not all places are urban, that the grand project of modernity, the depopulation of rural spaces, is incomplete and resisted by many individuals whose cultural capital is negotiable in local markets, spaces into which they are "born and bred." As rurality and small community habitus play together with class and gender we see that individuals saw different sets of possibilities, different visions of the self that might be attained. Through the 1960s and on into the mid-1970s, enacting a credible masculine identity in the space of the coastal community was not compatible with protracted schooling, and as a result most men dropped out of school.

This analysis suggests that the nature of a staples-oriented community and its economic base influences the way schooling is perceived by the people who live there. Staples capitalism in this coastal community provided traditional occupational and social roles for a significant proportion of young men through the 1960s and 1970s. A central problematic facing young people in coastal communities has always been to stay or to go, because these communities themselves operate at the margins of something bigger. The vision of that larger world and how one might access its opportunities is not equally distributed among individuals. In order to consider the "options," one must first be able to observe them and then have the resources to access them. The accounts of this cohort show how these "options" were not equally accessible or even visible. Most "had to" work or quit school, and others "wanted to" fish, get married or take secretarial training. The point is that both desire and compulsion are constructed in the context of the habitus that organizes resources at hand, structuring an array of socially "reasonable" options.

For the 1963–1974 cohort of stayers in the coastal communities along Digby Neck, post-secondary and even secondary education sat in an ambivalent position. The community contained an established core of elite fishing families, who found economic success by intensive and extensive adaptation of local knowledge to modern harvesting technologies. Stories of the economic success of hard-working fisherman of this generation who achieved independence and even wealth without formal education represents a powerful community myth that continues to have educational consequences. Men who possessed the requisite cultural capital learned this curriculum rather than the one on offer in school. Women who stayed did so mainly because they saw few other realistic options. This lack of options must be counterbalanced with the prosperity and activity in the local fishery, which needed the active support of a cadre of hard-working, multi-skilled women who would stay and do the work of social reproduction and child-rearing in the community. Because the family was the central locus of productive activity for the small-boat fishery through this period, women's work added direct support to the main economic activity of the community. I demonstrated in Chapter 3 that relatively few women who grew up on Digby Neck stayed to marry local men. They were more likely to migrate short distances to marry men "around here." Digby Neck fishermen typically married "women from Digby" or from nearby communities "across the (St. Mary's) Bay." More research could be done into marriage and migration patterns in the "around here" region.

Neither men nor women felt victimized by their "choices." Most feel secure and content for themselves, but they worry about their children because the community-based cultural capital that has sustained them and previous generations is now of questionable value, even "around here." This is not new; the Stirling County research team found the same sentiment in the area in the early 1950s (Hughes et al., 1960). Work and entrepreneurial skills, along with deep local knowledge of fishing grounds and strategies, had visible payoffs for successful fishermen who were able to take advantage of strong family networks. But the precarious nature of the contemporary fishery led many to conclude that this knowledge and these skills will have limited value for upcoming generations of the "born and bred."

Community and family-based strategies of production have remained prominent for stayers in this cohort, mirroring ethnographic findings from similar kinds of communities (Lofty, 1992; Kearney, 1993; Porter, 1993; Lawrence, 1998; Johnson, 1999; Binkley, 2002). While the numbers of families able to survive restructuring in the fishery have declined, traditional patterns of initiation and inheritance remain. The 1963–74 cohort now have children old enough to take up the inheritance. As it was with their fathers, some boys are able to stay and take advantage of remaining fisheries. As it was with their female relatives, most girls must leave to seek their fortune elsewhere. As this parent/educator commented, speculating on the future of a capable young Digby Neck women from the high-school graduating class of 2000:

> It's a shame to say it but I'd like to see her go because I think that she has [pause] she's smart. There's no one here on the Neck to get in with to stay. There's no boys, no one. I mean if she wants to

> find someone she's going to have to get out and she's not going to bring him back. Usually it's the boys who have the job around here. Nobody's going to take him on. (ES-FE)

In *Learning to Labour*, Paul Willis tried to explain why the working-class boys seem to interpellate themselves into what he considered to be miserable, meaningless work. My data suggest that in coastal communities, the equation of manual work and meaninglessness is not nearly as simple as Willis suggests. I am not romanticizing manual labour; in fact, no respondents explicitly mentioned the mental/manual work dichotomy. The fishery of the 1960s and early 1970s offered machismo but also petty capitalist entrepreneurial opportunity to a wide variety of young men on Digby Neck, while those born into elite fishing families integrated into larger scale economic possibilities in the emerging dragger fishery. Willis understands the power of the working-class network to integrate the young into its routines and its value system. However, his description of the alienating nature of factory work for the "lads" is not what I found in the coastal community.

Social meaning is generated in coastal communities through manual work and an intimate knowledge of the physical and social geography accompanying that work (Durrenberger, 1997; Gatewood, 1985; Matthews, 1976, 1993; Palsson, 1999; Pocius, 1991; Porter, 1993). Fishing is not a simple monolithic occupation. As other researchers have pointed out, there are many different types of employment and work relations within any given fishery (Davis, 1991; Kearney, 1993). These range from captaining and owning a large offshore vessel, to owning and operating a small-boat inshore "rig," to crewing on a large corporate-owned vessel, to crewing on a small family-owned inshore vessel, to working in a fish plant, to working onshore in temporary fishing support work, either for cash or for free to a family fishing operation. These are essentially class positions, and they carry with them different rewards and different access to community-based resources, particularly fishing licences, and non-community-based resources, like higher education credentials. In order to leave the coastal community and follow the path to elsewhere, one needed either money or family connections, and preferably both. Without these it was virtually impossible to "blaze the trail" to elsewhere.

Education was clearly one form of transit for this cohort, but class-based financial restrictions combined with a lack of social and cultural capital made the transition from the coastal community and into post-secondary education very difficult for all youth, particularly those from families whose connection to the fishery was marginal and based on selling labour. Not only did potential leavers need the financial resources to meet tuition and living costs outside the community, they were also required to establish social networks without support while constructing an identity that would allow them to "pass for middle class," as one leaver put it. Different communities provide youth with different familial, or what Bourdieu called "cultural capital," resources. The cultural capital resources that were at the fingertips of urban university students were missing for most of their rural counterparts, who were faced instead with a series of social puzzles and unfamiliar routines as fundamental as dealing with public transit and smog, living among strangers in cramped spaces or finding rooms in large buildings.

For stayers, this "deficit" in middle-class, schooling-oriented cultural capital became increasingly apparent the further they progressed in their secondary school careers. For males who had strong connections to the fishery, the increasingly obscure academic expectations and subject matter of the high school came to be perceived as irrelevant. The further they went in school the more esoteric the knowledge seemed to become. So paradoxically, at the very point in their personal lives when they felt that education ought to have become more focused on the practicalities of a career, the exact opposite happened, and Shakespeare and algebra entered their lives. Many accounts juxtapose the "naturalness" of learning to fish for the "born and bred" fisherman with the strained and abstracted schooled learning of secondary and post-secondary education.

At the same time, Digby Neckers were experiencing a stigma connected to their community and personal identities that served to reinforce the idea that they were rough and rude and not the "kind of people" who stayed in school, followed its rules and believed in what it had to offer. The culture of the fishing community was subtly and overtly undermined and criticized in both the formal and informal culture of the school. The results were often a predictable retreat from the ethereal content of academic subjects into the practical and immediate rewards of the community occupational structure.

It is too simple to suggest (as some educators I interviewed have) that through the 1960s and early 1970s, the possession of a Digby Neck identity was a source of some measure of self-conscious shame. A Digby Neck identity seems to have been an ambivalent possession for this cohort. Digby Neckers had specialized knowledge of a particular social and economic geography in which they knew what to expect and how to "turn a buck." This is cultural capital or knowledge that is limited in its portability. On wharves and on boats, men get together to do their specialized work. This work defined manhood. The nature of this work, its routines and challenges (and the stories that surround it) are common-sense, local knowledge. City people, tourists and school teachers are among those species of pathetic, stupid creatures who do not know what "common sense" is and who become the butt of jokes not unlike those told by the Western Apache about "Whitemen" (Basso, 1979). This common sense was also evident in the calm competence of "fishermen's wives," who organized social gatherings and successfully managed complex financial and family affairs. Young people saw this adult competence and many of them worked to emulate it. But at another level, and often through their experience in school and via the mass media, young people also saw a wider social picture, a different set of possibilities and competences, a different kind of language. In the 1950s and 1960s particularly, this fishing-based identity was often associated with poverty, hard, brutal work in horrible conditions and with simple, rustic living. There was often a sense that other people were more sophisticated and had, in most ways, better lives. But the stigma was tempered by a sense of community, resilience, toughness, integration, intimate local knowledge and belonging that constituted the resources of survival and the basis of wealth for a select few.

Into the 1970s and 1980s, when incomes from the fishery improved, this fishing identity came to be a source of pride and a positive sense of difference. Both of these identity positions fostered resistant attitudes in school. In the former period, Digby Neckers resisted their portrayal as poor fishermen who were not capable of succeeding at school or behaving in a civilized manner. In the latter period, they resisted even more vigorously, perhaps because they could afford to. For them, schooling was thought to be of little practical value for working people and a less profitable personal choice even for those who could have afforded it. Both poverty and wealth provided a platform for resistance to protracted schooling and higher education. With limited formal education many Digby Neck males were able to use their local community cultural capital, the ability and willingness to work hard, to access the employment structure on Digby Neck and, until the 1980s, by migrating to take up working-class positions in other parts of the province and the country.

Families from all social classes on Digby Neck had little historical experience in higher education. The vast majority of those few individuals who had acquired post-secondary education prior the 1960s had moved to larger centres. Thus, the typical urban connection between middle-class incomes and formal education has never existed on Digby Neck. In fact, my analysis of income and schooling, using Census Canada micro data, shows how income may in some circumstances be negatively associated with formal education on Digby Neck (see Chapter 3). Local knowledge about the dubious "value" of schooling if one is to remain is apparently supported by this ethnographic data. Wealth acquired without much formal education implicitly justified acceptance of poor education performance and low-level education outcomes of many young men. In other words, while virtually everyone mentioned parental support for their education, it was generally the case that this support seldom went any further than mild verbal encouragement. Indeed, where else could it go, given that even extended secondary education was a new experience for most Digby Neck families in the 1960s and 1970s? For the children of working-class Digby Neck families the picture is more consistent with the literature on working-class resistance to schooling. They were marginalized in school, and they marginalized themselves because they lacked both the financial and cultural capital necessary to make higher education a legitimate possibility.

Gender plays an important role in understanding who stays and who leaves and who goes on to access higher education. Young women typically understood that they had to leave, but their routes out of the community differed according to family position. While young men of all social classes lacked the social and financial capital to make higher education a desirable life choice, young women from elite fishing families were encouraged to pursue higher education and to seek their futures away from Digby Neck. Unlike their male counterparts, young women from these families tended to want to leave home because they saw how they lacked the community-based "capital" that their brothers possessed. These young women grew up in families where lucrative fishing operations provided a good family income, but they had no opportunity to access the means of wealth generation. For these young women, education and professional careers, or alternatively, marrying into a middle-class family through social liaisons in university were actively promoted in the 1970s–1990s. These families used financial capital from fishing to buy the education credentials for female children that would allow them to rmaintain family economic position, albeit off Digby Neck.

For young women from working-class families, access to opportunities in the fisheries was similarly bleak. A minority remained on Digby Neck to marry into fishing families, although because of the small population base and questions of endogamy, this was often not encouraged. Those who stayed have worked in fishing support occupations on the Neck or found work commuting to Digby and the surrounding area. Education resistance made little sense for women in this cohort. Some of these women have acquired post-secondary credentials, and a couple of them university degrees. More women migrated to the "around here" and "not far" regions surrounding Digby Neck, marrying and settling in nearby communities. These women too were, for the most part, compelled to leave, but their migration routes did not typically involve higher education, but rather marriage and part- or full-time employment in the service sector. Even in cases where they apparently possessed the cultural capital and the strong secondary credential to access university, financial constraints and the weight of community and family habitus made it very unlikely that these young women would access high status post-secondary credentials. This was the common story of the "good student" who for no reason apparent (to teachers) rejected university for a one year secretarial course or for an early marriage. Like their male counterparts, many of these young women were unable to see the purpose of schooling. Unlike their male counterparts they were better "socialized" to "set still" to meet the demands of school and to be less openly resistant to the irrelevance they found there.

Finally, it needs to be said that this cohort of stayers are now the established adult members of the community of Digby Neck. They have lived through the relative economic prosperity of the industrialization and privatization of the fishery. Many of these families control fishing licences and fish quotas, which have been increasing in value in recent years. They have also seen how the commodification and privatization of fishing privileges has created the current situation, that has radically destabilized their own position in the fishery and particularly that of their children. Some families have benefitted from this process and they now hold considerable fish quotas and multiple licences. Many though, see that the life and the community they have built through their adult lives are in deep trouble, and they are in trouble because of what one fisherman called "these educated people." Contemporary attitudes to education are in large measure shaped by this generation of citizens who have stayed on to protect the culture, economy and social structure of Digby Neck.

Playing counterpoint to the iconic hard-working, independent fisher, there are two kinds of archetypical educated people who are particularly reviled. The first type is the bureaucrat who "sits" in an office and decides fisheries policy so that it favours corporate interests. These educated people want an "efficient" fishery, meaning as small a number of professional fishers as possible harvesting the available stocks. The result of this will be fewer seasonal workers and thus fewer people eligible for transfer payments. This contraction of the work force in the fishery and in coastal communities will essentially force out-migration into urban places where labour is needed. It is the old economically rational, water pump (Papastergiadis, 2000) model of migration. To many Digby Neck families, this entire process is effectively destroying the life they know.

The second type of "educated person" also sits in an office and controls fish. This person has bought fish quota on the open market. They may also have bought fishing licences that are supposed to be fished by an owner-operator, who must remain aboard the boat attached to the licence. But these educated people who "own fish swimming in the water" hire other educated people (lawyers) to draw up trust agreements that allow the corporate fisher, whose hands never cut a fish and whose feet would never enter rubber boots, to fish from a great distance. These educated people have massive supplies of money and they are intent on buying up as much quota and as many licences as they can so that they can control the market. They drive up the cost of entry into the fishery to the point where a young Digby Necker could never compete, and so getting into the fishery is impossible for them, except by crewing for the educated person.

All of this has happened within the lifetime of the members of this cohort. This generation understands how educated people in government and in big business see fishing as a business opportunity to be exploited rather than as a way of life. This cohort sees control of its communities and its family businesses eroding as a result of abstract state policies that stack the deck in favour of big players. Little wonder that formal education is such a conflicted and ambiguous possession. It is the smooth, educated, legalistic and abstracted capitalist rationality of the corporate fishers who never touch a fish that Digby Neckers of this generation understand to be destroying their communities. Part of this destruction includes the idea that young people need to be educated themselves because they are forced to leave.

Not many Digby Neckers sit in an office. Not many in this cohort finished high school, opting instead for the parallel system of apprenticeship in the fishery. Most of the men work aboard boats and wear oil clothes most of the time. When you see them around wharves or in their trucks they are generally wearing work pants and shirt. When you shake the hands of these men, you know by the feel of their hands that they are more accustomed to metal and rope than to a computer keyboard. They possess what Bourdieu called "a body for working," and they are not accustomed to "settin' still" for long. Conversations about the state of education almost always end up being conversations about the state of the fishery peppered with a mistrust of educated people and their abstract knowledge. I can remember one fisherman stopping cold in the middle of a tirade about Department of Fisheries and Oceans bureaucrats and looking at me to say, "Well, maybe you're one of these educated people yourself."

## Notes

1. This is the colloquial term for periwinkles.
2. Informants are identified by pseudonym, gender, migration status and the year of potential high school graduation (which serves as a rough approximation of age). For instance, KS-MS-71 is informant "KS," a male stayer who was a potential graduate of the class of 1971. FE-FL-73 is informant "FE," a female leaver who was a potential graduate of the class of 1973. Educators are identified by a pseudonym and by gender. For example, CD-ME is informant "CD," a male educator. Quotes taken directly from my field notes are indicated by "FN".

3. "Baiting trawl" is the process of placing bait on hooks for a longline fishing operation. The hooks are baited and coiled into a bait barrel so that the line will play out without snagging when it is set out. This work has traditionally been done by women and youth on shore and it provides them a significant part-time income. "Baiting bags" is filling mesh bags with lobster bait. The bait is scooped out of large barrels that are usually kept in bait sheds or in large covered outdoor vats. The bags are then secured on a spike inside the lobster trap. Most lobster fishermen pull and check their traps at least every two or three days if the weather allows, but less often in winter months when lobsters are said to "slow down" and move further off shore. The demand for baiting bags is great during December and in the late spring between mid-April and the end of May, when the lobster season ends on Digby Neck. Knitting heads is repairing the netting in the lobster trap head, which is prone to damage because this is the part through which the spiny bodied lobsters crawl.
4. The common term for school on Digby Neck and in the Digby area generally is "the school house." Even the large, institutional-looking regional secondary school in Digby is still called the school house.
5. This distance represents a comfortable two or three hour drive or bay ferry crossing from the home place.
6. This informant went on to clarify that this class wasn't "dumb," they just "didn't give a shit about school" and were there mainly to "raise hell" until they "got fed up" and walked out. This interview was crammed with stories of insubordination and general pranks and tricks.
7. One educator commented that when she was growing up on Digby Neck in the 1940s, fishermen, "always had more money that the ones who didn't fish" (OI-FE).
8. Blythe also found this quasi-religious education discourse in *Akenfield* (Blythe, 1969). One of his informants commented: "People look to education now in the same way as they once looked at religion. Are you saved? Have you got your O levels? It's the same thing — salvation" (Blythe, 1969: 190).
9. Historian Eugen Weber found identical rates of migration by gender in rural France at the turn of the twentieth century:

    > The young and the women felt the temptation [to migration] most… if the young men could not be persuaded [to move], the girls went alone. In one Eure village in 1900, 42 of 100 sons of agricultural workers stayed on the land against only 15 of 100 girls. (1976: 286)

Chapter 5

# The Boom Years

## The Classes of 1975–1986

> If you're going to further your career, it has to be for something that you see. You have to be able to say: I'd like to be that. It's hard when you're growing up and your parents are fishing and your brothers and sisters are fishing and your uncles are fishing. I think there would even be more people that would have done better financially by staying here than [pause] some of the ones that have moved away. (SM-MS-77)

> It wasn't until quite late in my adult life when I started getting out and I saw. You know, I'm in my mid-thirties now and I'm just figuring it out. I didn't feel any different going to Acadia than I did in school because I didn't really realize what it was about. I just didn't have the underlying basis on why this was an important thing to do. That came a long time later. (EM-ML-80)

From the early 1960s, in the social and economic structure of Digby Neck, young men and women sorted out their lives in the context of an expanding and industrializing fishery. By the mid-1970s, the dragger and small-boat fisheries were providing ready employment for large numbers of young men and women on Digby Neck. Young men were able to access jobs as crew on draggers, longliners, on lobster boats, or hand-lining. Those who had what is considered to be a "direct" connection to the fishery (i.e., inheritance rights to licences) sometimes went directly from school to captaining family- or self-owned vessels. For those with less direct connections, large catches of groundfish and shellfish through this period also meant ready work in fish plants and in support work on shore.

From the mid-1970s to the mid-1980s, the relationship between schooling and community took on a different cast. As we saw in Chapter 3, out-migration rates declined rather dramatically, reflecting lucrative and widespread opportunities in the fishery. This decline was accompanied by lower rates of high school completion for male Digby Neckers, most of whom remained "around here." More young women also quit school early in this cohort compared to either of the other two cohorts. On the other hand, the expansion of the post-secondary education system, enhanced school guidance programs, improved transportation links, more money in the community (especially for licence-holding fishing families) and the path broken by the previous generation of out-migrants all contributed to promoting the visibility of options in higher education outside the community. More out-migrants of both genders began to access post-secondary education.

> Back in the seventies and eighties when the fishing was good there was money around and they didn't think twice about the cost of tuition. (FL-FE)

Educators remember this period as one in which there was a transformation in the formerly stigmatized Digby Neck identity. The "poor fisherman" came to be transformed to the "rich fisherman," and being a fisherman's son or daughter took on new meaning indicating economic privilege by local standards. The idea of relative privilege is important here. Family incomes continue to be low on Digby Neck relative to provincial and national averages, but compared to local norms, some families have relatively high incomes. The fishery, which provides the bulk of family income on Digby Neck, has an uneven structure of rewards, generating substantial wealth alongside poverty in fishing communities. This unevenness in incomes is reflected in the large number of people accessing government transfers. Those who "don't fish" in a coastal community tend to earn very low incomes. In comparison to minimum-wage alternatives available "around here," fishing is a relatively lucrative occupation. It is among the best of jobs. Relative privilege is said to have created a strong inducement for early school leaving for boys, supplementing lingering, strong anti-school attitudes, which were prevalent for men in the previous cohort.

> I can remember principals' meetings, going over the [standardized] tests.... And some of the teachers were really concerned that these kids were getting ready to quit school and talking about how they could make more money going out on the scallop draggers than the teachers who were talking about how important education was. And I can remember them saying that if you could make that kind of money what are you talking about getting your education for . (HL-FE)

## Gender, Work and Schooling

> She had an impulse to shout.... Get out of this Anna, for God's sake get out of it! Away from the whole of it. Dirty dishes and crumbling minds, the curiosity, the sympathy, the sneers.... Away from hurt and temptation, away from the shore. (Bruce, 1954: 113)

This cohort of stayers saw clearly the role of family position in the fishery in terms of its impact on the work opportunities of young people. As Davis suggests, by the 1980s, clear class divisions were emerging on Digby Neck (1991). Interviews with the 1975–1986 cohort reveal an awareness of difference in terms of employment and social opportunities across gender and class and a sense that the "community" contained individuals with unequal advantages. Teachers too were aware of the social-class dimensions that characterized the region, including Digby Neck.

> In the Digby area things are very diverse; diverse economically is what stands out most in my mind. There are isolated pockets of what I would think would be great wealth, or reasonable security, and then the larger majority would be, I would think, people who live on the margins. There are perhaps even greater pockets of poverty in hard times.... I think the Neck kind of shifts a bit more, because they're particularly involved in the fishery and that has its own kind of structure in terms of who gets the money and who doesn't. And I think that even in that system there are still very few... most of the people who live there are just making a basic living working for someone, or working in fish plants or those kinds of things. I think the ones that own the plants, or own the boats, or own the licences are fewer than the mass of the population. (CD-ME)

The fishery continued to "push" or "pull" differently positioned participants out of or into life in the coastal community. Women of this cohort articulate a clear and more critical structural understanding that entry into the fishery is a male "inheritance" and prerogative.

> My father passed his fishing rig on to my brother. That's how it goes down here. And my husband, he got his rig from his father. When you think about it, that's not fair to the women is it? Most people around here, they never think about that, it's just the way things are. Most men [pause], the older men, don't believe that a woman should [pause] they don't believe in women working anyway. (BF-FS-84)

Elite fishing families passed licences and expensive fishing rigs on to their male children, sometimes at a very early age. This generation of "born and bred" individuals understood not only that they had cultural capital, but that they could anticipate very lucrative economic capital of ownership rights in a limited-entry fishery. For young men in this position, these ownership rights allowed them to resist formal education and develop an "independent streak" at an early age. Educators remember young men who could leave school in adolescence and move directly into a fishing job. Unlike the stories told by the 1963–1974 cohort of entry into a developing fishery where hard work and a small investment could bring some measure of security and community respect, some men who entered directly into a family-owned, established fish dragging operation in the mid-1970s and early 1980s reaped significant financial rewards.

> And when I was sixteen my father had a little boat that he got running and he let me take it out. I couldn't even mend [nets] or anything. I didn't know about fishing or anything but I took it out and the first two trips I pretty near loaded it. So they said, well this fuller, he's gonna' be something, he's gonna' be a good fisherman. I just got lucky I guess. Not long after that my father gave up fishing.... So I was seventeen years old and I walked in the wheelhouse of the biggest steel boat in the fleet. My wife's mother came down to meet me one time and she said, that little boy's got that great big boat? (ES-MS-82)

This inheritance structure in the fishery exacerbated the gender divisions described for the 1963–1974 cohort because in the state-regulatory regime of the 1970s and 1980s the value of this inheritance increased astronomically.[1] Educators generally regarded young women in this cohort as more open to education, but paradoxically, less inclined to use it to open up the options out-migration might provide them. Out-migrants would, after all, be leaving Digby Neck just at the time of its greatest economic prosperity. Marrying a fisherman during this period could mean having considerable family income by local standards.

For young people from working-class families whose employment history was in the small-boat fishery or in fishing support work, there was still "lots of work," but it was of a very different sort. Fish plants were booming and processing record catches from both the small-boat dragger and the inshore fleet. In addition, young men could find work crewing on both types of boat. The transition from school to work was equally easy for men from this type of family, and they describe quitting school young and moving directly into employment.

> I first started workin' when I was sixteen, when I quit school. The first place I went was down the road there to the fish plant. And I worked them for awhile and then I went to Joey's and worked them for awhile. Then I started nettin', gill nettin' and for herring, trawling and lobstering. I stayed with William Robinson for quite a few years. Then after that I just come back to the plant an' then I went

> back to fish draggin', scallopin.' I done it all, right from the time I was sixteen. All fishin', lobsterin', draggin', trawlin', anything. (TR-MS-77)

The decision to drop out of school continued to be seen on Digby Neck as a "natural" event for young men. Women, who stayed in school longer as a group, report simply noticing from time to time, as a matter of course, that certain boys were no longer on the school bus, only to find out through inquiries that "oh yeah, he quit." This was the normal male career trajectory on Digby Neck for this cohort: a few years of secondary schooling, usually (but not always) a bit more than one's parents. In fact, male stayers in this cohort have the lowest high-school completion rates of any of the three cohorts, at 24.2 percent. Typically, young men's school careers were marked by more or less resistance, a final blow up and then entry into the fishery.

> That was the attitude. A lot of people did say (to the teachers): "Screw you, who the hell are you, I've got better options than this." And up went the middle finger and out they went. And they didn't get any pressure from the parents, because their parents didn't have any schooling either, most of them. (CF-ML-86)

The decision to leave school for fishing was not unusual; it was expected for most boys and there was no stigma attached to early exit from school. It was considered a logical choice and a "natural" thing for a young man to do.

> I found that we weren't judgmental of the choices of the young men who dropped out. There was a tacit agreement. You know you would be getting yourself in a lot of trouble for saying you're stupid for dropping out of school. (LS-FL-83).

> Look at my brother, a typical dropout. The first time he became a captain he was twenty-two and running a million dollar vessel, 150 miles away from land. The responsibility, it just blows me away now I look back on it. How could he have ever done that? I don't think I could've done it. My brother dropped out in grade eleven. (BF-FS-84)

During this period, young men continued to be able to access opportunities in the fishery through family connections and recommendations. While the fishery was becoming more capital intensive, traditional patterns of recruitment through families continued to be the principal means of finding employment for young men. Work was plentiful and post-secondary education was seen by male stayers as an irrelevance and a form of specialized training that did not relate to life in the fishery or success in the coastal community. This educator who raised her own children in the community describes the lure of the lucrative fishery in the 1970s and 1980s for young men. Her account also demonstrates how the industrialization of the fishery provided good financial opportunities that meshed with established traditions of masculinity and work, forming a potent attraction for young Digby Neck men.

> I can take my own family, or my husband's family for example, and Charles Smith, three generations. Charles was a fisherman from the time he could get into a boat. That's Phillip's father. So when Phillip came along, he would be sitting in school and all he could think about was the fishing. OK, so Jim came along... he went into Digby and all, and in grade nine his mind was no more on school than anything. His father says you don't need an education, I've done good and I've only had grade seven. So Jim got this in his head and he thought, why do I need an education? I've got a job, I can do this now.... And remember, the money was good. (ES-FE)

The pursuit of formal education did not relate experientially to financial success; in fact, it was perceived to be just the opposite. One had to "go to work" to make money and catch fish "before they're gone." The nature of the resource and the way it was managed, the application of intrusive and lucrative industrial harvesting technologies, the demand for a "skilled," "born and bred" fisheries labour force and the lure of money all conspired to create a kind of desperate "gold rush" mentality among young fishermen in this cohort.

> We were what, sixteen or so, and most of the guys were quitting. Most of the guys from the Neck would quit school and go to work and make more than most of the teachers made in five years in one year. And they were driving new trucks. I remember one guy I knew went one weekend and made 30,000 dollars. Back in the early eighties. That's a lot of money back then. So the old saw about how you'd better stay in school because if you don't you're not going to become anything, well.... It was a gold rush. (DE-ML-81)

The perception among this cohort was that abundant money could be made by men in the fishery of the 1970s and 1980s. This was true for male stayers in elite fishing families and for those working as wage labour crewing on boats or working in fish plants. The reality is, according to most informants, that a few families and individuals "did real well" and "watched their money," but the majority just worked hard for a decent living wage and made money for the captain or the fish plant owner. For people interviewed in this cohort, work was like a religion; it was an obsession and a moral responsibility and a way to establish manhood and a legitimate identity as a Digby Necker. Male cultural capital continued to be intimately connected to the physical work of fishing and the ability to "stand" working hard on the water. School, on the other hand, is not "real work."

> I think they see school as something divorced from working a lot of times. These kids know about work. The boys have been brought up around fishing. They don't lay around. They may not be very engaged in school and they may even seem painfully lazy there, but when it comes to getting to work at fishing, get out of the way. The girls too, they know how to work because they see their mothers keeping everything together and girls work in the fish too. So school, [pause] to them, it's not real work and that's what they look for when they evaluate what's going on in an educational program. What's this going to get me, how will this lead to money? (NS-FE)

While the structure of rewards varied in terms of family position, everyone was seen to benefit in relative terms. The perception of readily available "big money" helped to lure a willing labour force out of school and into the fishery. With relatively low education levels, as well as a very specialized sort of work experience, many of the stayers of this generation have since regretted their decision to leave school, a decision that seemed so logical when it was made.

> One year I set in the class and talked with one of the teachers and I told him what I made that year and he said, "that's more than I make." I had a brand new car when I was going to school there. My father never bought me anything. I don't think he ever bought me so much as a pair of socks from the time I was thirteen. Any time I wanted to make some money I'd take a day off school and get a first class job on a fishing boat. I'd go out and make $400. So that's how I kept going. The thing about it was that I kind of got a false sense of reality. I mean you never really dreamt of being anything else. (ES-MS-82)

This former dragger captain argued that for him, and for others in his position, staying in school was really an irrational decision, which would have meant foregoing significant income. Indeed, he claims the only men who stayed in school were those who could not stand the seasickness and hard physical labour of fishing. They could not endure the rigours of the sea that legitimate masculinity entailed. This account demonstrates the ambivalence that men in this cohort exude; they feel the need to justify their decisions, which now seem irrational to observers who "weren't around" through the boom of the early 1980s.

> I don't think anybody ever said I think I'm gonna' go to college because it was the best way to go. They said, hey I can't make it as a fisherman. It was, I just couldn't do that in the winter or in storms and in gales and I get too seasick. You know, I think most people that chose not to be fishermen couldn't stand the work. Now I'm not saying that that was the best way to make that decision, but it was the decision that made you some money. You'd have to be a pretty good talker to talk somebody out of it when you could drop out of school and jump right aboard a boat and make fifty or sixty thousand a year. You'd have to be able to talk him out of that and make him go to school for ten years when he had to pay for it and pay for it and pay for it. Why you'd have to be a pretty good talker to change his mind and sell him that, wouldn't you? That was the problem, the fishery was too good and too easy to get into. I can remember jumping right aboard a boat and making sixty or seventy thousand in my first year. My brother one year back in the eighties made $127,000. He jumped right out of school and made $127,000. I mean, people with ten years' college wasn't making no more. (ES-MS-82)

For young women, who did not have the same access to fisheries work and especially licences, education was coming to be seen as an important way to improve employment prospects. Like the 1963–1974 cohort, women in the 1975–1986 cohort "did better" in school in terms of staying in longer and achieving better in high school according to all informants in this cohort. This analysis is supported by my survey data reported in Chapter 3.[2] While young men had ready access to money and work opportunities, young women increasingly saw education as a fundamental career support.

> The boys could get out and go to work and they could make good money. Why spend that money on education when you could make that money now? That's how I saw it when I was growing up. Somebody would always hire them on. For us girls it was different. We had to hope school would give us something. And I think most of the girls I went to school with did graduate. I think that's what you'll find. (TC-FL-79)

Women of this cohort report having been more directly steered into prospective occupations that their parents thought would be good for them. Rather than floating aimlessly through high school for no apparent reason, these women were expected by their families to access a menu of gender- and class-specific options, which included hairdressing, secretarial work, nursing, teaching and social work. Women in this cohort do not report feeling as though they were expected to marry and set up housekeeping at an early age. While young men could fit into pre-established identities in the booming space of an industrializing fishery, young women were faced with having to construct educationally-supported tenuous-project selves. Education and sometimes mobility were promoted to many young women as the favoured route to a better life. Education was also seen as a means through which a family could control the life trajectory of a girl in a changing world.

> They even had what I was gonna' be: a secretary. Where that come from I'm not quite sure but that's what their expectations was. They wanted me to get an education and move far away as you can get. Far away as you can get, don't be stayin' here. There ain't nothin' for you here they always said. (BF-FS-84)

Educators were particularly troubled by the decision-making of young women. Teachers saw very few options for young women in the community so they felt that the decision to leave school early would result in highly limited future prospects. All high-school educators commented in slightly different ways about the young women in this cohort who quit school "because she got pregnant" or who "no sooner cleared the stage" from graduation and was "pushing a baby carriage." Educators wondered why this incongruous trajectory was so prevalent among some "really nice" girls who were "excellent students." These young women were seen to be resisting the liberal "options" oriented agenda of secondary schooling, typically by their own passive acceptance of gendered life roles and traditional femininity. This educator cast this common lament in liberal terms:

> I like to think what I define as success is that kids have options and make conscious choices.... It's the kind of dull eyed women who aren't even twenty-five yet who are shoving strollers up and down the front road that bother me because I really don't have a sense that they really had options or allowed themselves to exercise any kind of options.... What did we do for them? Young women are the part of the population that I see the school system failing in my particular circumstance at least in terms of the outcome I'd like to see. And that's where the heart wrenching examples are. I mean given the parameters of their world the young men definitely have

> favoured status. So those ones who decided to stay are happy with it and why wouldn't they be? (SR-FE)

Yet, a considerable proportion of Digby Neck young women did exercise the option of post-secondary education. Nearly one in three women from Cohort 2 has some post-secondary experience. Among elite families, who were positioned to take financial advantage of the booming fishery, higher education was coming to be seen as a way of providing opportunity to female children. One woman commented, for example, that her brothers were given fishing licences, boats and gear, while she was given a university education. Her brothers remain on the Neck and she now lives in central Canada. The gift of an education was offered with some reservations though, because this would mean that the young woman would have to move.

> I went home from school that day and I said, "Dad" [pause] and you know I can remember so vividly. I said, "Dad, I think that I would like to be a reporter." And he was thinking: the *Digby Courier*, was that what you mean? And he said, "Well, where do you go to school for that?" And I said, "Well there are some different schools, there's a school in Halifax called King's College and they have journalism program. And there's another one that's well known in Ottawa." He said, "Jesus Christ, Ottawa." I think that in a lot of ways I was kind of a mystery to my father. He understood the boys so much better. (LS-FL-84)

The ambivalence about the connection between mobility and higher education remained prominent through this period for young people and their families. Most women understood that post-secondary education would lead them out of the community, and some families did encourage their female children to migrate. Some of the women in this cohort rejected this directive, while others embraced it.

> It was "get your education so you can become something." And that was always a big thing of mine. I always wanted to be something and that was always a big thing when we went to school, to be something. And one of the first things every child would say when they came out of school was: "and I'm not going to be stuck on Digby Neck." And here I am [laughs]. (LF-FS-81)

In this cohort, gender distinctions remain pervasive and plain. Men experienced an intensified "pull" into the fishery caused by rapid industrialization opening up work on draggers and increased opportunity in booming fish plants, to supplement existing opportunities for independent petty production in the small-boat fishery. Women, on the other hand, experienced an intensified "push" and the understanding that "there's nothing here for you." The fishery offered young men both the security of a "steady" industrial wage in fish plants and crewing on draggers, as well as the established inducements of independence and money in the small-boat fishery, along with an identity that was sexy, valued in the community and in conformity with male cultural machismo.

> They're tough and they're proud that they're tough. If you talk to some of these guys about how they see the world and about men being men and the world being the world.... We go out there and work our guts out and go hard twenty hours at a stretch and come in and get drunk and we're tough. We want to help these people rise up above this, but really, is that such a bad life? This is what these guys know as manhood. Is that so different from what you find in the video store? (CD-ME)

As opportunities for young men expanded on Digby Neck, young women became increasingly marginalized and aware of their relative disadvantage. They saw their brothers and male friends making money in fishing through the boom period. Many leavers particularly resented this gender-divided structure of opportunity in the community. This awareness of disadvantage became a prime motivation for both education achievement and out-migration in women in this cohort.

> My father was strict and kind of old-fashioned. He forbade me from working in the fish plant. This bothered me at the time because I could see my brother and my friends making good money working in the fish while I was cutting a few lawns and babysitting for pocket money. You know, I thought that was really unfair, but he said that the fish plant was no place for a young woman. (US-FL-80)

Women in this generation, particularly leavers, were much more aware of the social limitations and prejudices of their communities. They tended to feel uncomfortable with what they saw as the narrowness of the people, a narrowness that was often set in contrast to the physical beauty of Digby Neck. These women saw education as a way to "escape," but the way was blocked for some young women by powerful and even abusive informal social forces. Leavers of this cohort identify Digby Neck as a "male space," a place where long traditions of gender inequality and men's exclusive occupational and economic position in their fishery gave them considerable power. Male racism and sexism for instance could impede not only boys' school careers, but those of girls as well.

> The worst that I can remember; and this left a real psychological scar on me as a child, were [pause] there were two series of incidents. One was the racism and another was the sexism. The racism [pause] there were some girls from the Neck, two sisters who were very pretty girls and they liked Black guys. At the time there was incredible segregation in high school. There were 40 kids out of 800 who were Black. There were actual gang fights going on at the school, gangland style fights going on at the school when I went up there to go to school. It was ugly, it was like Cole Harbour.[3] And so there were these two girls who liked Black guys and I remember one day they had to go on our bus because there was something wrong with theirs. But they were being taunted by other kids on the bus who were yelling at them calling them nigger lovers. That sounds like something from the Deep South doesn't it? And these girls both dropped out of school. And the boys calling them names dropped out of school too.

What is remarkable about this quote, apart from the rawness of the description, is its rarity in these accounts. This was the single instance in which race was invoked as a significant issue. The two youngest cohorts attended a regional secondary school in which racism was the subject of two separate inquiries (cf. Frank, 1998). Yet, the hegemony around solidarity and community makes this account an anomaly. The loud silence around race and racism in these accounts seems to me to indicate how the community and the relationships it represents were exclusively White. It could be that because Digby Neck was mono-racial, my informants considered that questions of race did not apply to their community. It could also be that they wished to suppress this kind of data. It seems rather obvious that the expansion of educational access to minority youth (i.e., Black youth) in the regional secondary school in the 1970s and 80s did generate new tensions on Digby Neck, as well as alternative self-definitions, forms of desire and control of women through overtly racist engagements. This is clearly an area that deserves more systematic study in mono-racial communities like Digby Neck. It is also clear that racial conflict remains an important issue in both the regional secondary school in Digby as well as in the relatively homogenous "White" and "Black" villages that send youth to this school.

While stayers and male leavers continue to speak of the "community" as a unitary entity, some women saw cracks in the solidarity of place. This vision of difference came both from literate interaction with wider communities via books and social experiences, as well as from the experience of being denied opportunities that were "naturally" passed on to men in the social conventions of family and community. These women saw their brothers and male relatives reaping advantages and access to work and social privileges they were simply assumed to deserve, and by questioning the social order they became uncomfortable in the community.

> I knew I couldn't stay there from a pretty early age. You've got to think of this from a woman's point of view, which is totally different from yours. I could never understand why it was just handed to boys without a question. They were taken on the boat and they were told stories about fishing and everybody would call them little fishermen all their lives. That really pissed me off because all of that ended up giving them money. They could go out and make a lot of money, and what could I do? Cut a few fish once in awhile and baby-sit. I did it but it bored the shit out of me and I swore I wasn't going to be doing that for the rest of my life. (TC-FL-79)

Despite this insight into the problematic nature of gender relations on Digby Neck and in the fishery, women in this cohort still spoke fondly of family connections and their intimate, nostalgic relationship with the physical setting of Digby Neck. For the most part their discourse is not explicitly feminist. Only one of the women I interviewed spoke about the influence of women's issues in the larger social context or identified herself as a feminist, or as having feminist ideas. Yet, a deep ambivalence runs through women's accounts of life on the Neck, and it is clear that both stayers and leavers have engaged in practices that challenge traditional gender roles. A movement out of the home and into paid employment is a central feature of accounts of members of Cohorts 2 and 3. Indeed, in the eastern end of Digby Neck, women's individual incomes were higher than the provincial average in 1996. Like men, women who remained on Digby Neck have also engaged in multiple forms of labour. Some of this labour fits into the traditionally feminine work located in the home, but some does not. Female leavers understood it as a place in which they could not remain or return to on a permanent basis. At the same time Digby Neck is a place that holds memories and deep connections that are still very important. Digby Neck is home, but like Tom Wolfe's protagonist, these informants cannot go back home again. Sometimes this ambivalent sentiment is framed in positive terms as a desire to recover a lost solidarity.

> The Neck is my home. We are a very close family. There's no other place that I will ever call home and when I die my bones will be up there in the graveyard with my family. It must sound weird, but that kind of gives me a good feeling to think about that. But I've been thinking about home lately and [pause] I've been thinking

> that home is the people and when the people aren't around any more then it isn't quite the same. The place is still there and so are the memories, but it's different. I'm only living where I am now because I have no choice. If I won the lottery I'd be back on the Neck in a minute. (US-FL-80)

And in some accounts it is framed as justification for staying away.

> I love the Neck. I love the physicality of the Neck. I love the Fundy shore; I love the St. Mary's Bay shore. I just feel so alive when I'm there. But sometimes the people really get on my nerves, the narrow mindedness of some of them. And the jealousy.... That's not to say we don't have it up here. And I want to say right up front, for everything that's wrong about the Neck, there's something that is right. And there are more things that are right than are wrong. But there is a real pettiness in some communities about who's got what. I think that it stands out in stark relief against all the things that are good. Here in Toronto there are so many things that are wrong, there are so many shitty things and I really don't like it here. And you just take the bad with the bad. You know, the backbiting and the one-upmanship.... You don't expect it to be a community. (LS-FL-84)

Female leavers in this cohort penetrated the habitus in the community by developing a critical analysis of sexism on the Neck. Because they were children of relatively privileged families, they were able to use higher education as a means of mobility out of the gender-stratified community social structure. As relatively privileged female youth, they expected to have advantages and education, which provided them with an avenue to acquire the middle-class dividend not available to them in the community. The community was defined with ambivalence, a place that is at the same time comfortable and profoundly uncomfortable. Male leavers, on the other hand, saw a comfortable community, economic potential and a family support structure that was difficult to resist because of the comforts and opportunity it offered. This comfort is a marker of the extent to which the space is so deeply gendered.

> The support structures down there are so good. My mom would have been perfectly happy if all of her sons were still living at the house, right. That would have been the cat's meow for her. And I said to her, mom, sometimes you've gotta' let them be adults. I guess it's good in a lot of ways. You go back, you know, and it's a very strong community and as far as emotional support, there's

> just a lot of stuff there. And so if you're of the personality that, that's what makes you feel comfortable, then it's really hard to go anywhere. (EM-ML-80)

For many young men of this cohort, Digby Neck was a hard place to leave and my analysis in Chapter 3 shows that more of them stayed than in the previous cohort. Masculine privilege here is no academic point; it is supported by the raw demographics of staying and leaving.

## Defining Security: Education, Identity and Work

> So... I mean it's beautiful geographically, and I think they feel like they're special in a way because of their geography. It makes them special in a sense [pause] and secure. (CQ-FE)

> There's something about Digby Neckers. They have very close families and they stick together. They really know who they are because they really know where they are. (NS-FE)

A recurrent theme for this cohort of Digby Neck natives is the idea of security as it relates to lifestyle. As the fishery industrialized, a more secure and affluent consumer lifestyle became possible for at least some Digby Neckers. People felt as though they were "doing good" in the 1970s and 1980s. The fishery was flourishing, apparently more secure than ever before, and the resource seemed endless. Fishing families spent money, modernized their homes, bought expensive vehicles (particularly 4-wheel drive, half-ton trucks) and treated their children to luxuries they themselves could never have imagined as children. Some paid off boat loans and mortgages, while others invested in high status consumer goods and "lifestyles," as several informants put it. With lucrative fishing and rapid social transformations in trade, transportation and communication, the Neck effectively entered consumer society during the 1970s and 1980s. Life in the single-industry community offered a new range of opportunities and challenges for those who chose to stay. For the male children of elite fishing families, security was defined in terms of access to financial opportunities and the feelings of camaraderie that accompanied life in the fishery. This feeling was reported by male leavers as well as stayers. For these individuals, the fishery offered security, both at the level of financial returns, but also at the level of living within a culture of masculinity that offered social rewards as well.

> It's a physical challenge and it's a challenge and it's a gamble. The stakes are pretty high you know. You're looking for fish and if you strike them there's a big payoff. And you never know if you're go-

> ing to get in [to port] or not. It's a real rush you know. I've never felt the way I did when I was fishing and I've done a lot of things in my life. It's an adrenaline thing that I've never experienced since, the danger, the gambles and the pay-off. And you're out there with your buddies, you work together and you drink together, you know party and stuff. There's real camaraderie there. There's nothing like it anywhere else. (DE-ML-81)[4]

> Oh yeah, it's the camaraderie of all your friends are doing the same thing. It's competitive, you know and it's hard work and there's nothing like the hard work that makes you feel like a man — right? (CF-ML-86)

These young men came from established, licence-holding fishing families. For male leavers in this cohort, there was a safety net hanging under their forays into post-secondary education. They had the financial resources from summer fishing and the certain knowledge that they could always "fall back" on fishing and the "tough comfort" of life in the community. Most male leavers say they left either because they did not like fishing, because they were simply bored by the routine or because they sensed insecurity in the way the resource was being exploited.

> I graduated in '81 and that was at the peak of the fishing. There was huge money to be made in the fishing industry. So on the financial side of things, there wasn't anything pulling me away. I mean a deck hand could make six figures, and you had very little responsibility. And most of the guys were running around with new vehicles and could afford to buy new homes and cottages. There's still people that survived all that. A lot of the money went down the tubes with drinking and the lifestyles and all that, but some of them played it smart. But the other thing about that is [that] I found it very boring. The fishing was exciting. I mean, there is certainly the romance of the sea life. But once you got ashore there was very little. I don't know, I found it very limited, there was lots of alcohol and partying and nothing beyond that. I guess I wanted something bigger. (DE-ML-81)

For stayers, there seemed little sense in acquiring much formal education because the fishery seemed to them totally secure. While the fishery was booming it seemed that life would continue much as it had for generations and the application to new technologies would not significantly reduce stocks or jeopardize the way of life on the Neck. This tradition and the security of following what seemed like a "natural" course for young men in coastal fishing villages combined with lucrative income potential made possible by new technologies.[5] Through this period the state was also contributing to the sense of security by actively supporting the industrialization and modernization of the fishery by financing the expansion of harvesting and processing capacity. As one dragger owner/operator (who is reputed locally to be a multimillionaire) commented: "You can't blame us for what happened to the stocks in the seventies and eighties, we just played by the rules, we didn't make them. If it wasn't me, it would have been somebody else" (FN). This potent mix of the known and the new created conditions of both security and prosperity for young men whose families held licences and owned fishing rigs, but also new problematic questions about staying and leaving. This parent/educator saw the dilemma facing young men and women in the 1970s and 1980s.

> Well, we know that the school plays an important part. They start here and decide whether they're going to slide into the community or slide out. It's stressful for a lot of them, mostly the boys but a lot of girls have left too but I can see those boys not wanting to leave home, not wanting to leave here. My parents have done this and I'd like to stay around. I can't remember anyone actually saying it, but you just know, you can tell that they want to stay. If they haven't given you notification, that well I'm going to [leave].... You know if they're going to go away they tell you very young: "when I get through here, well I'm not staying around at all." But if you don't hear that, well then you know they are going to stay. (ES-FE)

People had fished for generations and fished as hard as they could with the tools that were available to them. The tradition was one in which the harder you fished, the greater the rewards. This generation was the first to be in a position to exploit emerging technologies *en masse*. They believed, and a few continue to believe, that these new technologies would provide them with additional security and increased incomes indefinitely. Security was not evenly distributed though, nor was it interpreted in the same way by all Digby Neck boys. Several leavers described a "hunter mentality" and masculine identity constructed on the basis of machismo and a belief in the inexhaustible bounty of the ocean. By this time though, many Digby Neck leavers were beginning to question the sustainability of the hunter mentality.

> And if you've been out on a boat, especially in the days when the dragging was around—if you've been out on a dragger and you've seen the way the bosses and the captains reacted. You pull a net of fish up and you get couple of bags of fish, you want to get that

> thing back in the water just as fast as you can and catch and catch and catch. And you come in on a Friday night and you drink till you have to go back out again. And you do that until the weather gets bad. It's a hunterish kind of mentality, and I always wondered how long it could last. (EM-ML-80)

In this context it is not difficult to see how education was given a low priority by most stayers, particularly the men. The fishery was considered to be so secure and so lucrative that education was an irrelevance for men who had "direct" connections to the fishery and who could anticipate inheriting licences and fishing rigs.

> Dad never encouraged me to quit, but he never encouraged me to go to school either. He never made me do my homework. I guess he just thought like I did, well, "he's got the fishery." I think actually dad wanted me to become a fisherman so he could have somebody to run his boat. I don't think he [pause] I know my sister, he used to really plan her going to college and this and that. He paid her way all through and she was guaranteed to go to college because she was a girl. But me being a boy, I don't think I was ever even thought of as being anything but a fisherman. (ES-MS-82)

For men whose connection with the fishery was more tenuous, the fishery was defined in terms of insecurity. Contrasting the comments of the dragger fisherman above, this leaver, who was a member of a large family in the small-boat inshore lobster fishery, saw the industry as a tremendously insecure way to make a living. Dependent on the availability of fish and the caprices of the marketplace, this individual felt insecure and vulnerable as a fisherman. For him, education provided a "portable" sort of credential, which seemed to him more predictable and potentially lucrative than the fixed credential of a fishing licence. Marxist analysts of the Atlantic fishery have consistently pointed to the proletarianization of the small-boat fishery (Clement, 1986; Brym and Sacouman, 1979; Sacouman, 1980; Fairley, Leys and Sacouman, 1990). This quote supports the sense that small-boat fishers had little control over prices and thus their total employment conditions.

> In fishing, like there's a body of water with a limited resource, a finite resource. If you didn't harvest them first, somebody else will. I was thinking it would be like having one big field for the farmers and whoever got the harvest first got everything. Because in fishing, you either do really well or you get nothing and it's [pause] you know lobster season, if your motor breaks down the first day of the season.... You're shit out of luck. We'd come into the wharf

> and tie up, and the guy would say lobsters just dropped a dollar a pound today. I mean it was like I always felt so weak and out of control when something like that happened. My brothers told me of scenarios where they spent a lot of money gearing up for a season and then having them tell him the day before that there's going to be no season that year. I found that a really emotionally stressful thing. (EM-ML-80)

Leavers tended to define security differently than stayers, and they tended to see in the mechanization and expansion of the fishery the seeds of danger. Where stayers saw opportunity and rewards, leavers tended to see limitations and potential for tremendous insecurity and even immanent collapse. These perceptions cut across class lines, and to a certain extent the difference is that children of elite fishing families were virtually the only Digby Neckers in a position to easily choose higher education. But for these families, the choice of investing in higher education for their male children made little sense because they were the very people benefitting most from the industrial fishery. This is an important irony. Those men with the greatest access to higher education were the same people who had the greatest access to the fish stocks in the 1970s and 1980s.

Female stayers have more ambivalent memories about the connection between education and sustainable futures. They defined security in terms of staying, but their sense of staying had more to do with the importance of community linkages and relationships than with opportunities in the fishery. They found marriages, employment in the service industry and occasional fisheries-related employment, e.g., gathering "winkles" (periwinkles), baiting bags or trawl and working in fish plants. The community is defined as a sustainable, albeit "tough," economy if one is willing to work hard and a great place to raise kids.

> People here are [pause] you'll always get help from somebody, like if you break down on the road. Not a lot of opportunity, but we still have a school, we still have churches, we still have our fire hall, we have stores, we now have [pause] actually there's probably more to tell about Digby Neck than when I was growing up 'cause it was all to do with the fisheries. Well it still is today, but I mean it's different. You know we've got two salmon hatcheries now. It's a great place to live. You can always find... like I say there's always something that you can do once you get to know the people. I don't think we'd ever starve or go homeless here. You know I don't even hear people talk about getting their kids off of Digby Neck like when I was growing up. (LF-FS-81)

Women of this cohort did not speak of security in terms of connection to a successful fisherman, but rather in terms of the way they could acquire education credentials or local work experience which would allow them to earn an independent income. The presence of an independent income was the measure and indicator of security for these women. Yet, these women all married, and virtually all of them married fishermen. Female stayers were typically more able to see the direct connection between formal schooling and income than men, whose cultural capital was focused on the fishery. This informant illustrates how women combine formal education credentials with more traditional family connections and work ethic to make a living in the community.

> I've always wanted to work. I've never wanted to be stuck as a housewife. You know I wanted to be a career person, you know, pay your own way. I've never depended on anybody, I'm very independent. I didn't actually know what I wanted to be till I got out in the world and experienced it. I've done everything from logging, to helping in schools, to cooking.... The experience is how I found out what I wanted to do. Everyone on Digby Neck is a hard worker. Hands-on, hard work, do anything to work. Like I say, if worse comes to worst, you can always look after someone's kids or go down the road and [pause] well in lobster season, walk in the door and bait bags. There's always something to do. (LF-FS-81)

Female stayers defined the community as a place where a flexible, multi-skilled person can always find something to do. This response mirrors the multi-skilled emphasis of men in the 1963–1974 cohort. Women in the 1975–1986 cohort are highly active in the labour force as well as in more "traditional" gendered roles in community organizations. They work in a wide variety of occupations, both in the fishery and in service-sector employment, mainly in nearby Digby. Some educators commented on the versatility of these women, praising their ability to "carve out a niche" in the community to provide themselves with some income. Most educators see this change as a kind of women's entrepreneurship. "They're workers," everyone says, and this designation carries with it elements of pride and apology, admiration and scorn. This educator, on the other hand, questions the extent to which women's multi-occupational activity represents a real departure from traditional roles in coastal communities.

> It's just a different organization and spin on what they've been doing all their lives. I find when the word entrepreneurship comes up and the educators got a hold of this one about ten years ago, when it tends to be applied in rural areas to women what it amounts to

> is: I do something that I do at home, or it's more in the domestic scene. And what I find interesting in this is that I'm still very closely tied to home, I've still got a rope around my ankle. I may do catering and I may make Phentex slippers or whatever. (SR-FE)

Women on Digby Neck have a long history of work outside the home. As the fishery boomed in the 1970s, the labour of women became a more integral and necessary part of the Digby Neck economy. There was at this time more work than people to do it. And it was urgent work that needed to be done in order to unload and prepare bait for boats fishing virtually around the clock. Fish then needed to be processed quickly and efficiently before they spoiled. Women have always been a part of this activity in the family-based fishery. As more and more men were attracted to high wages in fish and scallop dragging, more opportunities opened up for women to get paid for doing fisheries support work, work they had often previously done for free in the family-based fishery of the 1950s and 1960s. As the fishery industrialized, there was more for women and children to "support" (Binkley, 2002). The ability to work hard when needed is the mark of a good worker in the fishery, male or female. Just as fishermen needed to be on the deck at 4 or 5 a.m., the boats needed bait and supplies.

Unlike the women stayers of the 1963–1974 cohort, these women did not anticipate marriage as either a path they were expected to follow or as a means to economic security. Women of this generation expected to work, and most saw the community as a place that held potential for them to make work for themselves. The notion of flexibility for women included formal and informal education, and both of these kinds of learning were respected. They tended to be very much immersed in the work ethic and the idea that it is hard work that provides security.

> Around here you've got to be willing to work.... You gotta' be there, you gotta' work. If they gotta' have eight tubs [of baited trawl], you gotta' have eight tubs and you stay there till the eight tubs are done. The first time you went somewhere else: that's it you're done. If they weren't done for the next day, that's it, you're done; they'd just find somebody else. So you gotta be pretty flexible and whatever they want done you gotta' do it. You gotta' be there. You say, "the next day I'll have it done," well you're done. You gotta' be reliable. (BF-FS-84)

This informant went on to justify her decision to stay in the community in terms of opportunity and security as well as the comfortable feeling of living in a known space. The community not only provides opportunity for those who are well integrated into its routines and work structures, it also provides the kind of high visibility and security of a community where "everybody knows everybody else," described by Bonner (1997). Stayers take pride in having been able to survive transitions in the economy and in the fishery, and this pride is reflected as both a personal achievement and an indicator of the resilience of community.

> You succeed by surviving. You know you look at a lot of people around here and you think, I don't know how they've done it, how they've held out here this long. It's been hard. Things were just moving along and then bang, the fish plants are gone. But we're still here and we're still surviving. (LF-FS-81)

> A friend wanted us to go out west. I said no, you go, cause I can survive here. I can survive here myself if I have to, with two kids I can survive. I make money every day. I wouldn't have to worry come the end of the day if I wouldn't have a toonie 'cause there's something out there to do and I know that. But if I go somewhere else, to a strange place, I wouldn't do it until everything was checked out, and yes, you do have place to live, and yes, you will have a job doing something. Other than that I would never, never leave here. My house is paid for if nothing else. There's always something you can do here if you want to make a living. If you wanted to make yourself 30-35 dollars today you grab yourself a periwinkle bag and go down to the shore and you go pickin' and you will have that 30 or 35 dollars. But if I go somewhere else, a strange territory, I don't know what I'm getting into. I don't know anybody there, all my family and friends are here. I know the school and the kids they hang around with. So I'd never take my children out of here unless I had guaranteed there is a job there for ya, and it would have to pay. I wouldn't leave that because that's my security. To ever take the kids somewhere where I have to think, well what shall I do today. I could never do that unless someone says: you have a good job year round. You have to guarantee work and guarantee your kids will have a good school. But you're not gonna get that guarantee I don't think. (BF-FS-84)

In the insecure economic climate of the contemporary Canadian (or global) economy, the kind of assurances and security this woman demands is only available in the known spaces of home. Women saw the direct connection between both learning and life in the community. In fact, two of the three female stayers interviewed in this cohort left the community to pursue post-secondary training in order to establish themselves more securely within the community.

> I thought that if I was going to stay in the area, because I was with my boyfriend and he was a fisherman, like if I was going to stay in the area, what could I do so that I could make decent money? I looked at that, well you had a hospital there that was pretty functional. And you had teaching. And what else did you have? You had a fish plant to work in. You know, there was secretarial work. But, you know, those seemed to be what you were limited to if you're a woman. (FS-FS-77)

Formal education was seen by both female stayers and leavers as one means of security that might complement or replace work in and around the fishery on Digby Neck. Women from this cohort saw formal education offering a kind of enhanced security that would allow them to remain in the known community. Unlike male stayers, who saw formal education as being disconnected from gendered work in the community, women tended to see education as a vehicle for achieving occupational and economic security that was denied them in the fishery, both "around here" and in more distant locations. These women had been "released" from the traditional roles of wife and mother in domestic spaces and into the multi-occupational space of the community; they were the first cohort to experience (almost universally) the two-income phenomenon that now characterizes most Canadian families. They do fisheries support work, labour in service industry jobs and acquire relevant credentials that allow them to access "more permanent" or "good" jobs. Sometimes the education strategy worked in terms of leading to professional employment, and sometimes it did not.

> In my own case I am bitter about the way my education turned out. I figured that if I went and got a good education that I would be able to come back here and get a good job. That's what I always believed and that's what people said to me, get your education and you can do anything. Well, that's not true around here and I'm kind of an example that people use. They say, look at her, she's got all that education and she's back here. I feel like one of those grade nine dropouts: a failure. (US-FL-80)

This story is a testament to the dubious value of "too much" formal education for stayers. She understands herself and is seen in the community as someone "overqualified" for existing positions and professional service in the local area, and as a result she must move.

The ability to stay in the community and find a reasonable living was differentially available to men and women on the basis of gender and class. Different definitions of security emerged out of the differential structure of opportunity faced by individuals of different genders and in different social classes. While males from elite and licence-holding fishing families had the opportunity to access higher education, they typically saw security in pursing their exclusive opportunities in the fishery. At the same time leavers needed to have sufficient family income and support in order to access opportunities in higher education. Unlike the situation of the 1963–1974 cohort, these people were not trailblazers in quite so stark a sense. University and the menu of higher education opportunities were within their sights, and their families had sufficient funds to allow them to access high-status post-secondary credentials. All of the leavers interviewed from this cohort attended university and all of them have acquired at least one degree. Leaving continued to be traumatic for many Digby Neckers of this generation, even when they understood from a very early age that they "had to leave." The stress was particularly acute when leaving was combined with post-secondary education, where one's identity was challenged at a very deep level.

> I think if you buy into it [university education], and in the sense of rural communities, you have to give up who you are. And have faith that, yeah, an education does mean that there are going to be bigger and better things and... you buy into something that you can't see in these kinds of areas, you can't really see and reflect on and think about for yourself. For a lot of these kids to buy into the educational dream, it means giving up what they know is solid, dad does it, mom does it and they can see it. And there is a sort of scale of wealth and poverty built into that, but it's real and it's relevant. Then we ask them to buy into this other thing that says that: yeah, I know that if I go and study, and if I do this and I do that, and as I work my way up through training and education that, yeah, there is a whole vast world out there. (CD-ME)

## Family/Class

> The more we look at the working-class life, the more we try to reach the core of working-class attitudes, the more surely does it appear that the core is a sense of the personal, the concrete, the local; it is embodied in the idea of, first, the family and, second, the neighbourhood. This remains, though much works against it. (Hoggart, 1957: 33)

Family structure is closely connected with the various fisheries on Digby Neck. On the top of the class structure of the fishery that had developed by the mid-1970s was the elite dragger owner/operator, fish plant owners and their families. These families had "all the toys," the satellite dish, paved driveways, late model cars and four wheel drive vehicles (sometimes even for the children), new or fully renovated classic houses, manicured grounds, snowmobiles, boats, cottages and all the indicators of material success in a consumer society. Owner/operators of small-boat fishing operations like lobstermen, gill netters and longliners also prospered through this period, albeit in smaller measure. Many of these families also displayed, and continue to display, the accoutrements of consumer success. The class of worker that laboured onboard another man's boat or in the fish plants of Digby Neck also found "lots of work" through this period, and their success was directly connected to that of all other classes of fishermen and fish plant owners. Social class divisions in a coastal community are both subtle and integrated in the sense that those at the top of the structure often (but not always) have a sense of *noblesse oblige* to the people they employ because these are their neighbours and even family members. Along with the consumer privileges, this cohort of families was the first to be able to consider higher education for certain of their children, particularly their girls.

> More of them started to think about educating their kids.... Mostly the girls because they took to school more [pause]. Well the money certainly never stood in the way for certain families I could name. They were considered successful in the area and money wasn't a problem. (FL-FE)

Many informants in this cohort report that they could have pursued post-secondary education and that they were encouraged to do so by their families. By the mid-1970s, the post-secondary system was as open as it has ever been with a variety of offerings that ranged from trades training in vocational schools to a relatively accessible, expanding university system. Government student loans were available to prospective students of higher education in Nova Scotia, and for those who could imagine the possibility of university and who could complete the endurance test of secondary schooling in the face of a booming fishery, there were education opportunities. The leavers in this cohort all took advantage of parental money and/or the system of student loans and went to university. Those children of elite fishing families who remained in the communities defined security in terms of growing opportunities in an expanding industrial fishery. Most of these were men. They actively resisted schooling because they had "better options." Female children of elite fishing families tended to opt for post-secondary education and the out-migration this entailed. As was the case in the previous cohort (1963–1974), there was a cadre of stayers from more marginal families who had no clear picture of the possibility of post-secondary education. These were individuals whose family/class position in the fishery did not situate them where they might seriously consider post-secondary schooling of any sort. These people lived to labour and anticipated nothing more than a lifetime of manual work in the fishery. Their schooling tended to support their reproduction as labour for an expanding industrial fishery.

> We worked, my whole family. My father had a little boat and he fished it. Me and my brothers we always worked around. It was always like that as far as I can see. I mean for us anyway, that's all we ever done. You didn't need no college for that. Could you see me sittin' at a desk chewin' on a pencil? [laughs] (TR-MS-77)

For people like this man, formal education continued to be an irrelevance rather than a tunnel. Manual work and the ability to labour long hours continued to be highly valued among this cohort. The good, steady worker is a theme that resonated among stayers. This was the kind of person who could survive in Digby Neck without the support of formal education or family money and "direct" access to the fishery. Survival was achieved through an application of multiple skills and through the flexible, hard, steady work required by local employers. Parents were silent about formal education. "Real" education did not happen in school; it often was understood as the ability to watch what people did locally and learn from them and apply that learning.

> They [parents] didn't say much about school. They didn't discourage you, but they didn't encourage you either. Dad never had that much education anyway. Mom did go to, I think she went to grade ten. Dad never ever really talked about it because he never ever went there. He just figured it was a waste of somebody's time and the place for you was out workin' and not sittin' behind a desk pushin' a pencil. And my brother was out [by the] time he was thirteen. The day he turned fourteen he was out of school and on that boat. But he learned a lot though on his own. Now he can do carpentry work and everything, you know, what he learned on his own, talkin' to other people. (BF-FS-84)

It was through this period that the observant, practically intelligent, "steady," "smart" worker could make what was considered to be a decent living and establish the survival skills. Family support for individuals whose connection to the fishery is less "direct" spoke in terms of mutual aid and sharing work. The silence around formal education was interpreted by these people as testimony to its lack of utility. Or, if education was a path to a better life, it was understood as one that was only open to certain privileged people. When I asked the question, "what do people around here say education is for?" one stayer responded immediately, "for the rich." In fact, "success" was defined differently by differently placed individuals.

For many stayers, success meant being able to persist in the community, while for many leavers, success meant being able to leave it. And staying meant being able to remain in a place where family and friends are there to share and trade with in a familiar environment. Intimate knowledge of the natural and social environment counted as resources for those whose family connections to the fishery were not established through licences. In the course of most of my interviews on Digby Neck, there were continuous "interruptions" caused by the normal flow of visiting, bartering, mutual aid and phone conversations. These interviews were held in kitchens, which, along with wharves and "the store" (local village convenience stores), are the social hub of families and communities.

> Well, I like it here. It's only a small village and people is quiet. You can walk up and down the road and there's always somebody waving to you or saying "hi." And they'll do anything for you. We got to take care of each other 'cause we ain't got much. (TR-MS-77)

For leavers, family support was more often defined in terms of money and encouragement. But leavers, all of whom have completed higher education, reported that they were not given significant counselling by their families about the array of options that stood before them. They had to "figure it out by themselves."

> High school was very uncomfortable for me. I felt like I was marking time a lot of days. And I look in envy at the education that my [Southern Ontario born] husband got and he [pause] I don't think he takes it for granted, he worked hard for what he got, his family wasn't wealthy and he had scholarships. But the access to knowledge, the mentorship was incredible. My parents did not mentor me. I realize now that they couldn't because they could only see so far. (LS-FL-84)

Through the boom period of the 1970s and 1980s, success for less privileged families meant being able to labour hard and meet the challenge of abundant labour opportunities in the fishery. School was for "other people" people who couldn't or wouldn't work or who were wealthy enough not to have to. Hard physical labour was a source of pride for some and a source of contempt for others. Women whose families were reaping the economic benefits of the industrialization of the fishery described a community in which they saw "nothing for me." Parents' expectations were somewhat contradictory and mixed:

> I hate to say it but I just knew there was nothing for me there. The best you could hope for was a good marriage. Well, you looked at

> those guys around and they were pretty wild most of them. Sure there was lots of money and partying and excitement when they were ashore. But then you thought, if I stay here I'll be stuck on my own a lot, a fisherman's wife. It's not much of a life, you don't have much independence and there aren't any decent jobs for miles. No thanks. (TC-FL-79)[6]

In later years, success for people whose connection to the fishery is indirect means being able to find enough work to survive. For more privileged families, success could mean either developing the family fishing business, looking at expanding tourism related opportunities or leaving the Neck in pursuit of a profession or other sorts of business opportunities.

> They've maybe started their own business or around here it was mostly people who went into fish dragging. Fish draggers were the successful people around here because they were the ones making the money. It's just to do with money and making a good living and supporting other members of the family. Their kids goin' to college or [pause] success, I don't know success [pause]. It'd be a lot of people around here because there's a lot of people that do for others. But then when you talk about, when they talked about when I was growing up, the ones that went away and went to college, and they said, "now he's a doctor, or now she's starting her own business, that was considered a success." (LF-FS-81)

Still, members of this cohort retain highly instrumental attitudes toward education as well as the clear sense that formal education is a tenuous route to economic success. This view is shared by both stayers and leavers, who see both the difficulty of making a living in urban places with a good education and the money that elite fishing families made during their formative years.

> In my mind, money's what makes things happen, if you want a lifestyle, you gotta' have money. There's lots of fine learning and fine arts and everything, but dammit, if you want a lifestyle you have to make money and I can count off the top of my head how many millionaires are on Digby Neck. There's a lot of them and they don't lead the extravagant lifestyle but they're extremely successful people and they made a lot of money, yeah. (CF-ML-86)

These comments also speak to the class divided nature of the Digby Neck community in the present day. As one fisherman commented, "It used to be everybody drove old trucks; now we got a few driving Cadillacs and the rest walk" (FN). As parents themselves, educators in this sample see the influence that they have had and how their overt or covert assumptions have had a profound impact on the education and mobility decisions of their own children. As the children of middle-class professionals, the children of teachers are "naturally" placed (or perceived themselves to have been placed) outside the community in the future that their parents imagine for them. Teachers are, in coastal communities, the quintessential stranger described by Simmel (in Coser, 1980); they live in established communities like those found on Digby Neck, but their reference points are always elsewhere.

> My own younger daughter cast up to me one time in recent years the pressure she had felt about going to university. And it was an unspoken pressure, just because both their father and I were university grads and teachers the assumption was that she would go to university. Well she did go and she poked along and got her degree finally. And then she went and did a two-year course in something that she was interested in all the time. You're right I said, I just did make that assumption. (GG-FE)

Young people need support to leave their families and "go on" to pursue further formal education. The community provided a backdrop and a functional social and economic support structure that needed to be actively resisted by leavers. By the same token, the school offered, at some level, the possibility of mobility to all students. Formal education is the chance to become a stranger,[7] and some Digby Neckers took it. This offer needed to be resisted by students who were content or destined to stay in the local milieu. Consciously in the 1960s and 1970s, and more unconsciously by the 1980s and 1990s, middle-class students and select working-class students in the regional high school have been systematically or implicitly expected by educators to be mobile. This finding is consistent with leavers' own perceptions of their own situations. If leavers felt subtle pressure or a "hand on the shoulder," educators understand that they have played a part in providing that subtle support to students they thought "capable." Such members of "mobile families" experienced secondary school as a progressive ushering out of the community and on to other places.

## The Mobile Family

> These analyses [of schooling and social class reproduction] fail to capture the notion of family-school linkages with — to use an analogy — a small, rarely-used pathway in one community or a large well-travelled pathway in another. Researchers need to study the size, nature and purpose of these home-school "roads," as well as the number of travellers using them. Having the company of many

> others may shape the nature of the journey by focussing primarily on individual travellers, researchers have missed these possibilities. (Lareau, 1989: 6)

The most mobile communities are Sandy Cove and Little River. Educators understand some families to be more outward looking than others. These families are known to be non-traditional or mobile. Non-traditional families possess and value books, have access to elite cultural activities and academic pursuits and have at least one parent who has no involvement in the fishery and often who either originated or works outside the community. But in the view of educators in this sample, most significantly and consistently, non-traditional families travel more often and further. A number of social theorists view mobility as a marker of both modernity (Giddens, 1995, 1996) and post-modernity (Bauman, 1991, 1992, 1999). Mobility complements choice, and as Bauman points out, contemporary consumers are "doomed to choose" everything from the products we use to the selves we construct (1999: 134).[8] Children from those families educators saw as "traditional" had an array of choices that were relatively limited compared to the more "worldly" family. Children of "mobile families" could choose from a larger, more extensive menu of options.

> If the family is, how shall I say it, worldly, you see this. These days you can be quite worldly with the internet and so forth without ever going very far, but there's nothing like the real experience of travelling there and doing it.... One of our students went to Ottawa on one of these programs and when she got to grade twelve, no problem. She wanted to take a program that was offered at Algonquin College in Ottawa. Yes, it's still a ways from home, but I've been away from home and I know what it is like. (CQ-FE)

In the case of female children it was generally considered imperative that they study hard and focus on a mobile, educationally rich future. Both non-traditional and many traditional parents tended to discourage female children from involvements in the working community and especially male dominated activity "down to the shore." This "protection" of daughters from the male dominated world of the fishery effectively reinforced the gender segregation that marks much of the east coast fishery and that continues to buttress gender inequality in coastal communities. By keeping girls and women away from the locus of action in the fishery, wharves and fish sheds remained male preserves.

> This was the way it was in quite a few families. They didn't want their girls in the fish plants and running the roads. We were more

> strict with her that's for sure. Three boys and one girl and we wanted her to not be like... well the boys. That's ok the way they are, but we just wanted her to have a different experience and do something that we ourselves couldn't do. (ES-FE)

As young women were kept away (and kept themselves away) from the working surface of the fishery, it became clear to many of them that schooling was the route to employment. In the context of nascent feminist mass media messages about women's potential careers, young women in elite fishing families saw significant limitations in "traditional" women's roles, which they realistically saw as the only option for them on Digby Neck. Women in this cohort reported that they integrated well in the regional secondary school and that while they may not have been able to see clearly the purpose of their education and where it might lead them, they knew that a direct slide out of school and into the fishery or marriage was not a viable option for them.

Educators drew a connection between mobility and the ability of individual children to integrate into larger communities, including the larger space of the regional secondary school. Some children were able to do this more readily than others who remained in a "clique" of Digby Neck students after entering the regional secondary school in grade seven. Those children who "integrated" with children from other communities, particularly with the academic and sports oriented middle-class "town kids," tended to stay in school longer and were thought to be more likely to access higher education and to become mobile.

> To a greater or lesser degree it was every year. Some years it would be just two or three kids who were insular. Some kids are just uncomfortable about or afraid to mix. And then there would be another group that would mingle. And I don't know, some of it may have come from the home situation and how comfortable children coming from a particular home were with meeting particular people. Some of it may have come from sort of general community attitudes that you get from time to time. You know, they say that everybody in Digby looks down on you if you're from here so just keep your guard up to some extent.... And the Digby Neck clique, they'd be the ones more likely to head into the fishery or get a job at the local garage. They had no notion, no desire to leave this area whatsoever and didn't see education as a key to getting away because they weren't interested in getting away. They didn't see it as valuable as an end in itself because they didn't care about anything outside of the framework within which they had always existed and always expected to exist. (GG-FE)

The students who integrated better into the regional secondary school were, in the 1960s and 1970s, typically people who were streamed into the academic program. Educators implicitly understood that the academic stream contained those students defined as capable of "going on," i.e., leaving their community in the pursuit of higher education and professional jobs. In more recent times the sorting has been more subtle and the "mobile family," the family that had travelled and "seen a bit of the world" was the one that provided their children with crucial cultural capital and an advantage in school, both because of wider experience, but also because these children were better prepared for the mobility that accompanies post-secondary education. Children in mobile families were thought to be able to imagine more easily life beyond Digby Neck. Education is clearly seen as part of the picture for most mobility-oriented young people because in the mobile futures they imagine, formal education is not only imperative but a "natural stepping stone," and the destination in the working-class tradition was a job somewhere.

> Well, I don't know. I think we all as teachers encourage children to get as much education as they can. But in the rural area, college was always for the ones who wanted to leave. College, for someone to go to college, it was always a stepping stone into a job, whereas I think of the more well-to-do people, it was just a thing you do to get well-rounded and have a career. (MS-FE)

Mobile families also tended to have contacts and connections in other places. This is a crucial factor in understanding why some people move and some people stay. The truly mobile family can be reproduced in other places, and supports can be set up in a destination off Digby Neck. The "hand on the shoulder" described earlier was also a hand on the chequebook and one that passed the mobile child along into the hands of supportive relatives elsewhere.

> The thing I notice more now too in recent years for those that want to venture off that way, they seem to have a broader family connection at least in what you'd call the middle area, between here and Halifax or whatever. You can see patterns sort of. Their aunt or some family connection somewhere is living in Bridgewater or Kentville or Fall River or somewhere and if they can get a program in something that they're interested in whatever area that person may be living — even though they may not live with them when they go to study — but there's somebody there, that kind of hand on the shoulder. (CQ-FE)

## Becoming a Stranger

> Every immigrant knows in his heart of hearts that it is impossible to return. Even if he is physically able to return, he does not truly return, because he himself has been so deeply changed by his emigration. It is equally impossible to return to the ahistorical state in which every village was the center of the world. (Berger, 1984: 64)

> I think we understand, or schools perhaps promoted that what it means to be a success, is to be like me and to be free to move off into the great world, but I think the other part of the reality is that that whole mythology is starting to fall apart. (CD-ME)

> The twenty-first century will be much more about staying where you are than about going other places. (Kunstler, 2005)

Leavers did not have to worry about survival; they originated almost exclusively from relatively privileged licence-holding families. As part of their family/class privilege they had the choice between staying on the Neck connected to the fishery and moving into middle-class professions and stable trades via higher education and migration. As I have pointed out in the first section of this chapter, for women from elite fishing families, this choice was relatively clear-cut. Female leavers knew from a very early age they would not be remaining in the community.

Female leavers also understood most clearly the connection between the acquisition of education credentials and out-migration. Seeing few opportunities for themselves in the community, they regarded higher education as their path into the kind of standard of living their brothers and male friends could access through the fishery. Additionally, these leavers experienced separation from many of their Digby Neck peers from the beginning of junior high school at twelve or thirteen years of age. The streaming system in the secondary school generated two sets of divorced and radically different secondary school experiences.

> Education does take you away. I always knew I was going to leave and go to university because I always wanted to be a professional and everybody seemed to know this. When I got to junior high I was put in the [pause] I don't know what they called it at that time [pause] the advanced class. There were only two other kids from Digby Neck who got into that class. I've always wondered about that. I know the kids from the Neck were no stupider than kids from Digby, but there they were, the kids from Digby I mean, all in the advanced class. And we went right through school together.

> Most of us went on to university or at least to some kind of training.... I don't know, it just seemed that you never saw them any more because they were all in those other classes, the ones who weren't going on. (US-FL-80)

By the 1980s, it was assumed that the majority of those students in academic classes would be leaving the community and "going on" to university or some form of higher education. Leavers report that the way school guidance discussions were conducted, the kinds of presentations that were made to the "advanced" students and the subtle assumptions built into teachers' comments all transpired to reinforce the idea that beyond grade twelve there was another set of education experiences. The education triage in a high school serving coastal communities is complex. For young men there were community economic opportunities and established male identity formations to adopt; for young women there were multi-skilled work opportunities mainly in gendered service-sector employment and romantic attachments to "rich fishermen." Some secondary school students, particularly males, actively resisted secondary and post-secondary education, but approximately four in ten female students came to accept a definition of the self that included both higher education and out-migration.

> I hung out with pretty smart kids. I don't know what happened but in my senior year I began to go a very different path than a lot of my friends. I hung around with one girl and her father was a minister. We were best friends from grade two up till grade nine. And she was a little different to begin with and she was a very smart girl. There was no question about her, she was leaving. There was another smart boy in our class who always made the honours program. And my cousin did too and him [pause] I don't know what happened, he became kind of a class clown and he dropped out of school pretty early and he went to work pretty early on his father's dragger. I knew pretty well that I was off. (LS-FL-84)

Just as family connections lured many young men into the fishery, a combination of education promise and family money offered young women a set of privileged opportunities beyond high school. Young women were also beginning to understand this privilege in terms of separating themselves from their families, friends and home communities, a process that began with streaming into general and academic programs in grade seven. Being streamed into the "advanced" class allowed female leavers to gain an external perspective on the Neck; they began to see the place from which they originated through the eyes of others. This sense of alterity distanced them from their peers as well.

> You sort of started to pick up attitudes [in secondary school]. [pause] This is really difficult to put into words. You started to almost look down on some of the people who used to be your friends. Nobody told you to do this, but you were just around a different bunch of people and the way they talked about Digby Neck wasn't very complimentary, even though they knew that's where you lived. (TC-FL-79)

For women, this alterity included an acceptance of the middle-class vision of the trajectory of education into higher education and professions, out-migration to urban areas and a definition of the self separated from the Digby Neck community. This perspective is highly ambivalent for both male and female leavers of this cohort, who love the community, the people who live there and the geography; but at the same time most are unable to imagine themselves living on Digby Neck ever again. Education has provided these individuals with a different perspective, not only on their own communities, but also about the world, learning and life in general. They became strangers in the course of their education, and they learned to define themselves as girls and women according to a set of standards not generated in their home villages. This leaver describes an educationally fuelled intellectual migration that, in important respects, has removed him forever from his home place.

> You get hungry for education, you get hungry for new challenges. You're constantly [pause] I find myself constantly [pause] I have to constantly mentally challenge myself because I think I've worked. The brain's like a muscle, you work it, it's going to grow stronger, and I find myself, I have to keep mentally challenging myself all the time now because I'm in that thought process that's an institution. You've taken all your life from the time you're five or six years old till the time you're twenty-one years old, you're in school, that's three-quarters of your life learning to learn, I mean to grasp, suck in knowledge, you can't just dump yourself out and go back aboard a boat. Your brain would die. (CF-ML-86)

Like their counterparts in the earlier cohort, leavers in the 1974–1986 cohort reported significant disorientation in the social space of university. As "country kids" they had to deal with social disorientation in addition to heightened academic demands in higher education. University was defined by many leavers as a traumatic experience that left them feeling like migrants and outsiders. For Digby Neckers the simple experience of being on a college or a university campus continued to be a very rare event. When the "tunnel" of education progress led there, leavers typically had to not only survive the transition but also construct a reason for being there as well.

> But I think that all comes back and kind of circles around with maybe how their sons and daughters maybe feel toward education. If your parents understand that it's a big world, and the more you know about this outside world the better you can deal with it, or the better you can meet obstacles when they show up, and the better off you are. I don't know how much that has changed, but I know when I went to, golly, I think, what was there two of us from my class in Sandy Cove that went to university? I was a total babe in the woods as far as knowing what to expect or knowing how to do well in school. (EM-ML-80)

Most Digby Neckers who confronted the challenge of university did succeed, like the six leavers from this cohort I interviewed. Community, Schooling and Migration Survey data show that among leavers, post-secondary participation rates range between 30 and 40 percent for all age cohorts. But they were faced with a "do-it-yourself" challenge: they had to construct an education trajectory out of raw cloth. While they could "afford" higher education, these leavers had no middle-class academic path to follow. For many leavers, education success distanced them from their communities and families. This is not to say that these individuals are not "close" to their families and communities, but rather that their connections are fundamentally different because they now see Digby Neck from a geographic and social distance. They are migrants.

> When I watch refugees on TV I always feel like I know what they're going through. I mean, it sounds weird but [pause] when I left home, for a long time I felt like I was lost. I didn't know anyone or what to do next or how to act even. I had to figure out how to live in the city on top of the stuff I was learning in university. Now when I go home it's kind of like that again unless I'm around my family. (TC-FL-79)

The realization that mobility is connected to higher education is highly problematic both for the leavers themselves and for their families, who retain the strong desire to "keep family close." Out-migrants from this cohort seem to exhibit the classic "marginal man" characteristics of migrants described in the 1920s by Park (1928). They struggle to become comfortable outside their communities and realize that they will now always be strangers back home.

> Mom phoned me last week and I hadn't talked with her since July

> or August. And it's not a reflection of how much I care for her or anything, it's just that, I don't know [pause] I feel like I've drifted apart because I've been away for so long. Every time I phone home that is a question that is asked: when are you coming home? You're becoming a stranger she says. I know she [mother] gets down a lot not having me closer. But that's the lifestyle back there. People don't move very far from their house basically. There's a lot of people on Digby Neck that can throw a rock to where they grew up, right? (EM-ML-80)

The kind of ambivalence that resonates in this quote demonstrates the problematic nature of education on Digby Neck. As this informant said, on Digby Neck the "support systems are just so good." By this he means that it was relatively easy for a young man to choose fishing as his life's work and remain in the community. Families provide material and emotional support, and friendship and mutual aid networks are extensive and well developed. Virtually all leavers comment: "a lot of my friends are still there," and "some of them have done well." Finally, the environment itself is a support because people know it intimately and they know a great deal about how to exploit its resources. All of these things are "supports." For young men, education was in competition with other forms of economic and social opportunity. For women the picture was much more limited. There were significant obstacles no matter whether they chose to stay or to leave. Women still said they "had to" leave, quit school or get married. Theirs is a discourse of compulsion, and it is one into which the necessity of acquiring education credentials fit nicely. Men continue to use the language of choice in their descriptions of the education and occupational trajectories, but these choices are contextualized within class boundaries and the menu of economic and social opportunity those boundaries frame. Stayers needed to learn to negotiate the complex environment of the local economy and manage to "survive." Leavers needed to exit the community and negotiate another complex social matrix, in higher education and in unfamiliar social spaces beyond.

## Conclusion

> Nothing may reduce the speed at which those on the transparent side of the one way mirror may move. The flexibility of the world for those on the move bears an uncanny resemblance to a rock-hard indomitable reality from the viewpoint of those who have been forced to stay. (Bauman, 1999: 26)

> The more education one can have, the more choices one can see. Presumably one will exercise those options more often than not.

> So of course, if you have more options than one, you are going to have a greater incidence of migration. (SR-FE)

Options are a luxury, unequally available possibilities liberal educators wrongly imagine anyone can access. Men and women of this cohort were able to see different opportunities for themselves based on their position in the class structure of the fishery and gender. Different class and gender positions gave the reality of community a different textures, and each group, in different ways, saw into different aspects of the structural conditions in which they grew up. These social positions carried with them different education expectations. These expectations were much higher for women as a group, largely because career opportunities "around here" were so restricted. For men, social class did not necessarily "determine" education experience. Male stayers from elite fishing families typically invested their energy, time and capital intensively in the fishery from a very early age. They understood themselves to be seeing through the false promise of schooling as insurance against a downturn in the fishery. In other words, like their predecessors in the 1963–1974 cohort, they saw the promise of economic security offered by schooling as a sham in the face of a lucrative fishery. They were in on the boom period in fish dragging, and many made very good (at least short-term) money while prosperity lasted. When the fishery turned down they came to question their youthful decision to choose the fishery as their sole means of support.

Male leavers saw the same opportunities but they read the future differently. They were able to reject what they saw as the false promise of the fishery, choosing to use their economic capital to acquire education credentials. By working through the summers in the booming fishery of the late 1970s and 1980s and by accessing student loans, these leavers were able to finance their post-secondary educations. They report seeing the precarious and fluctuating nature of life and incomes in the fishery. They were ambivalent about the fishery during the boom years and continue to be about the current situation in the fishery, expressing both discomfort with the riskiness and short-sightedness of the fisherman's hunter mentality, while at the same time remembering their own experience in that highly charged masculine fishing environment with great fondness. They also share stayers' analysis of bungled historical fisheries policies of the Department of Fisheries and Oceans and their impact on the communities of Digby Neck and its way of life.

Male stayers have remained more or less successfully in the fishery, usually in a "scaled down" fashion. Both elite fishermen and those employed more marginally have suffered through the downturn in the fisheries of the 1990s. They were "lured" in by opportunities created by the expansion of the fishery in the 1970s and 1980s, and they now consider themselves fit for no other kind of work. They tend to be fishing specialists to an even greater degree than men in the 1963–1974 cohort, although some of them also engage in multiple economic activities in order to make a living. Men in this cohort have few formal education credentials, with nearly three-quarters of them (74.7 percent) never finishing high school. Formal education was clearly not important to this group, in the context of an expanding fishery through the mid-1970s to the mid-1980s, when they were coming of age, and now many of them have regrets, mortgages and families to feed.

Female stayers are more difficult to categorize. They have found multiple ways of making a living on Digby Neck. Virtually all are married or living in long-term heterosexual relationships. Some have "survived" through formal education, going out for brief periods to acquire credentials and returning to Digby Neck. Others have followed the more traditional route of working in the fishery and in multi-skilled piecemeal jobs and managing to cobble together a living. Female stayers tend to relate staying with security, just as leavers relate leaving with security. They tend to be "entrepreneurial" and occupationally versatile, and report knowing and understanding how to find work and money from multiple sources in the community in a way that they probably would not be able to do outside it. They are the kind of women Porter (1993) describes in her analysis of Newfoundland women in fishing communities — tough, committed to community, family and to the survival of their way of life. The structural context they seem to have been able to penetrate is the idea that the inshore fishery and coastal communities are doomed to the forces of history and capitalist corporate concentration. These women are very active in community survival organizations such as community development organizations and projects, organizations of small-boat fishermen and school related organizations that are concerned with the survival of both economic and institutional structures on Digby Neck.

Female stayers tend to come from what might be called working-class families. They never took seriously (or saw as part of the realm of possibility) the idea that they might attend university like the female leavers in this cohort, either because of financial restrictions, academic obstacles or because they could not (or did not wish to) overcome the community habitus of life in the fishery. These women do not necessarily accept the gendered structure of employment on the Neck and in the fishery, but they do not see that there is anything they can do about it. This is not, however, a situation of powerlessness in the eyes of these women. They work in their "space" and use their skills to keep families together and surviving on the Neck. As one stayer put it: "bitching about what I can't do ain't going to put any money in my pocket." These women, who are now in their mid-thirties to mid-forties tend to value community and family attachments, have intimate local knowledge and relatively high education levels (compared to their male counterparts), which they use in community organizations and to access paid work in "town" (Digby).

Female leavers in this cohort all attended post-secondary institutions, and most have acquired professional credentials. Each of them came from elite fishing families and saw themselves as family trailblazers, cutting out the path to higher education and eventually to out-migration and professional careers. They can be both romantically nostalgic and critical (sometimes simultaneously) about Digby Neck, its lifestyle, their families and friends. They understand clearly how they were able to use formal education to establish their lives outside the community, and they also understand how difficult it is for youth from coastal communities to "make it" into higher education and survive there. They were highly aware of the direct connection between education and migration. For these women education opened up a range of options they could never hope to achieve on Digby Neck. As the children of elite fishing families, they expected to have lives that would continue to contain the accoutrements of the middle-class lifestyles they had become accustomed in their parental homes. Eschewing early marriage and dependence on men (i.e., not wanting to be a "fisherman's wife"), the only way they could see to achieve this was through higher education and professional training. Despite this, they still look at their mobile lives with ambivalence because leavers retain bittersweet Digby Neck attachments, and, at some level, each of them longs to return "home."

The importance of fishing licences to families on Digby Neck increased through this period, with the industrialization of the fishery and the new licencing and quota regime. In 1974 the lobster fishery followed most other Canadian fisheries and was made a limited-entry fishery, meaning that only those who had licences already could continue accessing the resource. This cohort came of age during the period in which this new regime was instituted. This regulatory regime made fishing a privilege limited to a diminishing number of established players. Fishing licences are, in many respects, the glue that holds the community and families together. In the regulated fishery, they have become the method through which the privilege to fish is passed on through the male lineage, insuring the continuity of communities and family-class position. Thus, it should come as no surprise that stayers, and not only those from this cohort, envisage a serious threat to their communities, families and way of life when licences are jeopardized in any way. The imposition of the Individual Transferable Quota (ITQ) system and Industry Allocations, which gave the corporate sector exclusive access to certain stocks in the 1990s, has begun the process of intensive commodification of fishing licences, and as licences increase in value, there is an escalating incentive for fishermen to "sell out" and leave the fishery. What results is concentration of ownership in fewer and fewer hands.

From the point of view of the Department of Fisheries and Oceans, such measures are implemented for the purposes of conservation of the stocks and to halt the "tragedy of the commons." From the point of view of small-boat fishers, regulation and ITQs creates a situation where they face both declining opportunities in the fishery and at the same time increased prices for their licences. The Marshall Decision in the Supreme Court has additionally had the two-pronged effect of producing a perceived threat of an unregulated First Nations fishery, while at the same time further contributing to the value of the fishing licence as a commodity as the state buys licences and quotas for First Nations groups. Members of this cohort of stayers feel vulnerable, more vulnerable than the 1963–1974 cohort, many of whom are now well established in their fishing operations. This cohort of men is old enough to hold licences but not old enough to be established and have "everything paid for." And so, they must choose between lucrative buyouts and an uncertain future in the fishery. Young fishing families now find themselves in the position of holding licences that are at present valuable commodities, while at the same time the fishery seems to becoming more precarious as a long-term, intergenerational means of income.

The result is a highly ambivalent discourse of nostalgic desire for a community-regulated fishery controlled by those who know it best (i.e., fishers themselves), and an aggressive confrontational resistance to the incursions of both the corporate fishery and First Nations' claims.

> And there's the Indians and that's a scary thing. We could lose the whole fishing [pause]. Here I am now thirty-five years old and I don't know anything but fishing [pause] never got an education in anything else. And now with the fishery going out from under me, that puts you in a hard situation with a family to feed. And right now those licences are worth something, but tomorrow, who knows? [pause] Anybody that had a boat wanted their son to take over their boat. That was your dream, to have your son walk into your boat. But I guess that's what most fathers in the area wanted, it was just that they have something for their sons and that something was the fishing boat. Like my little feller, I was going to sell my licences but my wife says, "Harvey you can't sell his rights to the ocean out." So it's just assumed that he's going fishing. I don't really want him to go fishing but she thinks we gotta' keep it for him. And he might want to go fishing. (ES-MS-82)

With the transferability of fishing licences and quota, the fishery has gone from a common property inheritance of the "born and bred," to be passed down from generation to generation, to a valuable commodity that can be bought or sold in the market. This has entirely changed the nature of community and the way Digby Neckers see fisheries resources, their children's future chances and their own opportunities. "What young man can afford to pay six or seven hundred thousand for a lobster licence?" they ask.

This quote also returns us to the loud silence of racial exclusivity that is the flip-side of community pride of place. Through the 1970s and into the late 1980s, Digby Neck remained the symbolic property of those who were "born and bred" there. The single racism-focused interview quoted earlier in the chapter seems to indicate that most of those who disagreed with this state of affairs found other places to live. Beneath the surface of solidarity lurks exclusion and a way of constructing a gendered and raced self for a particular social position in a traditional community. As the fishery declined and restructured in the 1990s and as the value of land as a commodity increased, it became increasingly difficult to protect spatial, social and cultural boundaries, and signs of deep change have begun to emerge. Today, Digby Neck is a slightly more multicultural place and it is likely to become more so as time goes on.

This in turn has influenced the way formal education is seen on Digby Neck. With the downturn in the fishery the rhetoric around the need for children to "get their grade twelve" has intensified. However, at the same time, the late 1980s and 1990s have seen the emergence of a new set of questions about the practical value of formal education. If they "need their grade twelve," the logical next question is, "what for?" In the fluid context of neoliberalism, postFordism, globalization and what is described as the "withering away of the state," parents and children now wonder if formal education can actually deliver on the promise it has always held out, a promise of financial and occupational security. Post-modern insecurity and manufactured risk are everywhere, and they are particularly acute in rural areas, where the insecurity of the metropolitan-hinterland imbalance has always made life unpredictable. One part of this risk is the way that Digby Neck is now more open than ever before to a wide variety of "outsiders," who have an equally wide variety of plans for development, change and for rural retreat. In this climate, formal education is typically presented as a form of risk management, and youth are chided to get their education for their own good and even for their own safety.

The result of this new climate of risk may be that youth in coastal communities will flock to extended formal education for the security it offers. On the other hand, media and experientially informed images of young people with worthless degrees flipping hamburgers are powerful symbolic forces leaving many people in this cohort to question the wisdom of trusting their children's future to the unknown, uncertain and apparently discredited processes of higher education. Higher education too typically means out-migration, and in order for families and individuals to place faith and resources in a college or university education, they need to believe that there is a job, and indeed a life, at the end of the process. For families on Digby Neck the stakes are high and through the past decade the ability of formal education to deliver on its promise of prosperity is in question. And this is the world facing the cohort of 1987–1998.

## Notes

1. Licences which originally cost less than a dollar are now valuable commodities worth as much as a million dollars.
2. Several parents of women who grew up in this generation commented in informal interviews that they were actually frightened that their daughters would settle on Digby Neck and marry a fisherman. For example, this excerpt from my field notes recounts the story of one of the few families who migrated to Digby Neck.

    > All of my kids were glad to get out of here. They weren't fishing kids, especially the boys. We were really worried about our youngest daughter because she was hanging around with boys from Digby Neck. You know, when we first moved here my husband had a professional position and he was making something like $23,000. He was counselling a young fellow from down here at that time, a seventeen-year-old boy who was fishing and making $25,000. My daughter wanted a car like some of her other friends, and we had to tell her that she couldn't expect us to give her the things that a fisherman's kid could expect, we just didn't have enough money. It was tough to try to push the idea that a young person needs an education to have something in their back pocket when they see this going on with their friends. You know, education is supposed to be the ticket to security and decent money. The girls found this really hard to understand. My boys never fit in here, they were never Digby Neckers so they were never lured to that lifestyle. They didn't fit into the culture. They fit into the Digby culture, but not the one down here. It was easier for the girls because they would just have to connect with a man. But all of them are glad now that they got out of here, very glad. (FN)

3. Cole Harbour is a suburb of Greater Halifax near the city of Dartmouth. The area high school serves a racially diverse population, and it was the scene of several highly publicized instances of overt racial violence in the late 1990s.
4. In his classic ethnography of life in rural England, Blythe described the deep satisfaction of work on the land that is missed by "leavers" (1969). Blythe found that it was the class dimensions of community life that decided young men against staying rather than the rigour of rural work itself. "It is… an inescapable status quo maintained by a poor wage and the social pressures exerted by a small community, which decide the bright boys against farm work. The work itself has never been despised and those that leave it know that they will never

find anything else which is so entirely satisfying (1969: 93).

5. Fishing is a high risk, capricious and dangerous occupation. Fishermen on Digby Neck often tell stories about particularly dangerous or lucrative voyages. In all of these accounts there is a strong sense of collective struggle and accomplishment, the sense of having faced adversity with one's mates. Kurlansky writes:

   > Fishermen like to talk about their espirit de corps, and it is true that there is a warm camaraderie, a sign of being part of an elite brotherhood. Fishermen are like combat veterans who feel understood only by their comrades who have survived the same battles. But fishing is a constant struggle for economic survival. (1997: 112)

   Another contemporary literary example is *The Perfect Storm* (Junger, 1999). The movie release of the screenplay of this book was a much-anticipated event for many Digby Neck fishermen. Several of my informants had read the book and one young man commented that it was the only book he had read since dropping out of school in grade nine.

6. This leaver's response is more typical of women from elite fishing family backgrounds. In fact she was able to access university education and establish a career in central Canada. An equivalent sentiment about becoming a fisherman's wife, expressed by a fisherman's daughter, who incidentally is a fisherman's wife.

   > B: Lots of people [women] think that way, oh yeah, we'll go get this rich fuller and marry a doctor and just get out of here and not be a fisherman's wife. That's what most young girls are thinkin'.
   >
   > MC: Why, what's wrong with being a fisherman's wife?
   >
   > B: It's boring. You spend most of the time by yourself. It's lonely. You talk to a lot of them and it's, not on your life, they say, I'm not gonna stay here. And some do, they just pack up and go get a job somewheres. Doesn't matter if it's not that interesting, it's just till they meet somebody or something. Yeah, a lot of 'em have moved out of here and moved to Yarmouth or Bridgewater. (BF-FS-84)

7. By "strange" I am using the term in the sense that Simmel used it to describe "the stranger." For Simmel, the stranger was the harbinger of modernity, the individual who entered ideologically cohesive communities, providing alternative points of view. Papastergiadis describes the significance of the stranger in understanding the transformation of social bonds in the age of migration.

   > The presumption that social bonds are defined by purity of origin, and based on an exclusive characteristic, is undermined, he argues, by the ambivalent presence of strangers. Simmel thereby claims that the most responsive visions of modernity are sustained, not by the consolidation of the unified Renaissance perspective, but through the dynamic incorporation of alternative viewpoints. (2000: 66)

Bauman's work also contains extended discussions of estrangement and strangerhood in contemporary societies (1991, 1992).

8. Bauman writes:

> Whether we like it or not we are doomed to choose, to go on choosing and to justify our choices and to be painfully aware that choosing and being pressed to prove ourselves right is our fate, since in a polycentric setting we are continually exposed to more than one image of the good life, more than one personal ideal pattern, more than one proposition how to tell apart the "should" from the "should not," and more than one credible story told of the world, past or present. (1999: 134)

Chapter 6

# Surviving the Crisis

## The Classes of 1987–1998

> Myself, I love to work with my hands and go in the woods. If I'm not at work, especially with fall coming on, I want to be in the woods until spring. I cut my own wood. I'm redoing the house as I can afford it. I'm doing my own carpentry work. I gyprocked the upstairs, and I did all the plumbing and wiring. I do all my own mechanical work. I keep it [his truck] running.... I just buy my parts and do the work myself. (TB-MS-88)

> And I think of fishermen and some of the people who didn't finish [high school]. I don't ever, and would never put myself above any of them because of formal education. And in a lot of ways I think that's just the way that I am, or the way that I'm made, I'm limited too. My only choice is to pursue a formal education. I don't know if I could do what they're able to do. I don't think quite that way. I don't think I have the tenacity to do what they do day in and day out. And they probably carry the whole heart and soul of Digby Neck with them. If everyone were to get a formal education, it could be gone. I think Digby Neck would die. (KF-FL-90)

By the end of the 1980s it was beginning to appear to many observers as though the fishery would not provide reliable employment for many residents of Digby Neck, no matter how they were positioned in terms of family, social class or gender. The ground fishery was in decline, and announcement of the Newfoundland cod moratorium combined with the "moral panic" of the federal Stay in School Initiative in 1990–1991 (Anisef and Andres, 1996; Roman, 1996) to generate a clear sense among Digby area youth that there was little future in the fishery and that education was the key to personal success.[1] Locally, the scallop fishery was in decline from the late 1980s to the late 1990s and the small-boat and dragger-based ground fisheries were considerably diminished. One would expect that these kinds of forces would conspire to create a climate ripe for massive out-migration from Digby Neck in the 1990s and much higher levels of commitment to formal education. Teachers assumed that a large percentage of young people would now be forced to move away from Digby Neck in the absence of fisheries related opportunities.

> The older ones, well they went fishing and naturally a lot of them stayed around. But the young people today, you know in their twenties [pause]. Well, most of them would be gone from here. There's nothing for the younger ones... is there? (NS-FE)

From the point of view of economic rationality, there appears to be little to hold Digby Neck youth. Yet, I discovered that Digby Neck youth, particularly young men, are becoming less mobile through time. This is to say that the two younger cohorts are less mobile than Cohort 1. The youngest cohort, Cohort 3, is also less mobile than Cohort 2. The members of this group were between the ages of twenty and thirty-two. Many of them, particularly those in their early to mid-twenties are not yet "settled." Several of the youngest among them are still completing high school and many are still engaged in some form of post-secondary education and training, or are planning to "go back to school." The younger part of this cohort is clearly a group in transition.[2] However, we should still expect to find a high rate of out-migration in this population because there are no post-secondary opportunities that are easily accessible from Digby Neck and young people taking training generally have to move. Large-scale studies of migration patterns have also shown that rural people between age twenty and thirty have been historically the most mobile element in the American population (Johnson and Fuguitt, 2000). Given this propensity of rural "twenty-somethings" to migration and current economic conditions on Digby Neck, Cohort 3 should be highly mobile, much more so than either of the two previous groups. Ironically, the opposite is the case on Digby Neck.

In this coastal community, young people appear to be resisting the "rational" economic compulsion to leave. If they were rational economic agents they would form a reserve army or "adjust" by moving outside the "around here" region with its high level of reliance of transfer payments and unemployment rates and relatively low wages. But fewer than one quarter of men and less than half of the women in Cohort 3 have settled outside the fifty kilometre "around here" circle. In this relatively weak propensity to move, Digby Neck youth may be part of a larger national (Finnie, 1998; Mendelson and Bollman, 1998) and international trend (Johnson and Fuguitt, 2000) in rural areas of North America. The fastest growing communities in Canada for instance are classified "rural non-farm" by Census Canada. Of course, this growth is occurring mainly in those "rural" areas within easy commuting distance of major centres, but in this coastal community, relatively isolated from any urban centre, there is a sharp decline in out-migration among the cohort that came of age in the 1990s. The teacher's question about, "nothing for the younger ones" is poignant. How and why are these young people staying in a coastal community that appears to be both in decline economically and well outside commuting distance of any urban area?

## What Is There For the Young Ones?

Cohort 3 was the first generation to have a clear sense of the "around here" region as their place of origin. The spatial sense of this group is profoundly different from the village-level focus of Cohort 1 and the sense of being a prosperous Digby Necker found in Cohort 2. The youngest group identify most clearly with the broader space of "around here" and do not differentiate themselves so clearly from their peers in other communities like Digby and the other villages that feed into the regional secondary school. Like the older cohorts, they went to secondary school in Digby and they integrated into that school far more readily and far more successfully than people in either Cohort 1 or in Cohort 2. As one teacher put it:

> I get the impression that there's a lot less of that, the sense of packing together, more integration. But I would agree that the kids who have integrated over the years are the kids who have tended to do better, a lot better. (SF-ME)

While this group mentions general problems of integration in the regional secondary, they report less feeling of difference and less discrimination against them as Digby Neckers. The Digby area was accessible to them because there is so much "traffic" moving "up the Neck" toward Digby. Most Digby Neck families make at least three or four trips to "town" each week and typically more.

> Most of the ones I went to school with are up in Digby or around there somewhere. You see them around working different places, or in the stores [pause] the club [local tavern], you know. I mean there's always somebody going to town, it's no problem to get up there. I can live home here and still get to work no problem. I got a car now. (HV-MS-98)

As was the case for previous cohorts, young men have more to hold them on the Neck (relative to women) and more opportunity to find work and social support while remaining close to home. But the sense of home is within the ambit of the "around here" region. The young man quoted below has lived outside the local area but never felt comfortable there. His description of the geography of home identifies the "around here" region very clearly. The vista from Deep Brook hill on Highway 101 and the Bear River bridge that separates Digby from Annapolis counties are often cited as the spatial markers identifying home for stayers.

> The whole time I was away I didn't want to be there. I've never wanted to be anywhere else. I grew up here, I know what it's like to live here. If you put up with the gossiping and the small town stuff. It's not perfect but you put up with it. I never wanted to leave here. Even in Digby, I still call it home. Even when I come home on the bus, when I got to that Digby County sign on the Smith's Cove bridge, I felt I was home. (KS-MS-89)

Women on the other hand report being encouraged to leave the Neck and sometimes the area around here. Even those who have remained on Digby Neck retain a highly tentative sense of attachment and claim that they stay in the area because it is difficult for them to make a life elsewhere, either for social, financial or family reasons. In this cohort, the categories of "stayer" and "leaver" become blurred, especially for women. n 1996, women's unemployment rates as two to three times higher on Digby Neck than the national and provincial averages. Men's unemployment rates on the other hand were right around those averages. Many women who remain on Digby Neck are there not because they want to be, but because they have no other options. This university-educated "stayer" for instance was encouraged to pursue education and to use that education to leave the area for places with more "opportunity."

> They [parents] loved me, they would love to be around me but they know that I have to make a life for myself and if it's elsewhere that you have to seek it then that's where you have to go. They knew that as I was getting older it was being seen that the economic or job situation I guess you could say, wasn't that great for women. They knew I wasn't the type of person that could stand to cut fish for a living. And they basically said that if you want more, then you're going to have to go somewhere to get it. (WC-FS-92)

University-educated women from this cohort were very much in agreement with the idea that there is nothing in the local area for them. Through the 1980s and 90s school success came to be linked with post-secondary education, and family and school expectations for higher education became more normalized. Their expectations of professional positions were simply unattainable in the local area, and they realized the necessity of moving outside the area in order to find suitable work.

> I applied for a job in Digby. I thought it would be neat to work in economic development or that kind of thing. There weren't any opportunities. That's why I decided I couldn't stay here. But I

> would have stayed here if I could have found a long-term position. (KF-FL-90)

Having completed higher education, leavers came to see the local labour market of the late 1980s to the late 1990s as inadequate in terms of opportunity and income. Their education placed them in a position where they had significant debt and significant investment in career trajectories that were not tenable "around here." Remaining in the area was out of the question for this group and indeed, there was "little for them" here. Another "stayer," who was at the time of the interview on the cusp of leaving to pursue post-secondary education, spoke of his parents' intention that he leave.

> Yeah, they do [talk about his leaving] a lot, they think you're better off leaving. There's more out there for finding something to do and higher paying jobs. That's for sure. You got to go to the city or something, you'll get a job no problem. They don't see many opportunities on Digby Neck. There's nothing here unless it's fishing or teaching or something. (HV-MS-98)

But despite this mobile discourse, most Digby Neck youth now also realize that it is difficult to leave, even if one has "the marks" (credentials and good grades). Male and female stayers both identified work and family and the connection between these two as the way they are able to remain on the Neck. Family traditions of working hard and supporting one another have allowed young people to be able to remain on Digby Neck.

> When I was growing up. Well, it was like that… we always worked. Everybody in my family worked. You know, that's how we were brought up. And they help us out, finding jobs and that. We're a really close family you know. (LL-FS-88)

Family also provides the kind of support that enables young people not yet "on their own" to live with a relative amount of dignity on limited funds. As informants are quick to point out, on the Neck there are no homeless people and there are many who "do for others." The story below provides a tangible example of this support, which stands in contrast to the assumptions built into my question about moving to a place where there is more work. The ability to find a job is only one of many concerns for a single mother and a move to an urban area would create tremendous insecurity in her precarious life. In her situation, staying is security, and leaving would be a considerable risk involving the abandonment of the very social supports that make her life situation tenable and keep her child's care within the trusted circle of the family.

> U: I take whatever work I can get. It ain't much, but babysitting, that's no problem. My mother and my grandmother and my sisters, they all help out. I'd be out on the streets somewhere if it wasn't for them.
>
> MC: Have you ever thought about moving maybe to the city where there's more work?
>
> U: [laughs] More work; yeah right! Who's gonna hire me? My grade ten ain't gonna' get me no job: MacDonald's maybe. And where would I live? I mean I'm better off here. I got a place to live and my family is close. (UR-FS-95)

Rather than seeing "nothing for her" on the Neck, this young woman sees nothing for her anywhere else. This woman's social capital is local, and she survives in a context of family caring and sharing, which is becoming increasingly essential with the erosion of state social supports. The world outside the "around here" area is defined as a "world apart" and one that is not congenial or even accessible for many stayers.

> It's a totally different world apart and I can easily see how someone might decide not to take that step and leave, and try to do those things because it is such a different world apart. (ET-ML-87)
>
> Most people that are there, they're set in their ways and they all like it down there. They like the Neck and I think most of them will stay there. They won't leave, not the ones that I went to school with. (HV-MS-98)

When I asked members of this cohort about the connection between education and leaving, their answers all confirmed that everyone understood the link in retrospect. And the link works both ways for this cohort: one needs to leave to be educated, and one needs to be educated to leave. Without education, leaving is virtually impossible. Without leaving, formal education beyond high school is very difficult to obtain. Youth who lack family support to finance higher education are virtually doomed to staying, regardless of their intentions. However, this link between education and leaving was not always understood consciously at the point where fateful life course decisions were made. When I raised the question, my informants were able to make the association between decisions taken for nebulous reasons and attachment to a particular way of life.

> I don't think they're going to think that the reason I'm quitting school is because I don't want to go anywhere. You know. I don't

> think they actually put that link together. How many people really understand why they do what they do? (WC-FS-92)
>
> To me it would be one of those hidden messages inside your body. It makes a whole lot of sense. Education means that you have to move. If you don't want to move, why get the education? (KS-MS-89)

Others understood clearly that the decision to remain in the area was implicated in their youthful decision to leave formal education. For those young men who had family and connections to the fishery and who had a very clear sense of purpose and direction in terms of locally oriented fishing opportunities, education continued to seem irrelevant. This stayer has mixed feelings about his decision to leave school well before graduation, but his life has unfolded much as he expected it would in his teens.

> I knew it was an important decision for me. I knew that at the time. Like when I decided that I was going to quit I knew it was a big decision. I decided well, 'cause I didn't want to go to college and I knew where I was going to end up and that was down here and fishing. And I just thought about it, what I'm going to get for education wasn't going to help me at least not at that time. It was only going to hold me back a couple of years if anything. (TB-MS-88)

Returning to the question, "what is there for the young ones?" the answer appears to be that for young men there are still opportunities in the fishery, albeit on a limited basis and at peak times. One of my key informants, an older fisherman, commented that during the lobster season it is often difficult to get anyone who "wants to work." He complained that, "with all this unemployment that's supposed to be around here you'd think it'd be no problem to find somebody to go fishing. Well I can't find anyone to work" (FN).[3] It is difficult for members of this cohort to stay in the local area doing seasonal or temporary work on a permanent basis due to changes in the employment insurance program. For this reason, some members of this cohort have become transient, moving between seasonal employment in the fishery and temporary employment in Halifax, western and central Canada. This makes the distinction between "leaver" and "stayer" problematic with this cohort. This informant, for instance, defines himself as a "nomad."

> It used to be that you could get enough work around here to make it right through the year. Not any more. So when fishing [lobster season] is over, I'll be going out west again. They fucked up the pogey [unemployment insurance] so you gotta' be a goddamn no-

> mad. It sucks, but what can you do? My father don't have a licence so I got nothing holding me here. (KF-ML-91)

For young men, the crucial connection that allows one to remain in the fishery is the family business and especially the "direct" connection of the fishing licence. An important part of this direct connection to the fishery is the expectation that a young man's destiny is fishing and part of his gendered privilege. This is a destiny that is not necessarily critical of education, but it precludes post-secondary education because of the sheer time the work takes and because education is still perceived to be unnecessary. Besides, young men still need to learn the craft and multiple skills of fishing.

> They have encouragement from their parents. You're going to be a fisherman, you're supposed to be fishing, that's your life, that's what I did, you know, and that's where you're going to make your money so stop screwing around in school and get to work. Help me out; I need help and you gotta' help me. They end up helping them for the summer and then just don't end up going back to school a lot of the times. (ET-ML-87)

Stayers who lack this direct "blood" connection, or who lost it through fisheries regulation changes, unfavourable quota allotments, death of a parent or some other means have a more difficult time getting into fishing in a permanent and sustainable way. While there continue to be opportunities crewing on "company boats" or for small inshore operators like lobster fishermen, the most direct connection to the fishery is through family licences. Those young men who grew up knowing that their fathers would "pass on their rights" via inheritance were pressured into fishing much more than young men who could not anticipate inheritance privileges.

> I find… I don't know, to have your father above you when you get a lobster licence, there's more pressure to go fishing. But without their father they wouldn't have the chance to go at all. (KS-MS-89).

The ability to work hard and to learn the complex of fishing-related skills remained the central focus of socialization to a life in the fishery for male stayers. This socialization also continued to be the principal justification for school resistance and the idea that, even in the 1990s, a young Digby Neck man did not need significant formal education. In fact, as education theorists as diverse as Tom Newkirk (2002), Lois Weis (2004), Nancy Lesko (2001), Daniel Cottom (2003), Paul Willis (1977) and Valerie Walkerdine (1990) have pointed out, many young men reject school and its structures and practices precisely because they have other ways of succeeding in the world that do not involve engagement with school. In the late 1980s, there continued to be a strong labour market locally for those young men "born and bred" in the fishery.

> It was no problem to get a job fishing. There was lots of work around. I think I caught the last end of it when there was lots of jobs around. My brother, he left when he was fifteen, younger than I was and he started right in fish dragging. He was on a sixty-five-foot fish dragger. And they made big money, it was really big money for a kid. (TB-MS-88)

Younger members of this cohort did face a more difficult labour market in the fishery. By the early 1990s, the availability of work in the fishery was very unstable except for young men who had direct access to family fishing licences. Telling the story of his return to the community from university in the early 1990s, this young man saw work opportunities but doubted that he would be able to access them.

> I never once missed university and I told him, that… the fuller you had to see before you left, and he would ask you questions about why you was going. I was wearing an Ultramar hat or something and he said it looks like you're going to go home and get a job pumping gas. I said, no, I got the hopes of going home and going fishing. (KS-MS-89)

By the end of the 1990s, there were few fisheries related opportunities for young Digby Neckers, but there was a growing menu of local service-industry jobs. For many stayers, any work is better than school. As one young man commented, wondering why I would want to continue working in schools, "working on a lobster boat ain't my favourite kind of job, but it's a hell of a lot better than goin' to school" (FN). But it is not just fishing that gives young people "something to do." Two major grocery chains and several fast food franchises moved into Digby in the late 1990s and these have provided new opportunities for stable but low-wage work. Tourism has also created new opportunities on the margins of the labour force for many youth who remain "around here." Part-time minimum-wage jobs combined with extended family support and a relatively low cost of living in rural Nova Scotia all contribute to making life "around here" as viable as anywhere else.

> You know there's some that get jobs waitressing. And they work at the new Superstore if they can get in there. Then there's Shaw's (a wood fabrication plant). I mean they aren't big money jobs, but they're jobs. (UR-FS-95)

Educators comment that students are not necessarily making the link between education and out-migration in the 1990s and that even fairly focused "around here" types are beginning to view education as a way of remaining in the community. This is perhaps an emerging trend for the educationally successful stayer.

> Well the young lady that I referred to awhile ago about now being focused spent two years at university and could have come home any time but since her summer placement this summer and knowing now that she's found an area of specialization and there's going to be opportunities to come back here and do that. Well now she will even go out of province for a year or two now that she knows she can come back and spend the rest of her life here. This is what she wants to do. (CQ-FE)

## Quitting in the 1990s: Finding Something to Do When There's Nothing to Do

> If you're not encouraged to do well in education, I think you become complacent and when you know that you've got something waiting there for you like a lot of people here did. If, you know, you get a fishing boat or whatever that you can go to, or if your family has money you don't have to think about these things. You know, they don't have to be concerned with what they have to take on as responsibility for their careers and education. It's the same in other small towns I've worked in. (KF-FL-90)

The federal Stay in School Initiative launched in 1990 was a well financed state propaganda campaign designed to create a "learning culture" for Canada and to convince individual youth that they ought to finish at least secondary schooling. While high-school graduation rates did climb nationally and in most Canadian provinces through the 1990s, young people continued to quit school because it seemed to them irrelevant. For many young people of Digby Neck, higher education and even secondary schooling were irrelevant (Corbett, 1991). In order for a course of action to seem relevant, it must be situated within a context. As the previous two chapters have shown, extended formal education was not a well integrated part of the male community habitus on Digby Neck in the 1960s, 1970s and 1980s.

> Yeah, they don't see education as kind of life long, or even beyond school. Or maybe community college for one or two years, that's what a typical student sees. And they don't know that they're going to be competing against university graduates for those seats in the

> community colleges. There are a lot of things that they just don't realize. (SF-ME)

Into the early 1990s this familiar male resistance remained powerful. Describing the attitude of her male peers, this young woman described male resistance to formal education that was built on the perception that education was unnecessary to earn a good living as a fisherman.

> I think they thought, I don't need this, you know, I don't. They put this big exterior barrier up and try to [pause] in their own minds; they're trying to tell themselves that that's reason why they're quitting, because they just don't need it [pause]. I can make money out there without having to put myself through this. (WC-FS-92)

However, by the middle of the 1990s, it was common for most people to parrot the Stay in School rhetoric and evoke the notion that "you need your grade twelve." Young women tended to act on this advice, as nearly 90 percent (88.1%) of girls in Cohort 3 graduated high school. For some children who came of graduating age in the 1990s, higher education did seem relevant. Some young women whose families could afford to send them on to university or community college could see the sense in acquiring a higher degree, which would allow them to access employment and social opportunities that Digby Neck could not provide.

> It's almost like there were two different groups of people from Digby Neck as well. There were people whose fathers owned their own fishing boat and had the satellite dishes and the new Ford trucks and the nice houses, and then there were those people whose parents worked in the fish plants. If you came from the first kind of family like I did, you wanted to keep your lifestyle and you knew you couldn't do that without education. (KC-FL-92)

A part of this privilege was the cultural capital, the family-based understanding that in order for women to reproduce economic and other forms of privilege for themselves they had to acquire higher education credentials. Their context was one of relative financial privilege. For these women, the path provided by financial comfort was an educational one.

> I guess we discussed university and what we wanted to do. It didn't have to be university but they wanted us to further our education so that we could better our lives. It always seemed like that's the way it was going to be. I was going to graduate from high school, and then after that I was going to go on to university. It just always seemed to be that path. (KC-FL-92)

Daughters of these licence-holding families, like their predecessors in the previous cohort, were expected to continue with their education and move away from the Neck. These expectations were sometimes stated but were also implied and made possible by associations these women "naturally" formed in the regional secondary school with other mobile young middle-class women. In this way these women used their economic privilege through the medium of formal schooling, where gendered traditions of school success for women were already established in previous cohorts. These young women were actively encouraged to take advantage of mobility and education opportunities that women who preceded them could only imagine. These young women were, after all, the children of the women of Cohort 1.

> I remember sitting down with mom and dad and talking about university. With mom especially now that I think about it. She wanted me to have chances she didn't have. (KC-FL-92)

> It was just that we all knew we were going to university. It was never instilled in me that you were going to university or to further your education. I was kind of on my own to figure it out. All of my friends in high school were from Digby. But people from here. They were fisherman. And I'm trying to think of the girls. I kind of broke from them as soon as I went to high school. And the guys were fishermen and they knew that this is what they were going to be doing. And for the most part they did. (KF-FL-90)

Other young men and women saw a more local set of options because their families were not in a position to allow them to reasonably expect that they could ever "go to college." For young men in the early part of this cohort, the fishery remained a viable option, but as this option lost its viability, other educationally related options did not necessarily become more attractive or accessible. Young women from less privileged backgrounds considered higher education outside the scope of their potential.

> You just can't decide you're gonna' go to college. I mean, you never thought about something like that. Where's the money gonna' come from in the first place? I mean, we just didn't go there. Nobody in my family got the brains to do something like that. That's something maybe you do if you're rich or something. (UR-FS-95)

The Stay in School literature of the 1990s was peppered with arguments of economic rationality attempting to convince youth that without at least a high school diploma, their future was limited and diminished. As one slogan read: "more education = more choices." This supposedly common-sense equation between education and employment and personal prosperity was not read by all Digby Neck students as it was intended to be understood. Those who were unable to access higher education because of poverty or a checkered academic career, or simply because they were following a well-worn family path, did not see higher education as something they could or would want to access. And as the fishery turned down, families that could in more prosperous times have afforded to send their children on to post-secondary education became more careful about the kind of education and training they would fund. Fewer and fewer families could afford the privilege of higher education in the 1990s.

> And the money is a big factor too now in the sense that it's not a real option for more and more children all the time. Tuition fees, textbooks and other additional costs for some programs, and then if you have to pay room and board for the whole week or part of the week, then you're looking at ten to twelve thousand dollars. That's hard to come by for some families. (CQ-FE)

Despite the force of the Stay in School rhetoric, many people in this cohort (particularly, once again, men) did not finish high school. The shallow cant of the anti-dropout rhetoric was no match for increasing tuition fees and diminishing student aid. Young men in the early part of this cohort were still able to access fisheries work, but what about those who came of graduating age in the 1990s? Although almost 90 percent of women in Cohort 3 graduated high school, why did more than 50 percent of men drop out? At one level, it is a problem of gendered environments of risk and security. Most women have been forced to take the risk and move away from home, but many young men are more protected from the need to acquire higher credentials (by their privileged positions in fishing families and the gendered structure of work) and more resistant to education. According to female informants, this male resistance was also fuelled by an unwillingness to take chances outside the known environment and the familiar structure of risk-taking in the fishery.

> I don't really know about the women, I can just remember the men because the majority of the men are still here. I think people that don't have education are kind of scared about what's out there [pause]. They're safe with their familiarity. I guess if you're willing to take the risk on having an education then part of you is willing to take the risk to move on to another area. (WC-FS-92)

Stayers' comments about their schooling evince a discourse of boredom, frustration, misbehaviour, disinterest and waiting until an opportunity to leave presented itself.

> Well I was just frustrated, I got bored. I lost interest in grade nine. I can say I was right at the top [of the class] and all my friends said, "well you're in with the nerds." All my friends skipped class and smoked. By the time I got to grade ten I just give it up. It was the lure of the loot I suppose [laughs]. They were sitting in school and I was making money. (TB-MS-88)

But the question remains: "what is there for them around here?" The fishery is the answer only for a limited number of the elder males in this cohort. Recently those opportunities have come in the form of service-sector work. Educationally resistant "bad" kids find work in a variety of low wage jobs in rural communities.

> I don't know, they were always kind of bad anyway most of them [laughs]. I know they found a lot of the [school] work hard, English and math and history. They had a very hard time with it all. They didn't know how to cope with it really. I guess they must have found jobs or something to do. You know, work in a store or pump gas or something like that. One or two of them might do a little fishing. (HV-MS-98)

> Most of 'em find enough work in stores and restaurants and stuff to get their stamps.[4] (UR-FS-95)

One of the reasons for increased graduation rates among young women is that many of the service-sector jobs available "around here" now require high-school completion. But there remain a significant number of low-wage service-sector jobs, particularly more manually-oriented jobs available to young men, that do not. The masculine "bad boy" persona (Kenway and Kraak, 2002) that typically leads to school failure can actually translate into the kind of risk-taking work behaviours, work orientations and discourse patterns that are valued on fishing boats and in other resource extraction workplaces. The idea that there's "lots of work" in Digby is cited by stayers, who see the expansion of the rural service sector as a way to piece together enough income to survive. This expansion also makes the lure of low-wage opportunities beyond the local area less attractive. One individual even used one of our interviews to get information on the local job scene, wondering if things had gotten better in Digby since he left more than a year before, prior to the opening of the two large grocery outlets.

> Well I know one of my buddies is working in the Sobey's. There seems to be quite a bit of work up in Digby right now. Do you think I could get a job there now if I came home? (FG-ML-97)

Through the 1990s, young Digby Neckers continued to quit school because they continued to see the disconnection between education and the community habitus. The local job market requires particular kinds of workers, and not necessarily workers prepared in formal education. Why do labourers, tourism workers, part-time and seasonal fisheries workers, gas pump attendants, chambermaids and supermarket cashiers require a high-school education? The argument that even these jobs now require high school graduation is taken as one very clear marker of the irrelevance and irrationality of the whole process of formal education. And how will post-secondary education help a community-oriented youth integrate better into occupational and social networks that are controlled by people whose education comes from local experience? These are questions of resistance. Education, for these stayers, was a series of disconnected abstractions delivered in a suspect institution. While the occupational sphere in the "around here" region has expanded to include service sector work in the growing retail sector in Digby, most "available" work that is seen as achievable is unconnected to formal education. Young people are staying in school longer because these new employers have slightly higher education requirements than many fisheries-related jobs have traditionally held, but the song remains the same, "You don't need much education to make it around here; what you need is to be able to work" (FN). However, for an increasing number of young people the notion of "making it" has changed to fit jobs that offer them a few hours of work a few days each week, just barely enough to survive while living with parents.

> Well, I got to live [at] home. I could never afford much on my own. I had a place in town [Digby] for a while, but everything went to the rent. So I come back home. But I want to get a place of my own. It's just temporary. (UR-FS-95)

This young woman's lifeworld is obviously far away from the world of the young women who describe growing up assuming that they would be going to university and leaving the area. The significance of the discourse around the importance of school is situated within the different experiences of differently placed individuals. Understandings of the self are not uniform among Digby Neck youth, even if they received the same education and mobility messages in school. Some individuals are positioned to access and act on the power/knowledge of the contemporary school and to understand why they ought to remain there until the end working to construct a mobile self. Others do not have that privilege and are forced into another track, constructing an immobile self, one that uses the natural and social assets at hand. All of this young woman's meagre resources are concentrated in the local social geography of Digby Neck. She has no portable resources, and as Charles Dickens' lawyer Pettifog kept reminding Pip, money is the most portable property of all.[5] What can be constructed as resistance to education can also be constructed as developing a gendered identity that fits with available opportunity in the changing but not necessarily "new"[6] circumstances of the rural economy.

## The New Reserve Army of Labour

> Well, I got a chance to try it up in Ontario. There was work up there when I left home. (FG-ML-97)

One of the most powerful theoretical explanations of out-migration from Atlantic Canada has been the reserve army of labour thesis (Veltmeyer, 1979, 1990). This thesis fits within the general structure of Marxist political economy and argues that social-class exploitation takes on a regional dimension within the modern state and that pools of labour are kept in "reserve" in peripheral predominantly rural areas, where they are warehoused until needed during periods of capital expansion in metropolitan regions. Veltmeyer argues that Atlantic Canada is a textbook case for this phenomenon and that population flows in and out of Atlantic Canada can be seen in terms of the needs of capital in industrial central and western Canada. When industry needs workers in the "core" they are siphoned out of the "periphery" only to be returned when the work is done. The key problem with this analysis is that it largely ignores communities and cultural forces in peripheral regions, arguing that people living on the rural margins are simply shunted to and from by the "needs" of big capital in other places (Southcott, 1999). While this political economy is presented as a theory of emancipation, it is, in practice, yet another theory that explains away the culture of coastal communities. In other words, it effectively denies the importance of the agency of rural inhabitants. This analysis shows that the population of the coastal communities on Digby Neck is mobile and out-migration from the villages of Digby Neck is significant, but the bulk of this out-migration remains within what Veltmeyer would describe as the periphery. There is only a relatively small groups of "nomadic" migrant labourers moving back and forth between the rural "periphery" of the coastal community and the metropolitan "core." Far more numerous are individuals working hard to become established "around here."

Does the reserve army in its traditional sense still exist in a rural place like Digby Neck? Cohort 3 is the most transitional group in this study. Many of them are still preparing for permanent employment by taking post-secondary programs or moving from job to job looking to "find themselves" and establish more permanent residence and occupational identities. This is true of both leavers and stayers and among younger members of this cohort there are few exceptions. For most young men and women who remain on Digby Neck, the mobility necessary to be "useful" as a member of the reserve army of labour does not appear to be evident. Young people on the margins in rural communities lack the portable resources necessary to move, even temporarily, to urban areas. They understand that marginal jobs in cities are not sufficient to support a reasonable standard of living and that the supports they have at home from family and friends can.

> I tell everyone down there, stay where you are. You can't get nothing to live in for less than five or six hundred a month. And the jobs up here [a southern Ontario city], they're about the same as what you could probably get in Digby, only thing is you don't know nobody. So why bother. I'll probably be coming home this summer. (FG-ML-97)

Part of the Stay in School rhetoric was the functionalist notion that formal education s necessary to escape a life of marginal, poorly paid, dead-end jobs. Yet, even for young people with higher education credentials the situation can be just as bleak. This young woman's story tells a tale of five years of transient work experience "away" from home. While she believes what everybody says, that "there's nothing here for you," her life experience has led her back to the supports available at home.

> I lived in Halifax for three years and then I moved away to Ottawa, tried to find work there but with a BA you need more now — you need a masters, in whatever field and I basically couldn't afford to stay out there just on my volunteer work so I came back home, and then years passed, I worked as a supervisor in Digby and then I got married and my husband got a job in Toronto so I moved out there and then he got laid off and [pause] money situation again, so we moved back down. (WC-FS-92)

Even for some well-educated individuals who have taken the plunge and pursued the higher education route, the economy of the 1990s proved a difficult environment in which to establish roots. The "jobless recovery" of the late 1990s did not provide the kinds of white collar "good jobs" that highly educated graduates from previous cohorts could access with relative ease. For those wishing to find anything other than marginal service employment "away," it does appear to be essential that they have some post-secondary credential.

> I got my ticket up at vocational and that's how I got on. But the work isn't steady out here [an Alberta city], so I'm back and forth.

> Sometimes me and my girlfriend we wonder where I'm going to land next month. She's out here because that's where her family is and she's got a job. But me, I could be anywhere between here and home. (KF-ML-91)

This transient "leaver" is a classic reserve army labourer whose work and location are determined by the "needs of capital" in western Canada. But he also moves into the coastal community during peak fishing periods to work in the fishery, sometimes leaving steady jobs in order to do so. It is not simply economic rationality that drives this man's decisions, he is also drawn back to his community, which is his home, and the way of life and work rhythms seem "natural" to him. His family connections provide him with a place to live, free meals and access to work because he is "known," connected by "blood," and welcome as one of the family.

> Oh Jesus, she [his girlfriend] gets some pissed off with me. She says, "what, you're gonna quit to go back there for a couple of months?" But she don't understand how I love fishing. I guess it's in my blood or something. And when I get that call to go home and go to work aboard a boat, well, like the song says, "you can take this job and shove it." (KF-ML-91).

The new reserve army seems perpetually in transition. Most informants in this cohort are ready to move when the right moment arrives. The trouble is that they have considerable difficulty breaking attachments and garnering the resources necessary to finance either higher education or a move to another part of the country.

> I would move in a heartbeat. Why? I know that's your next question — and I shouldn't probably say this with friends sitting in the room but… friends. I don't have the friends here that I used to have. After high school everybody moves on and all you got left is your family. Well that's important, but it wouldn't keep me here if a good opportunity came up. (LL-FS-88)

This recent graduate describes a life of working in manual jobs in a kind of holding pattern, working in minimum-wage jobs, saving and waiting for the right time to enter post-secondary education. Like many of his friends from Digby, he is "taking a year off," a year which has stretched into two. He also describes a common disjointed school-to-work-to-school trajectory which is now being taken by many of his "town" peers.

> Most of my friends are still here in Digby. But they're going away next year like I am. A lot of my friends have gone to university for

> one year and come back to work this year and uh, two of them have dropped out. One went back this year and another is going back next year. They failed actually. It's a lot of pressure. And it's so expensive, you can't just go and stay there until you finish. (HV-MS-98)

This informant also went on to claim that there is a good deal of work now available locally for a young person who is "not too fussy" and willing to "take what they can get." So the reserve army seems to have established a new encampment in the rural communities surrounding the newly developing regional service centre of Digby. These businesses have created the need for a pool of part-time and minimum-wage labour "around here" to supplement resource harvesting jobs and more established tourism and service-sector opportunities. The Stay in School rhetoric rings true for young women, who are now required to have "grade twelve" for cashier jobs. While these marginal jobs are acceptable to middle-aged women looking to re-enter the labour force on a part-time basis, they are transitional McJobs to many young people, who are waiting for something better or the chance at post-secondary training. Quitting school these days is not like it was in the 1980s, when there was money to be made in the expanding fishery. However the connection between school and steady lucrative employment is even more tenuous now than it has ever been. Given that this is so, it should come as no surprise that so many Digby Neckers stay around here waiting for things to improve and taking "whatever they can get" in the meantime.

## Getting Out: Class, Gender and Education

> I think part of it may have been income. It's perceived and it's true, college and university costs money and I think that Digby Neck certainly had two classes of people, two distinct classes. It had the people who owned boats and fish plants and they had people who worked on boats and in fish plants. I think there was a real dividing line there, a huge gap in income and I think a lot of the people who didn't have the income did not encourage their kids to get off Digby Neck. A lot of it was 'cause they didn't have an education either and they maybe didn't understand the whole concept of getting an education; but also, they didn't have the money to do that. (ET-ML-87)

Many of those families that have survived the crisis in the fishery in the past decade and who have managed to retain fishing licences and family-based fishing operations are the entrepreneurial middle class in coastal communities. While men's work is tough and industrial in character, it typically remains a small family business, albeit one operated by fewer and fewer families. The kind of independent, rugged character structure that was established as the standard for masculinity in the fishery remains the most prominent model for men who stay. Working hard, being tough and multi-skilled, highly dextrous and taking risks are among the skills needed for business success in fishing and fishing-related industries.

Like any business, it is the basis of a family's wealth, an inheritance for children and a valuable commodity all at the same time. Just as elite fishing families in Cohort 2 passed on fishing privileges to male children and educations to female children, young Digby Neckers in Cohort 3 faced different inheritances on the basis of family wealth and position in the fishery. As I showed in the first part of this chapter, the children of families whose connection to the fishery was through paid employment rather than licence or business ownership would never have considered the possibility of going to university any more than they could conceive of finding several hundred thousand dollars to buy him a fishing licence. Post-secondary education credentials are obviously marks of privilege, and they are bought at considerable expense. But they are presented less as privileges than as universally accessible choices or "options" by teachers. In the liberal analysis of many public school teachers, education is not a prerogative of any particular class, but the inalienable right of any individual who makes the right "choices." The importance of good choices is the hallmark of contemporary liberal educators' idea of what schooling ought to provide.

> Somehow the individuals have to have the usual sorts of liberal things that I value: knowledge, skills, they have to have the equipment of make choices and to recognize the implications of the choices they make. (SR-FE)

The difficulty with this liberal view is that it fails to address seriously the differential access that social class, gender and race represent in a given school. On Digby Neck, for instance, while school is taken to be fair, it is also recognized openly that some individuals have an advantage that stems from their family background. Secondary education was designed for those "moving on," and those who move on are those who can afford mobility.

> Being somewhat pushy by times I call some of these kids aside and say, do you realize that you have extraordinary abilities and powers in this and this and then and I say to them, it doesn't really concern me where you do this kind of thing, but that you shouldn't abandon it at graduation. And then there's kind of a nice little sweet smile and a shrug of the shoulders and they're off. (SR-FE)

Former students in this cohort are much more aware of how schooling is more easily dealt with by the children of professional parents. This is the habitus, the subtle nuances of taste and discrimination that mark out successful students' "intelligence" (Bourdieu, 1984a). In a coastal community, the professional class are "strangers" in Simmel and Bauman's terms; they often come from the "outside" and bring different values. This recent graduate's description of the kind of students who are successful in high school demonstrates a particular idea of what counts as "smart," but also a corollary vision of the kinds of families that understand the education system and help their children negotiate it. Significantly, and more than a bit ironically, teachers themselves are also identified as the very kind of "stranger" who can support their own children's education in a way that families whose traditions are rooted in the fishery cannot.

> Who succeeds in school? Smart ones: a lot of 'em, like, that had doctors or teachers or ministers for parents. I found that they did way better in school for some reason. Maybe it's because of the people they were around. You know, if your father's always fishing and working around boats or something. I found their marks were a little lower for some reason. There wasn't people around like encouraging them, people that went through university and had degrees and stuff that could sit down and help you. I found my parents, it kind of confused 'em. The parents that went to university and stuff found it easier to help out with projects and stuff. And if they had questions it was probably easier for them. (HV-MS-98)

If locally successful families have deep local knowledge, resilience and attachment to place, school successful families have a different array of knowledge and specifically what might be called an attachment to the multiform spaces produced in contemporary capitalism (Lefebvre, 1997). In the vernacular, they are more "worldly" or more "connected/wired" to the global scapes and flows (Castells, 2004; Urry, 2000) of late modernity. The discourse of education attainment is framed by most informants of this cohort in terms of families that "valued" education and those that did not. Families that valued education saw education connecting an achievable and desirable career trajectory for their children as opposed to families whose identity and day-to-day life practice was tied up in localized work. Educators distinguished between "work-focused" families and "education-focused" families. In this cohort family connections were seen as the lynchpin both for work opportunities and education opportunities. Employment opportunities are "family oriented," meaning that unless a young man has a direct family connection to licences, he may not have any opportunity to work in the fishery. In other words, the working class in the small-boat fishery is shrinking, leaving only family business opportunities for individuals positioned to inherit them and increasingly sporadic temporary work for the rest. The result is that the traditional fisheries "working-class," the individuals who crew or work in fish processing, are being squeezed out as family members and older "experienced hands" (who often have families to support) are given first priority for a diminishing pool of labour jobs.

> A few years ago I think you could have pretty well taken a job anywhere. Now it's harder and you've got to be almost family oriented because any man in this community, if they're in their thirties, or mid-thirties to forties, they've done this job before. For a young person starting out with no family connections it's hard. I know all about it. (KS-MS-89)

Families that "valued" work were those families that needed either labour in small-boat fisheries operations or who had a family history of working in the fishery. By the 1990s fewer families were in this position, and employment opportunities for work-oriented Digby Neckers decreased. Education-oriented families were those families that had acquired significant capital during the industrialization of the fishery and who saw schooling and post-secondary education as the most sensible path for their children, especially their daughters. As one informant commented, "The ones who made the real money don't care about the community; they're sending their kids off to college. They've got it made and their kids are gone" (FN). Those families who prospered were the ones able to afford to educate their sons and daughters and turn their financial capital into the social capital of education. In Cohort 3 this was the case and more children of elite fishing families did access higher education than in previous cohorts. Gender differences still remained significant though as 50 percent more women than men in Cohort 3 reached the post-secondary level. But at the same time the percentage of Digby Neck men who had the lowest levels of education credentials actually rose. So while more young men and women were graduating high school and getting post-secondary education in the 1990s (compared to Cohort 2), at the same time, more young men were quitting school before grade ten. This "anomaly" reflects the way social class works in terms of access to higher education and how the relevance of secondary schooling is constructed by individuals who see themselves as having no legitimate chance at accessing higher education and thus no need for the subject matter of a secondary school curriculum "all geared up" for those moving on and out.

> It was just boring and I hated it. It was all geared up for the smart ones, the ones that was goin' away. They didn't care about the rest

> of us, the ones still here. If you wasn't right smart, and you didn't dress rich and act like them snobs [pause]. I just never felt comfortable and I knew I didn't need none of what they was teachin'. It was all right up to grade nine but then it [pause] it got hard. (UR-FS-95)

In families where education was "valued" in this cohort, female children particularly were assumed to be moving on out of their home villages and into higher education. Leavers of this cohort identified a feminist element in the way they were encouraged by teachers, counsellors and sometimes family members to leave the community and to pursue careers. Leaving implied abandoning limited opportunities and dependence that marked women's roles.

> A lot of that had to do with your family life, whether or not basically you were able to go through with your education and how your upbringing was when [pause] like I say, women were taught to [pause]. I think a lot of mothers especially [pause] it was just getting to the generation where women weren't feeling so subservient to the man and they were feeling that if they only had the chance to continue to their education then maybe they wouldn't be in this situation. They would be more independent, they wouldn't be relying on men to take care of them so they tried to push that on their daughters. (WC-FS-92)

The vision of education as the path out of traditional roles continued to be a difficult topic for both stayers and leavers. But still, education and work histories of women in this cohort who left Digby Neck contain a strong sense of purpose and a strong desire both to become mobile and to acquire higher education credentials. This effectively mirrors what Lois Weis (2004) found in her ethnographic study of urban working-class white men and women in the United States. Women as a group were much more willing and able to use institutions of formal education to advance their life goals in a changing society that focuses on knowledge rather than industrial production. These women were on an entirely different "track" than stayers who remained in the area and typically married young.

> I had a friend here visiting from Alberta and I was asking my sisters about the different girls I went to school with and what they were doing now. And there was this one girl that I met in Digby. And then I said, oh, she must be married. Then the person I was with said, "I didn't know that was a career." And I didn't realize what I had said. (KF-FL-90)

The experience of these women contained conversations about "options" and the range of possibilities that lay before them. They entered into an enhanced, family-supported, middle-class tutelary system in "honours" programs and in "academic" classes where they were counselled in terms of seeing their lives as Giddens' project of the self. This, however, was part of the privilege of their family's elite position in the local class structure and not part of a "modern" form of consciousness, as Giddens suggests (1990, 1991, 1996).[7] The ability to incorporate education as part of one's life's project was unevenly distributed on the basis of family wealth. For these young women, money was not a significant concern. The informant quoted above believes that on Digby Neck money was not an impediment to young people of her generation who might have accessed higher education. For her the "decision" whether or not to go on to other places and to post-secondary education was entirely a question of personal ambition and the financial lure of prospects in the fishery.

> I don't think on Digby Neck [pause] I don't think it was financial reasons that stopped people from furthering their education. I think it was more that they wanted to stay where they were. I mean there was incentive, the money was good. (KC-FL-92)

The kind of "family planning" the informant quoted below describes happens in the context of a family committed to the notion that higher education is both necessary and accessible and who therefore initiated a long series of conversations with their child about a future that was assumed from an early age and assured by family capital. And like many young female leavers in former cohorts, her brothers were not party to any such conversations and strategic planning that included higher education.

> It was totally different with him. With my sister and I, it was always that we knew that we were going to go to university, and with him it's always been that he was going to take over the family business. And now he's running the boat. So why wasn't he geared the same way that we were? I don't know. I don't think it was deliberate. It was the expectation and it was very subtle. He just always wanted to do it from the time he was thirteen, fourteen, fifteen, his summers he would spend going fishing. It was just like a progression. They wouldn't have wanted him doing it if that wasn't what he really wanted. And he still wants it and he enjoys what he does. (KC-FL-92)

This young man was fortunate enough to be in position to be able to access dwindling opportunities in the fishery because of his "direct" family connections. As more and more licences are consolidated and sold out, fewer and fewer young men on Digby Neck have access to the fishery except as occasional labourers. Yet masculine identity constructions, even if they are now mythological, still have the power to define education as an unnecessary pursuit for virile men (Kenway and Kraak, 2004). Identity is not formed within a context of economic or any other form of rationality, it is forged in the furnace of practice (Bourdieu, 1984b, 1990), sexuality, habitus and activity. Decisions that appear as coherent in a particular community of practice, like that of the fishing, can only be properly understood in terms of the affordances and practices common in the community itself (Wenger, 1998; Palsson, 1998; Livingstone and Sawchuk, 2004). In addition, occasional, part-time and piece work in traditional physical male-dominated occupations, supplemented by federal government Employment Insurance, can provide what is considered locally to be a good wage (Johnson, 1999; McGrath, 2001). A nostalgic discourse about the entrepreneurial opportunities in the post-war fishery is more common and possibly more powerful among young men than what teachers see as forward-looking pro-education discourse.

> It's not that they're not listening, they just don't accept it because it's contrary to what they have always believed. I had a couple of young men as recently as three or four years ago [late 1990s] back when what was happening in the fishery was all over the media. Not only was it all over the media, it was the subject of supper table conversation, certainly at every house in Digby Neck. And I made the remark to one of these guys that you need to have an education whether you like that idea or not. One of these kids said, "I don't need any of this stuff. I have a job waiting for me, I can get into the fishery." I said, "excuse me but I know you and I know your parents. I know where you live. Why would you say something like that to me? I know what's going on in the fishery." "Well Frank Gibson done it." And I had to stop for a minute and I said, "do you mean Frank senior?" He said, "'yes." I said, "look, when Frank Gibson did that it could be done. It can't be done anymore. There are no more Frank Gibsons who are going to drop out of school in grade five or grade six and end up a multimillionaire, well-respected in the community. It ain't gonna' happen anymore." But this kid had grown up and he was fifteen, sixteen years old and he knew, he's heard all the conversations and he's still had in his head that if Frank Gibson did it fifty years ago, he could still do it. (GG-FE)

In the 1990s, the "natural" male transition from school to work in the fishery had become complicated and highly problematic, causing community elders and youth alike to wonder "what is here for them." For women the situation is not unlike in the previous cohort, where the "natural transition" for women from elite fishing families continued to be bound up with post-secondary education. Many young women integrated well with the middle-class academic stream in the regional secondary school, participating in sports and in what one leaver called "nerdy" cultural and social extra-curricular activities. Their identities as "fishermen's daughters" had become a sign of money in the 1970s and 1980s, and their parents still had the wealth necessary to provide them with ready access to higher education and careers no longer constrained by gendered role expectations.

> Oh, they'd say, you're a fisherman's daughter. You don't have to worry about money. That's how you were looked at. And they went into secretarial and hairdressing. I didn't want to be the wimpy hairdresser, that's why I went into fisheries. Most women around here don't want to do that, but I wanted to be different, I wanted to be able to get my navigation class 4 just like Billy Morgan did. I wanted to be right up there making the money like the guys did, not to show off, but just to show that I could do it. I got my dad behind me [laughs]. (LL-FS-88)

And as was the case with previous cohorts, these young people "integrated" better into the general population of the regional secondary school, never associating with Digby Neck focused "cliques."

> The ones from the Neck, I don't know [pause]. I made friends really quickly up there [the regional secondary] and we were [pause] I guess we were the good kids, you know, the ones the teachers like. We weren't into drinking and drugs and we did our work and that stuff. A lot of the kids from the Neck, they went kind of bad. (OS-FL-96)

The other side of the mobile clique was the immobile Digby Neck-focused clique. Women from Digby Neck who were drawn to the immobile cliques were not making the irrational decision to forego extended formal education for a life following their mother's footsteps. In fact, these young women were typically the most "resistant" and "wild" young women in their age group, choosing instead to focus their energies on "partying" and pursuing the lifestyles that could be had through an attachment to a "rich fisherman."

> The boys who went fishing had money and they had a fast car and they could spend money on them [girlfriends], sure, and we saw that in Digby. But it was a certain type of girl that would be

> attracted to that. I was in the honours class and there weren't any girls in my class that were attracted to that type of person. They were all going on. (ET-ML-87)

> I got to admit, I was a partier from the time I was fourteen or fifteen. I was pretty wild. It got me in a lot of trouble, but it got me in some good times too. Like they say: we're here for a good time not a long time. (UR-FS-95)

Contrasting this latter view was the mobile sensibility of this education-focused young woman, who saw "the good life" as being somewhere else. She also defined control in terms of getting away from the power granted to men by virtue of their relative wealth in the fishery. Women's accounts from this cohort demonstrate a much more overt and deliberate feminist consciousness.

> I always wanted to get out. A lot of people asked me, well why didn't you go out with anyone from down the Neck or marry a fisherman or [pause]. All I saw was pigs. They were too dominating. I didn't want to be in a situation where I wasn't in control of my life. That's the way I chose it. You know, I'm not saying that they're all like that, it's just my view I guess of how I see things sometimes. A lot of them drank and partied and made the big bucks so they figured they could waste a lot of it and do foolish things and give themselves some trouble. I just didn't have any interest. (WC-FS-92)

This young woman's choice to continue her education beyond the secondary level was supported by her family, who encouraged her to leave and planted in her consciousness that "there's nothing for you here." And her decision to leave and pursue liberal arts in university gave her the tools of a feminist perspective with which she could reflect on and use to redefine her youth. But like many young Digby Neck women, she also discovered that there was little for her elsewhere, either with or without higher education in the jobless recovery of 1990s Canada. And like others she found her way back home to the supports provided by family.

## Survival and Family

> Because boats in the kinship sector are family owned and operated… people continue to operate them as long as they can cover their costs. The labor force in the capitalist sector changes with conditions, while the kinship sector remains more constant because

> it can survive conditions that are lethal to capitalists. In some New England fisheries, the flexibility of the kinship sector to expand in good times and under employ people to maintain itself during bad times gives it a competitive edge over the capitalist sector. (Durrenberger, 1997: 160)

Stayers in Cohort 3, like their predecessors, take pride in having survived in an increasingly difficult economic climate on Digby Neck through the downturn in the fishery. They "like it around here" and feel comfortable in close proximity to a familiar geography, family and friends. They generally believe that the population of the Neck has taken a significant downturn from the late 1980s into the 1990s and Census Canada population figures confirm this trend. Population declined 23 percent between 1980 and 1990 and more than 15 percent between 1990 and 2000.. Family size is also said to be declining, contributing to decreasing population figures among those who persist on Digby Neck. The idea that there is no longer "enough work," especially for young people to "keep busy," is a common perception. Fishermen who once worked year-round in multiple fisheries and whose fathers and mothers had combined fisheries related work with "a bit of farming" or working on family wood lots now complain that they just "sit around half the year driving themselves crazy" (FN). To have survived all of this and to have been able to stay "around here" and to have avoided the necessity of having to move very far is viewed by many people as an accomplishment in itself.

> My family connections are all on the Neck here. We're survivors. Well, on my father's side here we're all on the Neck. We're a dying breed and there's four of us to carry on the family name. There's me and my brother and there's my uncle's two boys, who are the same age as me and my brother. They don't have no kids yet. Me and my brother too, but we both have girls. And that's the end of us as far as I know. It's tough to survive here in these times, but we're still here. (TB-MS-88)

Few males of this cohort have left Digby Neck. Those who have left speak of a harsh employment and social climate that allows them little of the freedom or comfort they enjoyed as children on the Neck. "I miss going out on my four-wheeler and tearing around in the wood and down to the shore," one young man commented (FN). While they feel forced to leave in order to find work, they feel trapped in the impoverished life available work provides them given the high cost of living in western and central Canadian cities. They find themselves paying for things that they are accustomed to getting for free and spending money more quickly than they can make it.

> I make good money out here you know. I'm getting' twelve dollars an hour. Nobody back home will pay you that for any kind of work, at least not steady. But you have to pay to park your car for Christ sake. Everything costs money out here and you can't get ahead. (KF-ML-91)

The experience of these male leavers is atypical because the strong majority of young men in Cohort 3 are still living "around here," within range of family and community "support structures" that provide at least marginal work, room and board for free or for low rent, and what is generally a low cost of living. However, everyone recognizes that staying also has its costs.

> Most people don't want to see their family disappear. If I have kids of my own I hope they don't have to go way out west to earn a living. But on the other hand, do I really want them to be here the way things are today… If I had the opportunity right now to leave fishing and make the same amount of money working a full year job, where I wouldn't have to move too far. I'd have to be able to leave fishing on my own terms. (KS-MS-89)

Staying presents challenges, but in order to leave, this young man requires more security than he can find locally by combining unstable but known employment and social benefits. The idea of relatively linear transitions from school to work that dominated the stories and perceptions of earlier cohorts is anything but evident in the youngest group.[8] Most of Cohort 3 remains around here despite the difficulty, and it is family support that allows them to do so. Dropping out, staying and working hard were still mingled together by members of this cohort. The majority who remained worked hard, partied hard and were supported significantly by their families.

> I can really say that everybody that I grew up with is still on the Neck. And either fishing, working in the fish plant, lobstering, some type of fishing industry. There was actually not too many that graduated, you know, a lot of them partied, didn't take it serious. It's just — education — I found with them wasn't that great and a lot of them dropped out. Yeah, they just dropped out and a lot of them still live with their parents. (WC-FS-92)

> I can always live home. Mom's always after me to come home. (FG-ML-97)

## Back to the Future: Surviving in the New Economy

> Overcoming the exodus of youth from rural communities and providing opportunities for young people who have left to return to the region is key to future growth and development. (Western Valley Development Authority, 1999: 18)

> Suggestions were put forward to encourage entrepreneurship training within the education system and to make sure that the courses being taught were relevant to the labour market realities within rural communities. (Canada, Rural Secretariat, 1999: 9)

For the past several years, the state has been promoting a vision of an emerging information economy, and it is apparent that the "vision" for developing the Canadian countryside is being framed within this matrix. Part of this "new economy" discourse around the contemporary rural community is supported by the statistical trend toward increased population growth in rural non-farm communities, as noted by Finnie (1998) and Mendelson and Bollman (1998) in Canada and Johnson and Fuguitt in the United States (2000). The argument is that, in the emerging information era, geographic location is becoming increasingly less important in terms of the generation of economic activity. Another part of the argument is that, as global ecotourism grows, rural places, their scenery and their culture become valuable commodities that can be sold to visitors. In the analysis presented in contemporary rural development or community economic development (CED) literature, "strategic planning," education and technological innovation become key assets that might allow rural communities to retain their youth populations. This attempts to reverse more established "brain drain" notions of schooling and higher education as a force for rural depopulation. In the "new economy," the educated, entrepreneurial individual is supposed to be able to overcome and even transcend the problems of geographic "isolation" and participate fully in a kind of economy that is not restricted in any way by place.

If this new economy exists in the context of coastal communities in southwestern Nova Scotia, it ought to be manifested in the lives of Cohort 3. It is fairly clear that the economy in the "around here" region has changed, but the transition is generally framed in negative language, in terms of what has been lost. But has something been gained as well? What does the new economy offer youth on Digby Neck? It is true that some entrepreneurial Digby Neckers have been able to exploit opportunities in tourism and in aquaculture.

> There has been transition for sure. I've seen people who were will-

> ing to make the transition to the so-called modern or post-modern economy. People are facing that issue because of the background in tourism with the Pines Hotel and other things around here. So some of these people are making the transition. (SF-ME)

But is this "new economy" really much different than the old one? Is aquaculture, for example, very different than fishing, from the point of view of the individual labouring on the working surface of the industry? According to one informant, the answer is no, and he describes an industrial work routine that requires many of the same skills needed by successful fishers. The new economy looks a good deal like the old one as "feed" replaces "bait," "cages" replace "traps," and fewer people have jobs.

> There's a lot of lifting. Right now we're feeding three times a day and there's a pallet of feed and there's forty bags a piece so it's 2,200 pounds. altogether. And we handle all of that, like them 55-pound bags, we handle them one by one. Like right now we're feeding about 120 bags a day to approximately 70,000 fish. I do a lot of mechanical work, you know, with the boat, and we deal with a lot of small engines. And I'm running a 36-foot boat with diesel, a 6-cylinder diesel into it. For instance, the other day we ran out of fuel and there we was with a 40-foot barge in tow, coming across the basin and we was just getting into the high tide at the time. So I had to play mechanic but things worked out OK. (TB-MS-88)

Other evidence of the new economy comes in the form of tourism and in the expanding service economy in the town of Digby. Tourism has been an important industry in the Digby area since the inter-war period, when the Pines Resort was constructed by Canadian Pacific Railways near the Bay of Fundy ferry to Saint John, New Brunswick, offering a luxurious rural retreat to middle- and upper-class tourists. People in the Digby area have worked in a variety of capacities in this and the area's other tourist resort, and in other tourism related services like restaurants, bed and breakfasts, hotels and motels, along with the centrepiece of local ecotourism, whale watching. The "new economy" is well established and it has used seasonal labour for generations.

The most significant development "around here" is the rapid expansion of retail services. In the year 2000 alone, more than a hundred mostly part-time jobs were created in an emerging grocery store war, which pitted the Sobey's chain against Loblaw's Superstore. If post-war, modern production-capitalism extracted raw materials from the Digby area as never before, post-modern consumer-capitalism is now returning manufactured goods. Both of these outlets are thought to be harbingers of development and rumours of "something big" coming to Digby were rife through the construction and grand opening of the new stores. It now appears more likely that the two corporate grocery chains are waging war for a grocery monopoly "around here," a war that has already seen the closing of two smaller grocery chain stores and the local co-op store. These new stores attract clientele from a distance of seventy to eighty kilometres in all directions. According to the Superstore manager, "They don't set these places up unless they know they're going to make money; it may take up to ten years, but we'll make money in the long run" (FN). All of this has created what is seen locally as a kind of new economy, a new set of consumer choices, a magnet for the area's rural consumers, who previously had to "do their mall crawling" in Yarmouth.

Yet, the new economy is very similar to the old one; it pays poorly and it relies on a steady supply of exploited and immobile labour. In addition to the expansion of retail services, the call-centre industry and small manufacturing have moved into the "around here" region, offering what is by local standards a great deal of opportunity. But much of this work is stressful and poorly paid. The principal work force is women tied to the local area by a combination of restrictions of social class, family responsibilities and the sense that the community is a safe and secure place, a good place to raise children. Fear of moving into insecure urban spaces, spaces that have become visible through the magic of cable television, is also a barrier to mobility and to higher education, which is linked with urban living and perhaps even urban sophistication, represented by cultural forms that extend beyond the folk sentiments of contemporary country music.

> Back home, people listen to country music and they are very sentimental about home [laughs]. They don't want to leave. Maybe they can't. Maybe they're scared. What do you expect when people watch Detroit TV news every night. That's got to make you think, who wants to live in a city? (OS-FL-96)

> They don't want to move, they're safe and secure. They don't want education. When you grow up in a small place you fear the unknown, you fear even Halifax because you've been protected and isolated in this safe little environment where everyone knows everyone. (KF-FL-90)

As Rothstein suggests, the development of the "new economy," with its downsized state apparatus and flexible accumulation, is creating the conditions where higher education is less accessible than ever and at the same time it is also appearing less "useful" than ever. The perception has been that there is little good work in urban centres regardless of how much schooling one has. How emerging social and economic developments such as economic boom in Alberta, declining birth rates, security-focussed restrictions on immigration, and the exodus of the baby boom from the labour force will play into the lives of the next "cohort" of young people is beyond the scope of this study. It is possible that all of this has already changed in a new labour-hungry national labour market. As the service sector of the local economy expands there are jobs, because "the labour of youth is an important part of the flexible accumulation that characterizes contemporary capitalism" (Rothstein, 1996: 361). This might help explain why fewer young Digby Neckers are now leaving home. Rather, they are making what they can of their lives "around here."

## Resistance

> Yes and the culture of school has rules and regulations that you're duty bound to follow. You say "up yours" and "you ain't telling me what to do." It's a culture of resistance. (GG-FE)

> The emphasis on experience, on self-worth, and on anti-authoritarian education would influence the 1960s. Most significant of all, however, was the real message of 1950s education: child-centeredness to an unparalleled degree.... The sheer numbers confirmed it: this society is designed for you. (Owram, 1996: 135)

A common perception among educators is that they operate within a culture of resistance. Students are now seen as less docile and less willing to submit to authority. The school is regarded as a part of a larger institutional complex often referred to as "society," and this complex of institutions is thought to be losing its grip. This is a functionalist vision. Another view of resistance posits that central institutions in the society are complexes that operate in the main to legitimate and support existing structures of social inequality. I have critiqued this view in Chapter 2. Both theories imagine a more or less monolithic society, which is driven by some central thrust, i.e., "order," in the functionalist tradition, or "class struggle," in the conflict or Marxist tradition. The resistance that these theories imagine is essentially an individual-level reflection of structural causation. Individuals resist the logic of capitalism or the functional society because they have been able to poke a hole in its logic — in Willis's terms, they have "penetrated" its facade.

In the Marxist tradition, Willis (1977), Hall and Jefferson (1976) and Corrigan (1979) documented this assistance in their studies of working-class youth (mainly boys) in urban Britain in the mid-1970s; Gaskell (1992) analyzed the way that young Canadian women found their way into marginal lives; McLaren (1980, 1989) documented another in the Jane Finch corridor north of Toronto; McRobbie (1991), yet another in her analysis of the resistance of working-class girls; indeed the list is long. More recently, Weis (2004), Hicks (2002), Smyth and Hattam (2004), Kenway and Kraak (2002, 2004) and Rose (2004) have used ethnographic methods to analyze how social class and gender play out in the lives and learning practices of contemporary adults. Ethnographies have never been much in vogue in the functionalist tradition. In a functionalist vein, there are few studies of schooling *per se*, but there are many studies of communities in which schooling figures prominently, and schooling is seen as one of the central socialization functions in the community, training, initiating and integrating young people into adult roles. In place of "penetration" one finds "integration."

The view of resistance that I proposed in Chapter 2 challenges this sort of theorizing. While I am generally supportive of critical theory in the Marxist tradition, I argue, following Foucault, that there is no singular discernible matrix of societal power either functional or entirely class based. Education institutions do not simply support the ruling elite or hegemonic class interests. Nor do they provide more or less uniform support for the social integration of everyone they process. Schools operate within a complex of lines of power and multiple modes of living, and in fact, it is the very difference that these multiple communities express that are brought more or less within the sway of the school's institutional power. Education systems are components of the state apparatus in that they purport to take individuals from different worlds and give them identical experiences. The attempt always falls short of the mark, as many longstanding traditions of research in education sociology have shown (Riordan, 2003). For instance, as Marxist ethnographers have shown all too clearly, social class and gender confound normalization efforts, and recalcitrant working-class youth "resist." As deCerteau argues, every exercise of power, every attempt to impose a set of practices upon a group, generates a reading and a tactical response, and it is this response that generates everyday life and resistance to power (1984). Walkerdine has shown, for instance, the multiple forms of resistance that operate in elementary school classrooms as social class and gender meet the institutional power of predominantly female teachers (1990). The capitalist development of the fishery caused individuals in coastal communities to become increasingly "proletarianized," as Sacouman (1980), Davis (1991), Kearney (1993), Durrenberger (1997) and others have shown, but how individuals and communities have responded and fashioned resistance to this power is not well understood.

Finally, Castells' (2004) account of communities of resistance to neoliberalism, bureaucratization and massification demonstrates how the very information technologies that are presently structuring global capitalism are also providing the conditions for a range of resistance movements. I think Castells is correct to suggest that the emergence of resistant communities of difference is at least as important today as was the emergence of civil society in the industrial era (2004: 421). Additionally, Castells points out that the "tragic irony" of network society and the retreat from the institutions of civil society that its emergence has signalled is that the emancipatory projects represented by state institutions like the public school are unlikely to fulfill their potential to enhance social justice and a greater measure of equality. The irony plays out in this coastal community in the form of resistant individuals, mostly young men, who have little connection to the formal education project beyond their elementary years of schooling.

The difference represented by multiple communities sets up multiple relations of power that attempt to change individuals and groups in a number of different circumstances. Young people are at once members of a class, a gender, a region, a village, a community, a family, a generation, a labour force and other social positions out of which identity is constructed. The members of this generation are not coherent, unified subjects who view themselves as "fishermen" or "housewives." Their contemporary identities are shaped in spaces that include the virtual space of the mass media, the local economy, the family and schools, which are becoming more "community sensitive" sites of normalization. In the modern school there is a concerted attempt to hold youth and normalize them, specifically by not promoting particular kinds of identity construction, but rather by opening the door to alternative possible identities. Yet, the known persona of the "born and bred" fisherman remains an attractive identity formation even in the context of a shrinking fishery and increasingly exclusive licensing system, and doom and gloom prognosis for the industry in general.

This program of community sensitive education generates multiple types of resistance, penetration and integration. The work ethic in the coastal community is both a reflection of a kind of male personality structure that is key to the capitalist development of the fishery and at the same time it is resistant to options offered in institutions of formal education. So integration into community and class relations in the fishery is at the same time resistance to schooling and the normalization project that schooling represents. The period of this study spans the transition from the pre-industrial fishery of the pre-World War Two period, to the initial industrialization of the fishery in the 1950s and 1960s, through the move offshore and heavy industrialization and regulation of the fishery in the 1970s and 1980s, to the 1990s, when concentration of ownership and the decline in stocks have choked off community-based opportunities for many people. Each of these stages in the development of the Digby Neck fishery generated different forms of resistance and integration.

As French historian Eugen Weber (1976) and Canadian social historian Bruce Curtis (1988) claim in different ways, formal education did not gain support in rural areas until it was seen as useful to country people. Formal education facilities were established in the early part of the nineteenth century but were sporadically attended until the latter part of the century. The change, Weber argues, happened with the industrialization of the society and the concomitant opportunities, communication and transportation that accompanied this process. In rural schools, though, the problem has always been fashioning an argument and a practice that are relevant, and so long as a strong manual labour market existed, formal education had a struggle to appear relevant. Before the existence of a locally understood reason for rural schooling, it was broadly resisted and seen as an irrelevance or an undesirable depopulation mechanism. In Weber's view, schooling is a depopulation mechanism; the question is whether or not depopulation makes strategic sense to individuals in rural communities. This question is complex, and it can only be answered by micro studies of the development of different kinds of communities as they become integrated into broader economies and polities.

Educators in this sample note a longstanding tradition of resistance to both school and to migration on Digby Neck prevalent among large numbers of students. Describing a typical resistant male, one educator noted the long history of traditional patterns in which formal education beyond junior high school was seen to be of little immediate utility. In the contemporary coastal community, educators' arguments about the need for extended formal education is couched in negative terms that stress what is no longer available for youth.

> You know, here's a guy who's twenty years old and he has a good job and it pays well. He may have a new truck and he can afford to make payments on a home. You know we're looking at getting ready to settle down and start a family. That has an appeal particularly in a rural culture where the previous generation regarded that as the norm of life. Somebody who went away to college or got a university education, that was a rarity in the forties and fifties. So by the seventies and eighties, although they did see a slightly different world, if they could hang on to that old world, they saw nothing wrong with that. It's just that this world has almost disappeared now. (SF-ME)

This situation did remain quite viable for particularly positioned individuals until well into the 1980s, but as he suggests, this world and its opportunities for education resistance and continued prosperity have all but vanished. But in the eyes of most educators, the change has only occurred significantly in the past decade. The following quote is from a teacher whose career began in the early 1980s.

> When I first started teaching it was nothing to see kids just graduated from school getting married. And the guy was on the boat and the girl was home keeping house and that was it. I think that doesn't happen so much any more. There are those who think: dad's going to give me his boat and his licences and he's got two or three boats in the water and I'm going to take one of them. That's just what's going to happen next. I think you also will see, even though they are looking around more, that a large percentage of the kids on Digby Neck do end up back in the community. (CD-ME)

Resistance to formal education has been grounded in family life in the community. This educator also reflects the common but not universal perception that most Digby Neckers do not move very far away. This perception is supported by the empirical evidence reported in Chapter 3. Most informants report that resistance to formal education among young men has traditionally been rooted in the practical orientation of students and the critique of irrelevance of education to the lives they saw around them and could imagine for themselves. Educators in the sample reiterate the novelty of the notion that everyone ought to finish high school; this is something that has "only just arrived" (FN) in this community and is still taking root. Virtually every educator in the sample saw Digby Neck culture as highly "materialistic" and very "practically oriented." People were only interested in education as an unproven tool for making money.

> It [education] hasn't been needed. They see wealth being generated through all kinds of ways that have nothing to do with education. Success, all those things that go with quality of life, happen in these areas without education being an active part in it. And traditionally, education hasn't been a part of it. We sort of came along after the fact in a lot of ways, and we've said we're the institution and we do it better. But the argument has never been proven to a lot of the local families that have been here hundreds of years doing what they've been doing and doing quite alright with it. And to say that my quality of life is better or worse [pause] better or the worse doesn't really enter into it. We can look at that and say what we want for them, but for those people who are experiencing it, that is life. (CD-ME)

Resistance to "higher purposes" of formal education, i.e., as a means of acquiring "culture" and "options," is, in the eyes of educators, yet another badge signifying a lack of family cultural capital in certain places.

> No, it's the same, well you know what rich people do, they take their children to Europe, they take them you know to all the operas and all the plays… educational books, good books and so on. And the rural people, they don't see any reason for doing that…. You'd get children to do projects and you'd have to provide all the materials for them, they didn't have any encyclopedias at home, they didn't have any magazines. There were a lot of homes where they had nothing. Not even the daily paper, maybe not even the weekly paper. (MS-FE)

Seeing the "higher purpose" of formal education is a part of class privilege and the economic security to be able to support a child through higher education. The "decision" to prolong formal education also forces a working-class youth to forego earning potential in their most physically vigorous years, when it is imperative to build their labouring credentials, reputation and general resume. This complexifies the rather simplistic "choice" rhetoric that is the foundation of much functionalist education theorizing. It also lends complexity, paradox and irony to the ever-pragmatic business of curriculum making and how-to pedagogy found in most instructional materials, textbooks and curriculum guides. Life itself is a non-standard pedagogy that makes education choices highly problematic.

> That's really a tough choice for some of those boys. And the ones who liked fishing, they were maybe just as secure as they would be in a profession. There is no guarantee for a good many years that they'd find a job after university. And I think this has discouraged maybe some that they look around and they see some big student loans to pay back and can't get a job. (MS-FE)

For practically oriented petty capitalist families who made their living by investing wisely and taking entrepreneurial risks, higher education has looked like a very questionable investment. The situation is somewhat different for young women, not so much because they are advantaged by being more compliant or "smarter" (which is generally thought to be the case), but rather because they lack man's access to power and resources in the community. In order to access a measure of control and power, women are forced to rely on formal education. When they could make a clear connection between formal education and sustaining a life in the local area, then the prospect of higher education became a lot more attractive.

> Well the young lady that I referred to awhile ago about now being focused spent two years at university and could have come home

> any time but since her summer placement this summer and knowing now that she's found an area of specialization and there's going to be opportunities to come back here and do that. Well now she will even go out of province for a year or two now that she knows she can come back and spend the rest of her life here. This is what she wants to do. (CQ-FE)

Education is increasingly being seen by young women as a way to remain "around here" as resource industries and opportunities in the fisheries diminish. Because family connections are so strong and so important on Digby Neck, contemporary youth are said to be becoming more interested in higher education not because they see it as a way to leave the community but as a way to stay in it. The discourse of rural education administrators is also becoming more focused on providing "relevant" curriculum as a way of keeping youth in school longer and extending the process of governance at least to the end of secondary education. In the words of one educator, this realization, combined with better road access via recently improved highways, has made the possibility of post-secondary education more attractive to many students. With transportation improvements, going into higher education does not necessarily imply leaving home for the first time. Community colleges in regional centers like Yarmouth and Middleton are both now within a ninety-minute commuting distance of Digby Neck.

Working-class youth must forego admittedly limited ready cash and known employment in a known place in order to attend post-secondary education, which is typically an unknown experience in an unknown place for highly questionable returns. As one educator comments, "We ask a lot when we ask them to go on, especially to university" (CD-ME). The reality is that even today, higher education is not part of the experiential scope of the lives of most Digby Neckers. As the above quote shows, the general consensus among educators is not so much that there is not enough money in the community or in families to finance higher education; the feeling expressed is that there remains strong reservation among less "well to do" families about the practical utility of post-secondary education. Resistance occurs when a student realizes that the program is not right and the expenditures are high, and in the present climate of occupational uncertainty, which program is "right?" As several stayers commented, they "couldn't see what it was going to get them." This vision referred to above is simply different for children from a rural area.

> Well they [urban children] have a larger perspective to begin with. These [rural] kids don't seem to realize that they're competing in this vast pool of people for ever diminishing good jobs. The only door to that is the educational door. And if you've got some edu-

> cation you can get a job and make some money. You don't need a whole lot of education, you don't need a PhD. School may not be a great way to educate kids but it fits into what's happening in cities and you might as well just try to go with it and get what you can out of it. (SF-ME)

To be able to see the practical application, work preparation and economic returns seem essential to many Digby Neck youth. The discourse of competitiveness is supposed to motivate young people to work harder and achieve more in terms of formal education, but it may also discourage rural youth who understand the cultural disadvantage they face.

> I always felt right stupid in school. Some kids, they could talk and the work was nothing to them. I just sat there scared somebody was gonna ask me something. Even talking to you makes me kind of nervous 'cause you're a teacher too, and I've been out of school a long time. You were asking about the ones who did good in school. I noticed that they could talk to the teachers just like they could talk to their friends. (UR-FS-95)

Several educators in the sample report that Digby Neck students very often have difficulty staying with higher education and that they resist by returning to the community and a known place precisely because they perceived the anonymity and competitiveness in higher education places as a "dog-eat-dog" environment. Despite its hardships and marginality, youth in coastal communities can at least see where work can be had "around here" and what they need to do to make money.

> I think they see school as something divorced from working a lot of times. These kids know about work. The boys have been brought up around fishing. They don't lay around. They may not be very engaged in school and they may even seem painfully lazy there, but when it comes to getting to work at fishing, get out of the way; the girls too. So school… to them it's not real work and that's what they look for when they evaluate what's going on in an educational program. What's this going to get me, how will this lead to money? (ES-FE)

This practicality shows itself in school as a highly critical, anti-authoritarian identity. This identity is the core of education resistance, and it is rooted in the availability of what are seen as good, practical alternatives for adult life, available without enduring the abstract and infantilizing experience of upper secondary and post-secondary education. The Digby Neck identity also carries with it a certain baggage with educators in the view of some informants. With official streaming no longer available for placing students according to their social backgrounds, more subtle forms of differentiation are at work. The quote below demonstrates how resistance is manufactured as children are marginalized by the subtle cues that work to make particular categories of marginal students "feel uncomfortable" in school. Referring to his own slow realization that marginal students' resistance is rooted in the complex and troubled context of their out-of-school lives, this administrator articulates how resistance is typically seen as "bad behaviour" and justification for stereotypes.

> I think certain family names elicit certain responses from certain long-standing teachers. And you have conferences with people about that and suggest to them that they might be a bit premature in their judgments when they say that, "oh, it's just another one." But many teachers have this insulated mentality. Somewhere along the line there is this misconception that if you're a teacher you've made the upper reaches of life and some teachers are not comfortable with certain communities we serve; they're not comfortable with the Neck, not comfortable with this or that place. (CF-ME)

In recent years resistance to formal education finds fertile ground in the perceived questionable utility of post-secondary education. Indeed those families with the resources to support their children will be much more likely to attempt to establish entrepreneurial opportunities (i.e., "a little business") for them in the local area than to invest in higher education. Higher education remains "invisible" training for invisible jobs in an elsewhere economy that has little tangible presence or discernible utility for traditional families on the Neck. Digby Neck students need more of a "guarantee" regarding the utility of post-secondary credentials before making the leap into uncertainty, precisely because of the chasm they have to bridge in doing so. But because of the location of their family-based supports, they actually have less of a guarantee than urban youth.

> Here at college I look around at the girls I've met. Most of them come from towns and cities and they always talk about going home when they graduate and they figure that there will probably be some kind of work for them. You know, some talk about going back to Halifax or Toronto. But me, where am I going to get a job on the Neck or even around Digby where I can use my degree? (OS-FL-96)

## Conclusion: The Mobile Discourse of Schooling

> I remember some of the teachers talking about other places and making it sound exciting and making us feel like Digby was the bottom of the barrel, your horrible little community where nothing important is going on. In grade twelve it was all geared to getting us to think about where we're going next year and what you're going to do next year. I wasn't going to be embarrassed. I wasn't just going to stay here. It wasn't a cool thing to do. If you wanted a career, a success story, you had to leave. (KF-FL-90)

The messages rural youth receive through the course of their education careers in community schools are highly mixed. They come to understand the limited prospects that their communities hold for them and the way that family, class and gender structure the menu of possibilities open to them. They also encounter what I have been describing as a mobile discourse, a discourse that presents their communities as peripheral places playing an ever diminishing role in an increasingly centralized and urban political economy. This is not presented to them as an overt political agenda or as a conspiracy but as a fact of life. Part of these facts of life are the idea that successful people are mobile and leave, while unsuccessful people are "stuck" and consequently forced to stay. In the first two cohorts, stayers were "stuck" in fisheries jobs and in marriages. In Cohort 3 stayers are increasingly seen as being stuck in the few remaining fisheries jobs and more commonly in low wage part time work, and/or in social welfare or family dependency. More than half of the young men in Cohort 3 have not graduated high school, and they make up the lion's share of the 76 percent of men in this cohort who remain "around here." Most members of this cohort are still single or living in common-law relationships with "Digby girls" or women from "across the Bay." Most either live with their parents or on family property on Digby Neck. This generation is in limbo, unable to commit to marriage, mortgages and raising children because the fishing economy is precarious and most other forms of available work pay such poor wages. One informant commented, "They call them Generation X, but I call them the minimum wage generation" (FN). When I asked people about how young people in the area who have limited formal education manage to survive, there is typically a long pause, lowered eyes and a sigh before the inevitable answer follows: "I don't know."

> Marginal employment and it's even more marginal than it ever was because we're now into the permanent part time because employers aren't willing to pay benefits. At least when you stick around you have friends and relatives who will help you over the hard

> times. When you're away you don't have that safety net. When you migrate, you're out there on your own. (GG-FE)

The comments of education migrants from earlier cohorts tell the story of being "out there on your own" in the social space of higher education and urban environments. These sentiments are repeated in Cohort 3, for example, this account of a stayer who spent a couple of years at university never really seeing the purpose of his education trajectory. The connection between higher education and actual work remained vague and undefined, and as a consequence he left before completing his degree to find work in the fishery.

> I never, ever thought where I'd go after I was done because I could never ever see myself getting anywhere. I was just wondering what I was doing, and the stuff that I was taking and doing these lab experiments in the organic chemistry class and stuff like that. What was I going to do afterwards; I had no plans. I didn't know what I wanted to do. As I grew up it was you… well you get your education, well you go to school and then you go to work. I was having the problem of where this education was taking me that I was going to be able to go to work. (KS-MS-89)

Higher education is such a major investment for most students who do not come from elite fishing families that it needs to be connected directly to some means of employment and very lucrative employment because of its cost. The paradox is that the kind of employment that pays the kind of money needed to finance an education was virtually unavailable "around here," for this cohort. Thus, higher education and particularly university was *de facto* considered to be an expensive exit from the community; indeed, it could be seen in no other way by individuals who would have to pay the costs after the fact when their student loans came due.

> If you've got an education you've spent thousands and thousands of dollars. What are you going to get here that's going to sustain what you've got to pay back? If you've got a student loan like I did, how are you going to pay for that staying on Digby Neck. There's very few jobs on Digby Neck that earn that kind of money other than fishing. So if you've got that education, you're going to look somewhere else. (KS-MS-89)

Even for children from elite fishing families, who could pay the cost of higher education "up-front," leaving their children with no debt to pay after graduation, the relevance of education still had to be constructed. For education to be relevant, leavers' discourse indicates that they had to acquire a mobile consciousness. Education was relevant precisely because it allowed one to be mobile and to "get out." Women spoke of the relevance of education in terms of the mobility it gave them, the opportunity to leave the community and access "bigger and better" things outside Digby Neck.

> I guess the relevance was that it [post-secondary education] was going to get me out. Not that I hated being where I was but I needed to move on and that was going to get me to where I wanted to go. Education took me out [pause] educationally wise but socially as well because it was going to take me out of the community and I was going to meet new people, different opportunities, things like that. (KC-FL-92)

These were the "good students," the ones who were "motivated," involved in a variety of school activities and who "got the marks." Teachers understood and supported these young people who were open to the mobile, options-oriented discourse of schooling. On the other hand most teachers were much less able to understand the desires, career trajectories and education decisions of young men whose identities and life circumstances were moving them into the fishery and into life in the coastal communities on Digby Neck. Their resistance and seemingly irrational decision to chase a few dollars in a declining industry seemed to most teachers incomprehensible.

> I think it was just a job to them, those teachers there in the high school [laughs]. I don't know what they're like now. I had one teacher and he used to be a fisherman himself. He could understand where I was coming from when I left. Most of them couldn't. I would say the teachers promoted anything but fishing, just get your education they would say. (TB-MS-88)

While many students have difficulty remembering specific teachers telling them directly about opportunities outside their communities and the education necessary to access them, teachers are generally conscious of the mobile nature of the discourse they use to describe successful and unsuccessful students.

> Even the language we use about this "to go further" is a positive kind of language about leaving. To move on, to go far, and I wonder if for some people even that language is intimidating, people who want their kids to stay. The words "he'll go far" might mean we'll never see him again. You know you hear people talking about somebody being a success and that means they've moved away, and somebody else only stayed here, or stayed down the Neck so

> they couldn't have been a success even though they have done well, they've got a nice home, they've supported their family, done alright, but it's still just alright, they haven't done well. (HL-FE)

If the mobile discourse of schooling was resisted by many stayers, it was embraced by many leavers in this cohort. Digby Neck students continue to pursue sets of options that allow them to use their personal and family-based social capital to cut out some kind of a living. Those from elite and licence-holding fishing families are much more easily able to access higher education credentials, which are portable and can be exchanged for professional positions off Digby Neck. Some younger members of this cohort hold out the hope that they may be able to use their post-secondary credentials close to home.

> I hope I'll be able to come back and get work around Digby some day; maybe even live on the Neck. I love it there; it's home.It's really confused for me right now though 'cause I know that if I come back home, like for good, that I've failed. I mean there's nothing there for me, just family. (OS-FL-96)

As the fishery declines and as ownership and licence rights consolidate into fewer and fewer hands, the cadre of young people who have access to the money required to make higher education a legitimate option declines apace. In fact, education credentials are now virtually essential as a support for migration outside the region around here. Forty-four of forty-eight of the young men and women in Cohort 3 who migrated into the "not far" and "away" regions have completed high school and more than 40 percent of them have university-level training. Education migrants struggle hard to maintain a Digby Neck identity while at the same time developing a mobile consciousness. For instance, this young woman commented that she feels layers of herself peel away with the time zones the closer she gets to home, and she arrives a self-reflexive migrant, a stranger when she arrives.

> Education does make us migrants if we choose to pursue it. I think it's unfortunate that some people say when they move from here to Toronto and they say that, well, Toronto's my home and Digby Neck, well, that's a place I'd rather forget. I think that's the dark side of education. I think they've migrated spiritually. (KF-FL-90)

But this young woman's story is also an account of a hybrid identity, one that has been formed by experience elsewhere as well as by experience and grounding in the home place. As Ryan claims, "While this global culture has a powerful effect on men, women and children, it does not simply roll over everything in a systematic fashion creating similarity as it does so" (1997: 47). Identity is now a creation of here and there, then and now, present and absent.

## Notes

1. Of course, such programs are not new in Canada. The "learn to earn more programs" of the 1960s are but one example (see Wilson, 1977). A definitive history of the "school dropout" in Canada has yet to be written.
2. I am currently undertaking a study funded by the Social Sciences and Humanities Research Council of Canada that includes a follow-up with this youngest cohort. This study is also investigating the migration and education decision-making of Digby Neck youth presently in secondary school.
3. This quote presages the more contemporary problem in rural Canada, the shortage of labour and the relocation of industrial and knowledge work to rural communities where labour costs are low (Winson and Leach, 2002). The "around here" area has seen the development of a call centre and some small scale manufacturing since 2000, and these industries are now experiencing difficulty finding workers.
4. "Getting their stamps" is Atlantic Canadian slang for working enough weeks to qualify for employment insurance benefits.
5. Or to quote Bourdieu on the portability of education credentials:

   > Educational qualifications, like money, have conventional fixed value which, being guaranteed by law, is freed from local limitations (in contrast to academically uncertified cultural capital) and temporal fluctuations. (1990: 132)

6. The notion of the "new rural economy" has become a mantra for rural development. I question how much of this change is really new.
7. Castells offers a similar critique of Giddens' project identity that I offer here.
8. Dianne Looker and her co-researchers have also noted the non-linear nature of contemporary school-to-work transitions for both rural and urban youth in 1990s Canada (Looker and Theissen, 1999; Looker and Dwyer, 1998; Looker and Andres, 1998). Young people's careers are marked by entry and exit from school-to-work-to-tertiary education-to work, etc. etc. (as funds and other commitments permit). Looker argues that the idea of a normal trajectory is becoming more problematic as idiosyncratic nonlinear transitions become common. Perhaps this is the unpleasant emerging face of a perpetually schooled, "learning culture" or what is commonly called, "life long learning."

Chapter 7

# Conclusion

> The goal is to be out of here.... One cannot explain why he is standing where he stands; why he is moving where he moves. But all this is irrelevant — as getting out is the *goal*. The only one to be had. (Bauman, 1991: 183, emphasis in original)

> "These youth show a very strong sense of identification with the locality, which, though it had a negative side, sprang 'from a familiarity with the geography of the district, and the feeling of being a cherished part of a close network of relationships'" (Coffield et al., 1986). The authors comment that in consequence of 'localism,' the quality of these young people's lives would have been lowered had they left the area. (Jones, 1999b: 3)

I began this analysis with the questions: who stays, who goes, and what role did formal education play in the distinction between staying and leaving. The answer to this question has several dimensions. First of all, women were both more mobile and more successful than men in institutions of formal education. This finding, which cut across the three cohorts, represents an established intergenerational social pattern in the community and mirrors broader patterns of gendered achievement (Weaver-Hightower, 2003; Arnot, 2006). Notwithstanding differences in social class and status, women were more comfortable at school, and they were more successful there. Their identity constructions were clearly more school friendly, and in families that had access to financial capital resources, there are now well-established patterns of converting family economic capital into education capital for young women who succeed in secondary school. Those women whose families lacked the financial capital to finance higher education still managed to take advantage of most of the state-supported, locally available education opportunities even if they had no plans or ability to move. Women have always needed education, whether they stayed or went, because the capital it can give them is negotiable in both local and distant employment markets. This is not to say that this educational success translated into economic advantage. Within the "around here" area this does not appear to be the case. Assessing the economic success of migrants is beyond the scope of this analysis.

In the case of men, there is no similar established habitus of education success. Across the three cohorts, there is a consistent pattern of education failure and more than half the male population in the youngest cohort still left secondary school before graduation (as opposed to about 10 percent of their female peers). The tradition with more privileged young men is that their families transfer economic capital — represented by fishing licences, quotas and gear — directly to male children. This reflects a patriarchal culture; it also continues to distance boys from the institutional routines of schooling. Given a growing, stable and prosperous fishery, this orientation may have some merit, but in the risky context of the contemporary fishery, the strategy is questionable. Regardless of whether or not this approach is economically rational, many young men on Digby Neck inhabit a cultural space that is virtually bereft of examples of men who were successful at school.

Education failure fit into a longstanding male tradition in many families, and being "born and bred" a fisherman included establishing an identity resistant to schooling. The myths of male identity construction continue to resonate even in the absence of a stable fishery. They have not yet been supplanted by identity options that are more congenial to, say, the development of the kinds of linguistic/literacy practice and presentations of the self that allow boys to succeed in school. Because "born and bred" identity constructions have been associated with both masculinity and economic power in the community and in the fishery, they tend to be entrenched. There is a powerful sense of disenfranchisement in men's stories about the decline of the fishery, with the evil triplets of corporate "big fellers," government bureaucracy and regulation, and the scientists generally considered to be at fault. Also, because of the cyclical nature of the fishing economy, men always seem to be waiting for the inevitable day when the "fish come back" and the boom economy of past years is re-established. Indeed, they have been proven right in the lobster and scallop fisheries of the late 1990s and early years of the present decade. The ground fishery is another matter.

The point is that the unstable nature of the economy does not seem to be influencing large numbers of young men in this community to engage more fully with formal education. In boom periods, education is unnecessary, while in bust periods, men wait for the Bay of Fundy to recover as it always has. In the meantime, a minority use formal education to leave the area. Given that "busts" or "downturns" are considered to be as much a product of state regulation and corporate concentration as greed and overfishing, there is a hope that through policy shifts and "common sense" management, the fishery can be made both stable and prosperous for the communities that have relied on it for centuries. Whether this kind of thinking is a rationalization or good sense is irrelevant. These are cultural patterns and the kind of indigenous knowledge that has supported people for centuries. Instability in the fishery has increased over the past several decades, and into the 1990s the Canadian state began a concerted effort to remove men and women from a partial or marginal reliance on it (usually supplemented by transfer payments). Some analysts claim that education will become part of the normal trajectory for young men from communities like Digby Neck when it is clear to them that the fishery is collapsing. Education is presented as a solution to the problem. It is, however, an ambivalent answer to a complex problem. From the perspective of established fishermen, schooling is in the realm of those "educated people" who have contrived to engineer the collapse of the fishery in the first place through corporate concentration and bureaucratic regulation.

## Place Matters

According to many contemporary theorists, a culture is no longer connected to any particular place. The idea of de-territorialization of culture stressed the declining importance of borders and the intimate connection that was supposed to exist between social identity and particular locales. Identity is forged in the "third space" between particular places, and global mass culture as migrations, travel and mass communications/media generate hybrids that range from the Donga Tribe, a loose multinational collection of wandering youth (Urry, 2000), to "world music," to the dozens of ethnic restaurants on a given block in any major western city. According to Papastergiadis (2000), ideal type modern/traditional categories are rooted in anthropological studies of small societies, which counterpoise a view of culture rooted in local practices, with the modern idea of culture as an "imposition" usually by nation states. Other anthropologists who study migration call for a view of culture that is not stuck in one closed place, but which is a more open system of "cross cultural negotiation and power differentials" (Papastergiadis, 2000: 104). However, Atlantic coastal communities like the one I have studied here, and the rural communities described by sociologists, historians and education researchers in the early chapters of this work, resemble in some ways those "small societies" built on face-to-face interactions to a considerable extent.

People living in these locales understand that they are under siege by cultural, economic and political forces that work to enclose and assimilate them. What emerges from the meeting of rural communities and the normalizing institutions and practices of late modernity (including the public school) is conflict, negotiation and an ambivalent intersection of purposes and values that is made all the more problematic by the way that the current phase (call it late modernity or post-modernity) simultaneously generates mobility and immobility. Communities are plastic constructions these days if contemporary theorists like Bauman, Giddens and Castells are to be believed. But like Theobald (1997), Ching and Creed (1997), Bonner

(1997), Porter (1996), Brandau and Collins (1994) and others, I found a strong strain of rural resistance that seems to fit well with Castells' idea of "resistant identity" formations that push against the "legitimizing identities" offered by formal education.

Both theories of reproduction and resistance in the sociology of education have tended to be theories of entrapment. In classic functionalist reproduction theories emanating from the work of Parsons, individuals were socialized and voluntarily integrated into particular roles and positions in the social structure. Their own voluntary "choices" integrated individuals into their "lot," and each individual choice generally worked to create social solidarity, harmony and a functioning society. Correspondence theory then developed in the 1970s, as a functional Marxist explanation of how and why particular youth found their way into particular stratified positions in the social-class structure (see Bowles and Gintis, 1976 and Apple, 1979). Correspondence theory saw schooling as a superstructural reflection of determining infrastructural relations of economy, power and hegemony. Again, the agents were trapped, the victims of social forces operating behind their backs, this time the forces not of social harmony, but of social class reproduction. Resistance emerged in the late 1970s as yet another theory of entrapment. Individual agents resisted the class content of their schooling, refusing to accept their interpellation into disadvantaged positions; they "penetrated" the facade of the emancipatory liberal rhetoric of schooling. The trouble is that in doing so they propelled themselves into menial jobs and trapped themselves in the working class anyhow. Structural entrapment was simply replaced by cultural snares.

A more subtle theory for explaining the nuanced way that particularly positioned social actors make the decisions they do is Bourdieu's *Logic of Practice* (1990). Bourdieu sees social actors creatively inventing their lives in differential circumstances. Bourdieu's social actors are positioned by "objective" circumstances of gender, race and class, and these circumstances are beyond their control. Bourdieu's research has mapped the nature of these forces (in French society) as well as the ways schools operate to promote opportunity but at the same time structure the availability of opportunity by privileging the cultural practices of particular groups. Despite the dynamic, even anthropological nature of his analysis, Bourdieu tends, like resistance theorists, to use agency to explain structure. Bourdieu's central concepts, like habitus, field, cultural capital and making a virtue of necessity, all construct a logic of practice that is at the same time creative and limited, but he ends up privileging and attending to the limitations and the predictable embodiments of practice a great deal more than the creativity that can be exercised within the habitus and under the pressure of the "coherent and convenient" choice. All action tends, in the end, to funnel into Bourdieu's structural categories of class domination and reproduction. Thus, Bourdieu's analysis is yet another discourse of entrapment.

While it is true that many of us who come out of working-class families "make a virtue of necessity," others make a virtue of many other things (e.g., commerce, religious observance, consumerism). The figure of the discerning consumer is at least as common as the "handy" bricoleur. At the same time, necessity is constructed in a number of ways. Contemporary discourse around the "necessity" of acquiring an education (a virtually universal discourse) often flies in the face of the pragmatics of survival in a rural community. As a perceived necessity, education is also constructed as a virtuous act in itself, turning Bourdieu on his head and making a necessity of virtue. Getting one's education and enduring the perceived irrelevance and inactivity of schooling is presented both in state Stay in School rhetoric and also in the language of Digby Neckers who do not trust the industrial-corporate fishery to sustain families into the future. It has always been seen as virtuous to stay in school, but increasingly it is understood as necessary.

Contrasted with local skills and intelligences, formal education continues to be perceived and experienced by many rural youth as a set of largely irrelevant experiences. But at the same time education is seen as a necessity because it confers mobility. In the local parlance, education is "light," "not hard to carry." In other words, education itself is mobile and negotiable across space, and despite its seeming irrelevance for solving known problems in the rural community and in the traditions of established families, it is begrudgingly considered necessary. Ironically, it is necessary because of the very forces that have unsettled the community.

What I found on Digby Neck is not a discourse of entrapment, but multiple discourses of strategic decision-making, which are more consistent with Castells' resistant identities and which are formed as a community-based response to big government and big capital. It is true that the habitus experienced by individuals growing up in particular communities did structure certain kinds of choices as "coherent and convenient," but this is not to say that the coherent and convenient choices were untroubled by competing discourses. To cite one example, youth in coastal communities have, for many years, been confronted with a negative discourse about the future of the fishery. Young men in Cohorts 2 and 3 established fishing families wondered whether or not they were making the right choice by deciding to follow their fathers into fishing, and very often their fathers were offering no encouragement to do so. There was no uniform sense of coherence and convenience; the "natural" path was increasingly seen as problematic. Even in a small, "close knit" single-industry community like Digby Neck, young people experienced multiple pressures, mediated by social class and by gender. Out of this matrix of ambivalence, a new sense of community pride and preservation developed through the 1990s.

Because resistance and reproduction theories each imagine a sovereign exercise of power and therefore develop only more or less tight discourses of domination, I have chosen Foucault's poststructural idea of power relation to understand the multiple oppositions that form the basis of education and migration decision-making on Digby Neck. I have found that each family is, in a certain sense, a habitus on Digby Neck, representing a particular history in the fishery, access to resources and a set of relationships and traditions. Children in particular families are presented at home and at school with a variety of "options," which seem to them more or less possible and attractive. Some options are accepted and embraced and others are resisted and rejected. Each habitus has its territory and more or less exclusive social, cultural and economic markets. Each competing habitus contains discursive patterns as well because it is produced and sustained symbolically, and for this reason it can be resisted. The habitus and normal middle-class life trajectory presented and valourized in school were seen by male stayers particularly as a feeble force, which was typically resisted because the community and the area "around here" presented "better options." For women, the education trajectory resisted the community habitus, but it was still seen to provide a "better option" for many women than staying and relying on the restricted range of options available to them on Digby Neck. Still other women and a few men followed the middle-class path only to return to the familiar geography of "around here" as professionals, white and pink-collar workers and entrepreneurs.

In chapters 1 and 2, drawing on Foucault, post-colonial theorists and the work of contemporary rural sociologists and historians, I presented the idea that rural communities are sites of resistance to the homeless, placeless assimilatory vision perhaps first described by Berger et al. in the early 1970s (1973) and developed by contemporary social theorists like Giddens and Bauman. While early school promoters were interested in establishing routines and normative practices of schooling within rural communities, there was a consistent and significant resistance to these efforts by rural dwellers who had other agendas. The crops needed to be brought in, father needed help with the fish, mother needed "help at home," the family moved from place to place in mining camps where there were no regular schools or teachers, homogenization, mobilization and the teacher quit and no replacement could be found, or the family needed money and a child of fourteen could sometimes earn close to an adult wage or make what amounted to an adult contribution to family income (Davey, 1978; Wilson and Stortz, 1995; Gaffield, 1987; Corbett, 2001b). All of these kinds of activity and their ordinariness across the developing rural landscape of Canadian communities created place-based traditions of resistance to schooling that juxtaposed practicality with academic irrelevance. These patterns have been part of the weave of biography and history, a "natural" transition from childhood to adulthood in rural Canada. Quitting school, being resistant while in school, working in the community and with family while in school, and seeing school as an impractical "waste of time" divorced from the "real" pursuits visible in a rural economy were (and remain) all part of this resistance.

In this study "stayers" are the back-bone of the Digby Neck community. Many of them are early school leavers who dropped out of school in order to drop in to life in their communities, a life that they take seriously, are committed to and want to protect in the face of forces marshalled against their survival on Digby Neck. The community has been remarkably resistant to in-migration and like many small, rural communities, it is a resilient space of racial, ethnic and religious homogeneity. The prototypical Digby Necker is a white man who is tough and independent, who knows the geography of land and sea, who is multi-skilled and rooted in multi-generational family networks. As Canada and the world have become what Mackey (2002) calls a "house of difference," increasingly multiethnic and multicultural, Digby Neck has remained a house of similarity that is challenged by forces originating in the wider society and in the geopolitics of economic globalization.[1] The majority of men in this group quit school and most of them are involved in some way with the fishery. They have learned to stay and learned how to survive, lessons that no one ever learned (or expected to learn) in school. They run boats and resist state efforts to make their industry more "efficient" by running them out of business and consolidating access to fisheries resources in the hands of a few elite fishermen and corporate interests.[2] The struggle is ongoing and continual and the threat of quotas, closures, the emerging First Nations fishery, fish stock collapse, corporate and government licence buy-outs, the loss of land to logging and to wealthy "outsiders," and other problems give these men and women a great deal to do and think about. They see themselves immersed in a political and ideological struggle for community survival that is much more difficult and complicated than the well-known struggle of getting a living from the sea.[3] As one fisherman put it, "All these meetings and sitting down with different people [interest groups] and working things out, that's the hardest work I ever done" (FN).

The struggle to protect these spaces and the resources they contain is also a women's struggle despite the fact that far fewer women raised on Digby Neck stay there. Women are among the most active workers in community survival organizations that seek to protect and preserve the institutional infrastructure of the community, particularly its elementary school. Just as men struggle to preserve their livelihoods, their "ocean spaces," women engage in struggle to preserve "community spaces." These activities all resist the forces of consolidation, concentration and community disintegration that have emerged in the retreat of the state from providing services to coastal communities. This, too, is an ongoing political/ideological struggle and hard, discouraging work which flies in the face of the discourse described by Berry (1977), Theobald (1997), Bonner (1997), Popkewitz (1998) and Ching and Creed (1997), a discourse that marginalizes rurality and that seeks to govern and reform if not destroy it. This resistant counter-discourse is the language of survival and community resilience that runs through these accounts. This survival discourse resists the persistent threat of the ongoing enclosure of rural spaces and common property (Theobald and Rochon, 2006).

Contrary to my expectations and to those of virtually all of my informants, popular discourse and the scholarly literature on schooling in rural areas, I found residents of Digby Neck to be less mobile at the turn of the 21st century than in previous decades. It is my contention that this decreased level of out-migration reflects a strong resistance to both the mobility imperative in rural schooling and to the discourse of decline that figures so prominently in the way Atlantic coastal communities are now described. These two capitalist-modernist discourses (the inevitablity of rural decline and the universal need for protracted schooling) are inextricably linked to generate a mobility imperative in contemporary educational thought and policy.

Through the 1970s and 1980s, the industrial fishery boomed, providing a strong economic reason for young men and for some young women to resist formal education. In this context, it comes as no surprise that out-migration rates fell. But, the late 1980s and 1990s was a period in which the prevalent discourse was that of fish stocks collapsing, rural Canada dying and general decline in coastal communities. This discourse of decline though, was received by Digby Neck youth in tandem with an equally pessimistic discourse of diminished urban opportunities, "downsizing" and industrial decay. Urban opportunities were made available principally through the acquisition of mobile education capital. The Basic Data Bank and the Community, Schooling and Migration Survey show that mobile out-migrant Digby Neckers who settled in the area outside the 50 kilometre "around here" zone have indeed acquired significantly higher levels of post-secondary credentials. On the other hand, those who remained inside the 50 kilometre circle seem very able to negotiate their lives with relatively low levels of formal education. The "around here" area and its occupational and social structure continues to provide a context within which resistance to higher education is supported, particularly for men.

Learning to leave was not generally a conscious process, although when

I raised the connection between formal education and out-migration, most informants were able to see the linkage. For many stayers, school was simply experienced as an irrelevance. Why it was irrelevant was generally not given much thought. Accounts from the interviews, though, trace the connection between formal schooling and out-migration, and leavers understood that they needed higher education in order to survive off Digby Neck. Leavers typically understood why education was relevant for them, and it was because they required it to be mobile. This was less true in Cohort 1, where the employment market for men particularly, in central and western Canada, could absorb large numbers of workers whose manual skills were more important than their education credentials. Women of all cohorts needed education to leave, as did men in Cohorts 2 and 3. Unless one was a young man coming of age in the 1960s or early 1970s, one had to learn to leave.

## Migration, Education and Ambivalence: Mobility Capital

> Few people anywhere in the world can any longer be unaware of the fact that their local activities are influenced, and somehow even determined, by remote events or agencies. (Giddens, 1996: 9)

What Bourdieu's conceptual scheme misses most in the context of rural economies is that capital must be transformed from fixed, locally negotiable capital, like fishing licences, boats, fish plants, quotas and gear in the case of a fishing community, into the mobile capital represented by formal education credentials. Even those families that had access to financial capital need to invest it in an intangible, trust-based and, to quote an educator from this study, "largely unproven" (CD-ME) form of symbolic capital that is only negotiable (with remarkably few exceptions) outside the life world of the coastal community and the "around here" region. Higher education does not just imply that children will leave; it is the "ticket" and the mobile capital now necessary to leave.

I argue here that schooling is a quintessential institution of disembedding, that schools are concerned with severing the attachments of individuals to particular places and making young people adaptable, flexible and mobile. Giddens writes: "(E)xpert systems are disembedding mechanisms because, in common with symbolic tokens, they remove social relations from the immediacies of context" (1990: 28). This study has shown how the discourse of mobility, or disembedding, is both accepted and resisted. Like all discourses, this one creates oppositions, it identifies individuals to be "educated," and it engenders a resistant set of tactical responses. When the education process "works," schooling mobilizes Digby Neckers and "re-places" them, if not physically, then at least by giving them an outsider's perspective on their own lifeworld. Leavers in this study expected their education to provide them with a larger sense of the world, and they see the inability of many stayers to contextualize their problems, and their biographies, in the larger context of national and global events as the root of many of their limitations.

> You know I look at the fishery as such a great example because there's a lot of very heartfelt emotional things that are happening there that a lot of Canada, 90 percent of Canada, doesn't even know is going on.... You know they [Digby Neckers] take their licking without even doing too much. They're not the kind of people that are going to stand there and throw their emotions in front of the TV camera. But the other thing is that there is the [pause] sometimes I just don't think they see what the outside would is like. (EM-ML-80)

The more schooling rural youth get the more mobile they become. In contemporary school systems, mobility takes on a moral character and comes to be framed both in terms of institutional advancement and in terms of a person's fundamental human worth and goodness. To have done well in school and to have persisted in formal education and moved on is to be a good, responsible person in this discourse. This is what I refer to as "making a necessity of virtue," the process of promoting a set of experiences that have no immediate or recognizable return. When schooling "fails," youth or when youth "fail" school, they remain in places like Nova Scotian coastal communities, and ambivalent "at risk" discourses about both these youth and these communities grinds on. On one hand, mobile, academically credentialed youth are praised while at the same time, community leaders bemoan the loss of the "cream of the crop" of potential entrepreneurs, consumers, producers, solid citizens and community leaders.

On the other side of the moral ledger of education policy and practice there is an equally persistent negative discourse about what will "become of" those youth who do not complete an education and become mobile. Teachers and parents alike wonder "what will they do?" in the economic space around here. The "dropout problem" is considered to be of crisis proportions by school board officials and "concerned" groups that formed and met with a fair degree of regularity through the 1990s in Digby County. Their target was always that simultaneously pathetic and frightening construction, the dropout, or the proto-dropout, the child "at risk," in danger of not becoming mobile and useful. The fact is that they do not fall off the map; rather they take advantage as best they can of opportunities available to them locally on the basis of their own particular array of social, economic and cultural capital. This at-risk discourse is not new. The resilience of the community serves as an indication that the social disintegration predicted for Digby County in the Stirling County Study (Leighton, 1963) in an earlier period of transition will not necessarily come to pass. In fact, as I demonstrated in chapter 3, wages on Digby Neck have actually risen relative to regional, provincial and national averages since microdata have been available for analysis. It is also apparent that the local economy continues to require a cohort of immobile labour that is either willing or forced to stay and work for depressed wages. In my analysis, this immobile group appears to be growing.

In the context of contemporary global culture, Digby Neckers are becoming less and less geographically mobile. Fewer students follow the expected path of this kind of mobile biography. And this creates yet another form of ambivalence among teachers, who are often surprised (and perhaps quietly disappointed) to find out how few of their former students have "moved on" and how many are "just around here." How do we explain this apparent contradiction? I claim that mobility is an accoutrement of privilege and economic power. In order to be mobile and see the potential for a life within a space broader than "around here" a young person needs to have access to the mobility capital necessary to leave. By mobility capital I mean those kinds of capital that are transportable across space but that also serve as "tickets" and confer mobility. Certain kinds of capital are mobile while others are not, and formal education credentials represent a quintessential form of mobile capital. Mobility capital is a combination of economic resources and secondary school education credentials; the former is a functional necessity for physical relocation into spaces of higher education, while the latter acts as a letter of reference that certifies that the bearer possesses sufficient mastery of academic space to "move on" beyond the locale. The possession of one does not necessarily mean the possession of the other, although without economic resources, education credentials appear as a virtuous and necessary accomplishment, but one that may lead back into local spaces and typically to low wages.

With the decline in the fishery, an ability to see the mobility path opened up by taking school seriously and dedicating oneself to mastering its discourse was constricted in the 1990s by a provincial and even national economy that seemed to offer little opportunity for families to realistically imagine that their children might survive elsewhere. Because they cannot see mobile futures, these children resisted or dismissed formal education, because for them, it led nowhere. And as Bauman points out, when the master narratives of modernity collapse, all forms of life become acceptable, one no better than another. In schools, it is no longer acceptable to "cream," "stream" or actively select mobile youth from families who have mobility capital. Teachers are now forced to adopt a discourse of community relevance that recognizes the "needs" of rural youth who want to stay "around here" and consequently modify their own mobility-oriented discourse to present staying on as a legitimate "option" and one that must be supported by a new form of community-sensitive "responsive" education and governance for those who remain.[4]

At the same time that this is happening, space outside the geographic parameters of Digby Neck and the known area "around here" is collapsing. Services are brought to people "around here" and they no longer need to go out in search of them. This helps individuals who see no possibility of moving outside the area to feel integrated into modernity as consumers and also feel that they have everything they need because everything that is available elsewhere is also found right "in their own backyards." One no longer has to go to Halifax or "up the [Annapolis] Valley" for consumer goods and services. The mobility of goods and services then serves to create conditions of immobility and greater insularity in the local area. As one informant commented, "People were more on the move a hundred years ago. They were on boats to Boston, all over the world really. It was a more cosmopolitan environment and it showed in the people" (FN). But surely, people have now become "cosmopolitan" (or at least cosmopolitan consumers) in a different and more intense way in the current epoch, if only because of ready access to mass media.[5]

Just as the concept of space is no longer located in any particular place, mobility is also unconstrained by geographic boundaries. The Internet is the most obvious example of a type of mobility that requires no geographic movement. This kind of mobility is becoming both a more accessible form of travel for youth on Digby Neck and at the same time a form of valuable cultural capital for those children in elite families who have at-home access to computers and the internet. To be mobile in this world also requires financial capital and the cultural capital of a "wired" family. Having computers and knowing how to use them is an unevenly distributed access to mobility within the created and expanding virtual spaces of contemporary capitalism. Electronic commerce and relatively inexpensive long-distance telephone service is also beginning to have an impact on mobility as well as allowing shoppers to access consumer goods "on-line" without the need to move physically. It is possible to live in a highly mobile world and benefit from some measure of its excitement and consumer pleasures, not because one is more geographically mobile, but precisely for the opposite reason, because anything is now accessible at the click of a mouse on the home computer, in the local convenience story video rack or in the grander shopping facilities in "town."

Like so many other places, Atlantic Canadian coastal communities have been drawn into an expanding global process of highly mobile goods, services, ideas and people which move rapidly across what Urry calls "scapes" or grids of transmission that range from airlines to fiber-optic cables (2000: 35–36; 63–64). Living in a context of radical mobility, it is possible to consume the products made available in the global marketplace while actually becoming less geographically mobile than in previous times. The increased proletarianization that Marxist theorists described in Atlantic Canadian fishing communities in the 1970s and 1980s is supported in this analysis. Fewer and fewer workers have been needed to harvest and process fish on Digby Neck, populations have fallen, and I show here how those remaining populations have become less mobile. The new reserve army of mobile young people are not the poor; in the context of this study they are more likely to be drawn from the privileged children of elite fishing families who use their financial capital to buy the mobility capital or "tickets" provided by the intersection of formal education and social class.[6] In late modernity, consumer society and the mass media seem to have penetrated even the most remote of communities generating ambivalence and immobility among those who remain.

## Ambiguity, Mobility and Resistance

Bauman writes that strangers are mass-produced in the "new intense and feverish mobility itself which arises from the state enforced 'uniformization' of vast spaces" (1991: 62). As movement and travel become normal, and strangers abound, localized spaces are changed by the invasion of unattached persons, who defy "the easy expedient of spatial or temporal segregation" (Bauman, 1991: 59). The stranger is notoriously restless and obviously placeless, an object of reform and at the same time responsible for their own reformation in the context of modern institutions and power/knowledge, unlike their opposite, the pre-modern "native," whose identity is fixed to place, habit, custom and tradition.

> Being a stranger means, first and foremost, that nothing is natural; nothing is given of right, nothing comes free. The native's primeval union between the self and nature has been sundered. Each side of the union has been brought into focus of attention — as a problem, and as a task. (Bauman, 1991: 75)

Bauman contrasts the experience and reflexive self-understanding of his stranger to that of the "native member of a community." The native lives within a structure that is socially scripted, and the self is effortlessly revealed to the individual in stages as part of the process of maturation and status passage in the community, "born as hc is 'into the community' and growing inside it without much challenge from the outside. His is the state of 'being saturated' or 'tuned'" (Bauman, 1991: 75). The stranger has none of this straightforward socialization experience; rather the stranger as a figure of modernity needs to be flexibly educated for a variety of contexts and a future that cannot be known in advance. Therefore, "he is denied the smugness of self-oblivion... the stranger is his own problem" (Bauman, 1991: 76). This is the modernist notion of the self as a project, as described by Giddens, an identity that one writes with one's "choices," choices we are "doomed" to make whether we like it or not (Bauman, 1999). Education credentials are the "objective" measures of one's suitability to a variety of contexts; they amount to references from academically certified strangers to other academically certified strangers that youth will necessarily encounter on their pilgrimage of choice. Increasingly, education is a prerequisite for a wide variety of established and emerging life projects. Education has taken as its object the "native," in the case of the study at hand, natives of Digby Neck, and attempted to write "options" onto their personality structures and to gauge the capacity of given individuals to adapt to particular kinds of changes, choices and specialized tasks outside a space where one is "known."

But what choices? There is no longer a single coherent habitus. Identity is plastic for the stranger, who is not rooted in either geographic or social place. The modern self floats free in the context of what Bauman calls the ambivalence generating "a priori displacement of the modern person" (1991: 207). Modern individuals must be equipped to become what modernity makes them: choosers, movers, workers, members of the optimistic/pessimistic terror-fixated consumer culture of the millennium and tacticians framing selves against a backdrop of multiple discourses. Bauman goes on to analyze the place of "expertise" in reflecting the self back to us for monitoring and choice. Again the system of formal education in western democracies takes the "individual" as its object in a psychologized discourse of adjustment to a universal strangerhood. Under these conditions ambivalence grows unchecked and nobody really expects order any more. This is good for the expert, particularly in fields that deal with the engineering of social behaviour like counselling, education, astrology, New Age "healing," health, "self-help" and religion. Ambivalence is the "industrial waste" of modernity, as Bauman says, and management of this waste has become a huge industry. What is there left for education as a central unifying governance mandate other than mobilizing people, or at least selecting and certifying some of us for mobility?

People on Digby Neck are aware of these "forces" that work to displace and integrate them and of how "experts" in schools have tried to help at least some of them become modern, functional, deployable strangers in the landscape of modern capitalism. This study is an account of the way that this project has been constructed in the discourse of schooling and embraced and resisted by generations of Digby Neckers. The role of the teacher in the coastal community is that of the stranger in the sense Simmel described it. Teachers enter the community, often as strangers from another community, calling the whole apparatus of the "native" community habitus into question, resisting the natural order of things by virtue of their alterity (Bauman calls this an "incongruent existential constitution" [1991: 76]), their "external" perspective on the community, and by promoting the mobile cultural capital that education credentials represent.

The educated eye, cultivated through the mobile discourse of schooling, the strangerhood of teachers and the increasingly national, pan-national and global nature of curriculum (Willinsky, 1998) is a feature of schooling that denigrates localism and marginalizes regional problems in Atlantic Canada (Kelly, 1993). A mobile sensibility is also inculcated, probably much more effectively and powerfully, in other mobile "education" discourses like the regional and national news programs, newspapers and magazines described by Williams (1958, 1961, 1973) and Hoggart (1957) in Great Britain. Mobile culture blends contemporary pop music made ever more accessible to privileged audiences via the internet and cable television, internationally accessible internet chat groups, inexpensive air travel, global youth culture, flexible "bund-style"[7] interest group associations described by Urry (2000), e-commerce and the ready availability of a virtually unlimited array of consumer products and services, among many other postmodern forces. An understanding of these features of the current epoch is a crucial part of a contemporary education and it is no more evenly distributed regionally or across social class lines than were the education technologies of any other period.

Williams argued that the state and corporate interests could produce just about any kind of human being it wanted by applying modern methods of social control, of which the education system was a key component. Bauman calls this the quintessential modernist dream, the notion of assimilation or the creation of a unified "society" (1991, 1992, 1999). But this is a project that has always contained the seeds of its own destruction for within every assimilatory initiative conceived in the context of modernity, including his favourite example, the Jewish Holocaust, the drive toward assimilation was met with resistance. In fact, resistance generates ambivalence, because without it power relations would be finished before they began (as Foucault pointed out), sterile, fascistic and uninteresting. Ubiquitous resistance (deCerteau, 1984; Castells, 2004) has put a sense of ambivalence at the centre of the project of modernity, an ambivalence that at least since the Holocaust, and particularly since the dissolution of the former Soviet Union, has become sharply defined and crucial as a psychological buffer against ever embracing any emancipatory ideology or modernist system too uncritically.

> Assimilation was the front line of social engineering, the cutting edge of the advancing order. With spontaneity discredited and nature's self monitoring capacity questioned, order became synonymous with monopoly of power, with control and repression of resistant "otherness." Ambivalence was that denial of order which the product of order in general, and its assimilatory arm in particular, could not help turning out in ever increasing volume. In the production of uniformity, ambivalence was the industrial waste. As with all refuse, it was shunned, viewed with disgust, and suspected of magic poisoning powers. (Bauman, 1991: 149)

Rural schooling has been such an assimilatory project. It has sought to do the missionary work of cultural elevation in the "backward space" like the coastal community studied here and it has consistently failed in this project. Dropout rates remain high, resistance remains common and people still continue to remain committed to staying where they are and learning a lot of practical knowledge about their locales rather than a little theoretical knowledge about places they have never seen. But through the years the nature of this project has changed. No longer are young people sorted on the basis of teachers' perceptions and judgments about their ability to survive outside the community or to "go on." Youth are now faced with making their own "choice." What was once presented to them as inevitability is now presented as choice, and it is the responsibility of each individual child to come to learn the modernist role of the stranger, which is to construct a life. As such, they are responsible, as individuals for their own failure and their ability or inability to have made the "right choices." This shift to individualization, introspection and a preoccupation with constructing a successful self has created, it seems, a generation that blames itself for its life outcomes. It is also a generation that walks with trepidation around big life decisions like post-secondary choices and, as the Hollywood film *Failure to Launch* illustrated, leaving home. These are the children of risk society (Beck, 1992) in a rural context, where they ultimately feel safe albeit bored.

Since natives no longer exist anywhere, no one is any longer "granted their existence, so that they can live in tranquility — to be rather than to become" (Bauman, 1991: 155). We are all strangers, we are all responsible for ourselves and we are all in motion. As the quote at the beginning of this chapter asserts, to be in motion is the only remaining goal. The ambivalence Bauman describes is a deep feeling of unease and unrest associated with the modern condition. Giddens also writes of the insecurity associated with living in a matrix of expert systems and networks of production and consumption that range from our dwellings, to our jobs, to our entertainment, to our illnesses, and to their cures (1990, 1991). Rural Canadians live as much in systems regulated by experts as in particular locales, and they need to struggle to keep control of territory, often against the hegemony of expert systems seeking to enclose rural places within the scope of their governance. Schooling is one of these expert systems, and one that I am arguing works to disembed and mobilize young people.

If getting out is the only goal, as Bauman suggests, perhaps the only remaining form of resistance is staying. It is precisely the vision of modernity so well described by Giddens and Bauman that Digby Neckers seem to resist. Giddens' "high modernity" is itself a discourse, and it is one that many Digby Neck stayers deplore. They detest and resist being drawn into abstract systems preferring to remain multi-skilled, hands-on, and community-based. Many women prefer to pitch-in and help rather than turn problems over to professionals, and many men prefer do-it-yourself problem-solving and sharing skills and knowledge to relying on experts. Digby Neckers' attitudes to problems of life in the matrix of expert systems is captured by their dismissive disinterest in the Y2K problem that gripped the international media through 1999. The abstract systems that were threatened were somebody else's problem.

My research shows that most Digby Neckers resist the mobility imperative built in to the idealized education trajectory and remain "around here." In the process they build alternative visions of success that involve persistence, survival and resistance to the forces that seek to displace them. As such, they create a moral order that confronts the mobility-focused sense of the "good person" that is predicated on achieving credentials and being mobile. It is easy to dismiss this process as Bourdieu (1984b) does, calling the whole thing "making a virtue of necessity," as though this were something specific to the working class. Wealthy fishing captains and those boys who idolize them mock the way teachers "make a necessity of virtue" when they pass on anti-school attitudes and demonstrate with their lives that economic wealth is not necessarily gotten by being a well-behaved, compliant and studious "good boy."

Perhaps the most important aspect of this apparently growing level of immobility is that rural schooling has lost direction and no longer understands its central mission, which has been to re-place and mobilize young people. If one place is no better than another, can rural teachers any longer shunt selected youth out and bemoan the situation of the rest being "stuck"? As one current teacher commented, "I don't know that we really ask them to go to Acadia [university] anyway. We do ask them to finish high school and then to see what they're going to do after that" (FN). Contrary to the fears of many rural sociologists and education theorists, the rural community, in at least some instances, is at least as stable as it ever was, and it is stable because its youth seem less enthralled with the siren song of the bright lights than most of us imagine. Rural schools can no longer admit to their role as institutions for "creaming," streaming," sorting and selection; they now require new narratives around which to organize governance, and in my view, they are still floundering toward finding this discourse.

## Resistances

> [S]chools have become "rational" in that "what education is good for" is often defined today with respect to expanded occupational possibilities and living standards possible by "obtaining a good education." At the same time, schools teach individuals that they are free from the constraints of local communities and families, since desirable economic and geographic mobility is theirs via the careers that good schooling has opened up to them. (DeYoung, 1995: 171)

Bourdieu's analysis seems much more appropriate for explaining the work and education histories of the two earlier cohorts in this study. Up until the early 1990s, there was a strong community-based habitus that drew young men into the economic orbit of the fishery. The habitus, however, is a problematic concept for explaining schooling on Digby Neck. Like Giroux and McLaren's resistance theory, Bourdieu's scheme is too tightly connected to a structural analysis of what he calls "objective" conditions and the logic of practice and habitus that arise from them. "Objective conditions" on Digby Neck have set the stage for a wide variety of education responses, including privileged young fishermen refusing the very real opportunity to access higher education because it was not sufficiently lucrative to attract them. But powerful ideas like Bourdieu's "habitus," Giddens "high modernity" and Bauman's "universal strangerhood" are all discursive productions and descriptions of particular sets of power relations. As such they represent plays of strategic vision and tactical resistance. This study looks into one small microcosm of these dynamic power relations and the resistances they contain.

For young women, the community habitus was, and continues to be, educationally focused. Girls have been expected to do well in school and to leave, if not for post-secondary education, then for work or relationships that allow for support. Because of this women "did better" in school, both in terms of credentials and in terms of experiencing schooling as a positive personal experience. Many women realized, at an early age, that their options were limited by staying on the Neck. For many of them this was a very difficult realization because it meant leaving behind crucial attachments and family support systems. Women also tended to have a strong attachment to place, commenting often on the natural beauty of Digby Neck. But, like Deborah Hicks' (2005) informants, they were also more likely to report wanting to "get out" or "get off the Neck" and experience a bigger world that offered women more opportunity and status. This was partly because of limited opportunities on the Neck but also partly because of the way they understood the position of women there. Most migrant women understood that choosing to stay on the Neck would mean living in a space that is dominated by men and in which men receive economic and social privilege. Women's out-migration was a form of resistance to the gender stratified opportunity structure in which they saw their mothers and some peers "trapped."

The consistent pattern for women is that nearly 50 percent migrate outside the "around here" region. Their superior education credentials allow these women to move further and access occupational positions and relationships outside the region. However, women who stayed both on the Neck and "around here" had nearly as high a rate of high-school completion as women who migrated further. Women who stayed "around here" were not, for the most part, education failures. Yet the relative success of women (compared to male stayers) in formal education did not translate into economic advantage. Census data showed that for all but one census enumeration area of Digby Neck, women's average income was significantly below that of men. The presence of many relatively well-educated women earning less money than their relatively poorly-educated male peers may have been yet another piece of local evidence that prolonged education was not of much value locally either to men or to women. Perhaps, education was irrelevant to economic success just as some people had always maintained. In the context of families, though, men's economic success is, in many cases, shared by women who support the entrepreneurial project of a family fishing operation. Thus, women are not necessarily oppressed by their relatively low personal incomes.

By the time Cohort 2 and especially Cohort 3 came of age, the vast majority of women were finishing high school. In Cohort 2 women's post-secondary participation rate peaked at over 24 percent of the population. This percentage fell slightly for Cohort 3. As interview data showed, many economically privileged families were investing their financial capital from the strong ground fishery into educating their daughters, an education that was often explicitly designed to take them out of the community and into middle-class lives elsewhere. By the 1990s this strategy was available to relatively few families, and as the fishery contracted and the cost of post-secondary education rose, so too did the ability of young Digby Neck women to access post-secondary education and resist being "forced" to remain close to home. The result is that the overall female population has become slightly less mobile, moving from Cohort 1 to Cohort 3. Resisting the gendered structure of economic welfare and social privilege that these younger women describe as characterizing life on the Neck became more difficult as the decade of the 1990s unfolded. Women sit more easily in the ambivalent space that education opens up in this rural community in no small part because of their relative economic disadvantage in the locale (Corbett, 2006a, 2006b).

Men who grew up in the 1960s, 1970s and 1980s rejected school because they considered it to be an impractical waste of their time. The gendered structure of labour in the fishery favoured them, and those born in families with different sorts of connections to the fishery moved into different positions in the industry. The male children of fish plant owners ran fish plants and got choice positions on company boats; the male children of licence-holding families worked the family rig, often with their fathers; the children of fish plant workers were brought "into the fish" at an early age and learned to be on the job when there were fish to cut, an availability that sometimes conflicted with school. Being born and bred meant having virtually exclusive access to family businesses, labour markets, family-based apprenticeship opportunities and socialization/education opportunities and traditions that taught young men how to be a Digby Necker and how to be a fisherman. If the ability to fish is "in the blood," then only those whose blood is pure can do the work and really inhabit the community. Racial, gender and ethnic exclusiveness were understood in terms the natural possession of an appropriate capital array (social, cultural, economic, etc.), of belonging to families, and of being connected to and established in a way of life that is under siege.

Women in each cohort understood the gender dimensions of this exclusiveness very well. What was much less well articulated were the racial dimensions of being inside the born and bred world. One marker of this exclusiveness is the absent presence of a discourse around race. While the regional secondary school experienced significant racial tension throughout the period dealt with in this case study, almost no one spoke of race as an issue. My data contain very little reference to race and ethnicity. Yet, there was one testimony in one interview that raised in a striking and powerful way the depth of racism and sexism in the community in the 1980s. Digby Neck was probably little different from many White communities in rural Nova Scotia. This account illustrates the level of racial intolerance that was documented formally in two studies done in the regional secondary school (Frank, 1998) and a provincial report prepared by the Black Learners Advisory Committee (1994).

It is interesting that Digby Neckers in the first two cohorts particularly identified themselves as something of an oppressed and misunderstood minority. The loud silence around questions of race and of ethnic difference more generally demonstrates both how tightly integrated the community continues to be but also how race was marginalized and perhaps suppressed as a topic of discussion and remembrance. It is clear that one effect of school consolidation, bussing and the expansion of education access to formerly disenfranchised groups has been to place in the same classroom people who have little experience with social difference. This has been, as Frank (1998) pointed out, compounded by multiple levels of difference and disadvantage. What is often read as racial tension or conflict can also be seen as an indicator of the frustrations of different disenfranchised groups butting up against one another in the context of school. It will be interesting to see how this history of mono-ethnic, mono-religious community solidarity and exclusiveness will survive the recent multicultural influx of tourists, summer residents, permanent residents and entrepreneurs. The character of Digby Neck will inevitably, albeit slowly, change. This change will undoubtedly have an impact on perceptions and habitual practices in formal education.

Resisting school was a "natural" thing for men in virtually every social position in the fishery because school interrupted the community habitus, the economic potential of a young man "willing to work" rather than "settin' in school." By the late 1970s and 1980s the booming ground fishery continued to offer employment to anybody who "wanted to work," and resistance to schooling continued in a fishery where young men in licence-holding families (and even those who crewed on draggers) could earn professional wages at the age of sixteen. These opportunities created a climate in which men's commitment to schooling as a path that led toward a career was generally weak, and those who did pursue schooling to the end of high school typically found their way out of the community, into post-secondary education and typically away from the "around here" region.

In Cohort 1 it was possible for men to leave the area with few formal education credentials and find employment. Booming economies in central and western Canada absorbed a considerable number of Digby Neck men at least temporarily. Fewer than one in five Digby Neckers stayed "away" (the percentages are nearly gender balanced). Women who left generally acquired formal education credentials, even in the 1960s. Most of these women took secretarial or "office" jobs and some went into expanding "helping professions." In Cohort 1, nearly 70 percent of female leavers graduated high school and this is in an era where the high school dropout rate was between 50 and 70 percent. This demonstrates that most Digby Neck women have always understood the importance of secondary education for their personal success. In Cohort 2, the high school graduation rate for women rose slightly to 70.1 percent, and in Cohort 3 it rose to 88.1 percent. In order for women to leave, education credentials were a virtual necessity, and if she did not have them, chances were that a woman would have to stay "around here."

This climate of economic prosperity in the industrializing fishery signalled the demise of the fishery in the eyes of most Digby Neckers. "We caught 'em all up," many men comment while at the same time arguing that if they were allowed to return to a strictly "fixed gear" fishery the stocks would once again rebound. As it was for women on Digby Neck, the 1990s was also difficult for young men. The community-based habitus and discourse around work in the fishery and the lucrative nature of fishing for the hard working, macho fellow with fishing "in his blood," an ideology that was supported in the booming ground fishery of the 1960s, 1970s and 1980s, continued to lead large numbers of young men out of school before graduation. Up until the early 1990s it was easy to resist education; it was "natural" for an adolescent to quit school and go fishing, it was an historical pattern, a well worn path taken by one's elders and one's peers. The young men's families seemed unsure how to support them staying in school beyond the "natural" quitting age of fifteen or sixteen, and they themselves typically seemed unable to "put up with" school. Through the 1990s the male dropout rate remained at more than 50 percent despite what appeared to be few fisheries-based employment opportunities. But for the "mobile" among the male population, those who moved outside the "around here" circle, dropout rates fell from 51.6 percent in Cohort 1 to 16.6 percent in Cohort 3. By the 1990s, if there were jobs outside the "around here" region, they could only be obtained by most men with the mobile capital of higher education. Thus, by the late 1980s and 1990s, learning had become a prerequisite for leaving.

For those who stayed "around here" the learning-earning equation was not evident. The "salvation" of this less mobile group has been the expansion of the service sector and mainly part-time, temporary and seasonal work in the "around here" economy. With the growth of the town of Digby as a service centre for the surrounding communities, retail activity has concentrated there, creating a variety of "McJobs," which have allowed a large marginally educated population to subsist and to continue to resist formal education. This resistance has its logic in that many of these youth have difficulty imagining themselves working at anything other than marginal jobs, regardless of their education qualifications. Living in the coastal community and in families whose whole intergenerational economic history and family habitus is connected with the fishery, many of these young men have never seriously considered doing anything but working as fishermen, a career that is built by "working around" and "helping out" and watching fishermen, and thus, getting an appropriate practical education. But like Lois Weis's (2004) post-industrial White working-class informants, many of these young men have been caught in an economic and social transformation.

The community habitus contained not only sets of restrictions and negative sanctions concerning one's "place" and one's "people," it also contained positive attractions like large (by local standards), albeit irregular pay-checks and masculine work identities and caring family-focused communities. What has remained constant through time is the resilience of different forms of resistance to schooling among Digby Neck men. Men resist schooling by staying "around here." While the logic of this resistance has been transformed, its content has not. What is also consistent is Digby Neck women's resistance to the gendered structure of opportunity on the Neck. Women resist by leaving and by taking education seriously, realizing that their "default option" is marriage and probable economic dependence. Many of the women in Cohorts 2 and 3 took their mothers' advice, tapping into community traditions of women's education success, and used formal education to position themselves favourably in a changing market. This women's resistance, however, is becoming harder to sustain because it became more difficult for young women to access post-secondary education in the 1990s, and more young women considered themselves to be "stuck" on the Neck and living with parents. Young men are also in this position, but their persistence is more "normal" as a community pattern. Most young men have always stayed, but young most women have always gone. And the fact that so many of these young people remain at home is not problematic for many families, who like having them around. As one informant put it, "I don't care if they never leave home and they stay in here with us. We've only got the two boys and they're a good help. We'd love to see them stay right here" (FN).

Bourdieu describes a sense of belonging, or being part of "people like us," in negative terms, in his discussion of the logic of practice. He details this feeling as a kind of restrictive sense of what one can accomplish and one's limitations grounded in habitus. Particularly in Cohort 3, it becomes difficult to distinguish this sense of integration in a community, class or family based habitus. Who indeed are "people like us" in the eyes of young Digby Neckers, who see themselves as part of a generation linked by new media to youth around the world? Even the most entrenched stayers are as likely to see themselves as residents of the Digby area or of southwest Nova Scotia as residents of Digby Neck. Greater mobility within the "around here" area has created a different sense of belonging and community, one that is spread at least into the fifty kilometre circle. As is the case with most people today, Digby Neckers' socio-spatial identities are moving on to a broader stage. While members of Cohort 1 tended to speak of their community as the particular village in which they were raised, and Cohort 2 tended to identify with "the Neck," members of Cohort 3 identified themselves with the "around here" region, where they work, socialize, shop and very often live. Youth from Cohort 3 were the most mobile of the three groups within the fifty-kilometre circle, mainly because of the employment and social opportunities available to them there. Members of Cohort 2 were very mobile as well, but their mobility often took them further, to shopping centers in Yarmouth, New Minas and Halifax in the 1970s and 1980s, when these facilities were not as well developed in the local area.

The influence of new media has also changed the sense of community among the younger members of Cohort 3 particularly. As modernity has progressed and infiltrated the rural margins, new possibilities have emerged and there are multiple relations of power at work in the life of any given individual; however, the concept of habitus tends to subsume these under a single umbrella. Bourdieu understands this, but it is my view that he never develops it in the context of his theoretical work because his work lacks a theory of resistance. It is my contention that the idea of resistances introduces the play of multiple social patterns converging in a given biography. For instance, Digby Neck students in all cohorts found themselves surrounded with discursive constructions that informed them in "common sense" terms that their communities were dying and that the way of life of their families was on the wane. Older people nostalgically yearn for a "simple life," a space outside modernity, outside the cut and thrust of new technologies and knowledges. The fisherman who saw the Y2K scare as entirely someone else's problem is a typical illustration. A "born and bred" identity is thought to contain with it the tools for resistance and survival in the physical space of the community. At the same time Digby Neckers confront other discursive formations, both local and through the course of their schooling, that present family and community as a space in which "people like us" belong and where we are "known," seen, comfortable, loved and cared for. It is only here that the skills learned from childhood are of value. While some youth accept this assessment, others resist it, and it appears that the latter group are growing as time passes. Yet the paradox is that into the 1990s the economic base of Digby Neck has declined, making it increasingly difficult for most young Digby Neckers to access the financial resources needed to acquire higher education and to migrate with any sort of security or reasonable chance of finding a living wage off the Neck.

Place continues to matter, in part by institutions of disembedding like school, the mass media, the corporate fishery and the multinational commercial chain store. In important respects, the idea of community is by now a largely a historical fiction (Giddens, 1990) and, ironically, a desperate response to the denegration of the importance of the face-to-face locale in contemporary life (Bauman, 2000). Yet, I continue to believe that community is, as Castells (2004), Scott (1985) Williams (1958, 1961) and others show, a space of resistance. For example, the community habitus has a very different set of messages and possibilities for men and for women. It also contains different sets of possibilities for members of different families by class. Children of elite fishing families face an entirely different set of "realistic" options than the children of marginal fisheries workers. However, as members of the same "peripheral community" space, all of these multiple discourses are still basically discourses of rurality. At one level most Digby Neckers share a fundamental mistrust of state apparatuses and big capital both. As members of community and as people who posses the core physical skills to harvest and process resources directly, many Digby Neckers continue to feel as though they do not need modernity, they do not need the state and they do not need formal education.

## Rural Schooling and Community

> Improvement is sought, not in the opportunity to escape from one's class, or to make a career, but in the general and controlled advance of all.... Not the individual, but the whole society will move. (Williams, 1958: 326)

In his discussion of the mass society he saw emerging from industrial capitalism and urbanization, Williams claimed that the concept of "mass" is derived from a way of seeing people, not from any tangible reality (1958). He claims that in seeing people at a certain distance we "mass" them, we construct them as a stereotypic "other," as part of a "herd" (1958: 300). What was interesting to Williams was discovering the conditions under which people become massified. He was also interested in resistance to massification, and he saw communities as sites of resistance in the sense that they represent experiential grounding against which mass communication is never entirely able to subdue. Much has happened since 1958, and massification has evolved, facilitated by technologies that were unimaginable fifty years ago. Communities have been transformed from the relatively self-contained lifeworlds described by the elder informants in this study to the geographically spread "around here" region, which is totally infused with global culture and products. Several television commercials play on this theme, showing rustic characters using laptops and an imagined wired world that has connected the urban poor in the United States, the rural poor in Africa, and a host of other stereotypes all bound together in a virtual global community. How, in this kind of space, can community be described as a resistant site? I think Williams had it right. Communities as actual physical places are containers of concrete experience as well as the mediated experiences now available. As Theobald (1997), Bonner (1997), Ching and Creed (1997), Berry (1977), Haas and Nachtigal (1998) and others argue, rural communities may hold the last chance for resistance to the homogenizing juggernaut of what Lefebvre (1991) and Castells (1998) call capitalist dominance of space.

Digby Neckers love their place because of its history, and their place in it, because of the geography and "oceanography" and also because it is not homogenized in the same way that cities are, it is not universally commodified in the sense that place becomes another product to be bought and sold and nothing more. Many Digby Neck men resist and reject schooling both because its practices are nonsensical and alien, but also because the entire organized project of civil society has never delivered on its promise to enrich life at home. What it has offered is an allegedly enriched life elsewhere. School offers youth its legitimized identities and its mobile credentials, but in the end these credentials have never been particularly attractive or inviting to born and bred community members, who have access to more immediate and familiar resources. Castells sees this paradox as the tragic irony of an unfulfilled dream of liberal democracy.

> The institutions and organizations of civil society that were constructed around the democratic state, and around the social contract between capital and labor, have become, by and large, empty shells, decreasingly able to relate to people's lives and values in most societies. It is indeed a tragic irony that when most countries of the world finally fought their way to access the institutions of liberal democracy, these institutions are so distant from the structure and processes that really matter that they appear to most people as a sarcastic grimace on the new face of history. At the turn of the millennium, the king and the queen, the state and civil society, are both naked, and their children-citizens are wandering around in a variety of foster homes. (2004: 420)

It seems to me that the ideology of the born and bred fisherman living and surviving in a coastal place waiting for the fish to come back and for justice to be done in the realm of fisheries policy is one such foster home, far from civil society and hostile to the state. These men do stay, in part because they see staying as their birthright, a birthright that has been usurped by cooperate concentration, engineered by the "big players," with the support the "educated people" in the bureaucracy.

In this final section I sketch out a few implications for rural schooling and community resistance. Williams was interested in communities as sites of resistance. Foucault encouraged us in an interview late in his life to look for those spaces in which resistance is likely to emerge. He writes: "The problem is knowing where resistance will develop. For example, in a working-class that will resist domination, will this be in unions or political parties; and what form will it take — a strike, a general strike, a revolution or parliamentary opposition" (quoted in Rabinow, 1997: 292–93). Arguing for a self conscious resistance against the consumer orientation embedded in advanced capitalism and the commodification of all aspects of the life-world, Bonner writes: "What is needed, therefore, is a critical and knowing resistance to the life world that Berger and associates merely describe[8] and by implication legitimize" (1997: 171). My own discussion of resistance so far has focused on the ways that people in a coastal community of Nova Scotia have resisted the mobility imperative in rural schools through more than three decades, but I have said nothing yet about the practical acts of resistance that seem to me to make sense.

First, it seems to me that rural schools need to adopt a more place-sensitive focus in the sense that schooling must be connected to the specific struggles and problems encountered in particular rural locales. These struggles include the challenge of environmental stewardship, the "whistle blowing" function of rural residents, who can see at first hand what is occurring in wild spaces (Berry, 1977; 2001), and the necessity of sustainable and fulfilling employment. Place-based education in this sense is not nostalgic or constructed in terms of immersion in a "traditional" way of life that sits outside modernity and in which young people learn to stay. Rather, I see it as an immersion in the contemporary transformations of rural spaces. As difficult as it may be, it is my troubled and ambivalent conclusion that an important part of a rural education is learning to leave because leaving is an opening up to possibilities and perspectives. After learning to leave, a person can always return.

A second caveat around place-based education is my contention that it is necessary for rural schools and communities to confront racism, sexism and constructions of masculinity and femininity that lead to oppressive and systematic inequality. It is now becoming increasingly apparent that the colonial history of places like Digby Neck will not remain buried. First Nations' claims to rural spaces, resource revenues and access will continue to present all residents of Canada's rural areas with a formidable challenge. We must, I think, recognize that the popular contemporary discourse of sustainable rural communities must be critiqued and problematized with further and deeper questions that have been raised by philosophical conservatives for generations about what is worth sustaining and conserving (Bowers, 2003). While incessant and rampant technological, industrial, social and economic change have been associated with rural decay, the answers do probably not reside in the kinds of backward looking conservatism that have characterized many rural political and social movements over the past century (McNichol Stock, 1996).

Education is always a tool of emancipation as well as of oppression. By taking school seriously and acquiring formal education, individuals resisted some things and capitulated on others. The same is true of refusing education and staying around the local area. It is important though to remember that educated people were seen, and perhaps continue to be seen, as trouble, both for the way they bring into communities their difference and their ideas, but also because they are more likely to be able to analyze and resist local power structures. If students in rural and coastal communities must leave in order to continue their education, they face an additional barrier, which compounds the other challenges faced by youth in a credential-focused society. If we do not offer additional support that levels this playing field, then we are inadvertently contributing to keeping rural youth "stuck" in their communities, forced to rely upon increasingly precarious local labour markets and family connections to sustain themselves.

Rural schools can and should be places where at least some of the complex intellectual work required to deal with these and other rural problems is done. Theobald has written a blueprint for this kind of rural education, tracing the philosophical roots of contemporary American schools to the ascendancy of liberalism as opposed to communitarianism. While there are problems with the bifurcation of the "community" and the "individual" in his account, the following kind of active political orientation for rural school seems imperative to me.

> Beginning at the elementary level, students must be socialized into the practice and habit of researching and deliberating answers to the questions that vex their communities at the moment... students should be able, if asked, to make the connection between ongoing work in the classroom or in the community and the issue of social justice. (Theobald, 1997: 134)

I quote this passage knowing full well how difficult this would be to implement and the kinds of political divisions in a community (and at other levels of governance) such an approach could engender. Communities are not the kind of unified entities Theobald seems to imagine. Communities contain within them multiple power relations and divisions, as well as tangible and virtual connections to other communities. But this is precisely why these multiple discourses need to be introduced into schools, so that children can work with them. I am also aware that this whole approach is largely at odds with the generic "outcomes" agenda that currently drives elementary and secondary curriculum discourse in all Canadian jurisdictions.

Next, it is essential to understand much better how rural schools transform economic capital into mobility capital for elite students. This can be understood if we see schools as travel agencies for those who can afford the tickets. We need more studies of specific rural communities as well as larger rural populations that investigate the connection between what Bourdieu calls "objective" economic factors and the acquisition of education credentials by particularly placed social actors. This transformation of one type of capital into another may not be so straightforward in rural areas as studies of class and schooling would suggest.

Rural educators also need to be aware of the way that the dominant narratives around the past, present and future of rural communities are used in and out of formal education settings, and what impact these discourses may have on their practice and on their students. The pervasive discourse of the decline and eventual collapse of rural communities has not been recognized as a force that drives curriculum and generates particular orientations toward rural youth and the places they live. This discourse of the "unstoppable" economic juggernaut that is destroying rural communities is far from politically neutral. When rural communities and forms of economic organization and resource access and harvesting are written off as dead or dying, youth are oriented to look elsewhere for their futures. This is not so much showing them "options" but presenting a life lived in the rural community as a non-option. This view of rurality is a discursive production, one that has a long history in rural schools, to the point where it is an act of resistance to face the way rurality is constructed. This, in the end, is the kind of resistance Foucault imagined, confronting the way one is discursively produced and daring to think differently.

Rural educators also need to be conscious of the paradoxical effect of the discourse of decline and fall. By presenting the community to rural youth as a diseased or deceased place, rural educators may unwittingly be encouraging education resistance by generating a kind of general hopelessness about the future. After all, rural children live in rural areas and so do their families. Nobody wants to live in a ghost town or in a place that is said to contain a past but no future. This general hopelessness is well supported and reinforced by a mass media focused on a running monologue of mostly urban violence and misery. Small wonder that so many rural youth decide that they are better off taking their chances in the dying community they know rather than in the imploding "outside" world they know not. In the discourse of rural education, those who remain are "stuck," left behind, they lack the necessary skills to move into the modern world, which is unfolding far from their home communities. This study shows however that many stayers resist this view and take pride in surviving where they want to be rather than where they feel they are supposed to go. Most of them do manage to survive and live well without post-secondary or even secondary education.

Finally, rural education needs to find a way to incorporate the "survivalist" discourse of rural communities into its own discourse space in a way that is neither backward looking and ignorant of modern global interchanges nor focused in a naive and jingoistic way on the wonderful opportunities presented to rural communities in the "new economy." Rural community survivalist discourse is often resistant to education as an "expert system" but not to rural schools themselves, which are very often considered to be the focus of community survival strategies (Wotherspoon, 1998).

Can we imagine rural schools as sites of resistance to the forces that threaten families and communities without at the same time falling back into simplistic notions about community. These simplistic notions form yet another discourse, one that has been used effectively to mask the power of vested local interests that have no stake in seeing anything change to the detriment of their own privilege. The idea of place-based education described by a number of contemporary educators (Comber, Thompson and Wells, 2001, Gruenewald, 2003; Shelton, 2005; Theobald, 1997; Haas and Nachtigal, 1998; Kincheloe and Pinar, 1991) contains both the intellectual seeds and the pragmatic examples for imagining and conducting education projects that engage particular students in particular places in a globalized, culturally hybrid, knowledge society. It is not as though the modern "contaminates" the traditional or replaces and homogenizes it through contact. As Appiah (2006) contends, contemporary villages contain seemingly contradictory but diverse hybrid combinations of well-established traditions and new forms of material and nonmaterial cultural artifacts from around the world.

> What John Stuart Mill said over a century ago in *On Liberty* about diversity within a society serves just as well as an argument for variety across the globe: "If it were only that people have diversities of taste, that is reason enough for not attempting to shape them all after one model. But different persons also require different conditions for their spiritual development; and can no more exist healthily in the same moral, than all the variety of plants can exist in the same physical, atmosphere and climate. The same things which are helps to one person towards the cultivation of his higher nature, are hindrances to another.... Unless there is a corresponding diversity in their modes of life, they neither obtain their fair share of happiness, nor grow up to the mental, moral and aesthetic stature of which their nature is capable." If we want to preserve a wide range of human conditions because it allows free people the best

> chance to make their own lives, we can't enforce diversity by trapping people within differences they long to escape.

The prevailing idea of standardized curriculum, standardized programs, programmatic pedagogies, standardized texts and standardized tests will continue to render school irrelevant for large numbers of students in rural, northern and coastal communities like the one I have been describing in this book. Furthermore, this education approach will reinforce the idea that education is fundamentally about learning things that someone, somewhere decides to be important. This ethereal somewhere is always, it seems, an urban place, and its abstract, standardized knowledge is necessarily divorced from the multiplicity of rural contexts. In the end, accountability will come to mean that children and teachers will be forced to render accounts to distant, powerful others, not to their parents, their communities and even to themselves.

We must be aware that when we set up programs and initiatives, we are building, once again a technology of power, another set of inclusions and exclusions. Yet, when one is aware of power/knowledge or the idea that everything is power and that power is everywhere, as Foucault suggested, there also can arise the idea that freedom is also everywhere and that power only emerges in its modern form to engage freedom. Resistance sometimes works, at least for a while, and the game is never over. G.H. Mead liked baseball analogies to describe symbolic interaction. Baseball has rules that are very restrictive and it is played on a fairly standard, spatially simple, constrained field, and yet, the possibilities for creative play are virtually endless. These possibilities obviously expand exponentially with the analytical distance achieved by stepping outside the game to find or imagine another one. Surely an understanding of the discursive basis of power opens up rather than closes down the possibility of human freedom. Included in this elusive freedom is the power to choose how and where to construct an identity and to discover where one belongs.

## Notes

1. One current example is a large rock quarry development project for Digby Neck, which, at this writing, is under review by the Canadian Environmental Agency. The ability of people in this community to remain even partly outside the influence of economic globalization is increasingly threatened as the quest for resources goes global, trade liberalization policy (i.e., NAFTA) and a provincial government desperate to create economic activity in rural Nova Scotia align to generate pressure to "develop" Digby Neck. The struggle over this quarry project, which is widely opposed on Digby Neck, particularly in the villages nearest to the project, is being closely monitored as a test case for similar kinds of multinational resource exploitation projects.

2. Examples of this kind of "force" are found in the way harvesting fisheries resources are thought about by the corporate sector. In a televised address at a recent conference on electronic commerce and business, corporate fisheries magnate John Risley commented that his company, which harvests some 30 percent of the total Canadian scallop catch, does so using seven vessels (CPAC [Canadian Parliamentary Channel] broadcast, 10 June, 2000). He then went on to argue that if they figure out how to manage offshore scallop ground more efficiently his company ought to be able to harvest the same quantity of scallops using only three vessels. These remarks were obviously addressed to a business audience that would be impressed with the way Risley is rationalizing his operation and increasing corporate profits by cutting costs. From the point of view of coastal communities, this kind of analysis is exactly what has destroyed both fish stocks and the small-boat fishery. The influence that Risley and others in his position have over state regulatory bodies is seen as the reason why the fishery has been "turned over to them fellers, so he can sit there in an office and send his boats out to catch his fish," as one fisherman put it.
3. Digby Neck poet and fisheries activist Arthur Bull has rendered the idea of struggle and community in a poem that serves as an introduction to a digitized collection of photographs, movie clips and stories from Digby Neck (Bull, 2000). Struggle, Bull points out, is nothing new to Digby Neckers; it is just that the field of struggle has shifted to an explicitly political stage. Bull writes:

   And now we know that this way of life won't stay here without
   Our dreaming and working together and fighting for it
   We know that our fishermen will not even be allowed to fish
   Even if the fish are plentiful in the water — without a fight
   It seems crazy really
   But at the same time it has always been that way
   There's nothing here that wasn't got without a struggle

   The internet site that contains this poem and the photographs that accompany it also serves as a virtual tour of the Digby Neck community past and present (cf. Bull, 2000).
4. In order to conceptualize the project of teaching as a communitarian enterprise these teachers will have to fight against what their training in teacher education has told them to be true and desirable. I have taken up this problem in an autobiographical account of my own teaching career in a series of rural communities (Corbett, 1999).
5. As Urry has recently argued, sociology has failed to understand with any clarity and in any depth, the impact of a mobility technology as mundane in the West as the automobile (2000).
6. The idea of the credential as a "ticket" is common nomenclature for both journeyman statuses in a trade as well as for professional certification. Informants sometimes used the example of my teacher's "ticket" to describe the kind of portable qualification I possess. The ticket is a mobile credential. Bourdieu also argues that the reserve army of labour has been extended out of the "lowest levels of competence" to the graduates of higher education (1998: 82–83).

This, I think, is a topic worthy of research.

7. Urry describes loose associations of mobile youth who create a kind of floating community both in cyberspace and by moving across geographic space setting up temporary physical communities in a variety of places. He describes these social organizations as "bunds" (2000: 143–47).
8. Bonner refers here to Berger and associates' *The Homeless Mind* (1973).

# References


Afsar, R. (1996). Rural-urban migration and development: Evidence from Bangladesh. In R.E. Bilsborrow (ed.), *Migration, urbanization and development: New directions and issues.* Norwell Park, MA: Kluwer/United Nations Population Fund.

Althusser, L. (1971). Ideology and ideological state apparatus. In L. Althusser, *Lenin and philosophy and other essays*. New York: Monthly Review Books.

Amit-Talai, V. (1993). Will they go? A study of intentions regarding migration among secondary V students in Quebec. *Canadian Ethnic Studies* 25, 1: 50–61.

Anisef, P., and L. Andres. (1996). Dropping out in Canada: The construction of a crisis. In D. Kelly and J. Gaskell (eds.), *Debating dropouts: Critical policy and research perspectives on early school leaving.* New York: Teachers College Press.

Anstead, C.J., and I. Goodson. (1993). Structuring and restructuring vocational knowledge: The commercial curriculum at the London Technical and Commercial High School, 1920–1940. In Coulter and I. Goodson (eds.), *Rethinking vocationalism.* Toronto: Our Schools/Our Selves.

Apostle, R., and G. Barrett. (1992). *Emptying their nets: Small capital and rural industrialization in the Nova Scotian fishing industry*. Toronto: University of Toronto Press.

Appiah, K.A. (2006). The case for contamination. *RSA Ejournal* April. <http://www.rsa.org.uk/journal/article.asp?articleID=719>. Accessed May 1, 2006.

Apple, M. (1979). *Ideology and curriculum.* London and Boston: Routledge and Kegan Paul.

Arnot, M. (2006) Gender equality, pedagogy and citizenship: Affirmative and transformative approaches in the UK. *Theory and Research in Education* 4, 2: 131–50.

Aronowitz, S., and H. Giroux. (1985). *Education under siege.* South Hadley MA: Bergin and Garvey.

Axelrod, P. (1997). *The promise of schooling.* Toronto: University of Toronto Press.

Bailey, T, K. Highes, and D. Moore. (2004). *Working knowledge: Work-based learning and education reform.* New York: Routledge.

Ball, S. (1987). *The micro-politics of the school.* New York: Routledge.

Banerjee, B. (1996). Migration, motivation, family links and job search methods of rural and urban migrants in India. In R.E. Bilsborrow (ed.), *Migration, urbanization and development: New directions and issues*. Norwell Park, MA: Kluwer/United Nations Population Fund.

Barber, B. (1995). *Jihad vs. McWorld: How globalism and tribalism are reshaping the world.* New York: Random House.

Barnes, C. (1997). *Getting out of town*. Fredericton, NB: Goose Lane.

Basso, K. (1979). *Portraits of "The Whiteman": Linguistic play and cultural symbols among the western Apache.* Cambridge: Cambridge University Press.

Bauman, Z. (1991). *Modernity and ambivalence.* Ithaca, NY: Cornell University Press.

_____. (1992). *Imitations of postmodernity*. London and New York: Routledge.

_____. (1995). *Life in fragments*. London and New York: Routledge.

_____. (1998). *Globalization: The human consequences*. New York: Columbia University Press.

_____. (1999). *In search of politics*. Stanford: Stanford University Press.
_____. (2000). *Liquid modernity*. Cambridge: Polity.
_____. (2004a). *Wasted lives: Modernity and its outcasts*. Cambridge: Polity.
_____. (2004b). *Identity: Conversations with Benedetto Vecchi*. Cambridge: Polity.
Beck U. (1992). *Risk society: Towards a new modernity*. London: Sage.
Beggs, J.J., V.A. Haines, and J.S. Hurlburt. (1996). Revisiting the rural-urban contrast: Personal networks in nonmetropolitan and metropolitan settings. *Rural Sociology* 61, 2: 306–25.
Beilharz, P. (ed.). (2001). *The Bauman reader*. Oxford: Blackwell.
Benko, G., and U. Strohmayer. (eds.). (1997). *Space and social theory: Interpreting modernity and postmodernity*. Oxford: Blackwell.
Berger, J. (1984). *And our faces, my heart, brief as photos*. New York: Pantheon Books.
Berger, J., and J. Mohr. (1977). *A seventh man*. Cambridge: Granta books.
Berger, P., B. Berger, and H. Kellner. (1973). *The homeless mind: Modernization and consciousness*. New York: Vintage.
Berliner, D. (2006). Our impoverished view of educational reform. T*eachers College Record* 108, 6 (June): 949–95.
Berry. W. (1977). *The unsettling of America: Culture and agriculture*. New York: Avon.
Bhabha, H. (1994). *The location of culture*. New York: Routledge.
Binkley, M. (2002). *Set adrift: Fishing families*. Toronto: University of Toronto Press.
Bird, W.R. (1956). *Off trail in Nova Scotia*. Toronto: Ryerson.
Black Learners Advisory Committee. (1994). *BLAC report on education: Redressing inequity, empowering Black learners*. Halifax, NS: Black Learners' Advisory Committee.
Blades, P. (1995). *Net destruction: The death of Atlantic Canada's fishery*. Montreal: McGill-Queens.
Blakie, A. (1997). Beside the sea: Visual imagery, ageing and heritage. *Ageing and Society* 17, 6: 629–48.
Blythe, R. (1969). *Akenfield: Portrait of an English village*. Harmondsworth, Middlesex: Penguin.
Bollman, R.D. (1999). Human capital and rural development: What are the linkages? In N. Walford, J.C. Everett, and D.E. Napton (eds.), *Reshaping the countryside: Perceptions and process of rural change*. New York: CABI Publishing.
Bonner, K. (1997). *A great place to raise kids: Interpretation, science and the urban-rural debate*. Montreal and Kingston: McGill-Queens University Press.
Bouchard, G. (1997). Marginality, co-integration and change: Social history as a critical exercise. *Journal of the Canadian Historical Association* New Series, 8: 19–38.
Bourdieu, P. (1984a). Le racism de l'intelligence. In P. Bourdieu, *Questions de sociologie*. Paris: Editions de Minuit.
_____. (1984b). *Distinction: A social critique of the judgement of taste*. Cambridge: Harvard University Press.
_____. (1990). *The logic of practice*. Stanford: Stanford University Press.
_____. (1998). *Acts of resistance*. Cambridge: Polity Press.
Bowers, C. (2003). *Mindful conservatism: Rethinking the ideological and educational basis of an ecologically sustainable future*. Lanhan, ML: Rowman and Littlefield.
Bowles, S., and H. Gintis. (1976). *Schooling in capitalist America: Educational reform and the contradictions of economic life*. New York: Basic Books.
Braio-Ureto, B.E., R.E. Quiroga, and J.A. Brea. (1996). Migration decisions, agrar-

ian structure and gender: The case of Ecuador. *Journal of Developing Areas* 30, 4: 463–75.

Brandau, D.M., and J. Collins. (1994). Texts, social relations and work based scepticism about schooling: An ethnographic analysis. *Anthropology and Education Quarterly* 25, 2: 118–36.

Brookes, A. (1976). Out-migration from the Maritime Provinces, 1860–1900: Some preliminary considerations. *Acadiensis* 5, 2: 26–55.

_____. (1981). The golden age and the exodus: The case of Canning, Kings County. *Acadiensis* 11, 1: 57–82.

Bruce, C. (1954). *The channel shore*. Toronto: Macmillan.

_____. (1959). *The township of time*. Toronto: Macmillan.

Bruce, H. (1988). *Down home: Notes of a Maritime son*. Toronto: Key Porter.

Brym, R., and R.J. Sacouman. (eds.). (1979). *Underdevelopment and social movements in Atlantic Canada*. Toronto: New Hogtown Press.

Buckler, E. (1952). *The mountain and the valley*. Toronto: McClelland and Stewart.

Bull, A. (2000). *Digby Neck in stories: A poetic and pictorial tour of Digby Neck*. <http://collections.ic.gc.ca/digby-neck/tour.htm>. (Accessed October 10, 2005.)

Bull, M.K. (1978). *Sandy Cove*. Hantsport, NS: Lancelot.

Burrill, G. (1992). *Away: Maritimers in Massachusetts, Ontario and Alberta: An oral history of leaving home*. Montreal and Kingston: McGill-Queens University Press.

Canada—Rural Secretariat. (1999). *Rural solutions to rural concerns: National rural workshop October 2–4, 1998, Final Report*. Minister of Public Works and Government Services Canada, Catalogue no. A22-171/1998-2E.

Casey, E. (1998). Production of space or heterogeneity of place. In A. Light and J.M. Smith (eds.), *The production of public space*. Lanham Maryland: Rowman, Littlefield.

Castells, M. (1998). *The end of the millennium*. Volume 3 of The information age: Economy, society and culture. Oxford: Blackwell.

_____. (2000). *The rise of the network society*. Volume 2 of The information age: Economy, society and culture. Second Edition. Oxford: Blackwell.

_____. (2004). *The power of identity: Economy, society and culture*. Volume 2 of The information age: Economy, society and culture. Second Edition. Oxford: Blackwell.

Catto, S. (2003). A slow death. *Time Magazine* (Canadian Edition). October 13: 48–57

Ching, B., and G.W. Creed (eds.). (1997). *Knowing your place: Rural identity and cultural hierarchy*. New York: Routledge.

Clement, W. (1986). *The struggle to organize: Resistance in Canada's fishery*. Toronto: McClelland and Stewart.

Coady, L. (1998). *Strange heaven*. Fredericton, NB: Goose Lane Editions.

Cochrane, (1987). Place, people and folklore: An Isle Royale case study. *Western Folklore* 46: 1–20.

Coffer, F., C. Borrill, and S. Marshall. (1986). *Growing up at the margins*. Milton Keynes: Open University Press.

Comber, B., P. Thomson, with M. Wells. (2001). Critical literacy finds a "place": Writing and social action in a neighborhood school. *Elementary School Journal* 101, 4: 451–64.

Connelly, P., and M. MacDonald. (1983). Women's work: Domestic and wage la-

bour in a Nova Scotian community. *Studies in Political Economy* 10.
Conrad, M. (1997). The 1950s: The decade of development. In E.R. Forbes and D.A. Muise (eds.), *The Atlantic Provinces in confederation*. Toronto: University of Toronto Press.
Corbett, M. (1991). *Dropping out in Digby*. Digby, NS: Digby District School Board.
_____. (1999). From here to uncertainty: A preoccupation with code. In A. Neilsen (ed.), *Daily meaning: Counternarratives of teachers' work*. Vancouver: Bendall Books.
_____. (2001a). *Learning to leave: The irony of schooling in a coastal community*. PhD Dissertation, Department of Educational Studies, UBC.
_____. (2001b). A protracted struggle: Rural resistance and normalization in Canadian educational history. *Historical Studies in Education* 13, 1 (Spring): 19–48.
_____. (2002). Against the tide of modernity: Poststructuralism, rural schooling, place and resistance. *trans/forms* 6: 24–59.
_____. (2004). I dreamed I saw Hilda Neatby Last Night: So little for the mind after fifty years. *McGill Journal of Education* 39, 2: 159–82.
_____. (2006a). *All kinds of potential: Women and outmigration in a coastal community*. Paper presented to the Canadian Association for the Study of Women in Education, York University, Toronto, ON, May 28.
_____. (2006b). *Where the girls aren't: Where the girls aren't: Education and outmigration in a rural community*. Paper presented to the Eleventh National Congress on Rural Education, Saskatoon SK, March 28.
Corrigan, P. (1979). *Schooling the smash street kids*. London: Macmillan.
Coser, L. ed. (1980). *The pleasures of sociology*. New York: Mentor.
Cottom, D. (2003). *Why education is useless*. Philadelphia: University of Pennsylvania Press.
Courchene. T. (1974). *Migration and the Maritimes*. Atlantic Canadian Economics Association Papers, 3: 1–39.
Critchfield, R. (1994). *The villagers: Changed values, altered lives: The closing of the rural-urban gap*. New York: Anchor Books.
Cruise, D., and A. Griffiths. (1997). *On south mountain: The dark secrets of the Goler clan*. Toronto: Penguin.
Cuban, L., and D. Tyack. (1995). *Tinkering toward utopia: A century of public school reform*. Cambridge, MA: Harvard University Press.
Curtis, B. (1988). *Building the educational state: Canada West 1836–71*. London, ON: Althouse.
Dale, R. (1989). *The state and educational policy*. London: The Open University Press.
Danahay, D.R. (1987). Farm children at school: Educational strategies in rural France. *Anthropology and Education Quarterly* 60, 2, April: 83–89.
Dasgupta, S. (1988). *Rural Canada: Structure and change*. Lewiston, NY/Queenston, ON: Edward Mellen Press.
Davey, I. (1978). The rhythm of work and the rhythm of school. In N. McDonald and A. Chaiton (eds.), *Egerton Ryerson and his times*. Toronto: Macmillan.
Davis, A. (1991). *Dire straits, the dilemma of a fishery: The case of Digby Neck and the Islands*. St. John's, NF: Institute for Social and Economic Research.
Davis, A., and J. Kearney (principal researchers). (1999). *Social research for sustainable fisheries*. Research proposal to the Social Sciences Humanities Research Council of Canada, mimeograph.
Day, D. (1990). *Young Women in Nova Scotia: A Study of Attitudes, Behaviours and Aspira-*

*tions*. Halifax, NS: Nova Scotia Advisory Council on the Status of Women.
Day, F.P. (1928/1989). *Rockbound*. Toronto: University of Toronto Press.
Day, G., and J. Murdoch. (1993). Locality and community: Coming to terms with place. *The Sociological Review* 41, 1 (February): 82–111.
deCerteau (1984). *The practice of everyday life*. Berkeley: University of California Press.
deFreitas, E. (1997). *Keel kissing bottom*. No place of publication cited: Random House of Canada.
Deleuze, G. (1988). *Foucault*. Minneapolis: University of Minnesota Press.
Demerath, P. (1999). The cultural production of educational utility in Pere Village, Papua New Guinea. *Comparative Education Review* 43, 2: 162–96.
DeVries, P., and G. McNab-DeVries. (1991). Ethnography in rural Cape Breton: Coping with postmodernism. *Canadian Review of Sociology and Anthropology* 28, 4: 483–502.
Deyhle, D., and F. Margonis. (1995). Navajo mothers and daughters: Schools, jobs, and the family. *Anthropology and Education Quarterly* 26, 2.
DeYoung, A. (1995). Constructing and staffing the cultural bridge: The school as change agent in rural Appalachia. *Anthropology and Education Quarterly* 26, 2: 168–92.
Dolby, N. and G. Dimitriadis (eds.). (2004). *Learning to labour in new times*. New York: Routledge Falmer.
Donaldson, G.A. (1986). Do you need to leave home to grow up? The rural adolescent's dilemma. *Journal of Research in Rural Education* 3, 3: 121–25.
Donzelot, J. (1979). *The policing of families*. New York: Pantheon.
Dublin, T. (1998). Working class families respond to industrial decline: Migration from the Pennsylvania anthracite region since 1920. *International Labour and Working Class History* 54, Fall: 40–56.
Durrenberger, P.E. (1997). Fisheries management models: Assumptions and realities or, why shrimpers in Mississippi are not firms. *Human Organization* 56, 2: 158–66.
Dyre, G. (2001). Visible minorities. *Canadian Geographic* 121, 1: 44–51.
Eagleton. T. (2003). *After theory*. New York: Basic Books.
Elder, G.H., V. King, and R.D. Conger. (1996). Attachment to place and migration prospects: A developmental perspective. *Journal of Research in Adolescence* 6, 4: 397–425.
Ellsworth, E. (1989). Why doesn't this feel empowering? Working through the repressive myths of critical pedagogy. *Harvard Educational Review* 59, 3: 297–324.
Egan, K. (2002). *Getting it wrong from the beginning: Our progressive inheritance from Herbert Spencer, John Dewey and Jean Piaget*. New Haven: Yale University Press.
Fairley, B., C. Leys, and R.J. Sacouman. (1990). *Restructuring and resistance: Perspectives from Atlantic Canada*. Toronto: Garamond.
Felt, L., and P. Sinclair. (1992). Everybody does it: Unpaid work in rural peripheral regions. *Work, Employment and Society*, 6, 1.
_____. (1995). *Living on the edge*. St John's, NF: Institute for Social and Economic Research.
Ferland, J., and C. Wright. (1996). Rural and urban labour processes: A comparative analysis of Australian and Canadian development. *Labour History* 71, November: 142–69.

Field, J.C., and L.J. Olafson. (1999). Understanding resistance in students at risk. *Canadian Journal of Education* 24, 1: 71–76.

Fine, M. (1996). Introduction. In D. Kelly and J. Gaskell (eds.), *Debating dropouts: Critical policy and research perspectives on early school leaving*. New York: Teachers College Press.

Finnie, R. (1998). *Interprovincial mobility in Canada: Who moves? A panel logit model analysis*. Working paper. Applied research branch, strategic Policy, Human Resources Development Canada (Document W-98-5E.b).

Florida, R. (2002). *The rise of the creative class: And how it's transforming work, leisure, community and everyday life*. New York: Basic Books.

Foucault, M. (1979). *Discipline and punish*. New York: Vintage.

_____. (1986). Of other spaces. *Diacritics* 16, 1 (Spring): 22–27.

_____. (1990). *The history of sexuality: An introduction*. New York: Vantage.

Frank, B. (1998). *External review of Digby Regional High School*. Report presented to the Southwest Regional School Board, October 8.

Frey, W.H. (1995). Immigration and internal migration "flight" from United States metropolitan areas: Toward a new demographic balkanization. *Urban Studies* 32, 3–4: 733–57.

Fukuyama, F. (1992). *The end of history and the last man*. New York: Avon.

Gaffield, C. (1987). *Language, schooling and cultural conflict: The origins of the French language controversy in Ontario*. Kingston and Montreal: McGill-Queens University Press.

Game, A. (1990). *Undoing the social: towards a deconstructive sociology*. Toronto: University of Toronto Press.

Gaskell, J. (1992). *Gender matters from school to work*. London: Falmer.

Gatewood, J. (1984). Actions speak louder than words. In J. Dougherty (ed.), *Directions in cognitive anthropology*. Chicago: University of Illinois Press.

George, R. (1970). *A leader and a laggard: Manufacturing industry in Nova Scotia, Quebec and Ontario*. Toronto: University of Toronto Press.

Ghemawat, P., and K. Mark. (2005). The price is right. Op-ed contribution. *New York Times*, August 3. <http://www.nytimes.com/2005/08/03/opinion/03ghemawat.html?thandemc=th>. (Accessed August 4, 2005.)

Gibbs, R.M. (1994). Rural youth outmigration: How big is the problem and for whom. *Rural Development Perspectives* 10, 1: 9–16.

Gibbs, R. (1995). Going away to college and wider urban job opportunities take highly educated youth away from rural areas. *Rural Development Perspectives* 10, 3: 35–44.

Gibson, R. (1986). *Critical theory and education*. London: Hodder and Stoughton.

Giddens, A. (1971). *Capitalism and modern social theory*. London: Macmillan.

_____. (1976). *The new rules of the sociological method*. London: Heinemann.

_____. (1979). *Central problems in social theory: Action, structure and contradiction in social analysis*. London: Macmillan.

_____. (1981). *A contemporary critique of historical materialism*. Berkeley and Los Angeles: University of California Press.

_____. (1990). *The consequences of modernity*. Stanford: Stanford University Press.

_____. (1991). *Modernity and self-identity: Self and society in the late modern age*. Stanford, CA: Stanford University Press.

_____. (1995). *Politics, sociology and social theory: Encounters with classical and contemporary social thought*. Stanford: Stanford University Press.

_____. (1996). *In defence of sociology: Essays, interpretations and rejoinders*. Cambridge: Polity Press.

_____. (1999). *Runaway world*. BBC Reith Lectures. <http://news.bbc.co.uk/hi/english/static/events/reith_99/default.htm>. (Accessed October 12, 2006.)

Giroux, H. (1981). Hegemony, resistance and the paradox of educational reform. *Interchange* 12, 2–3: 3–26.

_____. (1983). *Theory and resistance in education: A pedagogy for the opposition*. South Hadley, MA: Bergin and Garvey.

_____. (1988). *Teachers as intellectuals: Toward a critical pedagogy of learning*. South Hadley, MA: Bergin and Garvey.

_____. (1992). *Border crossings: Cultural workers and the politics of education*. New York: Routledge.

_____. (1994). *Disturbing pleasures: Learning popular culture*. New York: Routledge.

Goldscheider, F., C. Goldscheider, P. St. Clair, and J. Hodges. (1999). Changes in returning home in the United States, 1925–1985. *Social Forces* 78, 2: 695–725.

Gramsci, A. (1971). *Selections from the prison notebooks*. New York: International Publishers.

Grzetic, B. (2004). *Women fishes these days*. Halifax, NS: Fernwood.

Gruenewald, D.A. (2003). Foundations of place: A multidisciplinary framework for place-conscious education. *American Educational Research Journal* 40, 3: 619–54.

Haas, T., and P. Nachtigal. (1998). *Place value: An educator's guide to good literature on rural lifeways, environments and purposes of education*. Charleston, WV: ERID Clearinghouse on Rural Education and Small Schools.

Hall, S. (1976). Introduction. In S. Hall and T. Jefferson (eds.), *Resistance through rituals: Youth subcultures in post-war Britain*. London: Hutchinson.

Hall, S., and T. Jefferson (eds.). (1976). *Resistance through rituals: Youth subcultures in post-war Britain*. London: Hutchinson.

Harvey, D. (1965). *The economic base of Digby County*. Halifax, NS: Institute for Public Policy.

Harvey, David. (1990). *The condition of postmodernity: An enquiry into the origins of culture change*. New York: Blackwell.

Hawley, G., H.L. Harmon, and G.D. Leopold. (1996). Rural scholars or bright rednecks? Aspirations for a sense of place among rural youth in Appalachia. *Journal of Research in Rural Education* 12, 3 (Winter): 150–60.

Hektner, J.M. (1995). When moving up implies moving out: Rural adolescent conflict in the transition to adulthood. *Journal for Research in Rural Education* 11, 1: 3–14.

Hicks, D. (2002). *Reading lives: Working class children and literacy learning*. New York: Teachers College Press.

_____. (2005). Labour histories. *Educational Researcher* 34, 3 (April): 34–39.

Hodge, I., J. Dunn, S. Monk, and M. Fitzgerald. (2002). Barriers to participation in residual rural labour markets. *Work, employment and society* 16, 3: 457–76.

Hoggart, R. (1957). *The uses of literacy: Aspects of working class life with special reference to publications and entertainment*. Harmondsworth, Middlesex: Penguin.

Holloway, S., and G. Valentine (eds.). (2000). *Children's geographies: Playing, living, learning*. New York and London: Routledge.

hooks, b. (1994). *Teaching to transgress*. New York: Routledge.

Hornsby, S.J. (1996). *Tide and time: The transformation of Bear River, Nova Scotia*. Orono, ME: Maine Folklife Centre.

House, J.D. (1988). Outports and microchips: Peripheral regions in a post industrial age. In B. Flemming (ed.), *Beyond anger and longing: Community and development in Atlantic Canada*. Fredericton and Sackville, NB: Acadiensis and Centre for Canadian Studies.

Hughes, C.C., M. Tremblay, A. Rapoport, and A.H. Leighton. (1960). *People of cove and woodlot: Communities from the viewpoint of social psychiatry*. Volume 2 of the Stirling County Study of psychiatric disorder and sociocultural environment. New York: Basic Books.

Hussey, S. (1997). Low pay, underemployment and multiple occupations: Men's work in the inter-war countryside. *Rural History* 8, 2 (October): 217–36.

Hutchinson. D. (2004). *A natural history of place in education*. New York: Teachers College Press.

Jensen, J. (2002). *Post-secondary education on the edge: Self-improvement and community development in a Cape Breton coal town*. New York: Peter Lang.

Jentsch, B., and I. Dey. (2000). *Rural youth: The policy agenda*. Paper presented at the Conference on rural communities and identities in the global millennium. Malaspina University-College, Nanaimo, BC, May.

Johnson, D. (1999). Merchants, the state and household: Continuity and change in a 20th-century Acadian fishing village. *Acadiensis* 29, 1 (Autumn): 57–75.

Johnson, K., and G. Fuguitt. (2000). Continuity and change in rural migration patterns, 1959–1995. *Rural Sociology* 65, 1: 27–49.

Jolliffe, D. (1998). Skills, schooling and household income in Ghana. *The World Bank Economic Review* 12, 1: 81–104.

Jones, D.C. (1978). *Agriculture, the land and education*. EdD Thesis, UBC.

_____. (1979). "The little mound of earth": The fate of school agriculture. In G. Tompkins (ed.), *The curriculum in Canada in historical perspective*. Vancouver, BC: CSSE.

Jones, G. (1995). *Leaving home*. Buckingham, UK: Open University Press.

_____. (1999a). The same people in the same places? Socio-spatial identities and migration in youth. *Sociology* 33, 1: 1–22.

_____. (1999b). Trail blazers and path followers: Social reproduction and geographical mobility in youth. In S. Arber and C. Attias-Donfut (eds.), *The myth of intergenerational conflict: The family and state in ageing societies*. London and New York: Routledge.

Junger, S. (1999). *The perfect storm: A true story of man against the sea*. New York: Harper.

Kasabarian, J.A. (1996). Mapping Edward Said: Geography, identity and the politics of location. *Environment and Planning D: Society and Space* 14, 5: 529–57.

Kearney, J. (1993). *Diversity of labour process, household forms, and political practice: A social approach to the inshore fishing communities of Clare, Digby Neck and the Island*s. Doctoral dissertation, University, Laval.

Kelly, U. (1993). *Marketing place: Cultural politics, regionalism and reading*. Halifax, NS: Fernwood Press.

_____. (1997). *Schooling desire: Literacy, cultural politics and pedagogy*. New York: Routledge.

Kenway, J., and A. Kraak. (2002). Place, time and stigmatized youthful identities:

Bad boys in paradise. *Journal of Rural Studies* 18: 145–55.
_____. (2004). Reordering work and destabilizing masculinity. In N. Dolby and G. Dimitriadis (eds.), *Learning to labour in new times*. New York: Routledge Falmer.
Kincheloe, J., and W. Pinar (eds.). (1991). *Curriculum as social psychoanalysis: The significance of place*. Albany, NY: State University of New York.
Kirby, A. (2005). *What matters around here: Rural education, poverty and policy*. Paper presented to the American Educational Research Association, Montreal, May
Kristiansen, E. (1995). Time, memory and rural transformation: Reading history in the fiction of Charles Bruce and Ernest Buckler. In D. Samson (ed.), *Contested countryside: Rural worker and modern society, 1800–1950*. Fredericton, NB: Acadiensis Press.
Kulyk-Keefer, J. (1987). *Under eastern eyes: A critical reading of Maritime fiction*. Toronto: Macmillan.
Kunstler, J. (2005). *The long emergency: Surviving the end of the oil age*. New York: Atlantic Monthly Press.
Kurlansky, M. (1997). *Cod: A biography of the fish that changed the world*. Toronto: Alfred A. Knopf.
Lareau, A. (1989). *Home advantage: Social class and parental intervention in elementary education*. London: Falmer.
_____. (2003). *Unequal childhoods: Class, race and family life*. Berkeley: University of California Press.
Lawrence, B. (1998). *Working memory: The influence of culture on aspirations.* Unpublished PhD Dissertation. Boston University.
Leavitt, K. (1960). *Population movements in the Atlantic Provinces*. Halifax: Atlantic Provinces Economic Council.
LeBlanc, L. (1999). *Pretty in punk: Girls resistance in a boys' subculture*. New Brunswick: Rutgers University Press.
Lefebvre, H. (1991). *The production of space*. Cambridge: Basil Blackwell.
Lesko, N. (2001). *Act your age! A cultural construction of adolescence*. New York: Routledge Falmer.
Ley, J., S. Nelson, and S. Beltyukova. (1996). Congruence of aspirations of rural youth with expectations held by parents and school staff. *Journal of Research in Rural Education* 12, 3: 133–41.
Liaw, K.L. (1990). Joint effects of personal factors and ecological variables on the interprovincial migration patterns of young adults in Canada: A nested logit analysis. *Geographical Analysis* 22, 3: 189–208.
Livingstone, D., and P. Sawchuk. (2004). *Hidden knowledge: Organized labour in the information age*. Toronto: Garamond.
Lofty, J.S. (1992). *Time to write: The influence of time and culture on learning to write*. New York: State University of New York Press.
Looker, E.D. (1993). Interconnected transitions and their costs; Gender and urban/rural differences in transitions to work. In P. Anisef and P. Axelrod (eds.), *Transitions: Schooling and employment in Canada*. Toronto: Thompson Educational Publishing.
Looker, E.D., and L. Andres. (1998). *Constraints and choices: The effects of post-secondary structure on the participation of rural and urban youth*. Paper presented to the Maritime Provinces Higher Education Commission Conference on the State of Higher Education in the Maritimes, Moncton, NB, November.

Looker, E.D., and P. Dwyer. (1998). Education and negotiated reality: Complexities facing rural youth in the 1990s. *Youth and Society* 1, 1: 5–22.

Looker, D., and V. Theissen. (1999). *Investing in youth: The Nova Scotia school-to-work transition project*. Ottawa: Minister of Public Works and Government Services.

Lotz, J., and M. Welton. (1997). *Father Jimmy: the life and times of Jimmy Tompkins*. Wreck Cove, NS: Breton Books.

Lucas, R. (1971). *Minetown, milltown, railtown: Life in Canadian communities of single industry*. Toronto: University of Toronto Press.

Luke, A. (1997). The material effects of the word: Apologies, 'stolen children' and public discourse. *Discourse* 18, 3: 343–68.

MacDonald, M., and P. Connelly. (1989). Class and gender in fishing communities in Nova Scotia. *Studies in Political Economy* 30, Autumn: 61–85.

_____. (1990a). Class and gender in Nova Scotia fishing communities. In B. Fairley, C. Leys and R.J. Sacouman (eds.), *Restructuring and resistance: Perspectives from Atlantic Canada*. Toronto: Garamond.

_____. (1990b). A leaner meaner industry: A case study of 'restructuring' in the Nova Scotia fishery. In B. Fairley, C. Leys and R.J. Sacouman (eds.), *Restructuring and resistance: Perspectives from Atlantic Canada*. Toronto: Garamond.

Mackey, E. (2002). *The House of Difference: Cultural Politics and National Identity in Canada*. Toronto: University of Toronto Press.

MacLennan, H. (1951). *Each Man's Son*. Toronto: Macmillan.

MacLeod, A. (1976). *The lost salt gift of blood*. Toronto: McClelland and Stewart.

_____. (1999). *No great mischief*. Toronto: McClelland and Stewart.

Matthews, R. (1976). 'There's no better place than here': Social change in three Newfoundland communities. Toronto: Peter Martin Associates.

_____. (1983). *The creation of regional dependency*. Toronto: University of Toronto Press.

_____. (1993). *Controlling common property: Regulating Canada's east coast fishery*. Toronto: University of Toronto Press.

McCann, P. (ed.). (1982). Blackboards and briefcases: Personal stories by Newfoundland teachers, educators and administrators. St. John's, NF: Jesperson.

_____. (1994). *Schooling in a fishing society*. St John's, NF: Institute of Social and Economic Research.

McGrath, B. (2001). "A problem of resources": Defining rural youth encounters in education work and housing. *Journal of Rural Studies* 17: 481–95.

McKay, I. (1988). Among fisherfolk: J.F.B. Livesay and the invention of Peggy's Cove. *Journal of Canadian Studies* 23, 1/2: 23–45.

_____. (1993). Helen Creighton and the politics of antimodernism. In G. Davies (ed.), *Myth and milieu: Atlantic literature and culture, 1918–1939*. Fredericton, NB: Acadiensis Press.

_____. (1994). *The Quest for the folk: Antimodernism and cultural selection in twentieth century Nova Scotia*. Montreal and Kingston: McGill-Queen's University Press.

McLaren, P. (1980). *Cries from the corridor*. Toronto: Methuen.

_____. (1985). The ritual dimensions of resistance. *Journal of Education* 67, 2: 84–97.

_____. (1989). *Life in schools: An introduction to critical pedagogy in the foundations of education*. White Plains NY: Longmans.

McMahon, F. (2003). Rural development, an oxymoron: Preservation programs are bribes that trap young people in dead-end jobs. *Time Magazine* (Canadian Edition), October 13: 57.

McNichol Stock, C. (1996). *Rural radicals: Righteous rage in the American grain*. Ithaca, NY: Cornell University Press.

McRobbie, A. (1991). *Feminism and youth culture: From Jackie to Just 17*. Boston: Unwin Hyman.

Meighan, R. (1981). *A sociology of education*. London: Holt Rinehart and Winston.

Mendelson, R., and R.D. Bollman. (1998). *Rural and small town population is growing in the 1990s*. Rural and Small Town Canada Analysis Bulletin, 1, 1 Statistics Canada Catalogue no. 21-006-XPB.

Michalos, A.C. (1997). Migration and the quality of life: A review essay. *Social Indicators Research* 39: 121–66.

Moomis, R. (1990). *Schooling and rural transformation*. New Delhi: Vikas Publishing.

Mott, M. (1986). Confronting 'modern' problems through play: The beginning of physical education in Manitoba's public schools, 1900–1915. In N.M. Sheehan, J.D. Wilson, and D.C. Jones, (eds.), *Schools in the West: Essays in Canadian educational history*. Calgary: Detselig.

Mountford, A. (1997). Can a brain drain be good for growth in the source economy? *Journal of Development Economics* 53: 287–303.

Neis, B. (1999). Familial and social patriarchy in the Newfoundland fishing industry. In D. Newell and R. Ommer (eds.), *Fishing places, fishing people: Traditions and issues in Canadian small-scale fisheries*. Toronto: University of Toronto Press.

Newbold, B. (1996). The ghettoization of Quebec: Interprovincial migration and its demographic effects. *Canadian Studies in Population* 23, 1: 1–23.

Newbold, B., and K.L. Liaw. (1994). Return and onward interprovincial migration through economic boom and bust in Canada. *Geographical Analysis* 26, 3: 228–45.

Newell, D., and R. Omer (eds.). (1999). *Fishing places, fishing people: Traditions and issues in Canadian small-scale fisheries*. Toronto: University of Toronto Press.

Newkirk, T. (2002). *Misreading masculinity: Boys, literacy and popular culture*. Portsmouth, NH: Heineman.

Norman, J. (1989). *Loran Arthur Dewolfe and the reform of education in Nova Scotia 1891–1959*. Truro, NS: Atlantic Early Learning Productions.

Nova Scotia Department of Fisheries and Agriculture. 2006. *Statistics: NS Commercial Fish Landings*. Available at <http://www.gov.ns.ca/nsaf/marketing/statistics/landings/> (accessed 30 January, 2006).

O'Grady, W. (1995). A long holiday with pay? Youth unemployment on the edge. In L. Felt and P. Sinclair, *Living on the edge*. St John's, NF: Institute for Social and Economic Research.

Ong, R. (1987). *Spirits of resistance and capitalist discipline*. Albany, NY: State University of New York Press.

Orun, A.M. (1998). The urban imagination of sociologists: The centrality of place. *The Sociological Quarterly* 39, 1: 1–10.

Ovando, C.J. (1984). School and community attitudes in the Athapascan bush village. *Educational Research Quarterly* 8, 4: 12–29.

Owram, D. (1996). *Born at the right time: A history of the baby-boom generation*. Toronto: University of Toronto Press.

Pahl, R.E. (1966). The rural-urban continuum. *Sociologica Ruralis* 6: 299–39.

Palsson, G. (1994). Enskilment at sea. *Man* 29, 4: 901–27.

_____. (1999). Schooling and skipperhood: The development of dexterity. *American Anthropologist* 100, 4: 908–23.

Papastergiadis, N. (2000). *The turbulence of migration: Globalisation, deterritorialization and hybridity.* Cambridge: Polity Press.

Park, R. (1928). Human migration and the marginal man. *American Journal of Sociology* 33: 881–93.

Parsons, T. (1956). *The social system.* Glencoe, IL: Free Press.

Pinar, W., W.M. Reynolds, P. Slattery, and P.M. Taubman. (1995). *Understanding curriculum.* New York: Peter Lang.

Pittman, R.B., D. McGinty, and C.I. Gersti-Pepin. (1999). Educational attainment, economic progress and the goals of education in rural communities. *Journal of Research in Rural Education* 15, 1: 19–30.

Pocius, G. (1991). *A place to belong: Community order and everyday spaces in Calvert, Newfoundland.* Montreal and Kingston: McGill-Queens University Press.

Pollard, K., W.P. Oltare, and R. Berg. (1990). *Selective migration of rural high school seniors in the 1980s.* Washington, DC: Reference Bureau Inc. ERIC Document Reproduction service No. ED 332 840.

Popkewitz, T. (1998). *Struggling for the soul: The politics of schooling and the construction of the teacher.* New York: Teachers College Press.

Portelli, J.P., and A.B. Vibert. (2001). Beyond common educational standards: Toward a curriculum of life. In J.P. Portelli and R.P. Solomon (eds.), *The Erosion of Democracy in Education.* Calgary, AB: Detselig Press.

Porter, M. (1985). She was skipper of the shore crew: Notes on the history of the sexual division of labour in Newfoundland. *Labour/Le Travail* 15: 105–23.

_____. (1993). *Place and persistence in the lives of Newfoundland women.* Aldershot: Avebury.

Porter, M.K. (1996). Moving mountains: Reform, resistance and resiliency in an Appalachian Kentucky high school. *Journal of Research in Rural Education* 12, 2: 107–15.

Prentice, A. (1977). *The school promoters: Education and social class in mid-nineteenth century Upper Canada.* Toronto: McClelland and Stewart.

Press, H., G. Galway, and A. Collins. (2003). Maintaining Quality Programming in Rural Newfoundland and Labrador: A Case Study in Policy and Structural Change. *Education Canada* 20–23: 38–39.

Rabinow, P. (1997). *Michel Foucault: Ethics subjectivity and truth: Essential works of Foucault 1954–1984.* New York: New Press.

Raddall, T. (1957). *The wings of night.* Toronto: Macmillan.

Ranciere, J. (1991). *The Ignorant schoolmaster: Seven lessons in educational emancipation.* Stanford: Stanford University Press.

_____. (1995). *On the shores of Politics.* London; Verso.

Randhawa, B.S. (1992). Rural education: Opportunities and issues. In D.A. Hay and G.S. Basran (eds.), *Rural sociology in Canada.* Toronto: Oxford University Press.

Reay, D., and H. Lucey. (2000). I don't really like it here but I don't want to be anywhere else: Children and inner city council estates. *Antipode* 32 (4): 410–28.

Reed-Danahay, D. (1987). Farm children at school: Educational strategies in rural France. *Anthropology and Education Quarterly* 60, 2: 83–89.

Ricker, E. (1978). Towards and economic interpretation of schooling in Atlantic Canada. In E. Ricker (ed.), *Education and development in Atlantic Canada*. Halifax, NS: Department of Education Dalhousie University.

Rikowski, G. (1997). Scorched earth: Prelude to rebuilding Marxist educational theory. *British Journal of the Sociology of Education* 18, 4: 551–74.

Riley, B. (1992). Six saucepans to one: Domestic science vs. the home in British Columbia, 1900–1930. In G. Creese and V. Strong-Boag (eds.), *British Columbia reconsidered: Essays on women*. Vancouver: Press Gang Publishers.

Riordan, C. (2003). *Equality and achievement*. Upper Saddle River, NJ: Prentice.

Rogers, R. (1995). *The oceans are emptying: Fish wars and sustainability*. Montreal: Black Rose Books.

Roman, L. (1996). Debating dropouts: The moral panic and spectacle over "youth at risk." In D. Kelly and J. Gaskell (eds.), *Debating dropouts: critical policy and research perspectives on early school leaving*. New York: Teachers College Press.

Roman, L., and L. Christian-Smith (eds.). (1988). *Feminism and the politics of popular culture*. London: Falmer.

Rose, M. (2004). *The mind at work: Valuing the intelligence of the American worker*. New York: Penguin.

Rose, N. (1997). The death of the social? Refiguring the territory of government. *Economy and Society* 25, 3: 327–56.

Rothstein, F.A. (1996). Flexible accumulation, youth labour and schooling in a rural community in Mexico. *Critique of Anthropology* 16, 4: 361–79.

Roy, A. (2001). *Power politics*. Second Edition. Cambridge, MA: South End Press.

Ryan, J. (1997). Student communities in a culturally diverse school setting. *Discourse* 18, 1 (April): 37–53.

Sacouman, J. (1980). Semi-proletarianization and rural underdevelopment in the Maritimes. *Canadian Review of Sociology and Anthropology* 17, 3.

Said, E. (1993). *Culture and Imperialism*. New York: Knopf.

Schrank, W. (1997). The failure of Canadian seasonal fisherman's unemployment insurance reform during the 1960s and 1970s. *Marine Policy* 22, 1.

Scott, J. (1985). *Weapons of the weak: Everyday forms of peasant resistance*. Yale University Press.

Sennett, R. (1999). *The corrosion of character: The personal consequences of work in the new capitalism*. New York: W.W. Norton.

Sennett, R., and J. Cobb. (1973). *The hidden injuries of class*. New York: Vintage.

Seyfrit, C.L., and J.E. Danner. (1999). *Social vitality and ecological planning on Virginia's Eastern Shore*. Paper presented at the Conference on Rural Youth and their Transitions from School to Work, Old Dominion University, Norfolk Va.

Shanahan, M., R. Meick, and G. Elder. (1998). Changing pathways to attainment in men's lives: Historical patterns of school, work and social class. *Social Forces* 77, 1, 231–56.

Shelton, J. (2005). *Consequential learning: A public approach to better schools*. Montgomery, AL: New South Books.

Sinclair, P. (1992). Atlantic Canada's fishing communities: The impact of change. In D.A. Hay and G.S. Basran (eds.), *Rural sociology in Canada*. Toronto: Oxford University Press.

Smith, D. (1987). *The everyday world as problematic: A feminist sociology*. Toronto: University of Toronto Press.

Smyth, J., and R. Hattam. (2004). *Dropping out, drifting off, being excluded: Becoming somebody without school.* New York: Peter Lang.

Soja, E. (1989). *Postmodern geographies: The reassertion of space in critical social theory.* London: Verso.

Southcott, C. (1999). The study of regional inequality in Quebec and English Canada: A comparative analysis of perspectives. *Canadian Journal of Sociology* 24, 4: 457–84.

Sowell, T. (1996). *Migration and cultures: A world view.* New York: Basic Books.

Spaulding, A. (2000). Micropolitical behaviour of second graders: A qualitative study of student resistance in the classroom. *The Qualitative Report* 4, 1/2. <http://www.nova.edu/ssss/QR/QR4-1/spaulding.html>. (Accessed June 12, 2004.)

Stern, P.R. (1999). Learning to be smart: An exploration of the culture of intelligence in a Canadian Inuit community. *American Anthropologist* 101, 3: 502–14.

Stone, L. (1969). *Migration in Canada: Some regional aspects.* Ottawa: Dominion Bureau of Statistics.

Theobald, P. (1992). The concept of place in the new sociology of education. *Educational Foundations* 6, Winter: 5–19.

_____. (1997). *Teaching the commons: Place, pride and the renewal of community.* Boulder CO: Westview Press.

Theobald, P., and R.S. Rochon. (2006). Enclosure then and now: Rural schools and communities in the wake of market-driven agriculture. *Journal of Research in Rural Education* 21(12). Available at <http://www.umaine.edu/jrre/21-12.htm> (accessed Nov. 23, 2006).

Thornton, P. (1985). The problem of out-migration from the Maritime Provinces, 1971–1921: A new look. *Acadiensis* 15, 1.

Tilley, C. (1997). Performing culture in the global village. *Critique of Anthropology* 17, 1: 67–89.

Tolnay, S.E. (1998). Educational selection in the migration of Southern Blacks. *Social Forces* 77, 2: 487–514.

Urry, J. (2000). *Sociology beyond societies: Mobilities for the twenty-first century.* London and New York: Routledge.

Valverde, M. (1997), 'Despotism' and ethical liberal governance. *Economy and Society* 25, 3: 357–72.

Vanderbeck, R., and C. Dunkley,. (2003). Young people's narratives of rural-urban difference. *Children's Geographies* 1, 2: 241–59.

Veltmeyer, H. (1979). The capitalist underdevelopment of Atlantic Canada. In R.J. Brym and R.J. Sacouman (eds.), *Underdevelopment and social movements in Atlantic Canada.* Toronto: New Hogtown Press.

_____. (1990). The restructuring of capital: The regional problem. In B. Fairley, C. Leys and J. Sacouman (eds.), *Restructuring and resistance: Perspectives from Atlantic Canada.* Toronto: Garamond.

Vias, A. (2005). Bigger stores, more stores, or no stores: Paths of retail restructuring in rural America. *Journal of Rural Studies* 21, 3.

Walkerdine, V. (1990). *Schoolgirl fictions.* London: Verso.

Weaver-Hightower, M.B. (2003) The "boy turn" in research on gender and education. *Review of Educational Research* 73: 471–98.

Weber, E. (1976). *Peasants into Frenchmen: The modernisation of rural France, 1970–1914.*

Stanford: Stanford University Press.

Weis, L. (1990). *Working class without work: High school students in a deindustrialized economy*. New York: Routledge.

_____. (2004). *Class Reunion: The remaking of the American working class*. New York: Routledge.

Wenger, E. (1998). *Communities of practice: Learning, meaning and identity*. Cambridge UK: Cambridge University Press.

Western Valley Development Authority. (1999). *Building tomorrow: Multi-year community action plan for Digby and Annapolis counties*. Bridgetown, NS: Western Valley Development Authority Publication.

Wexler, P. (1992). *Becoming somebody: Toward a social psychology of school*. London: Falmer.

Williams, R. (1958). *Culture and society*. London: Chatto and Windus.

_____. (1961). *The long revolution: 1780–1950*. New York: Harper and Row.

_____. (1964). *Second generation*. London: Chatto and Windus.

_____. (1973). *The country and the city*. Frogmore, St. Albans: UK: Paladin.

Willinsky, J. (1998). *Learning to divide the world: Education at empire's end*. Minneapolis: University of Minnesota Press.

Willis, P. (1977). *Learning to labour: How working class kids get working class jobs*. New York: Columbia University Press.

Wilson, J.D. (1977). From the swinging sixties to the sobering seventies. In H.A. Stevenson and J.D. Wilson (eds.), *Precepts, policy and process: Perspectives on contemporary Canadian education*. London Ontario: Alexander Blake.

Wilson, J.D., R. Stamp, and L.P. Audet (eds.). (1970). *Canadian education: A history*. Toronto: Prentice-Hall.

Wilson, J.D., and P. Stortz. (1993). Education on the frontier: Schools, teachers and community influence in North Central British Columbia. *Histoire sociale/Social History* 52: 265–90.

_____. (1995). "May the Lord have mercy on you": The rural school problem in British Columbia in the 1920s. In J. Barman, N. Sutherland and J.D. Wilson (eds.), *Children, teachers and schools in the history of British Columbia*. Calgary: Detselig.

Winson, A, and B. Leach. (2002). *Contingent work, disrupted lives: Labour and community in the new rural economy*. Toronto: University of Toronto Press.

Wotherspoon, T. (1998). Education place and the sustainability of rural communities in Saskatchewan. *Journal of Research in Rural Education* 14, 3: 131–41.

Wylie, L. (1977). *Village in the Vaucluse*. Third edition. Cambridge: Harvard University Press.

Wynn, G. (1988). A share of the necessaries of life: Remarks on migration, development and dependency in Atlantic Canada. In B. Flemming (ed.), *Beyond anger and longing: Community and development in Atlantic Canada*. Fredericton and Sackville, NB: Acadiensis and Centre for Canadian Studies, 17–51.

# Index